A Research Agenda for Cities

Elgar Research Agendas outline the future of research in a given area. Leading scholars are given the space to explore their subject in provocative ways, and map out the potential directions of travel. They are relevant but also visionary.

Forward-looking and innovative, Elgar Research Agendas are an essential resource for PhD students, scholars and anybody who wants to be at the forefront of research.

Titles in the series include:

A Research Agenda for Management and
Organization Studies
Edited by Barbara Czarniawska

A Research Agenda for Cities
Edited by John Rennie Short

A Research Agenda for Entrepreneurship
and Context
*Edited by Friederike Welter and
William B. Gartner*

A Research Agenda for Cities

Edited by

JOHN RENNIE SHORT

School of Public Policy, University of Maryland, Baltimore County, USA

Elgar Research Agendas

 Edward Elgar
PUBLISHING

Cheltenham, UK • Northampton, MA, USA

Published by
Edward Elgar Publishing Limited
The Lypiatts
15 Lansdown Road
Cheltenham
Glos GL50 2JA
UK

Edward Elgar Publishing, Inc.
William Pratt House
9 Dewey Court
Northampton
Massachusetts 01060
USA

A catalogue record for this book
is available from the British Library

Library of Congress Control Number: 2016953954

This book is available electronically in the **Elgar**online
Social and Political Science subject collection
DOI 10.4337/9781785363429

ISBN 978 1 78536 341 2 (cased)
ISBN 978 1 78536 342 9 (eBook)

Typeset by Servis Filmsetting Ltd, Stockport, Cheshire
Printed and bound in Great Britain by TJ International Ltd, Padstow

Contents

Figures

Tables

Contributors

Jonathan V. Beaverstock is Professor of International Management at the University of Bristol, England. Trained as an economic-urban geographer, he has published widely across the social sciences, including world city network studies, and his latest books include *The Edward Elgar Handbook on Wealth and the Super-Rich* (2016) and *The Globalization of Executive Search* (2015). He jointly founded the Globalization and World Cities (GaWC) research group and network, and continues to investigate the competitiveness of cities' knowledge-intensive labour markets and global firms.

Lisa Benton-Short is Chair of the Department of Geography at George Washington (GW) University and a Senior Fellow at the GW Sustainability Collaborative. She is an urban geographer with a general interest in the dynamics of the urban environment with a focus on planning and public space, urban sustainability, globalization and immigration. Recent books include *Cities of North America: Contemporary Challenges in U.S. and Canadian Cities* (2014) and *The National Mall: No Ordinary Public Space* (2016).

Gavin Brown is Associate Professor in Human Geography at the University of Leicester, UK. He co-edited *The Routledge Research Companion to Geographies of Sex and Sexualities* (with Kath Browne, 2016) and is an editor of the journal *Social and Cultural Geography*. He is currently developing new research on the geopolitics of sexual orientation and gender identity.

James Farrer is Professor of Sociology and Global Studies at Sophia University in Tokyo, Japan specializing in urban sociology in East Asia, with publications focusing on sexuality, nightlife, expatriate communities and urban foodways. These include *Opening Up: Youth Sex Culture and Market Reform in Shanghai* (2002), *Shanghai Nightscapes: A Nocturnal Biography of a Global City* (with Andrew Field, 2015) and *Globalization and Asian Cuisines: Transnational Networks and Contact Zones* (2015).

Robert Freestone is Professor of Urban Planning at UNSW Sydney. His recent books include *Place and Placelessness Revisited* (2016), *Exhibitions and the Development of Modern Planning Culture* (2014) and *Urban Nation* (2010).

Oleg Golubchikov is Senior Lecturer in Human Geography at Cardiff University, Wales. His research interests and publications focus on urban political geography, critical and post-socialist studies, energy geography and sustainable cities. His current research and collaborations are in the post-Soviet and BRIC countries, the United Kingdom and Europe. He has advised the United Nations on aspects of urban development and sustainable housing. He has held a number of visiting positions, including currently at the National Research University Higher School of Economics in Moscow.

Andrew Gorman-Murray is a Senior Lecturer in Social Sciences and Leader of the Urban Research Program at Western Sydney University. His research interests include sexual minorities' experiences of belonging and exclusion in everyday spaces. His work analyses the intersections between queer politics, everyday experience, and urban and regional geographies. His books include *Material Geographies of Household Sustainability* (with Ruth Lane, 2011), *Sexuality, Rurality, and Geography* (with Barbara Pini and Lia Bryant, 2013) and *Masculinities and Place* (with Peter Hopkins, 2014).

Bernadette Hanlon is Assistant Professor in City and Regional Planning at Ohio State University, USA. Recent books include *Global Migration: The Basics* (2014), *Cities and Suburbs: New Metropolitan Realities in the US* (with John Rennie Short and Thomas J. Vicino, 2010) and *Once the American Dream: Inner-Ring Suburbs in the Metropolitan United States* (2010). She publishes in a wide range of academic journals including *Urban Studies*, the *Journal of Urban Affairs*, the *Journal of the American Planning Association* and the *International Journal of Urban and Regional Research*. Recent book chapters appear in *The New American Suburb* (2015) and *Cities of North America* (2013).

Phil Hubbard is Professor of Urban Studies in the Department of Geography at Kings College, London, UK. He writes on the intersections of society, law, culture and aesthetics in the contemporary city, with a particular focus on gentrification and sexualities. His recent books include *The Battle for The High Street: Retail Gentrification, Class and Disgust* (2016) and *Cities and Sexualities* (2012).

Tom Hutton is Professor of Urban Studies and City Planning in the Centre for Human Settlements, School of Community and Regional Planning, University of British Columbia. Recent publications include *Cities and the Cultural Economy* (2015) and *Cities and Economic Change* (co-edited with Ronan Paddison, 2015).

Ahmed Kanna is Associate Professor of Anthropology and International Studies at University of the Pacific, USA. His books include *Dubai, The City as Corporation* (2011), *Rethinking Global Urbanism* (co-edited with Xiangming Chen, 2012) and *The Superlative City* (2013). His articles and essays have appeared in *City, Cultural Anthropology, Journal of Urban Affairs, Jadaliyya* and many other publications. He is currently working on the rise of anti-capitalist, in particular Marxist, movements in US urban contexts.

Melissa Keeley is Assistant Professor of Geography and Public Policy at George Washington University. Her research focus is urban sustainability, particularly related to green infrastructure, stormwater management and green buildings. She is the author of numerous peer-reviewed articles on these topics.

Yeong-Hyun Kim is Associate Professor in Geography at Ohio University, USA. Her research interests include globalization, global cities, mega events and international labour migration. She is currently working on a comparative study of the lasting legacies of global sports events in Johannesburg and Seoul.

Lily Kong is Lee Kong Chian Professor of Social Sciences at the Singapore Management University, where she is also Provost. She is a social and cultural geographer, and her recent publications include *Religion and Space: Competition, Conflict and Violence in the Contemporary World* (with Orlando Woods, 2016), *Arts, Culture and the Making of Global Cities: Creating New Urban Landscapes in Asia* (with Ching C.-H. and Chou T.-L., 2015) and *Food, Foodways and Foodscapes: Culture, Community and Consumption in Post-Colonial Singapore* (with Vineeta Sinha, 2016).

Lina Martínez is an Assistant Professor of Public Policy and Director of POLIS (Observatory of Public Policies) Universidad Icesi, Colombia, with a specialization in educational and social policy. Current research focuses on informal workers in Colombia, urban policies and provision of public goods, social mobility and life satisfaction.

David Murakami Wood is Canada Research Chair (Tier II) in Surveillance Studies at Queen's University in Canada. He is a widely published specialist on the sociology and geography of global surveillance, and security and surveillance in cities from a comparative perspective, with a particular focus on Japan. He is Editor-in-Chief of the international, open-access, peer-reviewed journal *Surveillance & Society* and a co-founder of the Surveillance Studies Network. His main work, which started in 2014 and runs through to 2019, is a major grant-funded critical study of 'smart city' initiatives in Canada, the United States and the United Kingdom.

Catherine J. Nash is a Professor in the Department of Geography and Tourism Studies at Brock University, Canada. Her current research interests include changing urban sexual and gendered landscapes in Toronto; a focus on digital technologies and sexuality in everyday life; new LGBT mobilities; and a consideration of international resistances to LGBT equalities in Canada, Great Britain and Australia. Her books include *Queer Methods and Methodologies* (with K. Browne, 2010) and *An Introduction to Human Geography* (with E. Fouberg, A. Murphy and H. de Blij, 2015).

Linda Peake is Professor in the Urban Studies program in the Department of Social Science, York University, Toronto, Canada. Her most recent edited books include *Rethinking Feminist Interventions into the Urban* (with Martina Reiker, 2013) and

Urbanization in a Global Context (with Alison Bain, 2017). She has published in a wide range of academic journals and is a previous editor of *Gender, Place and Culture: A Journal of Feminist Geography*.

Edgar Pieterse is founding director of the African Centre for Cities (ACC) at the University of Cape Town and holder of the NRF South African Research Chair in Urban Policy. His most recent co-edited books are *African Cities Reader III: Land, Property and Value* (with Ntone Edjabe, 2015), *Africa's Urban Revolution* (with Susan Parnell, 2014) and *Rogue Urbanism: Emergent African Cities* (with AbdouMaliq Simone, 2013).

Bill Randolph is Professor and Director of the City Futures Research Centre at UNSW Sydney. He has 35 years' experience as a researcher on housing and urban policy issues in the academic, government, non-government and private sectors, and holds a PhD from the London School of Economics.

Xuefei Ren is Associate Professor of Sociology and Global Urban Studies at Michigan State University, USA. She is the author of two award-winning books: *Building Globalization: Transnational Architecture Production in Urban China* (2011) and *Urban China* (2013). She is completing a new book comparing urban governance and citizenship rights in China and India.

John Rennie Short is Professor in the School of Public Policy at University of Maryland, Baltimore County, USA. Recent books include *Urban Theory: A Critical Assessment* (2015, 2nd ed.), *Human Geography* (2014), *Cities and Nature* (with Lisa Benton-Short, 2013, 2nd ed.), *Stress Testing the USA* (2013), *Globalization, Modernity and the City* (2012) and *Cities and Suburbs*, (with Bernadette Hanlon and Thomas J. Vicino, 2010). He publishes in a wide range of academic journals and is a frequent contributor to *The Conversation*.

Thomas J. Vicino is Associate Professor in the Department of Political Science and School of Public Policy and Urban Affairs at Northeastern University, USA. A former Fulbright Scholar in Brazil, he conducts research on the political economy of metropolitan development. His recent books include *Global Migration* (2014), *Suburban Crossroads* (2012) and *Cities and Suburbs* (with Bernadette Hanlon and John Rennie Short, 2010).

Andrew Wheeler is a Senior Policy Analyst (Healthy Built Environments) in the New South Wales Ministry of Health. He has served as a Director of the Planning Institute of Australia and was Australian Planner of the Year for 2016.

Orlando Woods is an independent scholar, based in London. He is the co-author of *Religion and Space: Competition, Conflict and Violence in the Contemporary World* (with Lily Kong, 2016) and the author of numerous journal articles and book chapters on the socio-cultural politics of South and Southeast Asia.

Elvin Wyly is Professor of Geography and Chair of the Urban Studies Coordinating Committee at the University of British Columbia, Vancouver, Canada, and a past Editor of the journal *Urban Geography*. Recent papers include 'Gentrification on the Planetary Urban Frontier: The Evolution of Turner's Noösphere' (*Urban Studies*), 'Where is an Author?' (*City*), 'The New Quantitative Revolution' (*Dialogues in Human Geography*) and 'Please Do Not Cite This Article' (*Urban Geography*).

1 Introduction to the urban moment

John Rennie Short

This book provides a critical assessment of key areas of urban scholarship. In eleven provocative chapters, expert contributors examine a range of important pressing topics from sustainability and gentrification to feminist interventions and globalization and from security/surveillance to an interesting take on food issues. Eight more regionally informed reviews report on recent urban research in Australia, East Asia, Eastern Europe and Russia, Middle East, South America and sub-Saharan Africa. All the chapters provide polemical assessments of current work and signposts for future research.

The urban moment

The book is timely. We are living in a time of planetary urbanization. A majority of people now lives in cities. Big cities are at the heart of the global political economy, the setting for a refining of progressive politics and new ecological contexts of city constellations surrounded by rural hinterlands that provide natural resources, recreational sites and waste dumps.

Across the globe there is an urban growth change and resurgence. It is of such major and global significance that I have described it as a Third Revolution (Short, 2012). The first saw the invention of cities round 5,000 years ago and the second was linked with the Industrial Revolution. The present one is associated with three trends: rapid urbanization across the globe; the growth of large cities (there are now over 400 cities with a population of over a million); and a widening metropolitan reach as giant urban regions form well beyond the traditional city boundary.

The picture varies. In the US, selected cities that were losing population for decades are now experiencing an influx of people, and inner city areas, long the black holes of capitalism, are now sites of major investments. The great suburban shift that occurred from 1950 to 1990 is being replaced by central city resurgence. The population of New York City declined steadily from 1950, bottomed out in 1980 and has now bounced back. It is not just a US phenomenon: London saw a steady population decline from 1951 until 1991 when population growth began to surge past 1951 figures. A similar trend is apparent in Paris and Berlin. A select range of big cities are witnessing new influxes of people, quite literally revitalizing the urban experience.

1

But not all cities are experiencing this resurgence. Former industrial cities, such as Baltimore or Detroit, that are unable to replace the lost industrial jobs, continue to lose population and fail to attract investment. In 1950, Baltimore had a population of 950,000 and, like many cities in the US of the time, a vibrant manufacturing base providing jobs and economic security. The magnet of jobs attracted black migrants from the South. Since the mid-1970s, though, there has been a steady loss of manufacturing jobs due to offshoring, relocation to suburbs in non-union areas of the US and increased productivity. By 2013 Baltimore's population had declined to just over 622,000. There are of course many Baltimores. Within the city boundaries, there are old established elite areas such as Roland Park and more recently gentrified areas such as Federal Hill. The Baltimore of the riots of 2015 was only part of the city, a swathe of inner city neighborhoods impacted by job loss, poor education and aggressive policing.

But there are other Baltimores outside of Maryland. They include Akron, Birmingham, Cincinnati, Cleveland, Detroit, Pittsburgh and Toledo. It is not just an inner city problem. There is an inner ring of suburbs in crisis (Hanlon et al., 2010). There are also the bleak areas in the cracks of the metropolis: the trailer parks and suburban rental units that house those pushed out of the city by gentrification and redevelopment. Baltimores of economic neglect, massive job loss, aggressive policing and multiple deprivations are found across the country. They are the places of despair that house the voiceless of the US political system; the marginalized of the US economy and those left behind in the commodification of US society.

Across urban America, and throughout the world, we see pockets of gentrification and gleaming downtown towers beside persistent pockets of poverty and enduring marginalization.

Meanwhile, urban growth picks up pace across much of the global urban South. The rates of growth are staggering. In 1950, Dhaka had a population of 336,000. By 2015 it was 15.6 million and estimated to rise to 20 million by 2025. The swell of population has often overwhelmed the market's ability to cope or the local government's ability to organize, and the result is formal economies and housing markets that are simply inadequate to deal with the demand for jobs and the need for housing.

The picture varies across the global South. One of the chapters in this book (Chapter 15) deals with the differences between India and China while another notes significant variations among cities in Colombia (Chapter 13). In this volume the broad categories of global North and South are given a more rigorous interrogation so that they do not become the often used but rarely examined categories of so much of contemporary scholarship.

New subjectivities

A central tenet of traditional urban theory of the Second Urban Revolution was that urbanization, the process of people moving into the city, creates a citizenry that in turn creates the potential for a new social order. Cities, according to Marx and Engels, rescued people from the idiocy of rural life. The alienating experience of the agricultural work was replaced, at least in this Marxist reading, with the emancipatory and possibly revolutionary experience of urban life, as 'classes in themselves' turned into 'classes for themselves'. This is a major theme in E. P. Thompson's magisterial *The Making of the English Working Class*. It was in the towns and cities of industrial Britain that class-consciousness was developed and hardened (Thompson, 1963). In the Chicago School, and especially the work of Robert Park, newcomers to the city are seen as active agents in the creation of a new urban society (Park, 1928). A bedrock assumption of the Chicago School is that there is a symbiotic relationship between the assimilation of immigrants and the creation of a new urban order. In both of these foundational urban theories, there is an implicit relationship between urbanization and the creation of a citizenry. But in the Third Revolution we have counterfactual examples of urbanization without citizenship.

China has witnessed unprecedented urbanization during the last four decades, and more than half of the national population now lives in urban areas. However, Chinese urbanization is a process in which large segments of the native population are denied citizenship: that is, there is urbanization without citizenship, as newcomers to the city are integrated into the city as workers but denied entry as political bodies. They are economic agents but not political agents. They inhabit the city but are not citizens of the city. A number of other examples can be noted, including South Asian workers in the Gulf States and Filipino and Indonesian domestics in Hong Kong. In both cases there are severe restrictions on the ability of workers to become anything more than temporary workers, with all sorts of barriers raised to the possibility of them becoming citizens. In Hong Kong, for example, there are currently around 300,000 women from the Philippines and Indonesia working as domestic servants. They were long excluded from minimum wage legislation, becoming eligible only from 2011. In 2013 the Final Court of Appeal ruled that they were ineligible for permanent residency, no matter how long they worked in the city. The case was brought by a woman who had lived and worked in the city for 28 years.

The denial of citizenship, common in authoritarian societies, where foreigners can be effectively denied citizenship, raises interesting questions about the right to the city. Although Lefebvre (1996) extended the right to all those who inhabit the city, most commentators concentrate on active citizenship and on those with access to the rights and privileges of citizenship. What are the rights to the city for the quasi citizens given economic rights but denied political rights? What are the rights to the city if the basic political right is denied?

The main form of subjectivity noted in the urban theory of the Second Urban Revolution was that of class. It still plays an important role, witness the rising militancy of young female migrants to the factory cities of China's coastal belt; but it is interwoven with and undermined by traditional and new forms of identity including gender, ethnicity, faith and sexual orientation. A number of chapters deal with these themes.

The liberating potential of urbanization as predicted by Marx is a more complex affair with class-consciousness not the only source of political mobilization or personal subjectivity. Urban civil societies in the Third Urban Revolution are complex, with new and old subjectivities in the process of being and becoming in continual relational interaction.

Problems and opportunities

Cities are at the very heart of transformations of political economy, civil society and governmentality.

Metro areas in the US now house 83 percent of the population and are the main site for innovation and job growth. The 100 largest metro areas hold 69 percent of all jobs and are responsible for three-quarters of the nation's gross national product (GDP). The most dynamic parts of the economy, with more job opportunities and higher wage rates, are in the cultural creative economies of finance, advertising and all those sectors that require symbolic analysts. Data and narrative have replaced metal shaping and car manufacturing. This cognitive capitalism has a heavy urban bias, as it requires the close proximity of talented and creative people. There are strong economies of urban agglomeration because people living and working closely together generate the necessary increase in knowledge, creativity and innovation.

The possibility of urban transformation from low value to high value land use provides opportunities for great profit. This process, often lubricated, promoted and partnered by governments, attracts capital and investment from around the world. The frenzy of development, most of it speculative, can and does led to short-term and even longer-term property slumps and housing bubbles. Even in places such as Dubai, awash in oil money, property slumps are a threat.

There are costs to this urban transformation that include the displacement of the poor, the suburbanization of poverty, the creation of more divided cities and the long-term sustainability of global urbanization. The resurgent city can also be the city where the less powerful are further marginalized as house prices and rents are beyond the reach of all but the wealthiest.

Cities are of course sites of problems. In much of the global urban South, the expansion of informal employment and housing results from the inability of the formal sector to provide jobs or housing. But cities are also places for innovative solutions of civil society. In the past 60 years between one and two billion people have created self-build communities in cities all over the world. Cities are sites of regressive policies of neoliberalism but are also places of progressive political change as new communities emerge and new coalitions coalesce around issues of urban livability and the right to the city.

Consider climate change.

Cities and climate change

The high concentration of populations and investment puts cities at the very heart of climate change issues. Many of the world's cities are close to the sea, and many of the most vulnerable ones are those in coastal locations. Cities in the developing world, in particular, are often more vulnerable to natural disasters but less able to spend billions of dollars to upgrade their infrastructure to better withstand flooding or undertake similar measures. Cities such as Dhaka, Mumbai, Bangkok, Manila and Ho Chi Minh City are already in low-lying areas that now have the threat of increased flooding from extreme weather. The city of Jakarta, in Indonesia, is challenged by flooding that accompanies the yearly monsoons. But land subsidence from compaction by new skyscrapers, and increased groundwater extraction for a growing population, has caused the city to sink ten times faster than the Java Sea is rising because of climate change.

There is an unevenness to the risk; the urban poor, infants and elderly are most vulnerable.

The brute facts of climate change vulnerability in cities are prompting a new and more pronounced urban environmental sensitivity. People in cities are responding with both climate change mitigation and adaption. Mitigation focuses on reducing the concentrations of greenhouse gases by using alternative energy sources, encouraging greater energy efficiency and conservation, and through the promotion of carbon sinks by planting trees. Curitiba in Brazil is the showcase for many successful policies, including the integration of green spaces within the city, a widely used public transportation system and reduction of waste.

Separately, cities are adapting to the effects of climate change. Chicago has developed policies anticipating a hotter and wetter climate by repaving its roads with permeable materials, planting more trees and offering tax incentives to encourage green office roofs.

Why this shift? Part of it is a bottom-up movement from residents pushing for a better quality of urban life. Global climate change issues such as the shrinking ice sheets are real, but these problems are distant, long term and difficult for urban residents to solve. These residents, however, have an immediate experience of poor environmental quality in their city and a greater ability to leverage local polices to effect change. Global issues that seem distant yet pressing create a sense of anxiety without a clear route to immediate political response, since solutions struck in international negotiations can take decades. Cities provide a more amenable platform for civil society to enact real and positive changes.

The nation state, the political prize of progressive movement for the past 130 years, can be both too big to deal with urban issues and too small to affect global affairs. National legislatures, such as the US Congress, whose debates are shaped more by big-monied interests than the everyday needs of local citizens, can too often get locked in ideological disputes and policy paralysis.

By contrast, the city – and its government – is small enough to connect with citizens and tailor specific polices, while large enough to make a real difference. For that reason, cities are the ideal stage for developing policies and practices of sustainability compared with global and national bodies. Cities are the sweet spot of many progressive policies.

There is also growing competition among cities. As the world globalizes, cities are assessed by international standards in the competition for investment, skilled people and creative industries. Cities need to respond to the demands of an increasingly mobile and ecologically aware capital and global talent pool. Cities are now ranked, compared and assessed by the greenness of their environment and their success in moving toward more sustainable policies.

There is cooperation as well as competition. Cities are nodes in a global network of flows of people, ideas and practices. While the world is often described as a map of separate national states, it can be also visualized as a global urban network. Cities are learning from each other and testing policies, with the more successful ones diffused, adopted and adapted around the global network. Chapter 16 in this book looks at the context and circulation of the Singapore model of urban development.

By 2014, the US Conference of Mayors Climate Change Agreement included 1,054 mayors representing a total population of more than 88 million citizens. The C40 Cities Climate Leadership Group is a group of the world's largest cities committed to tackling climate change to reduce carbon emissions and to increase energy efficiency. Forty cities signed up in 2006, hence the name, but now more than 75 cities are committed to the project. Their combined population is over half a billion.

The remit

The city is now a crucial arena strategically located between global flows and national surfaces. We are living in an urban moment of some significance. The chapters in this book provide an indispensable and accessible guide to urban research across the globe at this crucial juncture.

I approached the contributors with a simple request: rather than writing a simple review they were encouraged to write a polemical piece outlining where we are now and suggesting possible avenues for research. The aim was to take stock, but also to shape current debates, not simply to report on them. The chapters give us a critical review of existing research. The book aims to stimulate discussions. The chapters have an open-ended sense of outlining avenues of future research based on what we know now after decades of urban research.

The chapters of the book

The remaining chapters are roughly classified into four sections. In Part I, *The Global City*, three chapters take different tacks on the nexus between globalization and the city. Yeong-Hyun Kim (Chapter 2) explores the conceptual and empirical limitation to global city research and highlights academic and public discontent with global city status. Jonathan V. Beaverstock (Chapter 3), a leading figure in the measurement of the globalization in cities, casts a critical eye over the field and identifies five challenges to understanding the city in global flows. David Murakami Wood (Chapter 4) sheds light on the panopticon formed in the nexus of globalization and urbanization, what he terms 'a planetary urban surveillance'.

In Part II, *The Lived City*, four chapters explore new subjectivities and different understandings of life in the city. Gavin Brown (Chapter 5) reviews the utopian promise that queer was believed to offer for alternative ways of living in urban space and answers the question 'where next?' for queer urbanism and the emancipatory promise it once offered. Phil Hubbard, Andrew Gorman-Murray and Catherine J. Nash (Chapter 6) discuss recent work on desire and the erotic in urban studies and explore the different ways of living and loving in the city. Linda Peake (Chapter 7) shows the deeply gendered nature of urbanization and makes visible the urban gendered geographies of inequality, poverty and social justice. James Farrer (Chapter 8) broadens the notion of urban foodways to show how food studies may uniquely contribute to urban studies. He draws from his own research on foodways in East Asian global cities, particularly Hong Kong, Shanghai, Singapore and Tokyo.

There are four chapters in Part III, *Changes in the City*. Elvin Wyly (Chapter 9) challenges the standard interpretations of gentrification and argues for a reassessment of the history, definition and future of gentrification as the leading edge of intensified, evolutionary human competition for urban space and life. Bernadette Hanlon (Chapter 10) assesses the measurement and examination of suburban sprawl and how the traditional metropolitan model is increasingly challenged by recent shifts in suburban conditions worldwide. Tom Hutton (Chapter 11) interrogates the concept of the creative city and excavates experiences of polarization, inequality and dislocation. Lisa Benton-Short and Melissa Keeley (Chapter 12) evaluate work on urban sustainability. They identify four opportunities for urban scholars to advance and support urban sustainability planning and implementation: governance and integration; setting priorities; benchmarking, measuring and mapping; and equity and access.

Part IV, *Cities in Place*, marks a change in focus. While the previous chapters were all acutely aware of the difference in the urban condition across the world, the chapters in this section take the difference as the starting point as they review urban research and urban trends in specific regions of the world. This is to counteract the usual Eurocentric bias of most urban books. Urban ideas are generated in specific places. This is often forgotten in the dominance of the Euro–US experience. The global North is given pride of place, an exalted position that is normalized to the point that US and European cities are the primary datum point and ground zero for theory on which to assess the progress and conditions of other regions of the world. The chapters presented here are reports from active research frontiers, and together they provide a more nuanced and comprehensive understanding of urbanization and urban research. The chapters undermine the taken-for-granted assumption that Eurocentric/US dominated models provide the royal road to understanding this urban moment. The chapters widen the debate about the nature of urbanization and open our eyes to a more global perspective.

Lina Martínez (Chapter 13) provides the most focused account as she recounts changes in Cali, Colombia. It is an example of research in cities in the global South. Data is used to show how the quality of life in Cali has changed over the last years. The analysis helps us understand traumatized cities heavily impacted by crime and drug-trafficking. Thomas J. Vicino (Chapter 14) reviews the history and characteristics of urbanization in Brazil.

Xuefei Ren (Chapter 15) compares urban work on China and India. Both fields have witnessed tremendous intellectual output in the past two decades, yet both are struggling to find a new vocabulary to better theorize urbanism. Housing policies toward informal settlements in Shanghai, Guangzhou and Mumbai are used as illustrations.

Orlando Woods and Lily Kong (Chapter 16) draw on the case study of Singapore as an example of the global circulation of urban models. They propose a future research agenda that focuses on the origin and circulation of policy and urban theory around the world. Edgar Pieterse (Chapter 17) outlines how various traditions of academic research have responded to the specificities of African urbanization. He advances a project for interdisciplinary research to make sense of the elusive nature of the African city and raises questions that form the core of a new research agenda. Ahmed Kanna (Chapter 18) surveys the development of urban studies in the Middle East and North Africa. He shows how research has shifted from identifying an Islamic city to more recent work that has a more sophisticated theoretical engagement.

Australia is one of the most urbanized nations in the world. Robert Freestone, Bill Randolph and Andrew Wheeler (Chapter 19) plot the emergence of urban studies since the 1960s as a succession of confrontations with urban planning and policy issues around themes of infrastructure, employment, housing, health, justice and environmental quality.

Cities in Eastern Europe have recently experienced extraordinary transformations associated with the politico-economic transition from state socialism to neoliberal capitalism. Oleg Golubchikov (Chapter 20) discusses how post-socialist cities represent a particularly fruitful lens to explore the entanglements of the urban and the ideological, including the workings of capitalism in reshaping societies and spatialities, and the centrality of the urban in the production of new social relationships.

Utterances and silences

The book packs a big punch. But urban studies are too varied and too numerous to be contained in one edited volume. Some may argue for more accounts of the postcolonial city, the right to the city or the political economy of the city, or for a consideration of even more regions of the world, such as Central America, North America and Western Europe. However, the present volume, intended as the start and not the end of a conversation about the urban moment, gives readers a sense of the range, dynamism and sheer variety of work on the city. The contributors provide us with the necessary intellectual tools to understand how cities are productive and competitive but also an empathetic response to how they could be and should be sustainable, livable and fair.

References

Hanlon, B., Short, J. R. and Vicino, T. J. (2010), *Cities and Suburbs: New Metropolitan Realities in the US*, London: Routledge.

Lefebvre, H. (1996), *Writings on Cities*, Oxford: Blackwell.

Park, R. E. (1928), *The City*, Chicago: University of Chicago Press.

Short, J. R. (2012), *Globalization, Modernity and the City*, London: Routledge.

Thompson, E. P. (1963), *The Making of the English Working Class*, Harmondsworth, UK: Penguin.

PART I

The global city

2 The global city and its discontents

Yeong-Hyun Kim

The global city is not a new research agenda for cities in the 21st century. Rather, it is a well-established research area in the study of the globalization–urbanization nexus since the 1990s. According to Acuto and Steele (2013, 1), the global city is indeed "one of the most successful terms that emerged from urban studies." While studying the most influential and economically powerful cities might not be particularly new or innovative in the vastly urbanized and globalized world of today, exploring various sources and forms of discontent with the theory and practice of the global city can open up whole new research agendas that promise to revitalize global cities research.

It is widely accepted that current global cities research owes much to Friedmann's (1986) world city hypothesis and Sassen's (1991) comparative study of New York, London and Tokyo, where "command and control" is produced and distributed to the rest of the world. The global city concept has been debated and expanded upon significantly over the years as more interest is paid to the role of leading global cities and their urban networks in the multifaceted and fast-changing process of globalization. While early studies focused primarily on identifying and ranking top-tier cities in the global urban hierarchy and their distinctive traits in a globalizing world economy, more recent research efforts have diversified substantially to explore various kinds of globalized or globalizing cities, connections between and among cities in the global urban networks, regional world cities and global city politics (Brenner and Keil, 2014; Kim, 2014).

Though a large number of articles and books continue to be published on key themes and debates related to the global city, some critics argue that the lack of convincing empirical evidence that global cities indeed command and control the global economy still remains unsolved, which eventually leads to "an impasse for global urban studies" (Smith, 2014, 106). In addition to strengthening the empirical basis of the existing literature, future research needs to explore multiple pathways to global city formation, as cities have deep histories and ties to their own national systems. While the notion of "command and control" casts an optimistic light on global cities, being a global city is not only about serving as a key node in the global network of finance capital and information. Global cities are extremely vulnerable to globally traveling risks, like infectious diseases, terrorists and other crises, which require further research. Additionally, such research has the potential of reshaping how global cities and their role in glo-balization are conceptualized. This chapter aims to, firstly, review how global cities research has highlighted the role of cities as critical sites in globalization. Secondly, it examines the conceptual and empirical limitations of global cities research that have been raised throughout its history. Thirdly, the chapter looks at the public's discontent with global city status, with particular focus on tax-payers' anxiety with global city making and aspiration. Fourthly, and lastly, it explores ways to break an impasse by proposing some future research agendas for global cities.

Global cities research

In global cities research, world cities and global cities are used interchangeably, with the latter becoming more common recently. It is useful to take a brief look at how urban scholars started using these terms and how their meaning and significance have evolved over time. The term "world cities" was used first by Patrick Geddes in *Cities in Evolution* (Geddes, 1915) to refer to large urban regions developed outside the United Kingdom. This term was reintroduced in Peter Hall's *The World Cities* (Hall, 1966) to highlight the concentration of the world's population and wealth in a handful of cities in the then industrial world, including London, Paris, Randstad Holland, Rhine-Ruhr, Moscow, New York and Tokyo. Taylor and Derudder (2015) view Hall's work as a major exception to the traditional state-centric urban studies of the 1960s, when most other scholars focused on the formation and evolution of national urban systems. It should be pointed out here that, though he successfully identified a shortlist of economic powerhouses and unofficial capitals of the world in the 1960s, Hall paid little attention to the connections or competition among them.

Academic attention to the concept of world cities exploded after John Friedmann's (1986) seminal work on the world city hypothesis. While arguing for a new research framework in which urbanization processes are linked to global economic forces, Friedmann attempted to draw a urban hierarchy indicative of individual cities' power and influence in the global, not just national or regional, economy. Despite much appreciation of a visualization of a rank ordering of major cities across the world, Friedmann has been subject to repeated criticism for the lack of empirical evidence to substantiate a hierarchical network of world cities (Derudder, 2006; Short et al., 1996; Taylor et al., 2013). Arranging cities hierarchically naturally begs the question of indicators and data to measure and compare individual cities' importance, position and service in the global economy. Peter Taylor and his Globalization and World Cities (GaWC) Research Network members have played a key role in addressing this data problem in global cities research and, more importantly, taken it in important new directions by formalizing a network analysis of global advanced producer service firms that assesses individual cities' global importance and connectivities and integration into the global urban networks (Taylor and Derudder, 2015).

Along with the efforts to map out an empirically grounded and systematically reasoned hierarchy of global cities, a great deal of scholarship has focused on the economic, social and spatial restructuring taking place inside the great and leading cities of the world. According to Brenner and Keil (2006, 82), Saskia Sassen became "arguably the single most influential and widely cited contemporary analyst of global city formation, primarily due to the massive international impact of her path-breaking book, *The Global City: New York, London, Tokyo* (1991)." Basically, Sassen saw these global cities as production sites of command and control functions of the global economy by housing a disproportionate and increasing share of the world's advanced business and financial services, and that global cities should be considered a new type of cities through which globalization would articulate. Building on Sassen's argument that globalization and urban change in global cities are mutually constitutive, many have taken a global perspective on urban economic, political and spatial restructuring and the effects of such restructuring on the growing inequality and social polarization in cities that are globalizing (Chiu and Lui, 2004; Ismail, 2013; Timberlake et al., 2012).

In the meantime, urban changes and processes in second-tier or even smaller cities have been examined with reference to globalization and in comparison to emergent global cities (Miraftab and Kudva, 2015). Indeed, long before "studying global cities in the global context" became a trendy research field in urban studies, cities had served as nodes in the social and economic networks spanning national borders, cultures and geographic distances – consider that Jane Jacobs' (1969) imaginary city New Obsidian emerged as the center of the long-distance trade of obsidian during the Paleolithic period. In addition, socioeconomic and spatial characteristics in the so-called Third World cities have long been understood and explained through concepts of dependent urbanization and (post)colonial urbanism (Davis and Tajbakhsh, 2005; Robinson, 2011). That is to say, various urban realities and challenges in large cities in the Global South of Africa, Asia and Latin America have traditionally been analyzed in terms of their respective positions in the capitalist world economy. Renewed by the recent scholarly interest in global cities, a growing body of research is investigating the globalization–urbanization nexus in megacities, primate cities and gateway cities across the developing world, with particular focus on their political quest for global city status (Ancien, 2011; Heng, 2015; Rogerson and Rogerson, 2015).

Academic discontent with the global city

The global cities literature, as reviewed in the above section, is classified into three major strands according to their research focus: global urban hierarchies and networks, urban changes in selected global cities, and globalizing cities, including those in the Global South. Understandably, concerns have been raised about a definitional discrepancy of the global city among these different research groups (Parnreiter, 2013). While some view it as a new type of city to have a strategic role in controlling the world's economy, others simply view it as a big city full of corporate headquarters, international flights and cosmopolitan communities. Some might attempt to go beyond a simple measure of corporate, financial headquarter locations to pursue a highly sophisticated analysis of the economic connections between global cities and to measure the degree of individual cities' integration into a global interurban network. Along with its definitional differences and difficulties, global cities research has been criticized for a series of empirical problems as well as theoretical ones. This section reviews three of the major academic criticisms directed at global cities research.

Firstly, since Friedmann's hierarchy of world cities (1986), the lack of convincing empirical evidence has proved most problematic for global cities researchers who suggested that a handful of elite cities might command and control the world economy and that cities across the world could be arranged in a hierarchical order of global control. Much of the problem results from the lack of comprehensive, consistent and internationally comparable data to measure individual cities' importance, position and service in a global capitalist world. Simply speaking, global rankings of cities are often asserted rather than justified by providing empirical evidence to support such rankings. Short et al. (1996) call it "a dirty little secret in the world cities literature" in which common assumptions about the list of leading cities and their role in globalization are merely repeated from previous works. Although rosters of world cities continued to be put forward in the 1990s (27 rosters reviewed in Beaverstock et al., 1999), global cities research was criticized for making little progress in overcoming its "evidential crisis."

Since the early 2000s, however, Peter Taylor and members of the GaWC have taken up the empirical challenge to open up new directions in global cities research by devising datasets on the locations and intrafirm networks of advanced producer service firms operating across the world – their most recent analysis covers 175 service firms across as many as 526 cities (Taylor and Derudder, 2015). Based on this empirical data analysis, Taylor and GaWC researchers have established a worldwide urban hierarchy in and through which those firms would plan, carry out and coordinate their business and personnel activities. They provide tables and maps of the world city network in which cities are ranked and categorized by global importance, urban network connectivities and strategic network connectivities. Along with global service firms, data on international airline passengers, global commodity chains, and energy and manufacturing production networks have also been analyzed in subsequent studies to assess individual cities' global connectivities and integration into the global urban networks (Derudder et al., 2008; Hesse, 2010; Krätke, 2014; Martinus and Tonts, 2015). There is no debate that Taylor and GaWC members have made a great contribution to global cities research in that they did not stop at addressing the empirical gaps, but started actively collecting and producing relevant data on the relations, linkages and interdependencies among a large number of cities. Although the GaWC has truly expanded the scope of interurban linkages beyond the small group of leading cities examined in many other comparative case studies, one may still argue that it is not enough to be called "a truly global-scale urban analysis," with so many places being left out (Krätke, 2014, 122). In addition, different studies employ different centrality measures that would capture "different dimensions of centrality in a global urban network" and, accordingly, present widely different rankings of cities, which adds a further layer of complexity and possible confusion to this approach (Sanderson et al., 2015, 176).

Secondly, despite much effort and progress made in overcoming the initial empirical shortcomings in the past 15 years, global cities research is yet to answer one very important question: whether the world economy is indeed being subject to control and coordination through global cities. In a short article titled "What is new about globalisation and what does it portend for cities?" urban scholar Hank Savitch (2002) argues that cities, whether they are a handful of global cities, a larger number of primate cities, or regional urban centers, "have made free trade much easier to accomplish, facilitated investments, and absorbed waves of migration. . . More than ever, cities serve as the command and control centers" of all the important wealth-generating strategic decisions. As such, global cities function as "efficient and enormously productive work stations" for the rest of the world. This reminds us of Sassen's notion of global cities as strategic places in the global economy and Friedmann's and Taylor's global cities at the apex of the worldwide urban hierarchy of global importance and connectivities.

While many have focused on what cities should qualify as command centers, how they would relate to one another and, more recently, how lower-level cities are incorporated into their global networks, few have asked whether housing quantities of globally operating financial and service firms, or any other assets for that matter, would "really amount to being in command of the world economy" (Smith, 2014, 104). Smith goes on to state that, without having analyzed any potential interfirm relations within cities, Taylor's world city network "contains no empirical proof" for global cities actually running the world economy and monopolizing global power. Basically, this calls back into question the fundamental assumption in global cities research that the global urban hierarchy is "a fundamental spatial infrastructure for the accelerated and intensified globalization of capital, including finance capital" (Brenner and Keil, 2014, 7). In an argument for more empirical researches on "most important inter-city links" in the global urban networks, Derudder et al. (2008, 6) contend that "global cities are key points in the organization of the global economy and increasingly derive their functional importance from their mutual interactions rather than with their proper hinterlands." As long as statements like this continue to be accepted without scrutiny, global cities research is likely to have another wave of crisis that may be more serious than the empirical crisis the GaWC has claimed to have overcome.

The third and last source of academic discontent concerns "multiple pathways" to and from global city formation. Following Sassen's analysis of how being a global command and control center should relate directly to higher levels of income inequality among its residents, many urban scholars have explored and tested the causal "effect of global centrality on income equality" in various global and globalizing cities (Monaghan and Ikeler, 2014). Basically, the so-called social polarization hypothesis states that the gap between the rich and the poor would be growing more rapidly in global cities than elsewhere, with increasing bifurcation between super-rich financial elites on one hand and low-wage, irregular immigrant workers on the other. This seemly insightful view of socioeconomic and spatial restructuring in global cities has frequently been criticized for its overemphasis on global economic forces at the expense of local and institutional factors like welfare programs, immigration regimes, and other traditional norms and practices (Chiu and Lui, 2004; Fainstein, 2011; Ma and Timberlake, 2013). The heavy focus on polarization might have a lot to do with the narrow scope of empirical studies conducted in the 1990s, during which a short list of global financial centers and their urban transformations were heavily investigated from a global perspective, while non-Western and/or non-global cities were largely neglected. That the vast majority of cities around the world neither house headquarters of global financial institutions nor undergo high-profile infrastructure work to be globally connected, their unique experiences and urban imaginaries in a globalizing age have not been fully investigated or adequately addressed in global cities research (Huyssen, 2008).

In more recent years, many have argued for a closer look at other dimensions of the global city than serving as centers of global capital accumulation, command and control (Acuto and Steele, 2013). Individual cities achieve differing positions, privileges and relationships with "multiple globalizations." Moreover, they all have a certain set of place-specific, path-dependent and political factors that would rework multiple global forces in particular ways (Ancien, 2011). Considering that all cities are global in the sense that they are connected with other parts of the world through networks of goods, services and people and that they are influenced by neoliberal capitalism, it makes great sense for global cities research to take a more fluid, less structured, "ordinary way" approach to the multiple processes that constitute a global or globalizing city. The recent rise of East Asian cities, such as Beijing, Hong Kong, Seoul, Shanghai and Singapore, as global corporate and financial centers and airline hubs, has prompted more and more urban researchers to explore multiple pathways to global city formation, as well as various outcomes and impacts of their rapid growth and advancement in the global urban hierarchy (Chubarov and Brooker, 2013; Roy and Ong, 2011).

Public discontent with the global city

While urban researchers have focused on addressing empirical and theoretical problems in the study of global cities, the defining features of global city status have been desired and debated in public and policy accounts as well. It is not uncommon to see urban politicians show a keen, persistent interest in improving their city's place in the global rankings of city competitiveness, however reliable and valid those ranking systems might be. In pursuit of economic success and global city status, mayors of the world's major cities have launched initiatives to refocus and prioritize actions and activities to enhance their city's global visibility and reputation and organize a bid for a large-scale sports competition like the

Summer Olympics. Naturally, it begs the crucial question of whether and how staging a sports event would bring global city status to the host place. However, the public is rarely invited to ask whether it is worth it at all, even if it were to succeed. Instead, urban policy makers, and their allies in business, media and management industries, form a coalition of powerful, self-serving interest groups that would command the authority to define what would be desirable for the city. Taxpayers and average citizens are increasingly frustrated that corporate words like global competitiveness, benchmarks, best practices and strategic planning are used in explaining the present state of their city and envisioning its future. This section reviews various forms and sources of public discontents with global city status and the projects and initiatives urban governments implement to achieve such status.

Let us take an example of Chicago, a solid second-tier global city whose government and local newspapers, as well as business leaders, often talk about how their city fares against other global cities and what it needs to work on to achieve first-tier status (Rodriguez, 2014). Among the city's public–private partnership initiatives created to rebuild and boost its global standing, Chicago's failed bid to host the 2016 Summer Olympic Games has been well publicized. Its current mayor is leading a public–private partnership called World Business Chicago to "advance Chicago's position as North America's global business center" by attracting foreign invest-ments (World Business Chicago, 2016). The Building a New Chicago program, a large-scale public work launched in 2012, has been upgrading the city's transporta-tion infrastructure, including the O'Hare international airport, so that it can be globally competitive again. Since 2015, the Chicago Council on Global Affairs has hosted an annual Chicago Forum on Global Cities "to discuss the power of global cities to shape the world's future" every summer, attracting a list of internationally renowned speakers. It might be the case that some residents and business owners in Chicago complain that the rest of the world has not yet recognized many of the global city qualities their city has worked to establish in recent years, and they feel that their city hall should do more to change world perceptions of Chicago. Yet, many others are unhappy with the cost and inconvenience the massive infrastruc-ture overhaul has caused and the high poverty and crime rates in its neighborhoods (Davey, 2016). Roadworks and homeless people are permanent features of life in downtown Chicago, while its 2016 Chicago Forum focused on the role and reach of the world's most influential cities.

Chicagoans would not be the only big-city residents to feel a mixture of frustration and pride with their city being ranked among the world's most globally competi-tive cities. Many around the world would resonate with the uncomfortable truth. Hundreds of thousands of people celebrate every four years when the next Olympic city is announced. However, the very same people are often forced to bear the brunt of tax hikes, cost overruns and traffic congestion caused by dozens of large, publically funded construction projects deemed necessary for a successful host. The level of public anxiety and frustration tends to get even higher when megacities in the Global South prepare to host a globally watched event, as happened to Seoul in South Korea with the 1988 Olympics and the 2002 World Cup and Rio, being the latest and perhaps most worrisome example, with the 2016 Olympics. Few national capitals and primate cities in the developing world are equipped with the operational capacity and physical infrastructure required to host a mega sport event. Yet, their political elites see competing to stage a major global event as a good and desirable policy choice on the grounds that their city is in need of a major turnaround to gain global recognition. This warrants a question: why is it so important for cities to be recognized as major global cities at a time when average citizens are more concerned about jobs, neighborhood violence, failing schools and overall public services?

An answer to this question can be found back in Chicago, where local politicians and policy makers showed unmatched enthusiasm about hosting, or even bidding for, a global sports competition. Their eagerness to host a mega event was vouched for and duly recommended by leading international consulting firms, as well as sports organizations. As a matter of fact, scores of consulting firms and think tanks collect data on individual cities' global competitiveness, based on which they hand out advice to city governments about what needs to be done to "ramp up the city's international profile" (Rodriguez, 2014). A.T. Kearney's Global Cities Index and Outlook, the Brookings Institution and JPMorgan Chase's Global Cities Initiative, the Economist Intelligence Unit's Global City Competitiveness and PricewaterhouseCoopers' Cities of Opportunity are only few of the many that promote and introduce best practices to become globally competitive and to get the attention of international business investors, creative talents, tourists and event organizers. This optimist bias that vastly overestimates the benefits of hosting a mega event, while underestimating its cost, is behind the increased advocacy and popularity of event-driven policies in urban governance.

There is now a large body of academic literature to point out the significant gap between pregame forecasts and postgame assessments and to warn candidate cities that hosting a global event might not bring much good at all (Hall, 2006; Short, 2012). We now see ordinary citizens feeling relief, rather than remorse, after they hear their city's Olympic bid end, as it was the case with Boston and Toronto among others. A *New York Times* article quotes Boston residents saying that they did not support their city's bid for the event because they were "too smart to be taken in by developers promising Olympic riches," and that the taxpayers worried about "bearing a huge burden" and ending up with "a lot of infrastructure that you don't use again" (Seeley, 2015). This is a telling example of what the public sees, or does not see, in Olympic and global city status. Once they comprehend that not getting such status would neither mean that their city is a stagnant city, nor that all cities are competing with each other over status, they would look closely at the price of being or becoming one of the globe's leading cities. More reservations about any policies and politics involved in planning, making and pursuing a global city would then be voiced.

As revealed recently in New York City, global city residents are indeed a lot more concerned about their vulnerability to infectious diseases and terrorist attacks.

They are well aware that global cities are particularly vulnerable to climate-related impacts due to population density and the built environment that includes high-rise office buildings and mega-size infrastructure facilities necessary for the global command and control functions. The anxiety and terror that come with global city status are under-researched and under-represented and should be prioritized in future research on global cities.

Future research agendas for global cities

It is evident from the abundant literature on cities and on globalization that the global city has now become one of the most exciting, if controversial, approaches to the study of urban change and policy development. The growth of research and teaching in the interdisciplinary field of global cities has enormously expanded since the mid-1990s, and so have criticisms. The global city has been criticized from two directions. On the one hand, critical urban researchers have addressed both conceptual and empirical challenges that global cities research has encountered. They include the longstanding debates on empirical poverty, the actual, not simply assumed or asserted, role of global cities in the current world economy, and the variety and multiplicity of global city formation. On the other hand, the fascination of global city status among urban leaderships across the world has led to increasing public discontent with the initiatives and policies designed to become or stay globally competitive. Building on these academic and popular discontents directed toward the global city, this section seeks to offer three new agendas for future research on global cities. By seeking to expand the horizons of global cities research beyond the traditional traits of command, connectedness and social polarization, and to offer more grounded approaches to understanding multiple trends and realities of global city formation, it is hoped that the role of global cities in today's global economy and in leading urban changes in other, globalizing cities can be better understood more fully and in detail.

Firstly, while much has been written about global cities coordinating global flows of trade, investment, information, ideas and people, little has been about their vulnerability to global risks. Research on the downside of global city status has focused mainly on social polarization and mega-event politics, but there is more to it. In an age of high mobility and ever-greater global connection, being a highly connected and densely populated urban center means high exposures to rapidly spreading infectious diseases, terrorism, financial risks, environmental problems and many other human security challenges. In addition, as the primary global media centers where most important news is first defined and disseminated, such cities are the very natural sites of global protest and activism (King, 2016, 196). The increasing globalization of security threats, health risks and illicit mobilities has indeed been researched and monitored in various disciplines, but the research findings are yet to be fully incorporated into global cities research. As clearly demonstrated in the outbreaks of Severe Acute Respiratory Syndrome (SARS) in 2003 and Ebola in 2014, for example, health problems that used to be more localized in remote areas of the developing world now spread rapidly and extensively over a vast region. Cities like New York, Paris, Singapore and Toronto that have long served as international gateway cities for large parts of Africa or Asia were among the first sites to have a public health emergency and, as importantly, to spread the disease to other cities through their national and global linkages (Ali and Keil, 2008; BBC, 2016; Heng, 2015). More intense research effort is needed to bring together the unconnected literatures on global urban networks, infectious diseases and immigrant communities in global cities to have a better understanding of the role of global cities in the globalization of health hazards and responses to them. The same should apply to research on other global risks like unwanted mobilities of terrorist groups and their financial transactions through and in global cities (Coaffee, 2009).

Secondly, though many have called for more research on the so-called non-global, non-Western cities to have a better understanding of their growth and integration into the global urban networks and their differences from, and similarities to, emergent global cities, we still need more research into the everyday urban experiences and practices of residents, migrant workers, policy makers and politicians, and business leaders in megacities and primate cities of the Global South. Consider large cities in Africa. In a time of unprecedented global integration, much has been assumed and discursively reproduced about their expanding linkages with other cities, whether their own kind in the region or another kind in the Global North. However, after the Ebola outbreak that claimed no fewer than 11,000 lives in West Africa, the international air connections of Freetown, Sierra Leone and Monrovia, Liberia have been unwanted, rejected and outright feared. A brief look at the International Civil Aviation Organization's (2016) statistics on inter-city passengers reveals that, even before the Ebola crisis, their air connections with global leading cities like London, New York and Paris had not recorded much growth. Instead, their connections with regional gateway cities like Accra, Lagos and Nairobi, and with the emerging one of Dubai, have intensified in recent years, presenting a case for further research into growing South–South relationships. It is believed that over the years, those who study global cities and, in general, the globalization–urbanization nexus have grown "in heterogeneity and multidisciplinarity" (Acuto, 2011). If so, it is time to see more stories, ideas, concepts and theories emerging from urban changes and policies in those diversified, heterogeneous, unconventional case study areas.

Thirdly, the reason for expanding the horizons of global cities research is not only to investigate those under-researched cities across Africa, Asia and Latin America, and smaller cities everywhere, but also to look into other, alternative dimensions of urban change in global cities that may not have already been captured by terms like competitiveness, connectedness, economic prowess or globalness. Comparative studies have been promoted in global cities research, but cities have been compared only when they are deemed comparable in size, global importance, history or architecture. Spencer (2015) argues that certain no-name rural places of Africa and Pacific Asia which remain important as part of the world's food production systems, tourist destinations and ecosystem services should be looked at. Indeed, it is rare for a small college town in the Midwest of the United States to be compared to a neighborhood in London, although both might share some traits of global fluency and progressive policy frameworks to promote human rights and global justice. The personal networks of diaspora and immigrant communities may link small towns and villages in Somalia of East Africa to cosmopolitan cities like London, Toronto and Minneapolis. Their cross-border, inter-city connections may not be measured by bank transfers, advanced services or even international flights, but rather by social networking services and other new forms of connections only revealed by further research.

References

Acuto, Michele (2011), 'Finding the global city: an analytical journey through the "invisible college"', *Urban Studies*, 48 (14), 2953–2973.

Acuto, Michele and Wendy Steele (eds) (2013), *Global City Challenges: Debating a Concept, Improving the Practice*, New York: Palgrave Macmillan.

Ali, S. Harris and Roger Keil (2008), *Networked Disease: Emerging Infections in the Global City*, Chichester, UK: Wiley-Blackwell.

Ancien, Delphine (2011), 'Global city theory and the new urban politics twenty years on: the case for a geohistorical materialist approach to the (new) urban politics of global cities', *Urban Studies*, 48 (12), 2473–2493.

BBC (2016), 'Ebola: mapping the outbreak', accessed 10 May 2016 at http://www.bbc.com/news/world-africa-28755033.

Beaverstock, J.V., P.J. Taylor and R.G. Smith (1999), 'A roaster of world cities', *Cities*, 16 (6), 445–458.

Brenner, Neil and Roger Keil (eds) (2006), *The Global Cities Reader*, London: Routledge.

Brenner, Neil and Roger Keil (2014), 'From global cities to globalized urbanization', *Glocalism: Journal of Culture, Politics and Innovation*, 3, 1–17.

Chiu, Stephen W.K. and Tai-lok Lui (2004), 'Testing the global city–social polarization thesis: Hong Kong since the 1990s', *Urban Studies*, 41 (10), 1863–1888.

Chubarov, Ilya and Daniel Brooker (2013), 'Multiple pathways to global city formation: a functional approach and review of recent evidence in China', *Cities*, 35, 181–189.

Coaffee, Jon (2009), *Terrorism, Risk and the Global City*, Burlington, VT: Ashgate.

Davey, Monica (2016), 'In deeply divided Chicago, most agree: city is off course', *The New York Times*, 6 May, accessed 8 May 2016 at http://www.nytimes.com/2016/05/07/us/chicago-racial-divisions-survey.html?_r=0.

Davis, Diane E. and Kian Tajbakhsh (2005), 'Globalization and cities in comparative perspective', *International Journal of Urban and Regional Research*, 29 (1), 89–91.

Derudder, Ben (2006), 'On conceptual confusion in empirical analyses of a transnational urban network', *Urban Studies*, 43 (11), 2027–2046.

Derudder, Ben, Frank Witlox, James Faulconbridge, and Jon Beaverstock (2008), 'Airline data for global city network research: reviewing and refining existing approaches', *GeoJournal*, 71, 5–18.

Fainstein, Susan S. (2011), *The Just City*, Ithaca, NY: Cornell University Press.

Friedmann, John (1986), 'The world city hypothesis', *Development and Change*, 17 (1), 69–83.

Geddes, Patrick (1915), *Cities in Evolution*, London: Williams and Norgate.

Hall, C. Michael (2006), 'Urban entrepreneurship, corporate interests and sports mega-events: the think policies of competitiveness within the hard outcomes of neoliberalism', in John Horne and Wolfram Manzenreiter (eds), *Sports Mega-Events: Social Scientific Analyses of a Global Phenomenon*, Malden, MA: Blackwell Publishing, pp.59–70.

Hall, Peter (1966), *The World Cities*, New York: World University Library.

Heng, Yee-Kuang (2015), *Managing Global Risks in the Urban Age: Singapore and the Making of a Global City*, Burlington, VT: Ashgate.

Hesse, Markus (2010), 'Cities, material flows and the geography of spatial interaction: urban places in the system of chains', *Global Networks*, 10 (1), 75–91.

Huyssen, Andreas (ed.) (2008), *Other Cities, Other Worlds: Urban Imaginaries in a Globalizing Age*, Durham, NC: Duke University Press.

International Civil Aviation Organization (ICAO) (2016), 'Data + on-flight origin and destination', accessed 25 January 2016 at www4.icao.int/NewDataPlus/.

Ismail, Ayat (2013), 'The hybrid outcome of urban change: global city, polarized city?', *Glocalism: Journal of Culture, Politics and Innovation*, 2, 1–38.

Jacobs, Jane (1969), *The Economy of Cities*, New York: Random House.

Kim, Yeong-Hyun (2014), 'Globalization and the city', in Lisa Benton-Short (ed.), *Cities of North America: Contemporary Challenges in U.S. and Canadian Cities*, Lanham, MD: Rowman & Littlefield, pp.143–165.

King, Anthony D. (2016), *Writing the Global City: Globalization, Postcolonialism and the Urban*, New York: Routledge.

Krätke, Stefan (2014), 'How manufacturing industries connect cities across the world: extending research on "multiple globalizations"', *Global Networks*, 14 (2), 121–147.

Ma, Xiulian and Michael Timberlake (2013), 'World city typologies and national city system deterritorialisation: USA, China and Japan', *Urban Studies*, 50 (2), 255–275.

Martinus, Kirsten and Matthew Tonts (2015), 'Powering the world city system: energy industry networks and interurban connectivity', *Environment and Planning A*, 47 (7), 1502–1520.

Miraftab, Faranak and Neema Kudva (eds) (2015), *Cities of the Global South Reader*, London: Routledge.

Monaghan, David and Peter Ikeler (2014), 'Global centrality and income inequality in U.S. metropolitan areas: a test of two hypotheses', *Sociological Focus*, 47 (3), 174–193.

Parnreiter, Christof (2013), 'The global city tradition', in Michele Acuto and Wendy Steele (eds), *Global City Challenges: Debating a Concept, Improving the Practice*, New York: Palgrave Macmillan, pp.15–32.

Robinson, Jennifer (2011), 'Cities in a world of cities: the comparative gesture', *International Journal of Urban and Regional Research*, 35 (1), 1–23.

Rodriguez, Alex (2014), 'Global city Chicago: how does Chicago stack up?', *Chicago Tribune*, 26 January, accessed 1 March 2016 at www.chicagotribune.com/news/globalcity/ct-global-city-chicago-nw-20140126-story.html.

Rogerson, Christian M. and Jayne M. Rogerson (2015), 'Johannesburg 2030: the economic contours of a linking global city', *American Behavioral Scientist*, 59 (3), 347–368.

Roy, Ananya and Aihwa Ong (eds) (2011), *Worlding Cities: Asian Experiments and the Art of Being Global*, Chichester, UK: Wiley-Blackwell.

Sanderson, Matthew R., Ben Derudder, Michael Timberlake, and Frank Witlox (2015), 'Are world cities also world immigrant cities? An international, cross-city analysis of global centrality and immigration', *International Journal of Comparative Sociology*, 56 (3–4), 173–197.

Sassen, Saskia (1991), *The Global City: New York, London, Tokyo*, Princeton, NJ: Princeton University Press.

Savitch, H.V. (2002), 'What is new about globalisation and what does it portend for cities?', *International Social Science Journal*, 172, 179–189.

Seeley, Katharine Q. (2015), 'Many in Boston feel relief as Olympic bid ends, but others see a stagnant city', *The New York Times*, 28 July, accessed 15 April 2016 at www.nytimes.com/2015/07/29/us/many-in-boston-feel-relief-as-olympic-bid-ends-but-others-see-a-stagnant-city.html?_r=0.

Short, John Rennie (2012), *Globalization, Modernity and the City*, New York: Routledge.

Short, J.R., Y. Kim, M. Kuus, and H. Wells (1996), 'The dirty little secret of world cities research: data problems in comparative analysis', *International Journal of Urban and Regional Research*, 20 (4), 697–717.

Smith, Richard G. (2014), 'Beyond the global city concept and the myth of command and control', *International Journal of Urban and Regional Research*, 38 (1), 98–115.

Spencer, James H. (2015), *Globalization and Urbanization: The Global Urban Ecosystem*, Lanham, MD: Rowman & Littlefield.

Taylor, Peter J. and Ben Derudder (2015), *World City Network: A Global Urban Analysis*, London: Routledge.

Taylor, Peter J., Ben Derudder, James Faulconbridge, Michael Hoyler, and Pengfei Ni (2013), 'Advanced producer service firms as strategic networks, global cities as strategic places', *Economic Geography*, 90 (3), 267–291.

Timberlake, M., M.R. Sanderson, X. Ma, B. Derudder, J. Winitsky, and F. Witlox (2012), 'Testing a global city hypothesis: an assessment of polarization across US cities', *City and Community*, 11 (1), 74–93.

World Business Chicago (2016), 'Who we are and how we help', accessed 10 May 2016 at www.world businesschicago.com.

3   The city of global flows

Jonathan V. Beaverstock

Cities are now theorized as relational spaces in a continual process of growth or contraction, flux and change, nourished by inflows of capital and labour, and different cultural and social practices. Technology is a catalyst for the reproduction of the city of global flows, but cities as relational spaces and economic, social and cultural processes are far more complex than first meets the technological-determinist eye! Urban theorists such as Manuel Castells, John Rennie Short and Peter Taylor, to name a few, have long advocated the significance of the city's relationalities, networks and connectivity, respectively, culminating in texts like *The Rise of the Network Society* (Castells, 1996), *Globalization and the City* (Short and Kim, 1999) and *World City Network* (Taylor, 2004). The establishment of the Globalization and World Cities[1] (GaWC) project has been at the forefront of such research. The last decade has seen a stupendous growth in theoretical and empirical work on the city in global flows, primarily from structuralist perspectives, encompassing both scholars and examples from the global North and South (the most recent being Parnell, 2016; Taylor and Derudder, 2015). Given that cities are the spaces that are affected by all of the contradictions of globalization in both the global North and the global South, there are significant challenges ahead for urban scholars in studying the city in global flows. In this chapter, I wish to briefly raise some of these challenges in the guise of new research avenues for theorizing and studying the city in global flows.

The rest of this chapter is organized in four sections. First, a potted history of cities in globalization and the genesis of the space of flows is briefly discussed, drawing on Castells' (1989; 1996) work in this field. Second, the contribution of the GaWC project in advancing urban scholarship on the study of inter-city relations and the city in the space of flows is critically evaluated. Third, the subject of *intra*-city flows, technology and inter-disciplinarity is addressed through a thumbnail sketch of the 'smart cities' and 'big data' debates regarding the new fascination with the so-called 'science of cities' (Batty, 2013a). In many ways, this scientific-driven agenda on the city as an integrated, real-time system provides the most significant challenge, both theoretically and empirically, to traditional ways of examining the city in global flows. Finally, I outline five main challenges for studying the city in global flows over the coming decade or so, revolving around the following questions: what flows to study? How to respond to the challenges of 'big' data? What should compose the space of flows 'of everything'? Where to study flows? And, how to incorporate inter-disciplinarity into studies of the city in the global space of flows?

Cities in globalization – flows, networks and nodes

Castells' (1989) *The Informational City* makes the first insightful interrogation of the concept 'the space of flows' in a context of the world economy's shift to services and the escalation of technology in the genesis of the information economy. Castells (1989) notes that the spatial logics and power of organizations, labour and the Informational City have produced a space of flows which is both place-bound and placeless, and perpetuated by the new information economy which, critically, has developed, '. . . [n]ew spatial forms, and even more important, a new spatial logic' (p. 167). Many of Castells' (1989) early conceptual ideas in the formation of the space of flows and the Informational City not only, obviously, set the underpinning for *The Rise of the Network Society* (Castells, 1996), but also allude to relationality and complement Sassen's (1988) analysis of the internationalization of advanced producer services, worldwide industrial restructuring and immigration in the rise of the so-called global city.

Castells' take on the space of flows and the accompanying new spatial logic is examined closely in his 1996 text, *The Rise of the Network Society* (n.b. 2nd edition, published in 2000). Space is defined as material social processes and practices, and flows are the essential make-up of society – 'flows of capital, flows of information, flows of technology, flows of organizational interaction, flows of images, sounds and symbols' – and Castells describes the space of flows as '. . . the material organization of time-sharing social practices that work through flows' (Castells, 1996, 412). Castells' (1996, 412–413, 415) space of flows is organized into three layers: the first layer essentially being information and communication technologies, 'a circuit of electronic impulses (micro-electronics, telecommunications, computer processing, broadcasting systems, and high-speed transportation)'; the second layer composed of 'nodes and hubs . . . refers to the analysis of the global city as a process rather than a place'; and the third layer '. . .the dominant spatial organization of the dominant, managerial elites (rather than classes) . . . the technocratic-financial-managerial elite'. Castells' (1989; 1996) writing on the space of flows and the *Informational City* is highly significant in theorizing the city in global flows precisely because it identifies the city as a new *relational* phenomenon constantly in a process of restructuring and change, as such nodes are unevenly affected by flows and network formations. Indeed, Castells' (1996) new spatial logic reaffirmed the place-based and bounded inadequacies of Friedmann's (1986) world city hierarchy and Sassen's (1988; 1991) global city thesis.

Twenty years on from the publication of *The Rise of the Network Society*, Castells' views on the space of flows and its layering in society are still highly relevant today. The space of flows is reaffirmed in the twenty-first century, particularly given the continual reorganization of industrial capital, the globalization of finance and financialization, the rise and rise of the internet revolution, e-commerce and social media, and the emergence of the so-called 'smart city', for example. The advent of a new kind of space of flows for the early part of the twenty-first century has reproduced the structural power of each of the three layers in the space of flows:

electronic exchange and telecommunications, nodes and hubs (effectively cities) and the all-powerful transnational managerial, financial and political elite (and also the super-rich elite – see Beaverstock et al., 2004; Hay and Beaverstock, 2016).

Like all innovative thinkers, Castells' seminal work on the space of flows and 'the Network Society' has received critique and stimulated discussion (see Smith, 2003a; van Dijk, 1999). But, importantly, as I shall note in the next section of the chapter, the GaWC project was heavily influenced by Castells' (1996) 'space of flows', which underpins many of GaWC's early work on the relational turn in the study of world cities and cities *in* globalization (see Beaverstock et al., 1999; 2000a; 2002; Taylor, 1997; 2001; 2004; Taylor et al., 2002).

The GaWC legacy

Inspired by Sassen's (1991) *The Global City*, Castells' (1996) *The Rise of the Network Society* and Short et al.'s (1996) 'The dirty little secret of world cities research', Peter J. Taylor and I, building on previous research (Beaverstock, 1994; Taylor, 1997), established the GaWC research group and network in the period 1997–98 to embark upon an empirical and conceptual quest to study cities relationally in the 'global space of flows'. By the mid-2000s, these two authors, with Richard Smith, Marcus Doel and Philip Hubbard, had produced a rich body of work which was driving evidence-based, conceptual thinking on cities in globalization and the global space of flows (Beaverstock et al., 1999; 2000a; 2000b; 2002). The pioneering shift in GaWC's thinking was the establishment of a new urban infrastructure, termed a 'world city network', which sought to examine the interlocking processes and actors that created the flows and networks that made world cities relational and responsive to external change. Taylor's (2001) and Beaverstock et al.'s (2002) world city network was a direct swing away from established thinking about world cities as isolated, hierarchical spaces, as illustrated in Friedmann's (1986) world city hierarchy and Sassen's (1991; 1994) analysis of the global city. GaWC's founding contribution to urban studies and urban geography was conceptual: to think differently about world cities (in fact, all cities) in globalization. GaWC brought a brand new relational aspect to theory and practice concerning cities and, significantly, their flows and networks in the global space of flows.

GaWC's second significant contribution to urban thought about cities in the space of flows was empirical. In a quantitative approach, Taylor's (2001; 2004) work on the specification of the world city network brought to the fray an interlocking world city network model which examined the connectivities of cities through a statistical analysis of advance producer service firms' office networks and predicted values of the importance of such offices around the globe. The advent of the interlocking world city network model has provided an evidence-based approach to quantifying the changing pattern of world cities since the early 2000s, producing a plethora of influential articles, books and edited volumes (see Derudder and Taylor, 2005; Taylor and Aranya, 2008; Taylor et al., 2007; 2011; 2013; 2014), most recently exemplified by the second edition of *World City Network* (Taylor and Derudder, 2015).

GaWC's quantitative contribution was also complemented by a string of qualitative and 'mixed methods' approaches, focusing on flows, networks and cities. For example, detailed work was undertaken on London and Frankfurt in the space of flows in the early 2000s (Beaverstock et al., 2005), the financial sustainability of London's financial district in relation to other global financial centres (Cook et al., 2007) and, more recently, the globalization of US advertising firms and how organizational change in these firms influenced New York's, Los Angeles' and Detroit's creative flows and networks (Faulconbridge et al., 2011). My own work in the field of elite migration studies continues to look closely at the mobility of highly skilled labour in the space of flows. The key component of Castells' (2000, 443) third layer in the space of flows, 'the dominant managerial elites', continues to play an integral role in sustaining and nourishing knowledge and capital accumulation in relational world city networks and global financial centres (see Beaverstock, 2007; Beaverstock and Hall, 2012; Beaverstock et al., 2005; Faulconbridge et al., 2009). In many ways, GaWC's primary legacy has also led the way for a relational approach or turn in many other geographical sub-disciplines, such as economic geography, which followed the spirit of the GaWC project from the early 2000s (see Boggs and Rantisi, 2003; Yeung, 2005).

GaWC's ground-breaking contribution to advancing conceptual and empirical thinking on the role of cities in the space of flows is not without controversy. GaWC's third major legacy has been its pivotal position in stimulating debate and critique about cities in global flows. Robinson (2002; 2005) and Smith (2003a; 2003b; 2013; also see Smith and Doel, 2011), from post-colonial and post-structuralist perspectives, respectively, have made very positive contributions to advancing knowledge and understanding of cities in global flows. Recent writings by Watson and Beaverstock (2014) talk of the empirical interlocking world city network model reaching a theoretical impasse and call on future GaWC data collections to embrace (once again) qualitative approaches to refresh their depictions of world city networks and connectivities. As they argue, '. . . we suggest that a combination of quantitative and qualitative methods, focused at either firm level and/or the level of the individual, will allow for the most holistic understanding of world city networking processes' (Watson and Beaverstock, 2014, 422).

We can categorically conclude that without GaWC's founding work on relationality and cities in globalization, the urban community's take on cities in the global space of flows would be a much poorer and inferior intellectual discourse.

Smart cities, 'big data' and the 'second' quantitative revolution

Following on from Graham and Marvin (1996), theorizing and visualizing the city of global flows has now become a quantitative science, first under the banner of 'smart cities', and now in the discourse of 'urban analytics' or 'urban futures', which has been swept forward by the new fad of 'big data' (see Batty et al., 2012; Glasmeier and Christopherson, 2015; Kitchen, 2014). Mike Batty's 'science of cities' research (Batty, 2013a; 2013b; Batty et al., 2012), drawing on geospatial data analysis, modelling and forecasting, argues that cities are integrated, complex systems of flows, both physical and electronic and internal and external, and has been instrumental in the advent of what I would term the second quantitative revolution in urban geography. In many ways, the city of global flows, built on the relational inter-city discourse, has now very much been superseded by studies of 'real-time' *intra*-city flows. The study of cities as complex urban systems is now populated by people from an array of engineering and scientific disciplines, such as civil engineers, mathematicians, economists (labour, transport), operations management specialists, geospatial scientists and statisticians. Importantly, the 'science of cities' has attracted much interest from government and scientific funding bodies (such as the United Kingdom's Economic and Social Research Council – http://www.esrc.ac.uk/research/our-research/big-data-network/, accessed 29.01.2016), city-based stakeholders (including regional and local government structures, non-governmental organizations (NGOs) and other not-for-profit organizations, and local universities) and private enterprises (engineering companies, telecommunications, transport). New York University's Center for Urban Science and Progress is one exemplar of the science of cities agenda being put into action through stakeholder partnerships (http://cusp.nyu.edu/about/, accessed 29.01.2016).

In my own university city, Bristol, England, the smart city agenda has quickly mobilized the University of Bristol and Bristol City Council, working in partnership with range of local stakeholders,[2] to analyse the city as a real-time, integrated system, drawing on the latest technology to study, visualize and forecast intra-city flows. The initiative is called Bristol is Open (http://www.bristolisopen.com/overview/), and its mission is to create an 'Open Programmable City-Region' and not get too carried away with the 'smart-city' and 'big-data' agenda:

> How cities work is changing. Developments in software, hardware and telecom networks are enabling more interaction between people and places and more machine-to-machine communication, creating an internet of things. Opening-up and making sense of this is giving citizens more ability to interact, work and play with their city. Using data sensors, smart city technologies will be able to respond in real-time to everyday events including congestion, waste management, entertainment events, e-democracy, energy supply and more. Together we are creating an open programmable city region. (http://www.bristolisopen.com/, accessed 29.01.2016)

Yes, it does have its place in our analysis of the city in global flows, both inter- and intra-city. But, this quantitative project has already generated much critique from the social sciences community (see Kitchen, 2013; 2015).

Looking ahead

Compiling a 'list' of burning avenues for future research and interrogation in the field of global urban flows and networks is problematic. Scholars, politicians, entrepreneurs, stakeholders and local communities can all identify numerous context-specific urban futures, but the list of research questions are possibly infinite and never ending, particularly as different countries, regions and cities are faced with differing combinations of challenges including climate change, economic and political disruption, new infrastructure, mass immigration, and energy, food and income security. Geography certainly plays a significant role in identifying the new directions of research in the thematic study of the global urban flows. Cities in the global 'North' certainly face many different challenges to those in the global 'South', and vice versa. In no way can I outline a comprehensive analysis of the urban futures for cities in the space of flows. But what I can do is offer several immense questions and issues that in my view will require further interrogation.

What global flows?

Year on year, the connectedness and speed with which material and immaterial flows circulate within the global urban system is mesmerizing. From the globalization of the financial system and the 'financialization of everything', to cities reaffirming their gateway status for new waves of international immigrants, and to the agency of social media whipping up instant, grass-roots communication and action in the form of crowd-sourcing and trending, cities have never been such fundamental nodes in the articulation of the global space of flows. But for the urban scholar, the challenge will be threefold. First, what constitutes a global flow, particularly in a new era of technology and communication, and geo-economic and geo-political change? Second, what distinctive global flows are crucial to the sustainability of the city-system in the global North and/or global South? Third, how can global flows be captured, measured and interrogated to provide suitable comparative urban data which the academy and policy makers can use effectively to formulate progressive urban policy and actions for not only the benefit of private enterprise but also for the social well-being of liveable and sustainable communities? These are simple questions that face the community of urbanists and policy-driven actors, irrespective of their local geography. But the answers are challenging and complex. Theorizing the city in the global space of flows is much easier in comparison to the challenges of collecting, analysing and interpreting inter-city data which falls out of the usual official statistical digests based on the nation-state (Beaverstock et al., 2000b; Taylor, 1997).

The 'big data' rebuttal!

Now that engineers and a reserve army of quantitative labour have re-discovered cities thanks to the advent of 'big data' and urban analytics, and the need to 'scientifically' make cities more resilient to natural and anthropogenic change, what goes on in the city has in many ways superseded theory and practice on the city in the space of global flows. Across the disciplines of the natural and physical sciences, technology and communication, engineering (particularly building and civil) and, to some extent, mathematics (often depicted as the STEMM disciplines[3]), academic scholars and the interested professionalized community (consultants, 'think-tanks', lobby groups and the like) have re-discovered the urban as a real-time, living 'laboratory' to collect data on both inter- and intra-city flows (e.g. commuting patterns, transportation usage, road tolls, inward investment, employment change), often using smart technology and sophisticated mathematical models to forecast and predict urban change, and thereby to offer solutions to make cities more resilient to future shocks. The challenge for urban scholars is to overcome the current structural bias in government funding and university investment in large centres and institutes which favour a 'big-data' and urban-analytics approach to studying the intra- and inter-city global flows, often in the guise of 'urban futures' or 'city futures'. It is imperative that the humanities and social sciences approaches to cities in the global (and local) space of flows are not left behind or sidelined by the STEMM disciplines jockeying for resources and the intellectual high ground. A key challenge for urban scholars is to continue to formulate transformative, process-led research and action that offers real solutions to the challenges facing the city in global change, which can, importantly, complement the race for 'big data'. 'Big data' doesn't necessarily provide the 'perfect, uncontested solutions' to understanding the complexities of contemporary and future urban life in both the global North and the global South.

The global space of flows of everything

Current and previous research on globalization and cities has looked at flows, networks and nodes all at different scales involving a multitude of case studies (e.g. firms, labour migration) and associated micro-processes. At a general level, the chronology was taken from the world city discourse (Friedmann, 1986; Sassen, 1991) and Castells' (1989) notion of the Informational City and, later, network society (1996), studying first nodes (world cities) and flows, and then as these debates matured, attention focused on the configuration and functioning of networks (in production, commodity, financial and global value chains) (see Brown et al., 2010; Coe et al., 2014). Importantly, these debates have spilled over into other disciplines such as economic geography, where global production networks involve the close interactions of flows, networks and nodes in the composition of firms' spatial organization and factors of production (see Coe et al., 2008). Looking forward, we still have the conundrum of precisely what to study and where to study it. Should our endeavours focus on the composition and material and immaterial nature and characteristics of global or local flows, or the make-up, sustainability and vitality of the actual networks or nodes? Or a combination of everything? A key area of debate when studying the city in global flows is how to study the city as an integrated system. Do you study the city to understand the city in the space of flows? Or should you study the flow or network to understand the processes ongoing in the city?

Where? Location, location, location

Geography matters (Massey and Allen, 1984). It is imperative that scholars engage in comparative work which goes beyond the global North. This is certainly a challenge on many fronts – intellectual, methodological and resource-based. It is clear from Robinson's (2002; 2005) seminal critiques of GaWC inter-city empirical depictions of the space of flows that urban scholars should embrace the global South in their studies of flows, networks and nodes (also see Parnell and Robinson, 2012). However, this post-colonial critique in itself neglects the significance of the emerging economies beyond the Sub-Saharan Africa city-system. Great inroads have been made in analysing Chinese, Brazilian, Mexican, Russian and Indian cities (see Derudder et al., 2013; Rossi et al., 2007; Parnreiter, 2015; Golubchikov, 2010; Chacko, 2007, respectively) in global flows using both quantitative and qualitative approaches, but more studies are needed with respect to global South cities (nodes) and those global South originated organizations (multinational corporations, NGOs, intergovernmental organizations (IGOs)), people and practices that generate and reproduce the flows and networks (see Parnell, 2016; Parnell and Pieterse, 2016). In order to make advancements in our knowledge of the city in global flows, it is imperative that researchers go beyond the saturated global North for new intelligence, data and policy-driven agendas. Outside of the GaWC project, Neil Brenner's Harvard University-based Urban Theory Lab[4] provides a compelling body of work on 'planetary urbanization' (see Brenner and Schmid, 2015; 2011) which complements traditional world city discourses advocating cities in globalization and in the space of flows. In the United Kingdom, University College London's Urban Laboratory[5] has been making similar inroads into advancing an inter-disciplinary approach to urban studies and the city, drawn from case studies from both the global North and the global South (see Gandy, 2011; Parnell and Robinson, 2012; Robinson, 2011). The BRICS economies,[6] while in relative slowdown, are still experiencing rapid growth in their city-systems, which presents an unparalleled opportunity to examine, both conceptually and empirically, the agency of their cities and the production of their global flows and networks. Cities like Rio de Janeiro, Sao Paulo, Moscow, Mumbai, Chennai, Pune, Bangalore, New Delhi, Kolkata, Tianjin, Guangzhou, Chengdu and Johannesburg, along with others like Abu Dhabi, Cairo, Istanbul, Ho Chi Min City and Hanoi, will provide fertile *relational* urban laboratories to develop new studies of flows, networks and nodes in the global space of flows.

Embrace inter-disciplinarity

The future is inter-disciplinary. Inter-disciplinary approaches are embedded in all of the above previous points made about the challenges of looking ahead in future studies of cities in the global space of flows. An inter-disciplinary approach is key to how we theorize and advance intellectual knowledge of the city in global flows, how we plan and execute data collection, analysis and interpretation, and in the mediums in which we disseminate findings and policy recommendations to the academy and stakeholder communities. Inter-disciplinarity will be driven not only by substantial academic agendas to embrace the STEMM disciplines to advance scientific knowledge of cities in the global space of flows, both internally and externally, but also by the academic and funding community who have embraced the second quantitative revolution of 'big data' and urban informatics to supposedly tackle the major challenges facing cities over the coming decades. Inter-disciplinarity will drive forward new and innovative ways of approaching and researching the city as a relational integrated system, whether in the global South or global North, and facilitate new collaborative partnerships with scholars and practitioners in the co-production of knowledge.

New research avenues – 'the space of flows of everything'

We are at a crossroads in the study of the city of global flows. In order to make a step-change in both theory and practice, the academy and policy community need to embrace new mind-sets for investigating the urban and city in contemporary globalization. Following on from the questions and burning issues discussed above, there are five key directions, or gauntlets, that I'd like to throw down to urban scholars, for future research and practice in studying the city in the 'space of flows of everything'.

First, a key question: what precise global flows will affect the city in the near and distant future, and how can such data be captured, analysed and interpreted to compile comparative inter-city data sets?

Second, it will be essential for urban scholars to embrace the 'big data' paradigm and use their social sciences and humanities theoretical and empirical approaches to help shape and transform the 'big data' debate.

Third, we need a better sense of what we should actually be studying – node, flow or network – to advance knowledge and understanding of the city in global flows 'of everything'.

Fourth, where we should do our research? The familiar or a fuller engagement with flows, networks and nodes that are in the rapidly emerging economies' cities and city-regions of the globe?

Fifth, there is a necessity to clasp inter-disciplinarity and foster collaboration with scholars and stakeholders from outside of traditional home disciplines like urban studies or urban geography.

The choice is yours!

NOTES

1 See www.lboro.ac.uk/gawc, accessed 20.01.2016.

2 Partners include nearby local government (e.g. Bath and North East Somerset), central government departments (e.g. Department for Business, Innovation and Skills, Catapult Future Cities, Catapult Digital), the Open Data Institute and many multinational, national and local technology companies (e.g. Dell, NEC).

3 STEMM is an acronym for the Science, Technology, Engineering, Medicine and Mathematics disciplines.
4 See: http://urbantheorylab.net/about/, accessed 19.01.2016.
5 See: http://www.ucl.ac.uk/urbanlab, accessed 19.01.2016.
6 Includes Brazil, Russia, India, China and South Africa. South Africa was added in 2010.

References

Batty, Michael (2013a), *The New Science of Cities*, Boston: MIT.

Batty, M. (2013b), 'Big data, smart cities and city planning', *Dialogues in Human Geography*, **3** (3), 274–279.

Batty, M., K.W. Axhausen, F. Giannotti, A. Pozdnoukhov, A. Bazzani, M. Wachowicz, G. Ouzounis and Y. Portugali (2012), 'Smart cities of the future', *European Physical Journal Special Topics*, **214** (1), 481–518.

Beaverstock, J.V. (1994), 'Re-thinking skilled international labour migration: World cities and banking organisations', *Geoforum* **25** (3), 323–338.

Beaverstock, Jonathan V. (2007), 'Transnational work: Global professional labour markets in professional service accounting firms', in John Bryson and Peter Daniels (eds), *The Handbook of Service Industries*, Cheltenham, UK and Northampton, MA, USA: Edward Elgar Publishing, pp. 409–431.

Beaverstock, J.V., M.A. Doel, P.J. Hubbard and P.J. Taylor (2002), 'Attending to the world: Competition, cooperation and connectivity in the world city network', *Global Networks*, **2** (2), 111–132.

Beaverstock, J.V. and S. Hall (2012), '"Competing for talent": Global mobility, immigration and the City of London's labour market', *Cambridge Journal of Regions, Economy and Society*, **5** (2), 271–288.

Beaverstock, J.V., M. Hoyler, K. Pain and P.J. Taylor (2005), 'Demystifying the Euro in European financial centre relations: London and Frankfurt, 2000–2001', *Journal of Contemporary European Studies*, **13** (2), 143–157.

Beaverstock, J.V., P.J. Hubbard and J.R. Short (2004), 'Getting away with it? Exposing the geographies of the super-rich', *Geoforum*, **35** (4), 401–407.

Beaverstock, J.V., R.G. Smith and P.J. Taylor (1999), 'A roster of world cities', *Cities*, **16** (6), 445–458.

Beaverstock, J.V., R.G. Smith and P.J. Taylor (2000a), 'World city network: A new meta-geography?', *Annals of the Association of American Geographers*, **90** (1), 123–134.

Beaverstock, J.V., R.G. Smith, P.J. Taylor, D.R.F. Walker and H. Lorimer (2000b), 'Globalization and world cities: Some measurement methodologies', *Applied Geography*, **20** (1), 43–63.

Boggs, J.S. and N.M. Rantisi (2003), 'The "relational turn" in economic geography', *Journal of Economic Geography*, **3** (1), 109–116.

Brenner, Neil and Christian Schmid (2011), 'Planetary urbanization', in Matthew Gandy (ed.), *Urban Constellations*, Berlin: Jovis, pp. 10–13.

Brenner, N. and C. Schmid (2015), 'Towards a new epistemology of the urban?', *City*, **19** (2/3), 151–182.

Brown, E., B. Derudder, C. Parnreiter, W. Pelupessy, P.J. Taylor and F. Witlox (2010), 'World city networks and global commodity chains: Towards a world-systems' integration', *Global Networks: A Journal of Transnational Affairs*, **10** (1), 12–34.

Castells, Manuel (1989), *The Informational City*, Oxford: Wiley-Blackwell.

Castells, Manuel (1996), *The Rise of the Network Society*, Oxford: Blackwell.

Castells, Manuel (2000), *The Rise of the Network Society*, Oxford: Blackwell (2nd edition).

Chacko, E. (2007), 'From brain drain to brain gain: Reverse migration to Bangalore and Hyderabad, India's globalizing high tech cities', *Geojournal*, **68** (2), 131–140.

Coe, N.M., P. Dicken and M. Hess (2008), 'Global production networks: Realizing the potential', *Journal of Economic Geography*, **8** (3), 271–295.

Coe, N., K. Lai and D. Wójcik (2014), 'Integrating finance into global production networks', *Regional Studies*, **48** (5), 761–777.

Cook, G.A.S., N. Pandit, J.V. Beaverstock, P.J. Taylor and K. Pain (2007), 'The role of location in knowledge creation and diffusion: Evidence of centripetal and centrifugal forces in the City of London financial services agglomeration', *Environment and Planning A*, **39** (6), 1325–1345.

Derudder, B. and P.J. Taylor (2005), 'The cliquishness of world cities', *Global Networks*, **5** (1), 71–91.

Derudder, B., P.J. Taylor, M. Hoyler, P. Ni, X. Liu, M. Zhao, W. Shen and F. Witlox (2013), 'Measurement and interpretation of the connectivity of Chinese cities in the world city network, 2010', *Chinese Geographical Science*, **23** (3), 261–273.

Faulconbridge, J.F., J.V. Beaverstock, S. Hall and A. Hewitson (2009), 'The "war for talent": Unpacking the gatekeeper role of executive search firms in elite labour markets', *Geoforum*, **40** (5), 800–808.

Faulconbridge, James, Jonathan Beaverstock, Corinne Nativel and Peter Taylor (2011), *The Globalization of Advertising: Agencies, Cities and Spaces of Creativity*, London: Routledge.

Friedmann, J. (1986), 'The world city hypothesis', *Development and Change*, **17** (1), 69–83.

Gandy, Matthew (ed.) (2011), *Urban Constellations*, Berlin: Jovis.

Glasmeier, A. and S. Christopherson (2015), 'Thinking about smart cities', *Cambridge Journal of Regions, Economy and Society*, **8** (1), 3–12.

Golubchikov, O. (2010), 'World-city-entrepreneurialism: Globalist imaginaries, neoliberal geographies, and the production of new St Petersburg', *Environment and Planning A*, **42** (3), 626–643.

Graham, Stephen and Simon Marvin (1996), *Telecommunications and the City: Electronic Spaces, Urban Paces*, London: Routledge.

Hay, Iain and Jonathan Beaverstock (eds) (2016), *The Handbook on Wealth and the Super-Rich*, Cheltenham, UK and Northampton, MA, USA: Edward Elgar Publishing.

Kitchen, R. (2013), 'Big data and human geography: Opportunities, challenges and risks', *Dialogues in Human Geography*, **3** (3), 262–267.

Kitchen, R. (2014), 'The real-time city? Big data and smart urbanism', *GeoJournal*, **79** (1), 1–14.

Kitchen, R. (2015), 'Making sense of smart cities: Addressing present shortcomings', *Cambridge Journal of Regions, Economy and Society*, **8** (1), 131–136.

Massey, Doreen and John Allen (eds) (1984), *Geography Matters!*, Cambridge: Cambridge University Press.

Parnell, S. (2016), 'Defining a global urban development agenda', *World Development*, **78** (February), 529–540.

Parnell, S. and E. Pieterse (2016), 'Translational global praxis: Rethinking methods and modes of African research', *International Journal of Urban and Regional Research*, **40** (1), 236–246.

Parnell, S. and J. Robinson (2012), '(Re)theorizing cities from the global South: Looking beyond neoliberalism', *Urban Geography*, **33** (4), 593–617.

Parnreiter, C. (2015), 'Strategic planning, the real estate economy, and the production of new spaces of centrality: The case of Mexico City', *Erdkunde*, **69** (1), 21–31.

Robinson, J. (2002), 'Global and world cities: A view from off the map', *International Journal of Urban and Regional Research*, **26** (3), 531–554.

Robinson, J. (2005), 'Urban geography: World cities, or a world of cities', *Progress in Human Geography*, **29** (6), 757–765.

Robinson, J. (2011), 'Cities in a world of cities: The comparative gesture', *International Journal of Urban and Regional Research*, **35** (1), 1–23.

Rossi, E., J.V. Beaverstock and P.J. Taylor (2007), 'Transaction links through cities: "Decision cities" and "Service cities" in outsourcing by leading Brazilian firms', *Geoforum*, **38** (3), 628–642.

Sassen, Saskia (1988), *The Mobility of Labor and Capital*, Cambridge: Cambridge University Press.

Sassen, Saskia (1991), *The Global City*, Princeton, NJ: Princeton University Press.

Sassen, Saskia (1994), *Cities in a World Economy*, London: Pine Forge Press.

Short, John Rennie and Yeong-Hyun Kim (1999), *Globalization and the City*, New York: Addison Wesley Longman.

Short, J., Y. Kim, M. Kuss and H. Wells (1996), 'The dirty little secret of world cities research', *International Journal of Urban and Regional Research*, **20** (4), 697–717.

Smith, R.G. (2003a), 'World city actor-networks', *Progress in Human Geography*, **27** (1), 25–44.

Smith, R.G. (2003b), 'World city topologies', *Progress in Human Geography*, **27** (5), 561–582.

Smith, R.G. (2013), 'Beyond the global city concept and the myth of "command and control"', *International Journal of Urban and Regional Research*, **38** (1), 98–115.

Smith, R.G. and M.A. Doel (2011), 'Questioning the theoretical basis of current global-city research: Structures, networks and actor-networks', *International Journal of Urban and Regional Research*, **35** (1), 24–39.

Taylor, P.J. (1997), 'Hierarchical tendencies amongst world cities: A global research proposal', *Cities*, **14** (6), 323–332.

Taylor, P.J. (2001), 'Specification of the world city network', *Geographical Analysis*, **33** (2), 181–194.

Taylor, Peter J. (2004), *World City Network: A Global Urban Analysis*, London: Routledge.

Taylor, P.J. and R. Aranya (2008), 'A global "urban roller coaster"? Connectivity changes in the world city network, 2000–2004', *Regional Studies*, **42** (1), 1–16.

Taylor, P.J., C. Catalano and D.R.F. Walker (2002), 'Measurement of the world city network', *Urban Studies*, **39** (13), 2367–2376.

Taylor, Peter J. and Ben Derudder (2015), *World City Network*, London: Routledge (2nd edition).

Taylor, P.J., B. Derudder, J.R. Faulconbridge, M. Hoyler and P. Ni (2014), 'Advance producer service firms and strategic networks, global cities as strategic places', *Economic Geography*, **90** (3), 267–291.

Taylor, P.J., B. Derudder, M. Hoyler and P. Ni (2013), 'New regional geographies of the world as practised by leading advanced producer service firms in 2010', *Transactions of the Institute of British Geographers*, **38** (3), 497–511.

Taylor, Peter, Ben Derudder, Pieter Saey and Frank Witlox (eds) (2007), *Cities in Globalization*, London: Routledge.

Taylor, P.J., P. Ni, B. Derudder, M. Hoyler, J. Huang and F. Witlox (eds) (2011), *Global Urban Analysis: A Survey of Cities in Globalization*, London: Earthscan.

Van Dijk, T. (1999), 'The one dimensional network society of Manuel Castells', *New Media and Society*, **1** (1), 127–138.

Watson, A. and J.V. Beaverstock (2014), 'World city research at a theoretical impasse: On the need to re-establish qualitative approaches to understanding agency in world city networks', *Tijdschrift voor Economische en Sociale Geografie*, **105** (4), 412–426.

Yeung, H.W. (2005), 'Rethinking relational economic geography', *Transactions of the Institute of British Geographers*, **30** (1), 37–51.

4   Urban surveillance after the end of globalization

David Murakami Wood

The planetary

The era of globalization is over.

This process, that was always fractured, contested and incomplete has neither suc-ceeded nor been beaten, but there is undoubtedly a scale of human socio-spatial activity that is now unavoidably and increasingly irreversibly global. The idea of the global has both an aspirational and a representational sense to it, and feels both abstracted and all too perfect. The concept of the global is descriptively and theo-retically inadequate. In the emerging era that is being termed the Anthropocene, in order to emphasize the deep physicality of the impact of humanity on planet Earth, the materiality, the environmentality, of the situation demands a focus on the planetary.

Prediction is fraught with dangers. However, Neil Brenner and Christian Schmid (2015) have already made a strong case that the urban can now be seen as a plan-etary condition, such are the interconnections within, and effects of, the global urban network (Taylor 2004). However, this network is not simply a generalized kind of urbanism or indeed necessarily going to be a familiar form of urbanism. Using the computing architecture metaphor of 'the stack', Benjamin Bratton (2016) has recently issued a massive and persuasive call for thinking of computing as a planetary condition too. Enabled both by conditions of urbanism and perva-sive networked communications, the planet is becoming a new kind of cybernetic system, with computing overlaying and interpenetrating existing social and eco-logical systems.

However, the initial inspiration for this chapter did not come either from Brenner and Schmid or from Bratton but via an interest in science fiction, from exobiology – from the perspective of astronomers interested in the possibility of life on planets other than Earth. In particular, it came from a speculative 1964 piece by the Russian astronomer Nikolai Kardashev, who proposed a typology of possible alien civilizations (Kardashev 1964). The typology was largely based on energy use and had a hierarchical three-stage model: Type 1 civilizations were able to harness the energy available on their entire planet; Type 2 their solar system; and Type 3 their galaxy.

In the spirit of J.G. Ballard's famous 1962 argument that Earth is the true alien planet (Ballard 1962), the American astronomer Carl Sagan made some crude calculations in the early 1970s of where Earth might stand on the Kardashev scale (Sagan 1973). In order to do so, a 'Type 0' civilization had to be understood, one that stood below the planetary scale. Given that the total solar energy from the sun hitting the Earth is approximately 174 Petawatts (1.74×1017 watts), Sagan calculated that human civilization stood at about 0.7 in 1973. However, crucially, Sagan added another variable. Drawing on Claude Shannon's Information Theory (Shannon 1948), he created a logarithmic scale of information processing capacity, with each order of magnitude defined by a letter, starting with a level A informational civilization with access to 106 bits (1 megabit) of information. In 1973, Sagan estimated that Earth was at level H (1013 bits).

Sagan's calculation and its sociopolitical context are highly symbolic. Massive social, political and economic upheavals were shaking both nation-states around the world and the international economic system that had persisted since the end of World War 2 (WW2). This was the time of the Oil Shock, international recession, and the final collapse of the fragile post-war truce between Capital and Labour that had resulted in what Eric Hobsbawm (1995) called the 'golden age of Capitalism'. It was the end of Fordism and the beginning of the era of neoliberal restructuring and the contemporary globalization of capitalism. It was the time when a sense of the planet as a single thing, that was first made visible in the famous 'earthrise' picture taken by astronauts on the moon, had started to be part of the collective (un)consciousness, and when the first steps towards international environmental management began with the World Conference on Environment and Population in Stockholm. It was also, according to Gilles Deleuze (1992), in his short piece, 'Postscript on the Societies of Control', the end of Foucault's 'Disciplinary Society' and the beginning of the era of 'Control Society' with computing and databases starting to afford new kinds of subjectivity and modes of ordering. In this regard, this period also saw the beginning of two extensible forms of networking, both of which had begun in military experimentation in WW2: first, modern logistics and the advent of global container systems of distribution; and then the earliest form of networked computer communications, ARPANET, which eventually would become the Internet.

In other words, it was in multiple ways the beginning of the planetary era or, in geological-environmental terms, the Anthropocene, an era which remains imminent rather than present, but whose imminence must now be foundational for any social or political theory. Now, in the big data age, with organizations like the US Department of Defense allegedly aiming at yottabyte (9.67140655691724 bits) storage capacities,[1] human civilization is at a much higher informational level. It has also, more modestly, increased its energy mastery, measured through the proxy of total world energy consumption, which in 2012 stood at 17.54 Terawatts, equating to nearly 0.725 on Sagan's version of the Kardashev scale. Importantly, I do not refer to this here in a crude quantitative or a predictive way, let alone a moral way – not least because, currently, energy consumption is not a good proxy for 'control' of planetary energy resources, rather, it indicates the speed at which we are under-mining the ecological bases of human civilization, leading to the horrific possibility of civilizational extermination (Thacker 2011) – but rather as a heuristic, to help get a sense of the extent of planetary urbanism and planetary computing.

Theorizing planetary urban surveillance

What I want to argue in this short chapter is that surveillance is crucial to this new planetary urban condition and, consequently, to propose specific research direc-tions. In this, I will build not only on Brenner and Schmid, and Bratton, as well as Gilles Deleuze, Michel Foucault, Giorgio Agamben, Achille Mbembé and Simone Browne, but also on the recent recasting of historical materialism by Japanese philosopher Kojin Karatani, work in urban geography by Steve Graham and Rob Kitchin, and my own previous work in which I have tried to put the pieces together in slightly different and inevitably less successful ways – since they were both pro-duced before Brenner and Schmid's and Bratton's more recent work.

In the first piece, in *Geoforum*, I outlined a theory of global surveillance, (re)combining work on social complexity and global assemblages with political economy to argue that neoliberalization was producing a global surveillant assemblage which worked not simply in the obvious way, to monitor and control people, groups and things at the global scale, but also to secure the global itself as the seemingly 'natural' scale of neoliberal capitalism (Murakami Wood 2013a). In this sense, global surveillance is not panoptic (Foucault 1977), but oligoptic (Latour 2005) – incomplete, fractured and particular – and perioptic (Lianos 2010) – self-regarding and reinforcing. In the second, in the collection *Global City Challenges*, I argued, based partly on a case study of Rio de Janeiro, that the global city network exists between the biopolitical and necropolitical, the former caring and/or productive inclusion and the latter uncaring and/or destructive exclusion (Murakami Wood 2013b). Urban surveillance operates in both modes simultaneously depending on the identification of the subject popula-tion as one to be protected and marked for life, or excluded and marked for death.

Here I wish to combine these and go beyond them, to argue that this early stage of the age of planetary urbanism is marked by a constant modulation of the biopoliti-cal and the necropolitical and that surveillance operates not only to mark all kinds of people and places for life or death, but also to give the impression of complete-ness, effectiveness and necessity to this mode of ordering, even while it continually fails and remains incomplete in practice. I want to expand on this first of all by disposing of three critiques of the general theory that I am deploying here. These criticisms are often made in a banal or automatic way, but answering them is essen-tial as it necessitates strengthening the underpinnings of the theory.

The first critique is that of technological determinism and/or teleology. It would seem quite clear that the era of planetary surveillance has multiple causes: it is one of complexity, whether one calls the ongoing results an actor-network, a hybrid collective or an assemblage of heterogeneous elements. However, that is not to say that either in general, or certainly not in specific cases, that particular elements or causes or forces or dispositions might not predominate. It seems clear that the economic, in other words, Capital, remains a powerful driver. But we have also seen how the particular situations from which Capital seeks to gain advantage are not entirely determined by relations of production in the way that Marx, and more significantly, Marxists, claimed. I share much of Kojin Karatani's (2014) concern with re-emphasizing the role of the Mode of Exchange over the Mode of Production and understanding that the current situation is evolving out of what he calls the triple "Borromean knot" of Capitalism–Nation–State. Each of these components represents very different Modes of Exchange and facets of human existence – economic, communal-societal and military-bureaucratic – without any being 'structural' or 'superstructural' in relation to the others.[2]

At the same time, Karatani's critique is still not cognizant enough of the environmental and technological. I would never go as far as Heidegger (1977) in claiming that technology has some kind of 'telos' or destiny, nor more recently Silicon Valley cheerleader Kevin Kelly (2010) in arguing that we should follow 'what technology wants'. However, it would seem undeniable that we are enmeshed in relationships with multiple technologies, that go far beyond dismissing technologies as either simply tools or McLuhan's 'extensions of man' (McLuhan 1994), but rather, after Langdon Winner (1986) and Bruno Latour (2005), are sociotechnical hybrids which afford certain openings and restrictions of possibility. It is still useful to consider planetary surveillance from the viewpoint of 'surveillance itself', that is, the functionality of the socio-technical-environmental collective that constitutes the surveillant assemblage. This is neither to endorse the trajectories described, nor to assume a vitalistic approach, nor consider such things as expressions of any conscious will to act of such an assemblage. Instead, the accurate description of the potential functioning of any surveillant assemblage aids in the construction of a critical challenge to such a trajectory while it is in process. This is especially important because while these relationships are not teleological or destined or simply 'linear', they sometimes appear so, particularly in retrospect, as path-dependencies emerge within assemblages that create trajectories that are increasingly irreversible over time. However, they also generate new trajectories that were unavailable before. Once a particular trajectory is followed, it progressively writes over or erases the facts of its own emergence, the knowledge of which would have allowed us to see the non-linearity of sociotechnical history and the conditions for other possible trajectories which had previously existed (see Delanda 2006).

This leads to the second critique, the idea that a 'grand narrative' style of theoretical intervention such as this must somehow lack a place for understanding difference, distinction and identity. Largely a product of New Social Movement critiques of the supposedly failed class-based Mass Movement politics of the mid-20th century, such critiques have contributed, since the 1970s, to a reaction against 'big theory' in general. We all know the story from innumerable graduate social theory classes. It should be clear already that I reject such binaries at the outset. In many ways, the argument is over, we just don't know it. In practice, identity politics and intersectional theories of oppression continue to be vital – and I mean that in the powerfully material sense of giving life to people and things that Capital-Nation-State, collectively or individually, would otherwise necropolitically cast out, reduce to bare life or eliminate (Agamben 1998; Mbembé 2003). However, deriving more general theories of historical change from such vital and immediate politics is fraught with dangers, and such theories are often in danger of producing new determinist forms of analysis, merely replacing 'class' or 'the economic' or 'technology' with, for example, 'whiteness' or 'cis-heteronormativity'. In contrast, what I would argue is that we can hold all of these ideas at the same time, bring them into conversation, and open up new avenues of explanation through those conversations. A superb example of this is Simone Browne's electric work *Dark Matters* (2015) in which, among many other insights, she shifts the focus of diagrammatic histories of surveillance away from notional white bodies of prisoners under surveillance but marked for productive life in Bentham's inclusionary, biopolitical panopticon reformatory scheme, to the real black bodies under surveillance and marked for exploitation and death in the diagrams of exclusionary, necropolitical slave ships. At every stage of its development, deployment and existence, planetary surveillance is involved in relationships which shape, refine or produce sociotechnical possibilities and reduce or eliminate others. It (re)produces relationships, and it also separates. It empowers some people, groups and things, and disempowers, dehumanizes and oppresses others.

The third critique, which relates more specifically to urban geography and urban studies, is that there is nothing particularly 'urban' about surveillance. Previous work I have conducted showed that surveillance did indeed originate as a mode of ordering from the building of early cities which, far from acting as merely defensive systems, were in fact designed as devices to concentrate, monitor and order otherwise unruly populations for a whole variety of reasons (Coaffee et al. 2008). These include, the way in which surveillant assemblages (Haggerty and Ericson 2000), as noted earlier, operate perioptically, self-referentially, always looking back at themselves to justify the situation in which they operate (whether a city, a nation-state or the planet) as 'natural' or 'normal' but, paradoxically, in need of further surveillance to ensure this normality. Further, as Karatani (2014) and Peter Taylor (2013) both point out, the early city did not just mutate into the city-state but from its inception was already the first form of state. The city was the exemplary spatial diagram of the mode of ordering (Law 1994) associated with Karatani's Mode of Exchange B[3] and the rise of Empires, which resulted in the conquest but subsequent simultaneous domination and protection of populations. In other words, the city represented a kind of offer that people could not refuse without harsh consequences, but whose acceptance entailed an increasingly irreversible integration into a subordinate role in emerging hierarchical class systems. And, of course, arguing that surveillance is urban does not exclude it also having many other characteristics.

Planetary urban surveillance: an agenda for research

What will an era of planetary surveillance mean for individual cities and urban places? The idea of a planetary urbanism does not necessarily mean one city-planet, and for the foreseeable future, recognizable individual cities, city-regions or clusters of cities will continue to exist as will identifiable urban places. So, attention to empirical detail and all manner of individual and comparative studies are still essential. Furthermore, the differences within cities will increase as urbanity as a homogenizing general condition spreads to a genuinely planetary condition, so one might be speaking of different types of individual and comparative study, and not simply those based on categories like 'city' and 'nation-state'.

Surveillance certainly plays a role in the maintenance of certain kinds of standard global urban places as meeting expectations of safety and predictability. One of the key surveillance processes to be studied in such a planetary urban society is the role of surveillance in territoriality: the making, maintenance, breaking and remaking of boundaries and borders. As new kinds of urban spatial conditions and territorial entities emerge, their identities, as well as frequently their virtual and material boundaries, will be contested. Surveillance, in its strange but important perioptic capacity noted above, in its monitoring for self-justification, to ensure the continuance of the conditions which gave rise to the surveillance, is crucial in these processes.

With urbanity as a planetary condition, it no longer makes sense to exercise control via the protection of the city against external forces; indeed, that has been an approach that has been obsolete for some time. Instead, technologies and practices of surveillance must be scalable, that is, similar wherever they are deployed and across whatever area, and compatible systems must be able to function at all scales. In other words, surveillance must be an intimate property of every level of the stack and also function between the levels. Scalability can mean nesting, hierarchies, distributions and many other configurations.

The most obvious conjunction of computing, surveillance and urbanism right now is in the networking of ordinary objects and existing infrastructures in what is broadly called the 'Internet of Things', defined by global standards body the International Telecommunications Union as 'a global infrastructure for the Information Society, enabling advanced services by interconnecting things based on, existing and evolving, interoperable information and communication technologies' (ITU 2012), but which has its specific urban utopian instantiation in the concept of the 'Smart City'. Smart Cities are the latest in a long line of efforts to recombine the digital and the material. Technocentric Smart City visions are characterized by depictions of pervasive wireless networks and distributed sensor platforms from video surveillance to meteorological stations, monitoring flows from sewerage to traffic to criminal activities and providing information in real-time or in anticipation of risks. Smart City initiatives vary in their depth and breadth worldwide. One of the most advanced whole-city projects is Rio de Janeiro's Smart City project, directly sponsored by US computing firm IBM, with a central control room bringing in data from multiple sources, and lauded by the current Mayor, Eduardo Paes, in a widely viewed TED presentation, as providing him with the ability to manage the city from anywhere in the world (Paes 2012; for some analysis see Murakami Wood 2013). Rio is only one of many branded IBM Smarter Cities projects, and their extent and relative smartness varies considerably, often being far less impressive when examined more closely. As with many such programs, it may be that securing involvement is in itself viewed as a marker of success in the competition for status in the world city network (Taylor 2004).

Smart City initiatives constitute surveillant assemblages, wherein a complex arrangement of people, technologies and processes permeate everyday urban life in often invisible, unreadable and incomprehensible ways. Relying on increasingly opaque software operations, they encode urban life and replay the results of those encodings onto urban spaces and people (Kitchin and Dodge 2011). As many commentators have pointed out, such initiatives have the potential to change the way in which both space and subjectivity are produced towards a more automated and standardized model. Of particular concern is the way in which in an anticipatory logic, something that has its roots in military cybernetics (Graham 2010), is embedded in automated urban control systems, leading to processes of social and spatial sorting on the basis of possibilities (Amoore 2013). Kitchin and Dodge (2011) refer to the resulting city as 'code/space', which occurs 'when software and the spatiality of everyday life become mutually constituted, that is, produced through one another'.

As Deleuze (1992) pointed out in his seminal essay on contemporary surveillance logic, the control society is based on flows. It is not so much that a discipline is imposed for moral reasons, rather flows are modulated based on organizational efficiency. As IBM say, 'Smarter cities of the future will drive sustainable economic growth. Their leaders have the tools to analyze data for better decisions, anticipate problems to resolve them proactively and coordinate resources to operate effectively' (IBM 2012).

The general conditions outlined by Deleuze for the 'Society of Control', which he saw emerging from the general social and technological conditions of early neoliberalism, are already starting to break down. Flow, the defining feature of Deleuze's schema, is problematic. Alex Galloway (2004) has already pointed out the relatively short lifespan of the society of control vision, for rather different reasons. However, in the planetary urban context, it is not so much that everything must flow and be merely modulated, *governed* (in the machinic sense), but that new forms of spatial blockage and division take the place of both the historical city walls and current national borders. Wendy Brown (2010) has also observed how boundary-making practices seem to be increasing with the imminent demise of the nation-state, and while she attributes this to the fact that borders are one of the few things that an increasingly powerless nation-state has to control, it could in fact be an emerging feature of the combination of planetary urbanism and planetary computing. Internal micro-division becomes pervasive and ever more complex precisely because of the embedding of technologies of pervasive surveillance, quantification and anticipation in the urbanized environment.

Some of this reinforces existing socio-spatial class divisions and boundaries in the manner identified by Teresa Caldeira (2001) and often termed 'enclavism'. In this continuously 'splintering urbanism' (Graham and Marvin 2001), those able to enclose themselves, and to monitor those boundaries, for their own protection, will do so, and those who cannot will be expelled, as Saskia Sassen (2014) recently argued. But Sassen is hardly the first to observe this. In many ways, the urban legacy of globalization has been the generalization of a colonial model of the city, as detailed by Anthony King (1990). Back in the 1990s, Scott Lash and the late, much lamented, John Urry observed an emerging pattern of that they called 'tame and wild zones' (Lash and Urry 1994), and International Relations scholar Barry Buzan (2008) identified a similar transformation of the geopolitical situation, something that was made very clear in the US Department of Defense's so-called 'new map' of the world in the late 1990s. And in the late 1990s, Giorgio Agamben (1998, 2005) observed what he attributed to the horrors of the Holocaust and the Nazi extermination camps, the extension and hardening of 'states of exception', which allowed extralegal management of populations to take place, marking some for life and others for what he called 'bare life' or conditions where only death and survival could be considered.

This division between those spaces (at every scale) can be understood as a dual form of governmentality, with one zone managed through what Foucault called biopolitics, the production of life, and the other through what Achille Mbembé called necropolitics, the production of death. The role of surveillance, in this context, is a constant process of sorting to determine the destination of particular bodies. Because this process is, again, nested, bodies in particular contexts can be marked for life in City A but for bare life/death in City B or at a global scale, or can be similarly contextually marked in particular spaces within any given city. The body's attributes in urban space are likewise changeable. The more precarious one's conditions of existence and one's class, racial, gender – and so on – identity, the more that such markers become *identifications*, the result of processes of control, and less *identities*, the product of self-definition.

However familiar the outcomes, the methods used to produce them will not all be so recognizable. In physical urban space, the eyes and ears of police and security guards, and video surveillance cameras on walls and gates and doorways, are already known to us. Then there are the rarer but emerging surveillance systems, such as handheld body-scanners, biomimetic robot surveillance drones that look like birds or snakes or insects, and sensor nets of microscopic radio frequency identification (RFID) powder. Finally, there are the currently very strange: hybrid biotechnological systems, at the moment only expressed in examples like genetically modified plants which change colour in the presence of particular chemical cues. However, in a planetary urban society, even one with significant 'restoration' of natural ecosystems or 'rewilding', what is left of 'nature' will be increasingly subject to forms of surveillance for our and 'its' own good, and could become integrated into the planetary stack. This blurring of boundaries will grow as cities and urban technologies become increasingly biological and the distinction between what is natural and what is urban begins to disappear. This is as true in computing as in anything else. We are only just beginning to understand how data can be encoded in living systems, in cells and complex molecules like DNA, and its seems that for all the hope for quantum computing, it is actually in biological computing that major advances in the storage of bigger and bigger data may well be made. Ironically, perhaps it is only when the entire biosphere becomes urbanized and is recast as a reservoir of data that we might acknowledge its essential, already existing, but so often unconsidered, value to humanity.

However, planetary computing may render such surveillant sorting only accessible or comprehensible to human beings insofar as the information gathered can be understood and interpreted and there are technical-legal regimes to enforce rules in favor of the common good. Instead, the rise of ever bigger data means that the systems of monitoring themselves must be automated and programmed and thereafter increasingly left to learn for themselves, and as Kitchin and Dodge (2011) observed of the code/space of the city, the results of such informated exchanges are increasingly only interpretable to other automated systems and may never be 'translated' for humans. This will be urban surveillance – but not as we know it.

So, on the one hand, urban surveillance specialists therefore should probably swallow their fear of being accused of technological determinism and spend more time attending, infiltrating or haunting the fringes of industry technological expos and conferences. Researchers will as a result have to become more familiar with technologies of surveillance, without losing sight of the fact that all such technologies are bio-socio-technical systems which are produced within, and which serve to variously challenge, undermine, produce and reproduce particular political-economic systems, governmentalities and environmentalities.

Researchers should simultaneously pay attention to what Shelton et al. (2015) call 'the actually existing smart city' – in other words, the reality of utopian presentations of an always on, always connected city beyond the prototypes, plans and glossy brochures. However, it is not necessarily about 'exposing' failures or secret exclusionary plans. In increasing numbers of cases, the utopian is in reality openly about creating exclusive enclaves for an emerging technologically enabled, if not actually technologically savvy, class. One key case, which is threatening to serve as a bad example to others, is the 'hundred smart cities' promise of Indian Prime Minister Modi, which, as Ayona Datta (2015) has shown, is rooted in a strange but increasingly common combination of belief in free trade, high technology, and an intolerant and hierarchical social and/or religious order.

Like all utopian schemes, or trajectories, among others, what will result are oligoptica – islands of intense and effective operation – surrounded by seas of partial coverage and partial functionality – and a fringe of entirely broken and malfunctioning operation. These will most likely correspond to the human distinction between those included and managed biopolitically, and those excluded and managed necropolitically. For a useful analogy, one might consider mobile phone systems now, and the overlapping and incompleteness of their coverage. If one imagines such 'coverage maps' multiplied many layers deep for all kinds of networked things, one can get some sense of how connectivities afford multiple forms of surveillance, but not the same surveillance, or the same levels of surveillance everywhere. However, perhaps the intensity of the combination of planetary urbanism, planetary communications, planetary computing and planetary surveillance will come to be defined by the depth of these layers – itself a representation of the stack – in particular places. Urbanity will become something more modular and variable than can be defined by current conceptions of city/urban–rural/countryside–wild/wilderness. Thus, what Taylor (2013) calls 'cityness' could be increasingly supplemented by considerations of 'stack depth'.

Planetary urbanism and computing will not mean a frictionless, homogenous modernity, but an often atavistic and divided set of visions of superiority, ironically rooted in the same kinds of intelligent technologies of control. In such cases, the role of the academic is inevitably political and activist. Here, I return to Kojin Karatani (2014), who shares with the Italian Autonomist Marxists not the old Marxist idea of a single and massive revolutionary moment but the idea of an 'escape' from capitalism, through the discovery of what Deleuze would call 'lines of flight' (1992). Many such lines might exist, ranging from those which favor a more just and empowering kind of urban surveillance and smart urbanism, new varieties of 'right to the city' (Lefebvre 1996), to those which reject this kind of technocentric urbanism *tout court*.

Conclusion

Urban surveillance as we have known it is already mutating into forms which are at once familiar and unfamiliar. On the one hand, we see the familiar in new spaces and at new scales such that its familiarity might be masked by extent and depth. On the other, we encounter the genuinely unfamiliar and new, that might still post similar and familiar problems, and exacerbate existing socio-spatial inequalities, or indicate something much stranger. This strangeness will be perhaps not simply some combination of capitalism, urbanism, computing or surveillance on a planetary scale, but something post-capitalist, post-urban, post-computational and post-surveillance. These combinations will require new theoretical development and methodological considerations.

NOTES
1 Although opinions and estimates vary (Novet 2013), yottabyte storage capacity is at least now a realistically conceivable scale of data storage for the very near future.
2 Karatani's Modes of Exchange are, briefly, Mode of Exchange A (reciprocity – societies characterized by gift and counter-gift); Mode of Exchange B (plunder and redistribution – where conquest, war and domination are characteristic and societies, once conquered, are offered the dubious 'protection' of empire); Mode of Exchange C (commodity exchange – or capitalism in its various forms); Mode of Exchange D ('X' – or the return of Mode of Exchange A on a higher level) (Karatani 2014).
3 See Note 2.

References

Agamben, Giorgio. 1998. *Homo Sacer: Sovereign Power and Bare Life*. Stanford, CA: Stanford University Press.

Agamben, Giorgio. 2005. *State of Exception*. Stanford, CA: Stanford University Press.

Amoore, Louise. 2013. *The Politics of Possibility: Risk and Security Beyond Probability*. Durham, NC: Duke University Press.

Ballard, J.G. 1962. 'Which way to inner space?' *New Worlds*, 118: 2–3.

Bratton, Benjamin. 2016. *The Stack*. Cambridge, MA: MIT Press.

Brenner, Neil and Christian Schmid. 2015. 'Towards a new epistemology of the urban?' *City*, 19(2–3): 151–182.

Brown, Wendy. 2010. *Walled States, Waning Sovereignty*. New York: Zone.

Browne, Simone. 2015. *Dark Matters: On the Surveillance of Blackness*. Durham, NC: Duke University Press.

Buzan, B. 2008. *People, States and Fear: An Agenda for International Security Studies in the Post-Sold War Era*. Colchester: ECPR Press.

Caldeira, Teresa. 2001. *City of Walls: Crime, Segregation, and Citizenship in São Paulo*. Berkeley, CA: University of California Press.

Coaffee, Jon, David Murakami Wood and Peter Rogers. 2008. *The Everyday Resilience of the City: How Cities Respond to Terrorism and Disaster*. Basingstoke, UK: Palgrave Macmillan.

Datta, Ayona. 2015. 'New urban utopias of postcolonial India: "Entrepreneurial urbanization" in Dholera smart city, Gujarat', *Dialogues in Human Geography*, 5(1): 3–22.

Delanda, Manuel. 2006. *A New Philosophy of Society: Assemblage Theory and Social Complexity*. New York: Continuum.

Deleuze, Gilles. 1992. 'Postscript on the Societies of Control', *October*, 59: 3–7.

Foucault, Michel. 1977. *Discipline and Punish: The Birth of the Prison*. Harmondsworth, UK: Penguin Books.

Galloway, Alexander D. 2004. *Protocol: How Control Exists after Decentralization*. Cambridge, MA: MIT Press.

Graham, S. 2010. *Cities Under Siege: The New Military Urbanism*. London: Verso.

Graham, S. and S. Marvin. 2001. *Splintering Urbanism*. London: Routledge.

Haggerty, Kevin D. and Richard V. Ericson. 2000. 'The surveillant assemblage', *British Journal of Sociology*, 51(4): 605–622.

Heidegger, M. 1977. *The Question Concerning Technology, and Other Essays*, pp. 3–35, New York: Harper & Row.

Hobsbawm, Eric. 1995. *The Age of Extremes: A History of the World, 1914–1991*. New York: Pantheon Books.

IBM. 2012. 'Smarter Cities brochure', formerly available at: https://www.ibm.com/smarterplanet/. Last accessed 01/04/2015.

ITU. 2012. *Internet of Things Global Standards Initiative*. https://www.itu.int/en/ITU-T/gsi/iot/Pages/default.aspx. Last accessed 21/10/2016.

Karatani, Kojin. 2014. *The Structure of World History*. Durham, NC: Duke University Press.

Kardashev, Nikolai S. 1964. 'Transmission of information by extraterrestrial civilizations', *Soviet Astronomy*, 8: 217.

Kelly, Kevin. 2010. *What Technology Wants*. New York: Penguin Books.

King, Anthony D. 1990. *Urbanism, Colonialism, and the World-Economy: Cultural and Spatial Foundations of the World Urban System*. London: Routledge.

Kitchin, Rob and Martin Dodge. 2011. *Code/Space: Software and Everyday Life*. Cambridge, MA: MIT Press.

Lash, Scott and John Urry. 1994. *Economies of Signs and Space*. London: Sage.

Latour, Bruno. 2005. *Reassembling the Social: An Introduction to Actor-Network Theory*. Oxford: Oxford University Press.

Law, John. 1994. *Organizing Modernity: Social Ordering and Social Theory*. Oxford: Blackwell.

Lefebvre, H. 1996. 'The right to the city', pp.63–181 in Eleonore Kofman and Elizabeth Lebas (eds), *Writings on Cities*. Oxford: Blackwell.

Lianos, Michalis. 2010. 'Periopticon: Control beyond freedom and coercion – and two possible advancements in the social sciences', pp.69–88 in Kevin D. Haggerty and Minas Samatas (eds), *Surveillance and Democracy*. London/New York: Routledge-Cavendish.

McLuhan, Marshall. 1994. *Understanding Media: The Extensions of Man*. Cambridge, MA: MIT Press.

Mbembé, Joseph-Achille. 2003. 'Necropolitics', *Public Culture*, 15(1): 11–40.

Murakami Wood, D. 2013a. 'What is global surveillance? Towards a relational political economy of the global surveillant assemblage', *Geoforum*, 49: 317–326.

Murakami Wood, David. 2013b. 'The security dimension', pp.188–201 in Michele Acuto and Wendy Steele (eds), *Global City Challenges*. Basingstoke, UK: Palgrave Macmillan.

Novet, Jordan. 2013. 'That NSA data center was never going to store a yottabyte of our data', *Gigaom*, July 25, https://gigaom.com/2013/07/25/that-nsa-data-center-was-never-going-to-store-a-yottabyte-of-our-data/. Last accessed 21/10/2016.

Paes, E. 2012. 'The four commandments of cities', *ted.com*, https://www.ted.com/talks/eduardo_paes_the_4_commandments_of_cities.html. Last accessed 21/10/2016.

Sagan, Carl. 1973. *Cosmic Connection: An Extraterrestrial Perspective*. Cambridge: Cambridge University Press.

Sassen, Saskia. 2014. *Expulsions*. Cambridge, MA: Harvard University Press.

Shannon, Claude E. 1948. 'A mathematical theory of communication', *Bell System Technical Journal*, 27: 379–423/623–656.

Shelton, Taylor, Matthew Zook and Alan Wiig. 2015. 'The "actually existing smart city"', *Cambridge Journal of Regions, Economy and Society*, 8(1): 13–25.

Taylor, Peter J. 2004. *World City Network: A Global Urban Analysis*. London: Routledge.

Taylor, Peter J. 2013. *Extraordinary Cities: Millennia of Moral Syndromes, World-Systems and City/State Relations*. Cheltenham, UK and Northampton, MA, USA: Edward Elgar Publishing.

Thacker, Eugene. 2011. *In the Dust of This Planet: Horror of Philosophy Vol. 1*. New York: Zero Books.

Winner, Langdon. 1986. *The Whale and the Reactor: A Search for Limits in an Age of High Technology*. Chicago: University of Chicago Press.

PART II

The lived city

5 The queer city

Gavin Brown

Introduction

Queer, as both a political practice and an intellectual methodology, originated in North American cities. In the late 1980s and 1990s, the emergence of a queer orientation to the world was believed to hold considerable potential for imagining new and alternative ways of organizing the lives of sexual and gender minorities beyond heteronormative imperatives. In this chapter, I want to reflect on why queer might have seemed to offer so much a quarter of a century ago, and to examine what became of that promise. In examining the place of queer in contemporary cities, I consider how the role of queer and the meanings attached to it have been altered by a range of social changes over recent decades. In this context, I question whether queer still holds emancipatory potential for living differently in cities.

One of the problems of writing a chapter on 'the queer city' is that queer has many meanings. In both its academic and its political incarnations, queer started as a conscious reclamation of a long-standing derogatory term thrown at sexual minorities (particularly those who broke conventional gender norms). By reclaiming this insult, queer activists sought to rob it of its power to hurt by positively celebrating sexual dissidence and gender variance. In academic contexts, queer is understood as a critical move for thinking about the (re)production of sexual and gender norms, and the saturation of the social and cultural order by normative assumptions that privilege particular expressions of heterosexuality. In the last decade or so, queer theorists have extended their critique to those 'homonormative' expressions of lesbian and gay identities that they see as increasingly aligned with, and offering little challenge to, heteronormativity. In many ways, queer activism was imbued with this critique far earlier, and frequently reserved its greatest anger for those 'assimilationist' gays who they believed were particularly complicit in the functioning of contemporary capitalism. Inspired by both these theoretical and political critiques, queer has also been claimed as a sub-cultural anti-identity which celebrates and values expressions and performances of sexuality and gender that are believed to challenge and contest both heteronormativity and homonormativity. Simultaneously, queer is frequently used as an inclusive, umbrella term for sexual and gender diverse people – a kind of synonym for 'LGBT', albeit often imagined to be broader and encompassing of those who might feel an affinity with lesbian, gay, bisexual and trans people, but not necessarily identify within those categories.

All of these connotations of 'queer' (and more) are used by geographers and other urban scholars. Indeed, some scholars have a tendency to celebrate the 'slipperiness' of the term, believing that difficulties in accurately defining 'queer' somehow add to its radical potential to undo the binary forms of thinking and categorization that maintain normative social relations. I now believe that this refusal to clearly define 'queer' has become problematic. Among the proliferation of different meanings of queer, this refusal to clearly define one's terms has allowed politically radical modes of queerness to add legitimacy to more socially conservative expressions of 'queer'.

In this chapter, I review the utopian promise that queer was believed to offer for alternative ways of living in urban space. I then elaborate a number of important social, legal and technological changes in recent decades which have undone and overtaken aspects of that utopian promise. In this context, I consider some of the important ways in which queer has changed in response to these changes, and how this has altered the form, function, presence and location of queer space in the city. Finally, I question 'where next?' for queer urbanism and the emancipatory promise it once offered for urban alternatives.

The utopian promise of queer

Queer activism emerged at the height of the AIDS crisis in the 1980s, the very particular political (mis)handling of the pandemic in the USA, and the rise of anti-gay prejudice that accompanied it (Brown 2015a). Queer sought to both challenge the prejudices and normative structures which were understood to limit the lives of sexual minorities at the time, but also to imagine alternative ways of living. Queer's emergence as a form of cultural and political praxis and its development cannot be separated from the changing social and epidemiological impacts of HIV in the Global North. In this section of the chapter, I sketch the development of queer over its first decade and a half, outlining the promise it seemed to offer to those who were concerned to find new ways for sexual and gender minorities to live in cities.

From the start, queer activism attempted to challenge the invisibility and marginality of gender and sexual minorities. Simultaneously, it questioned the aspirations and practices promoted by mainstream lesbian and gay politics. As an alternative to a politics of representation founded in fixed identities, queer promised an engagement with the world articulated through uncompromising resistance to regimes of the normal (Warner 1999).

This orientation to the world was proclaimed in an angry polemic entitled *I Hate Straights* which was distributed during the summer of 1990 at gay pride parades in New York and Chicago.

> Being queer is not about a right to privacy: it is about the freedom to be public. . . It is not about the mainstream profit-margins, patriotism, patriarchy or being assimilated. . . Being

queer is 'grass roots' because we know that everyone of us, every body, every cunt, every heart and ass and dick is a world of pleasure waiting to be explored. Everyone of us is a world of infinite possibilities. (Berlant and Freeman 1993: 200)

There are three key aspects of the polemic that I want to draw attention to. First, it positioned queer as an egalitarian public culture. Second, it positioned queer as refusing assimilation into capitalist markets and the American nation. Finally, and in distinction to proponents of assimilation, it celebrated the 'infinite possibilities' of a 'world of pleasure' founded in queer sexual and gender difference.

When the activist group Queer Nation took to the streets of New York City, their intention was to transform the everyday spaces of the city so that sexual and gender minorities might feel safe in all the sites they passed through and lived in, not just the bounded territories of 'gay' neighbourhoods (Brown 2015a). With this ambition in mind, they took direct action to challenge heteronormativity in a variety of spaces from sports bars to suburban shopping malls. Berlant and Freeman (1993: 199) have argued that, in this way, Queer Nation 'always refuse[d] closeting strategies of assimilation and [went] for the broadest and most explicit assertion of presence'. Through their direct actions and savvy cultural strategies, early queer activist groups attempted to open up new possibilities for engaging with sexual difference that moved beyond a rights-based politics that was founded on articulating 'sameness' with heterosexuals.

Inspired by this ethos, a growing number of academic commentators turned their attention to the study of 'sexual dissidence' and advocating the potential of dissident forms of sexual citizenship (Bell 1995). Bell and Binnie (2000: 9) favoured 'queering' the citizen. For them, this strategy would reengage debates around sexual citizenship with the 'erotic and embodied dimensions' of queer life, reclaiming and expanding 'spaces of dissident sexual citizenship that do not seek to deny the presence of such erotic topographies' (Bell and Binnie 2000: 20). In the face of ascendant homonormative politics, they advocated an alternative 'politics of rage' and a 'politics of the body' (p. 22) centred around sex-positive strategies of 'refusal' (p. 141) – refusal to act 'appropriately' or to accept 'liberal-statist grammars of rights and welfare' (p. 21).

For a while, in the late 1990s and early 2000s, writing on the queer city appeared to seek out and celebrate ever more marginal, occluded spaces of transgression, filth and unfettered desire. Suddenly, discussions of public (homo)sex, sex play and gender subversion were commonplace (Bell 1997, 2001; Binnie 2001). For example, drawing on oral histories, autobiographic memories and other representations, Bell (1997: 81) sketched 'an endless psychogeography of perverse possibilities', arguing that the erotic was central to sexual dissidents' engagement with and enjoyment of the city.

This was, however, about more than just celebrating transgression, or making visible those (public) sexual cultures that seemed to be an anathema to respectable advocates of lesbian and gay equality. It was a recognition and celebration of the ways in which sexual and gender minorities were engaged in an active process of experimentation to create spaces that could support the lives they desired. Binnie (2001: 107) assessed that,

> sexual dissidents are acutely aware of space in our everyday lives because we constantly have to re-create it from nothing. Heterosexual space and heterosexual desire are all pervasive – just *there*. Heterosexual identity is ubiquitous and thereby *placeless*. In this sense, queer space is intimately dependent on a sense *for* place for its realization.

The process of creating queer space is incomplete, insecure and open to new possibilities. For Ingram (1997: 40) 'queerscapes embody processes that counter those that directly harm, discount, isolate, ghettoize, and assimilate'. In contrast, Delany (1999) unambiguously locates queer urban space as being created and sustained outside of commodified social relations. He believed that spontaneous erotic contact between strangers in (semi-)public spaces was the foundation of urban queer life. While it is clearly possible to find un-commodified diverse economies shaping the lives of sexual and gender minorities in a variety of urban spaces (Brown 2009), this work attempted to make a serious point about the potential for challenging heteronormativity through an 'erotically charged *detournement* of the heterosexist city' (Bell 1997: 83).

In the late 1990s, public sex environments were increasingly under threat in North American cities (and elsewhere). These attacks inspired a new wave of queer activism. In 1997, SexPanic! mobilized to 'protect public sexual culture and safer sex in New York from police crackdowns, public stigma, and morality crusades' (SexPanic! Mission Statement cited in Shepard 2002: 202). They also made alliances with broader anti-gentrification campaigns to contest the 'Disneyfication' of Times Square and challenged new planning regulations that significantly curtailed where adult venues could operate (Brown 2015a). Increasingly, at the turn of the millennium, queer activist groups were forced to confront the complicity of mainstream gay politicians and advocates in furthering revanchist urban strategies of gentrification and social cleansing.

In response to these trends, some queer activists sought to experiment with building (temporary) alternative queer spaces. One of these experiments was Gay Shame, which was first held in June 1998 at a collective living/performance space in Brooklyn. This event offered an audience of several hundred people a mix of performances, political discussions and dancing. Afterwards, some of the participants produced a 'zine called *Swallow your Pride: a do-it-yourself guide to hands-on activism* that offered others practical tips on how to self-organize their own queer events and direct action politics. A year later, a Gay Shame event was held in San Francisco. The organizers described it as a 'queer autonomous space' (Brown 2007). For them, Gay Shame was a conscious attempt to reclaim public space in the city, during Pride week, in order to 'build something transformative, deviant, and dangerous out of alienation and desperation' (Mattilda 2004: 239).

Inspired by Gay Shame events in North America, British-based activists held 'Queer Mutiny' events, satirizing the mainstream Pride festivities in 2003 and 2004. In a free magazine circulated by organizers at the 2004 event, a commentator (Anon 2004: 4) reflected on the contradictory promises and possibilities of urban space for queer lives in the following terms:

> Cities are central to queer life. Most of us live in cities. Even if we don't, cities are the main locations where queer subcultures have developed. . .
>
> If the gay scene offers us hope, it also limits our possibilities . . . It is no wonder so many of us feel alienated by the commercial scene. Cities offer so many possibilities for queer folk that it seems a shame to shackle ourselves to that overpriced ghetto. Rather than limiting ourselves to the gay consumer playgrounds in major cities, let's go out and queer the whole of *every* city.

In the remainder of that article, they set out five methods for extending the queer potential of urban space. First was the importance of *celebrating our histories* as a call to foster intergenerational dialogue, to remember and learn from earlier experiments in LGBT community organizing, and to commemorate those histories in the urban environment as a means of challenging queer invisibility. Second, they advocated the importance of *engaging with cultural difference*, recognizing that diverse neighbourhoods can feel safest and most inclusive of sexual and gender difference, but that queer communities are then riddled with prejudice that needs to be countered through dialogue and meaningful engagement across difference. Their third point was the need to *defend sites of public homosex* as non-commercial sites that can foster new forms of communality across class and ethnic difference. Fourth, they highlighted the importance of *making time and space for play (rather than leisure)*, looking for the opportunities to learn through play, rather than con-suming ready-made leisure experiences on the commercial gay scene. Finally, they made a case for the importance of *creating autonomous queer spaces*, through the collective endeavour of queers of all sexualities and genders, as spaces in which to experiment with alternative ways of living in cities. The intention of this interven-tion, it seems, was to explore the queer potential of all kinds of quotidian urban space, to make the whole of every city queerer – 'not just friendlier or safer for well-behaved gay consumers, but more open to the limitless possibilities of gender and sexuality' (Anon 2004: 4). In doing so, the author(s) recognized that 'authentic' queer space does not exist and that such spaces always reproduce privilege and exclusions in some form (Oswin 2005).

In this context, queer urbanism functioned as a critique of existing expressions of gay (or LGBT) space in the city; but it also contained a utopian ambition for unleashing the potential for different ways of engaging with the city that were not limited by contemporary reified 'gay' identities. The queer urbanism articulated by Gay Shame and Queer Mutiny in the early 2000s was an anti-capitalist project in both its critique and its utopian imagination. But it was a utopianism of process not form (Harvey 2000) – rather than try to envisage what a queer city might look like, it explored the practices and relationships that might make the city queerer. Indeed, as Bell (2001) acknowledged, the shape of a queer city can only be glimpsed by collecting together the fragments of potential found in the present. Citing Golding (1993: 217), Bell (2001: 102) suggested that the queer city can be found in the 'creative and wild possibilities' that are (barely) contained within the urban form.

What changed?

If the initial utopian promise of queer arose out of (and in response to) the height of the AIDS crisis in North American cities in the late 1980s, and the heightened anti-gay prejudice of the time, it is important to account for the changes in sexual politics over the last quarter of a century and the ways these have impacted on the changing meanings, resonances and promises offered by queer. There are, at least, four main factors that I want to highlight here. First, the implementation of new 'equalities' legislation in many countries has offered new socio-legal recognition and protection for sexual (and gendered) minorities. There are a number of different dynamics that follow from this. Second, the ways in which these advances in civil rights are connected with wider political economic shifts over the last decade or so. Third, and relating to the origins of queer in the AIDS crisis, there has been the impact of anti-retroviral medications, which have changed the quality of life for many people with HIV (especially in the Global North). Finally, the development of new mobile digital technologies has altered the spatialities of sexual minority lives. Together, these four factors have significantly altered the terrain of sexual politics, as well as reconfigured those people, practices and places that are considered to be 'queer' (either because they contest, confound or transgress the altered social norms surrounding sexual and gender difference in the early twenty-first century).

Queer emerged with anger at a dark time for gay and bisexual men in North America. The urban 'gaybourhoods' that had been consolidated throughout the 1970s were being decimated by the impact of AIDS, and anti-gay prejudice seemed to be resurgent. Queer attempted to offer a joyful, transgressive alternative to this depressing period, without resorting to the staid conformism of more 'assimilationist' lesbian and gay politics. The first change I acknowledge is that, within two decades of queer's origins, throughout much of the Global North (and an increasing number of other countries too), the social and legal standing of lesbians and gay men, as well as some trans people, has changed considerably. In the 1990s some city governments took note of the growing 'gaybourhoods' in their municipalities, sometimes actively promoting them as part of the city's place-marketing and tourism strategies (Hubbard 2012). At the same time, breweries and other mainstream corporations took an increasing interest in capturing the imagined disposable income of gay men (and, later, lesbians too). As social attitudes to sexual difference liberalized, so more positive representations of lesbians and gay men appeared in the mainstream media (and those positive representations encouraged a further liberalization of social attitudes). As social attitudes changed, so politicians increasingly supported legislation to protect people from discrimination on the basis of sexual orientation or gender identity; to repeal existing unequal or repressive laws against homosexuality; and to extend legal 'equality' to sexual and gender minorities by, for example, allowing adoption rights, and civil partnerships or full marriage for same-sex couples. The ways in which these changes have occurred, where they have occurred, has varied depending on contemporary national contexts and the historical place of the family and religious orthodoxy within specific nationalisms (Di Feliciantonio and Brown 2015). Taken together, these changing social, economic and political arrangements in relation to homosexuality have been conceptualized as 'homonormativity' and interpreted as an expression of the sexual politics of neoliberalism (Duggan 2002), in which same-sex intimacy is privatized within the domestic sphere and mediated through responsible, marketized lifestyle choices. In this context, it is important to remember that neoliberalism is not just an economic, free-market ideology; it is also a form of governmentality that produces subjects who understand their relationship to society and others through marketized social relationships. Neoliberal governmentality encourages individual autonomy and personal responsibility through 'free choice' in the market for services. Neoliberal ideology claims to be intent on 'rolling back' the state from the provision of welfare and other services. While this is the case, states are increasingly interventionist in the incentives they offer to corporations to take on the privatized provision of these services. In these contexts, some gay people have become incorporated into state projects, by being seen to epitomize the responsible, self-reliant consumer in the contemporary world. I shall say more about 'homonormativity', and its consequences for queer urbanisms, shortly. But first, I want to acknowledge one of the potentially unintended consequences of the adoption of equalities legislation over recent decades.

Queer politics and sub-cultural milieu frequently presented themselves as a home for 'the queer unwanted' (Casey 2007) – all those sexual dissidents and gender variants who did not fit neatly into more mainstream lesbian and gay spaces, markets and political discourses. However, as Weeks (2007) has argued, it is not just homosexuality, but sexual diversity, that has 'come out' (and, to a greater or lesser extent, been accepted) in recent decades. Although much of the recent equalities legislation has been formulated with lesbian and gay identified people (and, even then, mostly couples) in mind, the current conjuncture has created a space for other sexual and gender minorities to make themselves visible and make equalities claims. It is perhaps not surprising that asexuals (De Lappe 2016), non-gender binary people (Hines 2010), and those in polyamorous relationships (Klesse 2014) have increasingly organized to have their identities recognized and validated in recent years. So, while 'homonormative' lesbians and gay men have become increasingly mainstream, there has also been a greater acknowledgement of sexual and gender diversity. Despite the valid critique that the inclusion of some sexual minority groups pushes others out of the 'charmed circle' (Rubin 2011), there is awareness of and openness to a wider variety of sexual and gendered lives than the mainstreaming of lesbians and gay men might suggest.

The major shifts in social attitudes towards sexual and gendered minorities, and the corporate interest in LGBT markets, occurred in the 1990s and early 2000s, while most of the major world economies were experiencing a period of growth. In contrast, the accelerated expansion of same-sex marriage and other 'equalities' measures has occurred since the global financial crisis of 2008 and in the context of the prolonged period of austerity that has followed it in many countries (Brown 2015b). This is the second major change that I want to highlight. In making this claim, I am (of course) aware that viewing austerity as an exceptional form of political economic arrangements is particularly Eurocentric and overlooks the impact of structural adjustment programmes in much of the Global South over several decades, and the shock doctrine that reintroduced capitalism to the post-Soviet countries in the early 1990s. In these diverse contexts, the neoliberal state seeks to retreat from many areas of welfare provision. In this process, in much of Western Europe, North America and increasing areas of Latin America, the state has accepted and supported those gay people who have been prepared to take responsibility for their own welfare provision within the privatized space of their household. This process has re-centred stable, long-term coupledom (now expanded to include same-sex couples) within social policy and has garnered the support of centrist politicians of all shades.

Early queer interventions into modes of urban life were marked by the impact of HIV and AIDS on urban gay communities and the sense of class dislocation experienced by gay professionals who suddenly found their social networks dying in unprecedented numbers, just as the expansion of urban gay neighbourhoods seemed to offer new possibilities for gay life and respite from the constraints of a homophobic society. The third major shift in the place of queer stems from this. If queer arose out of the anger and fear instilled by the high mortality rates in the early years of the AIDS crisis in North America and elsewhere, then the context of the development of queer cultures and politics has also been shaped by changes in the treatment of HIV infection. When queer ideas first erupted in the late 1980s, experimental treatments for HIV infection were only just becoming available and most people with HIV were expected to die of AIDS-related infections (Kearns 2016). The introduction of anti-retroviral combination therapies in the mid-1990s, and rapid improvement of these drug treatments in the intervening two decades, has significantly improved the life chances (and quality of life) of those people with HIV who can access and adhere to these medications. While there is still considerable stigma around HIV (not least of all amongst gay and bisexual men), HIV has become a manageable, chronic illness for most of those with the infection living in the developed world (and with access to either socialized health care or comprehensive medical insurance). Furthermore, the increasing availability of anti-retroviral medications used as 'pre-exposure prophylaxis' (PrEP) (in other words, as an HIV-prevention strategy for HIV negative people in 'high risk populations') has the potential to make a very significant impact on the lives of gay and bisexual men. As with the introduction of new 'equalities' legislation and changing social attitudes to sexual difference, this is likely to contribute to a reconfiguration of the fault lines of sexual politics – incorporating some previously disreputable social groups within the 'charmed circle' of normative socio-sexual relations, while chastising others. For example, there is already the beginning of a moral panic surrounding 'Chemsex' (a gay subculture found across Europe, North America, Australia and South Africa, in which crystal methamphetamine, GHB and/or mephadrone are used to enhance group sexual activity) (Andersson 2011; Frederick 2014). This panic worries that PrEP is encouraging men to take greater risks with their sexual health. But these panics (often perpetuated by gay men, as much as anyone else) judge that, despite the advances in legal equality, some urban gay men are pathologically substituting anonymous, drug-enhanced sex with strangers for the intimacy which is missing from their lives (Kirby and Thornber-Dunwell 2013).

The fourth (and final) change that has significantly reshaped the sexual life of cities since queer ideas and politics first arose (and even since the resurgence of queer radicalism as a distinct strand within the global justice movement of movements in the early 2000s) has been the development of new digital communication technologies. The internet and mobile apps utilizing geo-locative technologies have become a significant enabler and mediator of sexual relations in society (Brickell 2012). Indeed, the sex industry has been a significant driver of technological development on the internet (Hubbard 2012). These developments have spurred broader debates about the dangers of the internet for potentially skewing the sexual socialization of adolescents and undermining intimacy within established adult relations; but they have also been celebrated for their potential to educate about sex, relationships and sexual health, as well as their capacity to enhance human sexuality and expand the boundaries of normative behaviour (see Nash and Gorman-Murray 2016 for an overview of these contrasting debates). For my discussion here, though, I want to highlight two trends which I think are significant for considering how queer interactions with the city have changed over the last two decades. First, online dating sites and mobile hook-up apps now play a very significant role in how people (of all sexualities) meet sexual and romantic partners. These trends have important consequences for the relationships between online and offline spaces (indeed, they require a recognition that urban space is increasingly mediated). These technologies and applications are changing where people go to meet others, and the geographies of the relationships (and the sexual encounters) that they engage in. If earlier queer urban scholarship had an infatuation with the supposedly transgressive ways in which gay and bisexual men subverted the intended uses and meanings of urban space through cruising and their public sex cultures (Bell 1997; Delany 1999), then, more recently, scholars have recognized that these new technologies have contributed to the decline of these sites (or, at the very least, significantly altered how they are used) (McGlotten 2013; Mowlabocus 2010, 2016). These dynamics have also been assessed as contributing to the apparent decline of 'gaybourhoods' in North American cities (Ghaziani 2014). At the same time, and this is my second point, they have contributed to cohering new sex and gender identities, such as asexuality, and providing online spaces within which people can find each other, articulate their shared identity, and organize politically for it to be recognized within broader society (De Lappe 2016). Interestingly, the increasing participation of asexual groups within LGBT pride festivals demonstrates that collectives forged online are now beginning to shape offline space within cities.

Having elaborated these four drivers that have impacted on changing modes of queer urbanism and urban sexual politics, I now examine how queer has changed in recent years.

What became of queer?

There has been considerable debate about the current state of 'gaybourhoods' in cities around the developed world (Doan and Higgins 2011; Nash 2013). It has been posited that increasing social acceptance of sexual diversity, new equalities legislation, and the new modes of finding (sex and) community offered by digital technologies have rendered distinct inner city clusters of lesbians, gay men and other sexual minorities less necessary and, for many people, less desirable. While LGBT people are undoubtedly living more open, visible and integrated lives in a wider variety of urban, suburban and rural places than was previously (imagined to be) the case, it does not appear that this really means the end of lesbian and gay neighbourhoods – clustering still occurs, albeit for a wider range of reasons than before (Ghaziani 2014). Indeed, Ghaziani (2014) has argued that these neighbourhoods were never as territorially fixed as they have been imagined to be, and that all that has occurred in the last decade or so is that some of these leisure and residential concentrations have migrated to adjacent neighbourhoods, or have been reconstituted around a more diverse set of intersectional interests, shaped by race, class, generation and family status.

These changes and diversifications have implications for how queer urban spaces and queer modes of urban life are imagined. Although queer urbanism often critiqued the limits of (and exclusions from) the mainstream commercial bar scenes that were centred in gay neighbourhoods, it also celebrated the potential these spaces had to queer normative socio-sexual relations, and to serve as 'laboratories of love and friendship' (Bell and Binnie 2000: 132). While recognizing that many of these gay neighbourhoods had initially developed in (what were often perceived to be) run-down, derelict, and forgotten spaces, urban areas that offered both cheap rents and a degree of separation (and thus privacy) from heteronormative society, queer scholarship also frequently celebrated the transgressive potential of sites associated with dirt and dereliction (Bell 1997; Campkin 2007). Of course, many of the supposedly derelict areas in which 'gay neighbourhoods' developed did have resident populations. To see them as derelict and abandoned provided a justification to gentrifiers (gay or otherwise) to settle them and change their social character. While these associations with dirt and dereliction persist in some circumstances, they are less central to how contemporary 'queer' sites are understood. Previously, queer life was imagined to be found either as a distinct layer, a 'social overlay' (Ingram 1997: 40), that permeated the urban landscape, or as a set of practices and relations that emerged from the cracks in the mainstream social fabric. Today, in an increasing number of cities, distinct queer (or queer-friendly) neighbourhoods have become identifiable (and they are imagined to be distinct from both the heteronormative city and more established LGBT spaces).

Alongside its association with sex radicalism, public sex cultures and other transgressions of social norms around sexuality and gender, queer has (from the beginning) also been associated with avant-garde artistic and cultural production. This can be seen, for example, in the uses of high quality graphic art by ACT UP and Queer Nation in the late 1980s (Crimp with Rolston 1990), or in the overlapping connections between anti-capitalist radical queers and 'do-it-yourself' music and party scenes in the early 2000s (Brown 2011). Eleftheriadis (2014) has charted how a network of recurring queer festivals across Europe in the early twenty-first century helped sew together a transnational network of activists and cultural producers, and positioned certain urban neighbourhoods across the continent as being key nodes of creative queer life. While relatively marginal, these 'do-it-yourself' queer festivals are illustrative of a broader trend seen in many advanced economies – a layer of younger, highly educated (but often underemployed), people working often in the creative industries, have turned their backs on older LGBT 'villages' and neighbourhoods and created a space for themselves in more mixed, 'queer-friendly' and trendy urban neighbourhoods that accommodate and provide the social and professional infrastructure for a wider layer of people from similar class fractions (Nash and Gorman-Murray 2014). Informed, in part, by two decades of queer critique, these areas attract people who celebrate the fluidity of sexuality and gender identity, and may dis-identify with (what they perceive as) more mainstream expressions of lesbian and gay identities. Whether these areas are actually particularly more welcoming or inclusive of trans and gender variant people, queers of colour, or other members of the 'queer unwanted' (Casey 2007) is open to question and likely to be determined as much by one's ability to deploy the kinds of social and cultural capital validated by this class fraction as anything else.

At different points in the last 25 years, queer urbanism has been associated with different spatialities and spatial imaginaries. The early activism of Queer Nation and similar groups sought to confront and undermine heteronormativity in all its incarnations and make the whole city safe and accessible for all those whose existence challenged normative assumptions. Their practice and perspective sought to open up the whole city and refuse the corralling of sexual and gender minorities within distinct 'gay neighbourhoods'. In the mid-1990s, this ambition mutated slightly, and queer urban scholarship became more interested in those spaces and practices that transgressed both heteronormative social values and emerging expressions of homonormativity. In the last decade or so, those edgy spaces that offered a refuge in which queers could experiment with alternatives to mainstream lesbian and gay cultures have become increasingly gentrified. Although some self-identified queers might align themselves with social movements that are attempting to resist gentrification, and might protest the loss of long-standing LGBT venues to these processes, they are nonetheless complicit in the gentrification of these areas. The constellation of queer-friendly neighbourhoods in major cities around the world – Dalston in London, Neukölln in Berlin, Newtown in Sydney, and Queer West in Toronto, amongst others – are all experiencing heightened gentrification, and are home to similar class fractions with a shared habitus that includes, but extends beyond, a particular orientation to sexual and gendered difference. Queer's radical critique of normative social relations has increasingly been recuperated as an (urban) aesthetic and a cultural milieu. This milieu is increasingly materialized in certain types of 'hip' urban space.

This changing location and use of queer in the contemporary urban landscape reflects the playing out of some of queer's contradictions (Brown 2012). Although queer critique and practices have often been contrasted with more homonormative expressions of lesbian and gay life, queer is just as much the product of neoliberal times as 'the new homonormativity'. There was always a thin line between the 'do-it-yourself' ethos of the queer autonomous spaces and festivals of the early twenty-first century (Brown 2007; Eleftheriadis 2014) and the self-regulating, self-reliant citizen favoured by neoliberal modes of governmentality. Since its beginning, queer has highlighted the diversity of sexual and gendered subjectivities that are occluded by mainstream lesbian and gay identities (or even the more recent ubiquity of the LGBT acronym). While many queer activist projects of the 1990s and early 2000s stressed the potential for forging new collectives across difference, the celebration of difference always also contained the potential for fragmentation into ever smaller identity categories. Queer's celebration of difference often validated individual experience over collective knowledge. Without acknowledging these individualizing tendencies, and offering a strong counterbalance to them, it is hardly surprising that queer knowledge production has been subsumed and recuperated (Di Feliciantonio and Brown 2015). This is not to argue that queer has become devoid of politics, but to suggest that queer's original anti-identitarian stance has been weakened, and (amongst other, simultaneous connotations) queer has increasingly been claimed as an identity in itself. Rather than an ethics of radical openness to difference, queer politics and culture has become increasingly censorious of those modes of living in and interpreting the world that do not fit with its current vogue. Rather than actually challenging normative social relations, for some time now queer has functioned as a form of social and cultural capital by which a highly educated layer of sexual and gender minority people have staked a claim to access and reproduce class privilege in the city (while still presenting themselves as edgy, alternative and avant-garde). This has considerable implications for how to approach the queer city and the potential for 'queer' to actually challenge the normative structuring of sex, gender and other social relations in urban space.

Where next?

In considering where to take queer urban theory next, it is tempting to revisit the agenda proposed by the anonymous (Anon 2004) authors of *Dreams of the Queer City*. They proposed that queers should celebrate their histories, fostering intergenerational dialogue and learning about earlier experiments in LGBTQ community organizing. In relation to the first of these propositions, increasingly LGBT histories are being incorporated into some national heritage projects – for example by the National Park Service (2014) in the USA and Historic England (2015). How queer these heritage projects remain is open to question. Second, the *Dreams of the Queer City* also staked a claim for the importance of engaging with cultural difference, recognizing that persistent racism and other forms of prejudice within queer communities needed to continue to be challenged, but simultaneously recognizing that socially and culturally diverse neighbourhoods were important to a queer praxis that was founded within a radical openness to difference. Third, the dreamers argued for the defence of sites of public homosex as forms of queer commons outside of commercial interests that might foster free interactions across class and ethnic difference. As I have noted earlier in this chapter, the proliferation of digital geosocial hook-up apps has drastically altered the fortunes of many of the public sex environments that survived even a decade ago. Fourth, the dreamers advocated the importance of 'making time and space for place (rather than leisure)', imagining that the playful co-production of queer urban life outside of the commercial gay (or LGBT) scene might offer a qualitatively different mechanism for building queer collectives and cultures. Finally, the activists behind this manifesto argued for the continuing importance of 'creating queer autonomous spaces' through collective self-activity which could experiment with alternative ways of living, queerly, in cities. I still appreciate the utopian post-capitalist impulse underpinning some of these statements, but I read them less optimistically now than I did a decade ago. They may still seem necessary and desirable, but they also seem less achievable (in the sense that they were originally intended). In part, this is because the unfolding of changes in social policy and 'equalities' legislation in some national contexts, alongside new technologies and the changed social practices and relations they have produced, have overtaken the proposals made in 2004. At the same time, as I argued earlier, the place and social function of 'queer' has changed.

Too frequently over recent decades, scholars and activists have left definitions of 'queer' open and slippery. That might have served a productive purpose in the past, but increasingly it has allowed highly individualized and socially privileged articulations of queer praxis to predominate. For all of their radical pretensions, queer theory, queer subcultures and queer activism are as much a product of neoliberal times as the sexual politics and lifestyles that they critique and position themselves against. I fear that, over the last decade, as queer-friendly neighbourhoods have emerged in the trendiest corners of many major cities, the limits and contradictions of queer thinking have become visible in the very fabric of urban space.

Queer once played an important role in drawing attention to (and confronting) the ways in which heteronormativity was reproduced in urban space and the ways in which people of all sexualities and genders inhabited it. Since its inception, that same queer critique has been used to question more 'homonormative' expressions of lesbian and gay cultures that are complicit in the reproduction of heteronormative privilege. In contrast to these tendencies, both radical queer activists and queer urban scholars have tended to celebrate those urban sexual and gender subcultures and practices that can be seen to transgress and challenge normative social values. As Natalie Oswin (2005) has argued, this has led to a perpetual search for ever more authentically transgressive practices, people and places. I value this earlier work's focus on the marginal, the unwanted and the less visible; but I also recognize its limits. First, this work has tended to focus too much on spectacular expressions of sexual and gendered difference, rather than the negotiation of social values in more mundane and ordinary spaces of everyday life in a variety of urban locations. Second, queer's focus on difference can easily lead to a validation of individual experience over more shared or relational experiences of urban space.

In the current period, there is still value in studying urban sexual cultures and offering an uncompromising critique of mainstream sexual politics. However, I am increasingly cautious about the limitations of only using queer methodologies to approach these questions. I think it is time for urban scholars to expand our theoretical repertoires when it comes to the study of sexuality and gender in the contemporary city. This will probably entail a move away from placing 'the normative' at the centre of 'queer' critique. This has become a barrier to studying the diversity of lives (and locations) lived by people of all sexualities. It also lets 'queer' subcultures off the hook for their own complicity in reproducing (classed and racialized) privilege and redrawing the boundaries of 'the charmed circle' of sexuality in contemporary society.

References

Andersson, Johan (2011), 'Vauxhall's Postindustrial Pleasure Gardens: "Death Wish" and Hedonism in 21st Century London', *Urban Studies*, **48** (1), 85–100.

Anonymous (2004), 'Dreams of the Queer City', *The Pink Pauper* 2 (May), 4–5.

Bell, David (1995), 'Perverse Dynamics, Sexual Citizenship, and the Transformation of Intimacy', in David Bell and Gill Valentine (eds), *Mapping Desire*, London: Routledge, pp. 304–317.

Bell, David (1997), 'One-Handed Geographies: An Archeology of Public Sex', in Gordon Brent Ingram, Anne-Marie Bouthillette and Yolanda Retter (eds), *Queers in Space: Communities/Public Places/Sites of Resistance*, Seattle, WA: Bay Press, pp. 81–87.

Bell, David (2001), 'Fragments for a Queer City', in David Bell, Jon Binnie, Ruth Holliday, Robyn Longhurst and Robin Peace (eds), *Pleasure Zones: Bodies, Cities, Spaces*, Syracuse, NY: Syracuse University Press, pp. 84–102.

Bell, David and Jon Binnie (2000), *The Sexual Citizen: Queer Politics and Beyond*, Cambridge: Polity Press.

Berlant, Lauren and Elizabeth Freeman (1993), 'Queer Nationality', in Michael Warner (ed.), *Fear of a Queer Planet: Queer Politics and Social Theory*, Minneapolis, MN: University of Minnesota Press, pp. 193–229.

Binnie, Jon (2001), 'The Erotic Possibilities of the City', in David Bell, Jon Binnie, Ruth Holliday, Robyn Longhurst and Robin Peace (eds), *Pleasure Zones: Bodies, Cities, Spaces*, Syracuse, NY: Syracuse University Press, pp. 103–130.

Brickell, Chris (2012), 'Sexuality, Power and the Sociology of the Internet', *Current Sociology*, **60** (1), 28–44.

Brown, Gavin (2007), 'Mutinous Eruptions: Autonomous Spaces of Radical Queer Activism', *Environment and Planning A*, **39** (11), 2685–2698.

Brown, Gavin (2009), 'Thinking beyond Homonormativity: Performative Explorations of Diverse Gay Economies', *Environment and Planning A*, **41** (6), 1496–1510.

Brown, Gavin (2011), 'Anarchism and Amateurism in the Creation of Autonomous Queer Spaces', in Richard Cleminson and Jamie Heckert (eds), *Anarchism and Sexuality*, London: Routledge, pp. 200–223.

Brown, Gavin (2012), 'Queer's Contradictions (and Radical Sexual Politics for Precarious Times)', . . .*ment Journal*, 3, last accessed 18 October 2016 at http://journalment.org/issue/fragment-authorship.

Brown, Gavin (2015a), 'Queer Movement', in David Paternotte and Manon Tremblay (eds), *The Routledge Research Companion to Lesbian and Gay Activism*, Abingdon, UK: Routledge, pp. 73–86.

Brown, Gavin (2015b), 'Marriage and the Spare Bedroom: Exploring the Sexual Politics of Austerity in Britain', *ACME: An International e-Journal for Critical Geographies*, **14** (4), 975–988.

Campkin, Ben (2007),'Degradation and Regeneration: Theories of Dirt and the Contemporary City', in Ben Campkin and Rosie Cox (eds), *Dirt: New Geographies of Cleanliness and Contamination*, London: I.B. Tauris, pp. 68–79.

Casey, Mark (2007), 'The Queer Unwanted and Their Undesirable Otherness', in Kath Browne, Jason Lim and Gavin Brown (eds), *Geographies of Sexualities*, Farnham, UK: Ashgate, pp. 125–136.

Crimp, Douglas with Adam Rolston (1990), *AIDSDemoGraphics*, Seattle, WA: Bay Press.

De Lappe, Joseph (2016), 'Asexual Activism', in Nancy Naples, Renee Hoogland, Maithree Wickramasinghe and Wai Ching Angela Wong (eds), *The Wiley Blackwell Encyclopedia of Gender and Sexuality Studies*, Oxford: Wiley Blackwell.

Delany, Samuel (1999), *Times Square Red, Times Square Blue*, New York: New York University Press.

Di Feliciantonio, Cesare and Gavin Brown (2015), 'Introduction: The Sexual Politics of Austerity', *ACME: An International e-Journal for Critical Geographies*, **14** (4), 965–974.

Doan, Petra and Harrison Higgins (2011), 'The Demise of Queer Space? Resurgent Gentrification and the Assimilation of LGBT Neighborhoods', *Journal of Planning Education and Research*, **31** (1), 6–25.

Duggan, Lisa (2002), 'The New Homonormativity: The Sexual Politics of Neoliberalism', in Russ Castronovo and Dana D. Nelson (eds), *Materialising Democracy: Towards a Revitalized Cultural Politics*, Durham, NC: Duke University Press, pp. 175–194.

Eleftheriadis, Konstantinos (2014), 'Queer Activism and the Idea of "Practicing Europe"', in Phillip M. Ayoub and David Paternotte (eds), *LGBT Activism and the Making of Europe: A Rainbow Europe?*, Basingstoke, UK: Palgrave Macmillan, pp. 145–167.

Frederick, Brian J. (2014), '"Delinquent Boys": Toward a New Understanding of "Deviant" and Transgressive Behavior in Gay Men', *Critical Criminology*, **22** (1), 139–149.

Ghaziani, Amin (2014), *There Goes the Gayborhood?*, Princeton, NJ: Princeton University Press.

Golding, Sue (1993), 'Quantum Philosophy, Impossible Geographies and a Few Small Points about Life, Liberty and the Pursuits of Sex (All in the Name of Democracy)', in Michael Keith and Steve Pile (eds), *Place and the Politics of Identity*, London: Routledge, pp. 206–219.

Harvey, David (2000), *Spaces of Hope*, Edinburgh: Edinburgh University Press.

Hines, Sally (2010), 'Queerly Situated? Exploring Negotiations of Trans Queer Subjectivities at Work and within Community Spaces in the UK', *Gender, Place and Culture*, **17** (5), 597–613.

Historic England (2015), *Pride of Place: LGBTQ Heritage Project*, accessed 11 January 2016 at https:// historicengland.org.uk/research/inclusive-heritage/lgbtq-heritage-project/.

Hubbard, Phil (2012), *Cities and Sexualities*, London: Routledge.

Ingram, Gordon Brent (1997), 'Marginality and the Landscapes of Erotic Alien(n)ations', in Gordon Brent Ingram, Anne-Marie Bouthillette and Yolanda Retter (eds), *Queers in Space: Communities/ Public Places/Sites of Resistance*, Seattle, WA: Bay Press, pp. 27–52.

Ingram, Gordon Brent, Anne-Marie Bouthillette and Yolanda Retter (eds) (1997), *Queers in Space: Communities/Public Places/Sites of Resistance*, Seattle, WA: Bay Press.

Kearns, Gerry (2016), 'Queering Epidemiology', in Gavin Brown and Kath Browne (eds), *The Routledge Research Companion to Geographies of Sex and Sexualities*, Abingdon, UK: Routledge, pp. 263–273.

Kirby, Tony and Michelle Thornber-Dunwell, M. (2013), 'High-Risk Drug Practices Tighten Grip on London Gay Scene', *The Lancet*, **381**, 101–102.

Klesse, Christian (2014), 'Polyamory: Intimate Practice, Identity or Sexual Orientation?', *Sexualities*, **17** (1–2), 81–99.

Mattilda (aka Matt Bernstein Sycamore) (2004), 'Gay Shame: From Queer Autonomous Space to Direct Action Extravaganza', in Mattilda (aka Matt Bernstein Sycamore) (ed.), *That's Revolting! Queer Strategies for Resisting Assimilation*, New York: Soft Skull Press, pp. 237–262.

McGlotten, Shaka (2013), *Virtual Intimacies: Media, Affect, and Queer Sociality*, Albany, NY: SUNY Press.

Mowlabocus, Sharif (2010), *Gaydar Culture: Gay Men, Technology and Embodiment in the Digital Age*, Farnham, UK: Ashgate.

Mowlabocus, Sharif (2016), 'Horny at the Bus Stop, Paranoid in the Cul-de-Sac: Sex, Technology and Public Space', in Gavin Brown and Kath Browne (eds), *The Routledge Research Companion to Geographies of Sex and Sexualities*, Abingdon, UK: Routledge, pp. 391–398.

Nash, Catherine J. (2013), 'The Age of the "Post-Mo"? Toronto's Gay Village and a New Generation', *Geoforum*, **49**, 243–252.

Nash, Catherine J. and Andrew Gorman-Murray (2014), 'LGBT Neighbourhoods and "New Mobilities": Towards Understanding Transformations in Sexual and Gendered Urban Landscapes', *International Journal of Urban and Regional Research*, **38** (3), 756–772.

Nash, Catherine J. and Andrew Gorman-Murray (2016), 'Digital Technologies and Sexualities in Urban Space', in Gavin Brown and Kath Browne (eds), *The Routledge Research Companion to Geographies of Sex and Sexualities*, Abingdon, UK: Routledge, pp. 399–405.

National Park Service (2014), *Lesbian, Gay, Bisexual, Transgender, and Queer (LGBTQ) Heritage Initiative*, accessed 11 January 2016 at http://www.nps.gov/history/heritageinitiatives/LGBThistory/.

Oswin, Natalie (2005), 'Towards Radical Geographies of Complicit Queer Futures', *ACME: An International e-Journal for Critical Geographies*, **3** (2), 79–86.

Rubin, Gayle (2011), *Deviations: A Gayle Rubin Reader*, Durham, NC: Duke University Press.

Shepard, Benjamin (2002), 'Culture Jamming a SexPanic!' in Benjamin Shepard and Ronald Hayduk (eds), *From ACT UP to the WTO: Urban Protest and Community Building in the Era of Globalization*, London: Verso, pp. 202–214.

Warner, Michael (1999), *The Trouble with Normal: Sex, Politics and the Ethics of Queer Life*, Cambridge, MA: Harvard University Press.

Weeks, Jeffrey (2007), *The World We Have Won*, London: Routledge.

6   Sex and the city: sexuality and urban order/disorder

Phil Hubbard, Andrew Gorman-Murray and Catherine J. Nash

Introduction

Urban studies was slow to recognise that sex and sexuality are as important in the making of social and spatial orders as class, race or gender. Initial explorations of sex and the city were largely restricted to consideration of the distributions of 'zones of vice' and studies of prostitution (e.g. Kneeland 1913; Reckless 1926; Symanski 1974), and few foundational texts in the discipline made mention of sexuality. However, the increased visibility of lesbian and gay life in a range of Western cities in the 1970s and 1980s (notably San Francisco, New York, Amsterdam, Berlin and Paris) arguably thrust sexuality on to the agenda of urban studies, with Manuel Castells' examination of gay groups as a new social movement in *The City and the Grassroots* (1983) highlighting the importance of the city in the social, economic and political life of those outside the heterosexual 'norm' (see also Castells and Murphy 1982). The realisation that some 'gay neighbourhoods' were also spaces of incipient gentrification helped to bring the investigation of sexuality into dialogue with unfolding debates in urban studies about the important role of culture and lifestyle in driving processes of capital accumulation through property development (e.g. Lauria and Knopp 1985).

Studies acknowledging the sexuality of the city have subsequently become important in a body of work concerned more broadly with the relations of 'sexuality and space' (Bell and Valentine 1995). This sub-discipline – which draws on diverse perspectives in geography, sociology and planning about the spatial construction of sexuality – has become significantly more diverse in the twenty-first century by shifting focus beyond a fixation with the location of 'zones of vice' or 'gay neighbourhoods' to consider the broader ways that urbanisation shapes sexual practice, performance and identity (Browne et al. 2007; Doan 2011, 2015; Hubbard 2012). Indeed, in a context where many societies are more open about sexuality, and more accepting of sexual diversity, the opportunities for investors, developers and retailers to profit through the promotion of sexual consumption and 'queer diversity' appear more pronounced than ever (Bell and Binnie 2004; Kanai 2014). At the same time, the commodification of sex continues apace, mainly online, but also offline, with the sex industries visible in our cities in a variety of subtle and not-so-subtle forms, including sex shops, striptease bars and adult entertainment complexes (Maginn and Steinmetz 2014).

In this chapter we highlight how some of these changes demand attention from urban researchers. First, we focus on the flux (and even decline) of 'gay villages' (Brown 2014; Nash and Gorman-Murray 2014), which we argue challenges many existing theorisations of the role of particular neighbourhoods in the reproduction (and normalisation) of marginal sexual identities. Second, we advocate for the importance of considering not just LGBT spaces and lifestyles in the city, but recognising the diversity of heterosexual spaces that are understood as either spaces of conformity or 'perversion' and disorder. The third theme concerns the shifting relations of sexuality and the city in the contemporary era of 'dense' interpersonal connection and exchange – that is, an era of heightened internal and global migration, and of increasingly widespread use of digital, mobile and online technologies. Finally, we address the challenges these changes pose in terms of the methods we use to interrogate the relationships of sexuality and space, and we ask whether theories mainly worked through in the context of Western world cities can, or should, be adapted when examining the sexual life of cities beyond the urban West.

The 'moving' gay village

The historical emergence and contemporary status of so-called LGBT or, more often, gay villages in major cities in the US, UK, Europe, Canada and Australia has been the subject of a substantial body of research. Most of this argues that the foundations of such villages began in the West in the period after World War II, when gay men, in particular, and some lesbians flocked to the downtown or inner-city neighbourhoods of large cities, seeking affordable apartments and flats (rather than houses) (Adler and Brenner 1992; Lauria and Knopp 1985). However, subsequent analyses suggest this triggered the conditions for a gentrification that benefited property developers and corporations rather than LGBT populations:

> Many of these once-derelict neighborhoods, such as the Castro in San Francisco, West Hollywood in Los Angeles, Boys Town in Chicago, the South End in Boston, Chelsea in New York, the Gayborhood in Philadelphia, and Midtown in Atlanta . . . developed reputations as desirable places for LGBT people to live and recreate. At the same time, their renovation . . . made them more attractive to non-LGBT individuals in search of in-town living. Higher demand for property in these neighborhoods has resulted in steep rises in rents, frequent conversion of rental properties to condominiums, and competition for commercial space, which make it difficult for less affluent LGBT people and businesses targeted to the community to remain in the neighborhoods. (Doan and Higgins 2011: 6)

In many such cities during the 1970s and 1980s, deindustrialisation and decentralisation meant that inner-city neighbourhoods were somewhat marginal and run-down, providing a location where those 'alternative' lifestyles could co-exist with other marginal groups – for example, sex workers, drug addicts and the chronically unemployed (Knopp 1995, 1998; Lauria and Knopp 1985; Nash 2006). Despite the somewhat destitute nature of many such districts, some gay men and lesbians were able to find relatively safe locations to escape the largely homophobic nature of public urban spaces. While lesbians and queer women did (and still do) frequent gay villages, research also demonstrates that distinctive lesbian concentrations also emerged, reflecting specific socio-spatial relations in urban spaces (Adler and Brenner 1992; Nash 2001; Podmore 2001, 2006, 2013; Rothenberg 1995).

As gay men and lesbians increasingly benefited from anti-discrimination legislation and growing acceptance in mainstream society in the 1990s, cities also incorporated gay districts into tourism and marketing strategies. This mainstreaming of LGBT spaces and experiences has generated pointed arguments about the commodification of gay life and the development of an identity politics grounded in consumerist practices. Some scholarship also argues that gay villages are dominated by white, middle-class, gay male interests, and are thus perceived as exclusionary to lesbians, LGBT people of colour, older LGBT people and those of lower socioeconomic status (Duggan 2002; Richardson 2005). Hence, while gay villages are now considered completely interwoven into the fabric of inner-city life and touted as evidence of cities' tolerance and diversity (e.g. Florida's (2005) problematic 'gay index' as a measure of cosmopolitanism and creative economies), some critiques argue that only some LGBT people have gained acceptance through an assimilationist politic that 'privileges a middle-class aesthetics and monogamous, consumerist couple-dom' (Nash and Gorman-Murray 2014: 760). This arguably constitutes a form of 'homonormativity' that privileges some gays and lesbians over others – that is, those who are able to freely participate in commodified gay village spaces (Binnie 2014; Duggan 2002; Rushbrook 2002).

Many contemporary gay villages are in a state of flux (Brown 2014; Gorman-Murray and Nash 2014), losing certain gay businesses and populations as rents and taxes rise (Collins 2004; Ruting 2008). Some claim that with social, political and legal inclusions, LGBT people no longer need gay villages and are more comfortable moving beyond LGBT spaces. Indeed, a new generation of gay men and lesbians are connecting with others through new social media in ways that render the gay village superfluous (Mowlabocus 2010; Usher and Morrison 2010). Others claim that gay villages are, in part, victims of their own success, where, as commodified, consumeristic spaces, they are increasingly inhabited by heterosexuals looking for exciting nightlife or downtown living in relatively safe neighbourhoods (Binnie and Skeggs 2004; Casey 2004). A new generation of gay men and lesbians may also be finding traditional gay villages limiting, regarding them as an historical and political area that is no longer of relevance to them (Nash 2013a; Reynolds 2009; Sullivan 2005; Vaccaro 2009).

Whether gay villages will disappear is a matter of some debate and depends on a range of factors, including a given village's history, geography, and political, economic and social circumstances. Recent work comparing changes in Toronto, Canada, and Sydney, Australia, discusses these spatial differences (Nash and Gorman-Murray 2015a). Toronto's gay village, Church and Wellesley, has considerable support from the City of Toronto through its tourism and marketing initiatives, and has a strong Business Improvement Association (BIA) devoted to maintaining the strength and relevance of the gay village to current and future generations of LGBT people (Nash and Gorman-Murray 2015a). The Church and Wellesley BIA has raised funds to support a local planning study, make street improvements (parklets, street signage, commemorative statues) and support gay village businesses. The district also benefits from the advocacy of its openly lesbian city councillor, Kristen Wong-Tam, and is home to major LGBT institutions, including the LGBT community centre, 519 Church Street. By contrast, Sydney's gay village, Oxford Street, has been experiencing decline for some time (Reynolds 2009). Its daytime economy is struggling while the night-time economy is increasingly problematic, with numerous clubs and bars frequented by young heterosexuals (Nash and Gorman-Murray 2015a). Another Sydney inner-city neighbourhood – Newtown – is arguably becoming the new 'queer' district, offering a community feeling, vibrant street-life, and diverse and welcoming spaces, including a range of LGBT-specific and LGBT-friendly organisations and services (Gorman-Murray and Nash 2014; Gorman-Murray and Waitt 2009).

What is becoming clear is that the experiences of LGBT people in cities in the West are currently undergoing transformation, although it is difficult to tell what the ultimate outcome will be. Scholarship has certainly shown that some LGBT people are able to move into other areas of the city, more freely experiencing an openly visible gay or lesbian identity (Nash 2013a, 2013b; Nash and Gorman-Murray 2014). While these changes might suggest the decline of the gay village in favour of other neighbourhoods, it might be more useful to think about gay villages and new LGBT districts as mobile and relational, linked through expanding networks constituted by flows of people, goods and ideas. The increasingly mobile lives of some LGBT people, achieved through shifting social positioning as much as new technologies, are creating relationships both in and between historically important gay villages and the new nodes and pathways open to LGBT people (Gorman-Murray and Nash 2014; Nash and Gorman-Murray 2014, 2015b).

Heterosexual landscapes of the city

Given the normalisation and assimilation of LGBT values in many Western cities, it is tempting to argue that the city is becoming 'softer' as traditional sexual moralities and norms are challenged. The seeming diminution of the traditional family, the rise of divorce, and the legal recognition of same-sex civil unions or marriages all suggest something fundamental has happened to sexuality in recent decades, with the idealisation of the nuclear family being superseded by a wider range of possible household types and lifestyle choices. In its 'plastic' incarnation, sex has become recreational, with the trade in sperm and human embryos, in vitro fertilisation and reproductive technologies meaning that sex itself is no longer even required for procreation. The implication, seemingly, is that people are more able to choose sexual lifestyles and identities beyond the taken-for-granted norm of the married, co-resident, heterosexual couple with children. Giddens' (1993) identification of the dominance of 'confluent' love based on mutual satisfaction rather than life-long commitment highlights this putative shift in sexual ethics, something registered in the increased purchase of sexual services, the consumption of pornography, the use of online dating sites and the pursuit of hetero-flexible lifestyles (Attwood 2007).

But it is clear that this sexual 'diversification and dispersion' (Sigusch 1998) remains geographically uneven. Clearly, not all cities are equally open to sexual diversity, and even in the urban West there are still clear limits to sexual citizenship. The contemporary Western city remains highly normative, reproducing certain assumptions about the importance of love and coupledom: singleness remains suspect, whether people live alone by choice or appear unable to form relationships (Wilkinson 2014). This implies we should not aim to simply contrast the homosexual and heterosexual experience of the city, but adopt a queer perspective that considers the plurality of sexual identities that exist in the city. Literatures on the regulation of deviant or 'Other' heterosexualities within the city go some way to make this clear, particularly those that focus on the historical regulation of single mothers, prostitutes and 'hysterical' female sexualities (Hubbard 2011). In contrast, less has been said about the ways that cities have marginalised particular masculine identities and practices, though the way that perpetrators of domestic violence against women, errant fathers and male sex tourists are marginalised in social and spatial terms suggests an interesting line of enquiry here (see also the literatures on the spatial restrictions placed on male sexual offenders in the US city, for example, Berenson and Appelbaum 2011; Grubesic 2010).

There is then a strong case for further opening up the 'black box' of heterosexuality to explore the many possible articulations of heterosexual desire that are included or excluded within the city (Howard 2013). Literatures on prostitution are also helpful in clarifying how 'heteronormativity' is reproduced through the containment of commercial sex work away from 'family spaces' (the subtext here being that prostitution and pornography threatens to corrupt the innocent) (see Laing and Cook 2014). Overt policies of zoning and licensing hence exclude brothels and sex shops from the proximity of educational establishments, religious establishments and suburban 'family' areas (Hubbard et al. 2013), reproducing a 'moral geography' which separates the presumed disorderly from the ordered and respectable (Prior and Gorman-Murray 2014).

Yet there is much variation here: adult entertainment in the form of female striptease is apparently accepted at the heart of many successful urban economies in the form of 'gentleman's clubs' given that it can attract visitors and enhance the tax base (Maginn and Steinmitz 2014). Against this, there are others who regard the presence of such premises – and sexualised images in the cityscape – as offensive and intimidating, perpetuating ideas that women are always 'on display' as sexual objects (Lim and Fanghanel 2013). Feminist groups regularly oppose the opening of lap dance premises (see Hubbard and Colosi 2013), and many other business and resident groups typically portray sex businesses as bad neighbours (Hubbard et al. 2013). Such opposition portrays sexual entertainment as normalising retrogressive, male attitudes towards women, and suggests, perhaps wrongly, that the presence of clubs is associated with increased rates of both violent and non-violent crime (see Linz et al. 2000; Paul et al. 2001). Working through these debates, it seems that the identities and spaces that can be accommodated within normative heterosexuality are constantly changing. This said, there remains much more to be said about the apparently de-sexualised spaces of the 'family': for example, the suburbs, the mall, the 'family' resort and so on. Not all of these are monolithically heterosexual, of course, suggesting that work considering how they are lived, imagined and practised should be a priority.

World cities of sex

One of the starting points for any exploration of sex and the city has been the observation that cities – and especially big cities – are sites where disconnected people, perhaps drawn from different cultural and geographical backgrounds, are drawn into sexual relationships with those they find themselves living among (Hubbard 2012). While the assumption that people tend to partner with people within their own neighbourhood provides a launching pad for many studies of the sexual organisation of the city, these ideas must be held in tension with an awareness of the shifting mobilities ushered in by the technological changes associated with globalisation. Two trends are notable here: first, the improvement of transport technologies that allow many individuals to maintain transnational lifestyles and, second, the rise of digital, mobile and online communication technologies that allow individuals to maintain social and sexual relationships at a distance.

In relation to the former, it is evident that message boards and social networking sites like Facebook and Twitter are used by LGBT groups to communicate, make contact with others, organise events, create communities, and tell the stories of their lives (Pullen and Cooper, 2010), encouraging the movement of those of LGBT identification to specific cities and neighbourhoods. This may of course simply exacerbate the tendency for LGBT populations to gravitate towards the biggest cities, and the marketing of certain cities as spaces for 'gay tourism' is clearly a factor here (Waitt and Markwell 2006). However, Binnie (2014: 595) argues that 'given the intensification of networked links and resources within queer cyberspace, it is hard to retain the tenability of assertions of queer cultural life within one locality remaining uninformed by events, practices and values from elsewhere'. Here the suggestion appears that changing communication is enabling the globalisation of the gay lifestyles most vividly associated with metropolitan centres of the West. This implies that a persistent focus on the largest cities that are the 'hubs of a global network of sexual commerce around which images, bodies and desires circulate voraciously' (Hubbard 2012: 176) is perhaps misplaced: as Muller Myrdahl (2013) has argued, gay and lesbian lives are of course led in cities both small and large, with e-communication making it easier to feel part of a 'queer' community even if one is living in a small or remote town (see also Waitt and Gorman-Murray 2011).

More widely, Internet technologies allow for the production of intimacies-at-a-distance in all manner of ways, being tied into practices of coupling, partnership and sex itself (Valentine 2006). This means that distance does not necessarily bring intimacy to an end, with growing numbers of individuals 'living apart together' (Duncan and Phillips 2010), including commuter couples where one partner works away from home during the week, dual career couples who maintain individual residences in separate locations, and diasporic families whose members are scattered across the globe (Constable 2009). At a more local level, websites and phone apps appear significant in reshaping the parameters of dating and relationships, and it is widely assumed that they are providing a means for individuals to meet, and mate with, others from a wider range of social backgrounds and communities (Brickell 2012). While dating sites such as Match.com and 'hook up apps' like Grindr, Tinder and Blendr are widely used by a variety of audiences, others are more specifically designed with those with particular tastes in mind, sometimes tied in to the promotion of fetish and kink pornography sites (Attwood 2007; Mowlabocus 2010). Again, this means that residence in the larger towns and cities traditionally associated with fetish or swinging scenes is no longer necessary for individuals to become part of BDSM (bondage, discipline, submission and (sado)masochism) networks: in an important sense, such networks and communities have gone virtual.

This virtualisation of sexual relations poses important questions about the city as the primary site for sexual encounter, particularly in the realm of commercialised or paid-for sex (Cunningham and Kendall 2011). But this should not distract from the fact that most sexual encounters are embodied and proximate rather than virtual or at-a-distance, and that cities remain key meeting grounds where global business people, tourists, immigrant workers and hosts circulate and mix to varied degrees. Mai and King (2009: 297) remind us that 'beyond their common function as mobile workers within the global capitalist economy . . . migrants and other "people on the move" are sexual beings expressing, wanting to express, or denied the means to express, their sexual identities': cities characterised by high rates of in- and out-migration tend to be characterised by highly diversified sexual scenes and 'hybrid' sexual cultures (Oswin 2013).

Recent urban scholarship on cities under conditions of contemporary globalisation, informed by increasingly sophisticated understandings of the ways that cities exist as 'unbounded places', may then be valuable in considering the intersection of nationalism, ethnicity and sexuality. Here, relational understandings of space (Massey 2005) provide a way of approaching the city as a series of relatively disconnected and dispersed activities made in and through many different kinds of networks. This type of perspective has important implications for studies of sex in the city given it suggests that cities cannot be understood solely through reference to the nation-state in which they are located: it also challenges the idea that the city-state is a coherent actor by insisting it is a set of actors with different and often competing intentions, with policies being constructed and mobilised in a multiplicity of sites, both near and far. As Ward (2010) succinctly argues, this means we need to not only study cities, but also the relations that bind them together and push them apart. However, research has as yet said little about sexuality as something that binds particular cities together, despite the evidential importance of sex to the economies of cities and, conversely, the importance of cities in articulating flows of migration in which love and sex can be a significant motive for movement (Mai and King 2009; Morrison et al. 2013).

Research challenges: methods for studying urban sexualities

The above themes have notable implications for methods of studying the sexuality of cities. One traditional way in which it has been possible to consider the sexual organisation of the city is through mapping exercises, which, with varying levels of precision and via different technologies (e.g. see Brown and Knopp 2010), allow us to 'see' the emplacement of sex in the landscape. This important tradition introduces a 'spatial epistemology' into the study of sexuality, albeit such cartographic traditions have clear limits given they support a 'pointilist' view of the world in which identities are 'fixed' in places (Bissell 2013). As much work on the sexuality of the city insists, the sex life of the city is much more fluid and 'messy' than this implies. This is thought to be especially the case for LGBT populations, something Knopp (2007: 23) underlines when he argues that 'queers' lived experiences' entail a radically different relationship to notions like place and space than that of 'more sedentary non-queers'. As he notes, 'the visibility that placement brings' can make LGBT populations vulnerable to violence, meaning that queers are 'frequently suspicious, fearful and unable to relate easily to the fixity and certainty inhering in most dominant ontologies of "place"'.

Grasping the fluidity and messiness of queer urban life-worlds can therefore be challenging given the transient and semi-anonymous nature of the experiences central in reproducing both the erotic and social lives of LGBT-identified individuals living in different cities, noting that for some people such identifications are themselves deeply problematic: Kanai (2014: 4) states that being 'gay' 'seems to be a privilege of the urban middle-class affiliated to the central city's Eurocentric worldliness and benefiting from economic globalization'. In his view, sexual dissidents from disadvantaged metropolitan outskirts cannot afford the luxury of dissociating identity politics from more pressing concerns related to basic material needs and clear threats in their everyday lives. This suggests that methods need to be aware of the specific languages used to describe sexual identification and practice in different parts of the world, and the use of ethnographic methods capable of grasping the 'elisions, inequalities and erasures that trouble and disrupt' Eurocentric mappings of gay modernity in the city (Manalansan 2015: 566).

Such observations highlight what is perhaps the most significant challenge to the current literature on sexuality and space, namely the need for its practitioners to escape the confines of a Eurocentric world-view that typically privileges white, middle-class males, to the exclusion of trans people, people of colour and people of lower socioeconomic status. The failure of much of the literature to adequately acknowledge intersectionality remains notable, particularly in post-colonial contexts. Even a cursory overview suggests many of the discussions concerning sex in the city remain within a 'homonormative' frame that re-centres the position of the most privileged LGBT individuals (Puar 2006), often marginalising queers of colour. As Haritaworn (2008) shows, this often involves the analogising of race and sexuality: by isolating and comparing the experiences of 'gays' (white) and 'blacks' (heterosexual), these writers obliterate racialised queer subjectivities and the multiple allegiances to which they potentially give rise. Likewise, Spurlin (2000: 183) argues that 'with its narrow Eurocentric, and therefore imperialistic gaze, queer studies has not seriously engaged how queer identities and cultural formations have taken shape and operate outside of large metropolitan locations', suggesting the need for studies of sexuality to move beyond engagement with the 'proud, Prada-wearing, marriage-bound, tax-paying, legitimate citizens of the queer global city' (Manalansan 2015: 577) to encompass other citizens and other cities (see also Gorman-Murray et al. 2013). Kanai's (2015) suggestion that future research will need to take stock of the heterogeneity and contingency of urban sexuality in Latin America and elsewhere implies a need for comparative work which is not merely aware of difference, but which evinces the intersections of sex, class, gender, age and ethnicity that produce localised manifestations of sexual life in different cities (see also Brown 2008 and Browne and Bakshi 2011 on 'ordinary cities').

Conclusion

The literature on the relationship of sexuality and the city is now significant, having generated some sophisticated understandings of how the city is patterned and sometimes divided on sexual lines. Moving beyond dominant understandings of urban/suburban remains a challenge (Tongson 2011), and there is still much that can be said about heterosexualities in cities (Hubbard, 2000). Moreover, it is clear that the literature on cities still fails to adequately grasp the intersection of sexuality with class, race and gender, with many commentators ignoring the former in favour of the latter variables. And, as we have shown, much of the writing on sex in the city remains fixated on the global cities of the West, failing to consider the different inflections of sexuality in non-metropolitan, non-Western and more 'ordinary' cities (Brown 2008). Here, queer writing on homonationalism adds new perspectives on the ways that capital accumulation aligns with sexual, racial and class norms to produce particular representations of the sex life of cities (Puar 2006). It is clear from such queer critiques that many of our 'mappings' of sex in the city fail to grasp matters of desire and corporeality through methods that alert us to the diverse gendered, classed and racialised experiences of sexual space. This implies that much remains to be done in unpicking existing assumptions about sex in the city, providing fuller and more nuanced understandings of the role of sexualities in producing urban order and disorder.

References

Adler, S. and Brenner, J. (1992), 'Gender and space: lesbians and gay men in the city', *International Journal of Urban and Regional Research*, **16** (1), 24–34.

Attwood, F. (2007), 'No money shot? Commerce, pornography and new sex taste cultures', *Sexualities*, **10** (4), 441–456.

Bell, D. and Binnie, J. (2004), 'Authenticating queer space: Citizenship, urbanism and governance', *Urban Studies*, **41** (9), 1807–1820.

Bell, D. and Valentine, G. (eds.) (1995), *Mapping Desire: Geographies of Sexualities*, London: Routledge.

Berenson, J.A. and Appelbaum, P.S. (2011), 'A geospatial analysis of the impact of sex offender residency restrictions in two New York counties', *Law and Human Behavior*, **35** (3), 235–246.

Binnie, J. (2014), 'Relational comparison, queer urbanism and worlding cities', *Geography Compass*, **8** (3), 590–599.

Binnie, J. and Skeggs, B. (2004), 'Cosmopolitan knowledge and the production and consumption of sexualized space: Manchester's gay village', *Sociological Review*, **51** (1), 39–61.

Bissell, D. (2013), 'Pointless mobilities: Rethinking proximity through the loops of neighbourhood', *Mobilities*, **8** (3), 349–367.

Brickell, C. (2012), 'Sexuality, power and the sociology of the internet', *Current Sociology*, **60** (1), 28–44.

Brown, G. (2008), 'Urban (homo)sexualities: Ordinary cities and ordinary sexualities', *Geography Compass*, **2** (4), 1215–1231.

Brown, M. (2014), 'Gender and sexuality II: There goes the gayborhood?', *Progress in Human Geography*, **38** (3), 457–465.

Brown, M. and Knopp, L. (2010), 'Between anatamo- and bio-politics: Geographies of sexual health in wartime Seattle', *Political Geography*, **29** (7), 392–403.

Browne, K. and Bakshi, L. (2011), 'We are here to party? Lesbian, gay, bisexual and trans leisurescapes beyond commercial gay scenes', *Leisure Studies*, **30** (2), 179–196.

Browne, K., Lim, J. and Brown, G. (eds.) (2007), *Geographies of Sexualities: Theory, Practices and Politics*, Chichester, UK: Ashgate.

Casey, M. (2004), 'De-dyking queer space(s): Heterosexual female visibility in gay and lesbian spaces', *Sexualities*, **7** (4), 446–461.

Castells, M. (1983), *The City and the Grassroots: A Cross-Cultural Theory of Urban Social Movements*, Berkeley, CA: University of California Press.

Castells, M. and Murphy, K. (1982), 'Cultural identity and urban structure: The spatial organization of San Francisco's gay community', in N. Fainstein and S. Fainstein (eds.), *Urban Policy under Capitalism*, Thousand Oaks, CA: Sage, pp. 237–259.

Collins, A. (2004), 'Sexual dissidence, enterprise and assimilation: Bedfellows in urban regenderation', *Urban Studies*, **41**, 1789–1806.

Constable, N. (2009), 'The commodification of intimacy: Marriage, sex, and reproductive labor', *Annual Review of Anthropology*, **38**, 9–64.

Cunningham, S. and Kendall, T. (2011), 'Prostitution 2.0: The changing face of sex work', *Journal of Urban Economics*, **69** (3), 273–287.

Doan, P. (ed.) (2011), *Queerying Planning: Challenging Heteronormative Assumptions and Reframing Planning Practice*, Chichester, UK: Ashgate.

Doan, P. (ed.) (2015), *Planning and the LGBTQ Community: The Need for Inclusive Queer Spaces*, London: Routledge.

Doan, P. and Higgins, H. (2011), 'The demise of queer space? Resurgent gentrification and the assimilation of LGBT neighbourhoods', *Journal of Planning Education and Research*, **31** (1), 6–25.

Duggan, L. (2002), 'The new homonormativity: The sexual politics of neoliberalism', in R. Castronovo and D. Nelson (eds.), *Materializing Democracy: Towards a Revitalized Cultural Politics*, Durham, NC: Duke University Press, pp. 175–194.

Duncan, S. and Phillips, M. (2010), 'People who live apart together (LATs) – how different are they?', *Sociological Review*, **58** (1), 112–134.

Florida, R. (2005), *Cities and the Creative Class*, New York: Routledge.

Giddens, A. (1993), *The Transformation of Intimacy: Sexuality, Love and Eroticism in Modern Societies*, Chichester, UK: John Wiley & Sons.

Gorman-Murray, A. and Nash, C.J. (2014), 'Mobile places, relational spaces: Conceptualizing change in Sydney's LGBTQ neighbourhoods', *Environment and Planning D: Society and Space*, **32** (4), 622–641.

Gorman-Murray, A. and Waitt, G. (2009), 'Queer-friendly neighbourhoods: Interrogating social cohesion across sexual difference in two Australian neighbourhoods', *Environment and Planning A*, **41** (12), 2855–2873.

Gorman-Murray, A, Pini, B. and Bryant, L. (eds.) (2013), *Sexuality, Rurality, and Geography*, Lanham, MD: Lexington.

Grubesic, T.H. (2010), 'Sex offender clusters', *Applied Geography*, **30** (1), 2–18.

Haritaworn, J. (2008), 'Shifting positionalities: Empirical reflections on a queer/trans of colour methodology', *Sociological Research Online*, **13** (1), 13–26.

Howard, C. (2013), 'Building a "family-friendly" metropolis: Sexuality, the state, and postwar housing policy', *Journal of Urban History*, **39** (5), 933–955.

Hubbard, P. (2000), 'Desire/disgust: Mapping the moral contours of heterosexuality', *Progress in Human Geography*, **24** (2), 191–217.

Hubbard, P. (2011), 'Gender, power and sex in the world city network', *L'Espace Politique*, **13**, http:// espacepolitique.revues.org/1815 (accessed 21 December 2016).

Hubbard, P. (2012), *Cities and Sexualities*, New York: Routledge.

Hubbard, P. and Colosi, R. (2013), 'Taking back the night? Gender and the contestation of sexual entertainment in England and Wales', *Urban Studies*, **52** (3), 589–605.

Hubbard, P., Boydell, S., Crofts, P., Prior, J. and Searle, G. (2013), 'Noxious neighbours? Interrogating the impacts of sex premises in residential areas', *Environment and Planning A*, **45** (1), 126–141.

Kanai, J.M. (2014), 'Whither queer world cities? Homo-entrepreneurialism and beyond', *Geoforum*, **56**, 1–5.

Kanai, J.M. (2015), 'Buenos Aires beyond (homo)sexualized urban entrepreneurialism: The geographies of queered tango', *Antipode*, **47** (3), 652–670.

Kneeland, G. (1913), *Commercialized Prostitution in New York City*, New York: The Century Co.

Knopp, L. (1995), 'Sexuality and urban space: Gay male identity politics in the United States, the United Kingdom and Australia', in R. Fincher and J. Jacobs (eds.), *Cities of Difference*, New York: Guilford Press, pp. 149–178.

Knopp, L. (1998), 'Exploiting the rent gap: The theoretical significance of using illegal appraisal schemes to encourage gentrification in New Orleans', *Urban Geography*, **11** (1), 48–64.

Knopp, L. (2007), 'From lesbian to gay to queer geographies: Pasts, prospects and possibilities', in K. Browne, J. Lim and G. Brown (eds.), *Geographies of Sexualities: Theory, Practices and Politics*, Farnham, UK: Ashgate, pp. 21–28.

Laing, M. and Cook, I. (2014), 'Governing sex work in the city', *Geography Compass*, **8** (8), 505–515.

Lauria, M. and Knopp, L. (1985), 'Toward an analysis of the role of gay communities in the urban renaissance', *Urban Geography*, **6** (2), 152–169.

Lim, J. and Fanghanel, A. (2013), 'Hijabs, hoodies and hotpants: Negotiating the "Slut" in SlutWalk', *Geoforum*, **48**, 207–215.

Linz, D., Blumenthal, E., Donnerstein, E., Kunkel, D., Shafer, B. and Lichtenstein, A. (2000), 'Testing legal assumptions regarding the effects of dancer nudity and proximity to patron on erotic expression', *Law and Human Behaviour*, **24** (5), 507–533.

Maginn, P. and Steinmitz, C. (2014), 'Spatial and regulatory contours of the (sub)urban sexscape', in P. Maginn and C. Steinmitz (eds), *(Sub)urban Sexscapes: Geographies and Regulation of the Sex Industry*, London: Routledge. pp. 1–17.

Mai, N. and King, R. (2009), 'Love, sexuality and migration: Mapping the issue(s)', *Mobilities*, **4** (3), 295–307.

Manalansan, M.F. (2015), 'Queer worldings: The messy art of being global in Manila and New York', *Antipode*, **47** (3), 566–579.

Massey, D. (2005), *For Space*, London: Sage.

Morrison, C.A., Johnston, L. and Longhurst, R. (2013), 'Critical geographies of love as spatial, relational and political', *Progress in Human Geography*, **37** (4), 505–521.

Mowlabocus, S. (2010), *Gaydar Culture: Gay Men, Technology and Embodiment in the Digital Age*, Farnham, UK: Ashgate.

Muller Myrdahl, T. (2013), 'Ordinary (small), cities and LGBQ lives', *ACME: An International E-Journal for Critical Geographies*, **12**, 279–304.

Nash, C.J. (2001), 'Siting lesbians: Sexuality, space and social organization', in T. Goldie (ed.), *In a Queer Country: Gay and Lesbian Studies in the Canadian Context*, Vancouver: Arsenal Press, pp. 235–256.

Nash, C.J. (2006), 'Toronto's gay village (1969 to 1982): Plotting the politics of gay identity', *Canadian Geographer/Le Géographe canadien* (March), **50** (1), 1–16.

Nash, C.J. (2013a), 'The age of the post-mo? Toronto's changing gendered and sexual landscapes', *Geoforum*, **49**, 243–252.

Nash, C.J. (2013b), 'Queering neighbourhoods: Politics and practice in Toronto', *ACME: International E-Journal for Critical Geographies*, **12**, 193–219.

Nash, C.J. and Gorman-Murray, A. (2014), 'LGBT neighborhoods and new mobilities: Towards understanding transformations in sexual and gendered urban landscapes', *International Journal of Urban and Regional Research*, **38** (3), 756–772.

Nash C.J. and Gorman-Murray, A. (2015a), 'Recovering the gay village: A comparative historical geography of urban change and planning in Toronto and Sydney', *Historical Geography*, **43**, 84–105.

Nash C.J. and Gorman-Murray, A. (2015b), 'Lesbians in the city: Mobilities and relational geographies', *Journal of Lesbian Studies*, **19** (2), 173–191.

Oswin, N. (2013), 'Geographies of sexualities: The cultural turn and after', in N. Johnson, R. Schein and J. Winders (eds.), *The Wiley Companion to Cultural Geography*, Chichester, UK: John Wiley & Sons, pp. 105–116.

Paul, B., Linz, D. and Shafer, B. (2001), 'Government regulation of adult businesses through zoning and anti-nudity ordinances: Debunking the legal myth of negative secondary effects', *Communication Law and Policy*, **6** (2), 355–391.

Podmore, J. (2001), 'Lesbians in the crowd: Gender, sexuality and visibility along Montréal's Boul. St-Laurent', *Gender, Place and Culture*, **8**, 333–355.

Podmore, J. (2006), 'Gone "underground"? Lesbian visibility and the consolidation of queer space in Montréal', *Social and Cultural Geography*, **7** (4), 595–625.

Podmore, J. (2013), 'Lesbians as village "queers": The transformation of Montréal's lesbian nightlife in the 1990s', *ACME: An International E-Journal for Critical Geographies*, **12**, 220–249.

Prior, J. and Gorman-Murray, A. (2014), 'Housing sex within the city: The placement of sex services beyond respectable domesticity', in P. Maginn and C. Steinmetz (eds.), *(Sub)Urban Sexscapes: Geographies and Regulation of the Sex Industry*, London: Routledge, pp. 101–116.

Puar, J. (2006), 'Mapping US homonormativities', *Gender, Place and Culture*, **13** (1), 67–88.

Pullen, C. and Cooper, M. (eds), (2010), *LGBT Identity and Online New Media*, New York: Routledge.

Reckless, W. (1926), 'The distribution of commercialized vice in the city: A sociological analysis', *Publications of the American Sociological Society*, **20**, 164–176.

Reynolds, R. (2009), 'Endangered territory, endangered identity: Oxford Street and the dissipation of gay life', *Journal of Australian Studies*, **33** (1), 79–92.

Richardson, D. (2005), 'Desiring sameness? The rise of a neoliberal politics of normalization', *Antipode*, **37** (3), 515–535.

Rothenberg, T. (1995), '"And she told two friends": Lesbians creating urban social space', in D. Bell and G. Valentine (eds.), *Mapping Desire: Geographies of Sexualities*, London: Routledge.

Rushbrook, D. (2002), 'Cities, queer space and the cosmopolitan tourist', *GLQ: A Journal of Lesbian and Gay Studies*, **8**, 183–206.

Ruting, B. (2008), 'Economic transformations of gay urban spaces: Revisiting Collins' evolution gay district model', *Australian Geographer*, **39**, 259–269.

Sigusch, V. (1998), 'The neosexual revolution', *Archives of Sexual Behavior*, **27** (4), 331–359.

Spurlin, W. (2000), 'Remapping same-sex desire: Queer writing and culture in the American heartland', in D. Shuttleton, D. Watt and R. Phillips (eds.), *De-centring Sexualities: Politics and Representations beyond the Metropolis*, London: Routledge, pp. 182–198.

Sullivan, A. (2005), 'The end of gay culture: Assimilation and its meanings', *The New Republic*, October 24, 16–19.

Symanski, R. (1974), 'Prostitution in Nevada', *Annals of the Association of American Geographers*, **64** (3), 357–377.

Tongson, K. (2011), *Relocations: Queer Suburban Imaginaries*, New York: NYU Press.

Usher, N. and Morrison, E. (2010), 'The demise of the gay enclave: Communication infrastructure theory and the transformation of gay public space', in C. Pullen and M. Cooper (eds), *LGBT Identity and Online New Media*, Los Angeles, CA: Sage, pp. 110–135.

Vaccaro, A. (2009), 'Intergenerational perceptions, similarities and differences: A comparative analysis of lesbian, gay, and bisexual Millennial youth with generation X and baby boomers', *Journal of LGBT Youth*, **6** (2–3), 113–134.

Valentine, G. (2006), 'Globalising intimacy: The role and information and communication technologies in maintaining and creating relationships', *Women's Studies Quarterly*, **34**, 365–393.

Waitt, G. and Gorman-Murray, A. (2011), 'Journeys and returns: Home, life narratives and remapping sexuality in a regional city', *International Journal of Urban and Regional Research*, **35** (6), 1239–1255.

Waitt, G. and Markwell, K. (2006), *Gay Tourism: Culture and Context*, New York: Haworth Press.

Ward, K. (2010), 'Towards a relational comparative approach to the study of cities', *Progress in Human Geography*, **34** (4), 471–487.

Wilkinson, E. (2014), 'Single people's geographies of home: Intimacy and friendship beyond "the family"', *Environment and Planning A*, **46** (10), 2452–2468.

7 Feminism and the urban

Linda Peake

Feminism and the urban, even in the twenty-first century, are terms that to some still appear to be incongruous. Notwithstanding five decades of interdisciplinary academic and policy-based work by feminist scholars, there continues to be a struggle to show how the connection between feminism and the urban is indeed both long-standing and necessary. In this chapter I provide a brief overview of this work before turning to ask what, in the twenty-first century, are the necessary connections between the urban, urbanization and feminism and what this means for future research directions.

Feminist urban research in the twentieth century

Although the field of research on women in cities began with studies of the urban global south in the 1960s, its positioning within a developmentalist framework with an empirical focus on the 'immorality' of women who migrated to urban areas was decidedly not feminist. Feminist research on urban issues can be said to have begun with the Danish economist Ester Boserup in her 1970 book, *Women's Role in Economic Development* (Boserup 1970). Although better known for her agricultural and rural-based research, she presented what is probably the first typology of women's presence in urban areas in the global south, identifying different kinds of 'male' and 'semi-male' towns (Moser with Peake 1995). Publications on women in cities of the global north also started to emerge in the early 1970s, and by the late 1970s was well established: witness the wide range of journal special issues that blossomed across both urban and women's studies, including, for example, the formation in 1976 of the *Women and Environments* journal; the *International Journal of Urban and Regional Research* 1978 issue on Women and the City; the *Heresies* 1979 issue on urban public space; the 1980 issue of *Signs* that identified women and the city as a specifically feminist and women's studies concern; and the 1984 issue of *Antipode* on women and urban issues (Peake 2009).

Tables 7.1 and 7.2 outline the trajectories of feminist urban research from the 1970s onwards. Feminist work on the urban global south was conducted within the framing of development issues and had a strong emphasis on women's employment, such as investigations into the relationship between the informal and formal sectors, the impact of structural adjustment policies, household structures, and

82

Table 7.1 Feminist research on gender in the urban global south

Research foci	1970s	1980s	1990s	2000s+
Women and urbanization processes, especially rural to urban migration	X	X	X	X
Women and work: formal and informal sectors; women as active in production and reproduction (in the 1970s with a focus on basic needs policy and in the 1980s with a focus on the implications of the New International Division of Labour); feminist critiques of women's work in prostitution	X	X	X	X
Land, housing and human settlements		X	X	X
Urban poverty; women's triple role in production, reproduction and community management		X	X	X
Household structures; household survival strategies; distribution of resources within the household		X	X	X
Urban politics, especially squatter movements; urban service provision such as water, childcare, and transportation		X	X	X
Domestic spaces; the home		X	X	X
Urban crisis survival strategies; impact of structural adjustment programmes; (with the introduction in the 2000s of urban citizenship)			X	X
Urban violence, domestic and economic			X	X
Specific groups of workers, especially transnational migrant workers and sex workers			X	X
Urban environments: degradation of urban environments; women farmers in urban areas; urban feminist ecology			X	X
Urban planning and women			X	X
Gendered nature of urban space			X	X
Urban health; women's reproductive health; AIDS/ HIV			X	X
Urban children and youth			X	X
MDGs and women in urban places; SDGs				X
Sexualities and queered urban spaces				X
Women in transnational urban families				X

Notes: MDGS = Millennium Development Goals; SDGs = Sustainable Development Goals.

Source: Adapted from Peake (2009).

the division of labour. In the global north work was taken up by feminist scholars for whom the impact of second wave feminism was spread across a range of urban-related disciplines, including geography, sociology, anthropology, planning and architecture as well as women's studies (see Box 7.1). Feminist urban geog-

Table 7.2 Feminist research on gender in the urban global north

Research foci	1970s	1980s	1990s	2000s+
Gender and urbanization; urban form: city centre versus suburbs; processes of production (paid work) versus reproduction (unpaid work); urban restructuring	X	X	X	X
Labour markets and work–home links, including child care; transportation and access to facilities; (as well as from the late 1990s studies of parenting, childhood and children, care giving and the ethics of care)	X	X	X	X
Urban planning, design and architecture	X	X	X	X
Women and urban politics; urban social movements; women's political participation (with the introduction in the late 1990s of urban citizenship)	X	X	X	X
Domestic spaces; the home		X	X	X
Urban based identities of gender, race, ethnicity and sexuality; urban geographies of patriarchies; social constructions of difference, especially in relation to femininities and masculinities (with the introduction in the late 1990s of issues of racism, whiteness and transnationalism)		X	X	X
Women's fear and urban places (with the introduction in the 2000s of issues of surveillance)		X	X	X
Urban poverty		X	X	X
Housing: homelessness and gentrification		X	X	X
Immigrant women, First Nations, Aboriginal women in cities; a focus on specific groups of workers such as domestic workers and sex workers			X	X
Lesbian and gay urban geographies; LGBTTQ spaces; queer geographies and, later, transgendered geographies			X	X
Embodied urban geographies			X	X
Urban public space (though earlier studies on, for example, women's access to parks date back to the late 1970s)			X	X
Women's spaces of pleasure/leisure, the female flaneur			X	X
Urban emotional geographies				X

Source: Adapted from Peake (2009).

raphers, for example, had a broad range of interests, from theoretical critiques of Marxist conceptions of production, social reproduction and urban form (Breughel 1973; Burnett 1973) to empirical studies detailing the everyday lives of women (and men), such as Palm and Pred's (1974) time-geography study of women's inequality in the United States. This literature has expanded greatly over the last five decades to address a large number of themes, and although, as Tables 7.1 and 7.2 show,

BOX 7.1   WAVES OF FEMINISM*

First-wave feminism is taken to refer to an extended period of feminist activity during the nineteenth and early twentieth centuries in Canada, the United States, the United Kingdom and France, that is, in those countries most urbanized through the industrial revolution. Emerging out of a politics of social justice, it was, despite its engagement with abolitionism, primarily a movement of and for white women in which the activities of women of colour, such as the African-American activist Sojourner Truth, were claimed for their own. This wave is best known for promoting political citizenship through securing the vote for (white) women, addressing the abolition of slavery (in the United States) and challenging the 'cult of domesticity', through granting to women the right to own property, to access to birth control and education, to secure a divorce, to retain custody of their children and to keep their income and inheritance. In the United States this wave formally began at the Seneca Falls Convention in 1848 and ended with the passage of the Nineteenth Amendment to the United States Constitution (1919), granting white women the right to vote in all states. In Britain the (working-class) Suffragettes and the (middle-class) Suffragists campaigned for women's right to vote and in 1918 the Representation of the People Act was passed granting the vote to women over the age of 30 who owned property while the Equal Franchise Act of 1928 gave women over 21 the same voting rights as men.

Second-wave feminism, the era of 'women's liberation', although often overlooked as a continuation from the first wave, is most commonly associated with the 1960s through to the late 1980s. This wave unfolded in the radical context of the post-colonial, anti-war, civil rights and environmental movements and the growing self-consciousness of a variety of women's groups. Women of colour and women in the global south refused to be represented by white women and raised their voices independently, often under the name of the social change perspective of womanism; a lack of acknowledgement of racism by white women was to prevent any mass solidarity or joint organizing between them and women of colour. Feminists focused on issues of gendered and classed inequality, coining phrases such as 'the personal is political' and 'wages for housework' in an effort to raise consciousness and to demonstrate that race, class, gender and sexuality oppression were political and societal issues. The second wave was increasingly influenced by feminist theory, based on both neo-Marxist and psychoanalytical theory, and the subjugation of women was associated with critiques of patriarchy, capitalism and heteronormativity. Sex and gender were also differentiated—the former considered biological and the latter a social construct that varies across place and over time. The black lesbian Combahee River Collective in 1974 created the theory of 'interlocking oppressions', arguing that the liberation of black women entails freedom for all people, since it would require the end of racism, sexism and class oppression. With the understanding of feminism deepening but the movement splintering, feminism came to be increasingly appropriated within state structures, its public voice less vocal, although remaining strong in the Western academy.

Third-wave feminism began in the early 1990s with the cultural shift that occurred when the men and women raised in the second wave came of age. The term is attributed to Rebecca Walker, the daughter of the novelist Alice Walker. It was informed by the perceived failures and rigidity of thinking of second-wave feminism as well as by queer, post-colonial and post-modern thought. Indeed, many third-wavers refuse to identify as 'feminists', a term they find limiting and exclusionary. In this phase the notion of a 'universal womanhood' was destabilized, and constructs of the body, gender, sexuality and heteronormativity were queered in a way that encouraged experimentation and creative thought. Judith Butler's work, for example, led to gender being understood in terms of performativity as opposed to binary categories, and trans people became prominent in some strands of feminism. The self-named 'riot grrrls' of the third wave appeared strong and empowered, eschewing victimization and defining feminine beauty for themselves as subjects, not as objects of a sexist patriarchy, including adopting dress codes that previous feminists had identified with male oppression. They were also, however, predominantly white. Their reappropriation of derogatory terms such as 'slut' and 'bitch', to subvert sexist culture, has been critiqued by women of colour, who argue they do not have the privilege to claim these terms. Second-wave feminists have also critiqued third-wavers' definition of empowerment as an internal feeling of power and agency for its lack of attention to external measures of power and control. The internet was adopted as a powerful tool of communication and E-zines have provided 'cybergrrls' and 'netgrrls' a space that permits users the opportunity to cross gender boundaries. This is in keeping with the third wave's celebration of ambiguity and refusal to think in terms of 'us–them'.

Fourth-wave feminism emerged out of the third wave, post the global financial crash of 2007, with (mostly) young queer/trans people of colour at its forefront, who view the third wave as either overly optimistic, exclusionary or hampered by an individualistic approach. This generation had grown up with the web and use it as a tool for internet activism, while also recognizing its role in perpetuating misogyny. New issues this wave addresses include gender 'deviance' in pop culture and public education. And issues that were central to second-wave feminism are moving out of academia back into the realm of public discourse and receiving national and international attention by mainstream press and politicians. These include problems such as sexual abuse, violence against women, the pornification of everyday life, the pressure on women (and men) to conform to a single and unrealistic body-type, unequal pay, and the realization that gains in women's representation in politics and business, for example, have not been substantial. Feminism(s) are now part of a call for global gender solidarity. For example, SlutWalks and the Everyday Sexism Project, via the internet, have taken off globally. And in this age of austerity, feminist movements are also increasingly linked to others, such as BlackLivesMatter and Occupy, concerned with uncontrolled capitalism, unemployment and under-employment, zero-hours contracts, and damaging rhetoric against people of colour, immigrants, the disabled and those who need support from the state.

Note: *The notion of waves is a contentious one and is not to be taken as a discrete chronological categorization. Rather, waves are overlapping and multiple and do not necessarily correlate with the age of any individual feminists.

Sources: England (2016); Harvey-Peake (2016); Munro (2016); Rampton (2015).

many research themes have a long legacy, new avenues of research have emerged as feminist scholars have increasingly faced their own biases and omissions, such as the pervading whiteness of the majority of its practitioners in the global north, and have engaged with new analytic frameworks, such as those of post-structuralism, post-colonialism, third wave feminism and critical race theory (see Box 7.1). The urban interface of feminism and queer studies has also been a productive one, not least in studies that recognize gender as a continuum as opposed to a hierarchical binary and being inclusive of categories of women that have traditionally been considered outsiders.

While feminist scholars are not in agreement about the extent to which the city is liberating or not for women (cf. Bondi and Rose 2003; Wilson 1991), there is acknowledgement that women's disenfranchisement reaches deep into the urban, that women form heterogeneous groups (Chant 2010, 2013) and that women's and men's experiences of the urban differ, played out through gendered norms and expectations

in the ways in which they use and give meaning to urban space; in the degree of restrictions placed on their mobilities and in levels of spatial exclusion; in their access to basic needs and employment; in their risk of encountering violence; in their exposure to environmental hazards; in ownership of land and property; and in civic disenfranchisement. (Peake and Pratt forthcoming, 2017: 291)

No doubt, there are other themes not yet documented or admitted into the predominantly northern feminist academic discourses that serve to regulate the content of Tables 7.1 and 7.2. Why there are separate tables for feminist literatures pertaining to the urban global north and south, however, is not in doubt. One of the most enduring legacies of feminist urban research in the twentieth century is the naturalization of this division; like the proverbial ships that pass in the night, these literatures have maintained the fallacy of these global regions as separate geographical containers, failing to engage with each other. Furthermore, as I argue, with Martina Reiker (Peake and Rieker 2013), feminist urban studies has mirrored the larger field of urban studies that Jennifer Robinson (2006) has defined as having 'a tendency to characterize cities of the global north as crucibles of modernism, and hence sites for engagement with critical theory, rendering cities in the global south as objects in need of development, representations of which emphasize poverty, culture and tradition and their populations as lacking or passive' (Peake and Rieker 2013: 1). The hegemonic nature of representations of northern modernity and southern developmentalism, and their pervasiveness in travelling globally, speaks to their continued influence on (some) feminist studies of urban places and their inhabitants. We argue that eschewing such a reification of difference requires a feminist revision enabling

> a theoretical engagement with gender relations and an empirical concern with women's everyday lives undertaken, not in separate spheres of north and south but in productive engagement with each other, within an analytical register that articulates these subjects as marked both by 'differences' in global, epistemic and material positioning and through global structures that render them mutually constitutive. (Peake and Rieker 2013: 4)

The rapidly shifting and increasingly globally interconnected urban geographies, which developed from the 1970s onwards, demand nothing less.

Gender and the urban in the twenty-first century

The tipping point into an urban world, and what is now widely referred to as 'the twenty-first century of the city', supposedly took place in 2008 when 50 per cent of the world's population was declared to be living in areas defined as urban, a figure that is estimated to grow to over 66 per cent by 2050 (UNPD 2015). If it can be argued that the future of the nineteenth and twentieth centuries was already urban, in what way is urbanization in the twenty-first century different and what are the implications for women?

First, twenty-first century urbanization is taking place within a new global development and policy environment, with the year 2015 marking the cusp of a watershed. The post-Millennium Development Goals (MDGs) era has a new global partnership based on the 2015 launching of the Sustainable Development Goals (SDGs), including the first global urban goal (SDG 11 *To make cities safe, inclusive, resilient, and sustainable*) (ICSU, ISSC 2015). Furthermore, Habitat III's *New Urban Agenda* (announced in October 2016) will determine how cities will be analytically located in relation to the SDGs with the potential to change the normative base of how urban issues are understood and acted upon by national and international bodies depending upon which one of three scenarios wins out. Cities may continue to be seen as one of many sites for sustainable development (alongside oceans, forests and farmlands), or as the new centres and most important locations in which distinctive challenges of sustainable urban development must be supported, or, more radically, cities may be framed as the absolute drivers of sustainable development in what amounts to an urban Anthropocene, an epoch in which humans living in urban areas are considered as the dominant drivers of global environmental change, and in which cities, as the locus of humanity, create the tipping points of global sustainability (Parnell 2016).

Second, urbanization in the twenty-first century is characterized by different geographies than those of preceding periods. Driven by natural increase and accelerating levels of rural to urban migration in the global south, catalyzed by push factors (e.g., climate change, land-use change, natural disasters, poverty and unemployment, war and conflict) and pull factors (e.g., higher income and increased access to infrastructures and facilities, promises of better employment opportunities), the growth in the urban population has shifted from the global north to the global south (Miraftab and Kudva 2014; Parnell and Oldfield 2014). Although academic attention has overwhelmingly been given to the mega cities (of over 10 million inhabitants) of the global south, it is also in small cities, with fewer than one million inhabitants, that urbanization is concentrated, with nearly half of the world's urban dwellers residing in provincial towns and agrarian hubs with fewer than 500,000 inhabitants (UNPD 2015). Analytical focus has, moreover, remained on the 'city' (as opposed to the city as one particular spatial container of the urban), while growing peri-urban and suburban settlements have received much less attention (Addie et al. 2015; Ali and Rieker 2010). Furthermore, the standard late-twentieth century factors used to theorize the shaping and growth of cities – for example, urban agglomeration economies and land markets – can no longer account for the increasing number and diversity of forms of urban settlements in the global south, where the needs of human social reproduction, overwhelmingly supplied by women's labour, are often the catalyst for urban extension (Roy 2003).

Third, in the late period of neoliberalism the increasingly unregulated nature of capital and the 2008 post-financial crisis economic growth is not only causing production and consumption to approach unsustainable levels, but is also resulting in increased inequality, manifested through large increases in wealth and income for the top one per cent and further austerity policies for the poor (Sen and Durano 2014). Although inequality is not new, in the twenty-first century it is characterized in many places in the urban global south by a range of new features: the increasing concentration of wealth at the apex of income distribution, leading to the fall of members of once affluent middle-classes into precarious lives (Dorling 2014); the incorporation of large numbers of poor rural migrants to the poorest urban communities (Miraftab et al. 2015; UNDP 2015), resulting in the urbanization of poverty within the first decade of this century (Craig and Porter 2006); and the feminization of the urban population through increased rural–urban migration among women, demographic ageing and rising proportions of female-headed households in urban areas (Chant and McIllwaine 2016), culminating in the feminization of urban poverty, experienced through a range of gendered economic, social and environmental insecurities. Indeed, some feminists argue that gender remains the most basic determinant of global inequality (Chant 2010).

Urbanization is indeed a deeply gendered process. The rise in inequality, the feminization of urban poverty and the proliferation of urban growth in mostly poor cities in the global south point to the need to engage with gendered insecurities and with those women who form the urban majority, the working poor (defined as those who earn an income and work for a living but live in households that lie below or close to the poverty line), who are central to addressing the sustainability of urban communities (Moser 1993; Roy 2010). These women also serve as a point of departure through which broader social issues of family, community and livelihoods are addressed in their relations with men, youth and children, and whose work is still most commonly the foundation of the economy, the community and the family (Peake and Rieker 2013). Indeed, feminists have argued that neoliberalism has built 'its regime of accumulation "on the cornerstone of women's waged labour" (Fraser 2009: 113), while simultaneously the maintenance of "traditional gender roles of social reproduction … create a third shift of voluntary, unpaid labour for women" (Roy 2010: 70), effecting profound changes in women's lives in cities everywhere' (Peake and Rieker 2013: 6–7). At the heart of the urban neoliberal project (that constitutes a policy orientation away from state regulation and management of urban processes towards governance mechanisms that seek to attune all aspects of urban life to the economic concerns of free markets) lies the individuated, entrepreneurial self that development agencies have gendered as female and targeted in the micro-financed income generating programmes that blanket the urban global south and position women centrally in thinking through the everyday in urban places. And yet urban theory and vast arenas of urban policy, both heavily masculinist fields, pay very little attention to women's lives or to the gendered dimensions of urbanization (Peake 2016a, 2016b). Hence, what remains underdeveloped about the current contours of urbanization is how gendered processes of production and social reproduction are being transformed, requiring new ways of theorizing the urban and urban subjectivities.

Feminist urban research in the twenty-first century

In this final section I outline some of the more pressing issues for future research agendas: what it means to engage with feminism in the twenty-first century; making visible contemporary urban gendered geographies of inequality, poverty and social justice; and feminism's role in urban theory and democratic futures.

Engaging with feminism

As Cornwall et al. (2007: 16) state, there are a variety of feminisms: 'feminist discourses and feminist actions are above all diverse, differentiated and themselves sites of contestation.' Indeed, the kaleidoscopic lineage of feminist activity in urban places speaks to vibrant multifaceted movements, particularly around issues of violence and urban public space, such as the Reclaim the Night marches that have been taking place in cities since the mid-1970s and more recently the SlutWalks and the Everyday Sexism Project of the 2010s (Peake and Pratt forthcoming). Feminism, and its application to the study of cities, however, has also been problematically entangled with projects of the state and of capital (Fraser 2009; Rottenberg 2014). Some feminists claim this engagement started in the early stages of second wave feminism, when liberal feminists institutionalized Ester Boserup's analysis of women's role in economic development into the development industry, espousing gender mainstreaming through WID (Women in Development), WAD (Women and Development) and GAD (Gender and Development) approaches to the study of women in cities in the global south. For others this entanglement developed later with the application of 'governance' (Halley et al. 2006) or 'neoliberal' (Fraser 2009) feminism in both the global north and south, seen most clearly perhaps in the gender–poverty nexus and the myriad micro-financing projects that have targeted women at the same time as states have abandoned macrostructural efforts to fight poverty (Roy 2010).

Fraser (2009) argues that despite increasing mainstream acceptance of feminist ideals – of, for example, gender equality and critiques of sexual harassment – there has been little movement within institutions to achieve them. Instead, increasingly divorced from a critique of capitalism, there has been a selective incorporation of certain strands of feminist demands for gender justice into the capitalist project. Drawing on the work of Luc Boltanski and Eve Chiapello (2005 [2009]), Fraser (2009: 109) outlines how capitalism

> periodically remakes itself in moments of historical rupture, in part by recuperating strands of critique directed against it. In such moments, elements of anti-capitalist critique are resignified to legitimate an emergent new form of capitalism, which thereby becomes endowed with the higher, moral significance needed to motivate new generations to shoulder the inherently meaningless work of endless accumulation.

The feminist critique of the family wage, for example, has been used to justify both working-class and middle-class women's increased engagement in the workforce: '[o]nce the centrepiece of a radical analysis of capitalism's androcentrism, . . .[it] serves today to intensify capitalism's valorization of waged labour' (Fraser 2009: 110–111).

This crisis in contemporary feminism is most starkly outlined in the global south, where women's movements have become unmoored, incorporated into neoliberal gender governance (whereby issues of collective concern are transformed into isolated and manageable projects, divorced from the context in which they take place), with the co-optation of feminists into non-governmental organizations (NGOs) a very real consequence of this disconnect (Peake and de Souza 2010; Sen and Durano 2014). Neoliberalism's ability to absorb difference and translate it into a question of governmentality, as Hardt and Negri (2000) argue, has constituted a significant challenge for feminist (and other) movements. Within this context the challenge is how to reanimate resistance to the contemporary neoliberal urban context by connecting with the hopes and desires of those women that form the majority urban group, the working poor, by situating demands for gender justice not only within a critique of contemporary capitalism but also within the context of women's right to the city (Peake and Rieker 2013).

The lack of an articulation of a gender perspective in the Lefebvrian informed right to the city (Lefebvre 1996 [1967]) debate has been noted by a range of feminist scholars and organizations, at scales from the urban to the global (Fenster 2005;

World Forum of Women 2004), who have argued that gendered relations of power and sexual divisions of labour result in women experiencing the city differently from men and that these differences need to be taken into consideration, as do differences between women, in ensuring women's right to the city. Based on central aspects to the right to the city – the right to use and the right to participate – criteria towards the realization of women's right to the city include their engagement in the democratic management of cities; safety in urban environments, including in the private spaces of the home; access to urban services, public infrastructure (including water and sanitation) and transportation; security of housing tenure; access to employment; and ensuring a connection to reproductive responsibilities. In order to guarantee that any of these criteria are met, it is vital that women are involved in decision-making processes, from their own local urban governance to the global scale of Habitat III.

Urban gendered geographies

Complex configurations of spatial scales have displaced the nation with the city as the site through which policy and the academy increasingly locate research questions pertaining to the social (Marston 2000; Smith 2004). While not denying the importance of nation states in framing the everyday life of gendered subjects, and not least, diasporic gendered experiences, it is the city that has become the space in which humanness is delineated and engaged, where neoliberal social contracts are engaged, imbricating the social and hence the gendered subject into discourses about the city in new ways. The modern city, as a site of spatial segregation and exclusion, always produced particular types of human: state endowed and legitimized, or not. The neoliberal city, though, is characterized by processes of the hollowing out and reconstitution of the social, marked by increasing inequality, regulatory (and increasingly securitized) infrastructure, violence, displacement of the poor, and the disintegration of family and community, witnessed through increases in social and economic distress. Such processes are giving way to urban forms whose notion of the social, or urban belonging, is increasingly unequal, structured around new frameworks of distinction, difference and segregation, and whether class, religion or ethnoracially based, these are experienced in gendered ways.

Gendered inequality has traditionally been open to investigation at the national scale through (limited) measurable indicators or through (instrumental) strategies for sustainability, divorced from the processes that give rise to it. But inequality is produced, reproduced and experienced in place through complex relations of injustice, domination and exclusion and can only be deeply addressed through democratic modes of transformation (Sen and Mukherjee 2014) that recognize women's right to the city. It is through a focus on urban place making and everyday life (Lefebvre 1996 [1967]) that the several intersecting inequalities, experienced by women through economic, social and environmental insecurities, can be brought into view. Place making is a deeply political process that can normalize and reinscribe power relations through, for example, senses of home and belonging. But in addressing 'multiplicities of space–time' (Massey 1995: 284), place making can also accentuate and reveal power relations that highlight the (re)production of urban inequality, revealing gendered geographies that extend beyond individual city limits to rural hinterlands and to city and global regions, that can trouble gendered norms and identities potentially producing opportunities for reducing insecurities (through remittances for example) and enabling women's strategies for their inclusion in urban life.

Feminist urban theory

While Boserup's argument (1970), that the costs of modern economic development were shouldered by women, has been echoed by feminists along the decades into the contemporary period, urban theory has paid scant attention to women. Invariably the building blocks of feminist urban theory – women, gender, the intertwining of the public/private spheres, social reproduction/production and gendered violence – have been ignored, paid lip service or left unproblematized, passed over for those of production, class, the public realm, structural violence and men. But both changing geographies of urbanization and the turn to comparative urbanism (McFarlane 2010; Robinson 2011) have led to calls for new global urban theory that resonates with feminist modes of knowledge production. Closing down the twentieth-century belief in a universally valid theoretical framework or hegemonic model that can explain how and why urbanization takes place based on a 'single case', comparative urbanism works not by attempting to 'control for difference' across sites, but by following the interconnections produced through a city's mode of integration into the world economy and by engaging with shared features (migration, 'slums', industrialization and so on) as well as variations across cities. Theorizing through comparative investigation, moreover, is always partial, mindful of the situated nature of theoretical insights (Haraway 1988) and open to multiple starting points, including recognizing new alignments of authority and expertise in terms of those who develop urban theory (Robinson 2016).

Understandings of all knowledge as situated, embodied and geographically placed also characterizes feminist geographic knowledge production. While feminist knowledge production of place making *within cities* can draw upon the research approach of feminist ethno-geography (a feminist ethnographic approach that has a particular sensibility to the role of place both in constituting subjects and the production of knowledge (Nagar 2014)), urban knowledge production *across cities* has much to gain from both Cindy Katz's (Katz 2001) method of counter topography and transnational feminist praxis (TFP) (Lock Swarr and Nagar 2010). Counter topography reinserts materiality into feminist theorizing through an insistence on studying the processes of global capitalism in particular places – of recognizing the historical and geographical specificities of particular places while also inferring their analytic connections in relation to specific material social practices. It is, moreover, common interests in these material connections (for example, deskilling) that serve as the basis for a feminist politics of connection across places. This work of connection, not only across place but also of imagining knowledge production through the mobilization of situated solidarities, is the work of critical TFP. It involves not only engaging in collaborative dialogues across national boundaries, being invested in alliance building across difference, and of being critically aware of the situated, embodied and geographically placed nature of knowledge production, but also of incorporating into knowledge production those who constitute the urban working poor, not as informants but as knowledge producers (Nagar 2014; Peake forthcoming). Such collaborative practice has often been marginalized in academia, but it can be a rich source of theoretical and methodological knowledge production. TFP, moreover, has the ability to exceed its methodological intervention, breaking down the hierarchical relations between theory and method through its focus on dialogue, storytelling and dialogical learning (Nagar 2014).

Such dialogical and open-ended modes of knowledge production, open to ongoing critique and collective reflection of its limitations, fits well with Robinson's (2011) call for new urban theory to be both provisional and revisable and for the reworking of urban theory through the development of new and creative methodologies for comparative work. A feminist mode of situated knowledge production engages with both the limits of urban theory (see, for example, Derickson 2016, Peake 2016b and Roy 2016 for a feminist engagement with the meta-theoretical narrative of planetary urbanization) and the urban as a site of praxis of everyday struggles of living and working, embedded in which are hopes for a better future, open to possibilities of the evolving but 'not yet' that mark generative knowledge.

Conclusion

The contours of urbanization in the twenty-first century are rapidly changing as urban growth continues to be marked by economic crisis and social uncertainty. Despite the now thoroughly global scale of urban policy, migration and capital accumulation, little is known about how they are serving to reconfigure gendered urban inequalities or of their impact upon gendered rights to the city, issues that speak to equity, belonging and justice, and which lie at the heart of democratic urban transformations. With the promises of the modern city – freedom and publicness – incomplete, contemporary urban forms may continue to inspire hopes for a better life but no longer define what this better life is. To understand how this better life can be realized in the contemporary urban era requires engaging with the everyday struggles of living and working of those at the bottom of the urban hierarchy, the working poor. This group constitutes the vast majority of women living in cities, and it is upon their ability to realize their hopes and dreams that the achievement of women's rights to the city must be judged (Peake and Rieker 2013). It is on this ground that feminist urban geographies can interrogate the twenty-first century quest for the urban, refusing any notions of fixed subjectivities or bounded 'urban' space in its interrogations of emerging urban geographies of belonging and being urban.

References

Addie, J.P., Fielder, R., and Kiel, R. (2015), 'Cities on the edge: emerging suburban constellations in Canada', in Filion, P., Moos, M., Vinodrai, T. and Walker, R. (eds), *Canadian Cities in Transition: Perspectives for an Urban Age*, 5th edition, Oxford: Oxford University Press, 415–432.

Ali, K.A. and Rieker, M. (eds) (2010), *Comparing Cities: Middle East and South Asia*, Oxford: Oxford University Press.

Boltanski, L. and Chiapello, E. (2005) [1999], *The New Spirit of Capitalism*, London: Verso Books.

Bondi, L. and Rose, D. (2003), 'Constructing gender, constructing the urban: a review of Anglo-American feminist urban geography', *Gender, Place and Culture*, **10** (3), 229–245.

Boserup, E. (1970), *Woman's Role in Economic Development*, London: Allen & Unwin.

Breughel, I. (1973), 'Cities, women and social class: a comment', *Antipode*, **5** (3), 62–63.

Burnett, P. (1973), 'Social change, the status of women and models of city form and development', *Antipode*, **5** (3), 57–62.

Chant, S. (ed.) (2010), *The International Handbook of Gender and Poverty: Concepts, Research, Policy*, Cheltenham, UK and Northampton, MA, USA: Edward Elgar Publishing.

Chant, S. (2013), 'Cities through a "gender lens": a golden "urban age" for women in the global South?', *Environment and Urbanisation*, **25** (1), 9–29.

Chant, S. and McIllwaine, C. (2016), *Cities, Slums and Gender in the Global South: Towards a Feminised Urban Future*, London: Routledge.

Cornwall, A., Harrison E. and Whitehead, A. (eds) (2007), *Feminisms in Development: Contradictions, Contestations and Challenges*, London: Zed Books.

Craig, D. and Porter, D. (2006), *Development beyond Neoliberalism? Governance, Poverty Reduction and Political Economy*, London: Routledge.

Derickson, K.D. (2016), 'On the politics of recognition in critical urban scholarship', *Urban Geography*, **37** (6), 824–829.

Dorling, D. (2104), *Inequality and the 1%*, London: Verso Books.

England, K. (2016), Personal communication.

Fenster, T. (2005), 'The right to the gendered city: different formations of belonging in everyday life', *Journal of Gender Studies*, **14** (3), 217–231.

Fraser, N. (2009), 'Feminism, capitalism and the cunning of history', *New Left Review*, **56**, 97–117.

Halley, J., Kotiswaran, P., Shamir, H. and Thomas, C. (2006), 'From the international to the local in feminist legal responses to rape, prostitution/sex work, and sex trafficking: four studies in contemporary governance feminism', *Harvard Journal of Law and Gender*, **29** (2), 335–423.

Haraway, D. (1988), 'Situated knowledges: the science question in feminism and the privilege of partial perspective', *Feminist Studies*, **14** (3), 575–599.

Hardt, M. and Negri, A. (2000), *Empire*, Cambridge, MA: Harvard University Press.

Harvey-Peake, E. (2016), Personal communication.

ICSU, ISSC (2015), *Review of Targets for the Sustainable Development Goals: The Science Perspective*, Paris: International Council for Science.

Katz, C. (2001), 'On the grounds of globalization: a topography for feminist political engagement', *Signs*, **26** (4), 1213–1234.

Lefebvre, H. (1996) [1967], 'The right to the city', in Kofman E. and Lebas E. (eds), *Writing on Cities*, Oxford: Blackwell, 63–184.

Lock Swarr, A. and Nagar, R. (eds) (2010), *Critical Transnational Feminist Praxis*, Minneapolis, MN: University of Minnesota Press.

Marston, S. (2000), 'The social construction of scale', *Progress in Human Geography*, **24** (2), 219–242.

Massey, D. (1995), *Spatial Divisions of Labor: Social Structures and the Geography of Production*, 2nd edition, New York: Routledge.

McFarlane, C. (2010), 'The comparative city: knowledge, learning, urbanism', *International Journal of Urban and Regional Research*, **34**, 725–742.

Miraftab, F. and Kudva, N. (eds) (2014), *Cities of the Global South Reader*, London: Routledge.

Miraftab, F., Wilson, D. and Salo, K. (eds) (2015), *Urban Inequalities across the Globe*, London: Routledge.

Moser, C. (1993), *Gender Planning and Development: Theory, Practice and Training*, New York and London: Routledge.

Moser, C. with Peake, L. (1995), 'Seeing the invisible: women, gender and urban development', in Stren, R. (ed.), *Urban Research in Developing Countries Volume 4: Thematic Issues*, Toronto: Centre for Urban and Community Studies, University of Toronto, 279–347.

Munro, E. (2016), 'Feminism: A fourth wave?', https://www.psa.ac.uk/insight-plus/feminism-fourth-wave. Accessed 2 February 2016.

Nagar, R. (2014), *Muddying the Waters: Coauthoring Feminisms across Scholarship and Activism*, Chicago: University of Illinois Press.

Palm, R. and Pred, A. (1974), 'A time-geographic perspective on problems of inequality for women', *Working Paper 236*, Berkeley, CA: Institute of Urban and Regional Development, University of California.

Parnell, S. (2016), 'Defining a global urban development agenda', *World Development*, **78** (February), 529–540.

Parnell, S. and Oldfield, S. (eds) (2014), *The Routledge Handbook on Cities of the Global South*, London: Routledge.

Peake, L. (2009), 'Urban geography: gender in the city', in Kitchin, R. and Thrift, N. (eds), *The International Encyclopedia of Human Geography*, London: Elsevier, 320–327.

Peake, L. (2016a), 'The twenty-first century quest for feminism and the global urban', *International Journal of Urban and Regional Research*, **40** (1), 219–227.

Peake, L. (2016b), 'On feminism and feminist allies in urban geography', *Urban Geography*, **37** (6), 830–838.

Peake, L. (forthcoming, 2017), 'Feminist methodology', in Richardson, D., Castree, N., Goodchild, M., Kobayashi, A., Liu, W. and Marston, R., *The AAG Encyclopedia of Geography*, Malden, Oxford: John Wiley & Sons, Ltd, 10pp.

Peake, L. and de Souza, K. (2010), 'Feminist academic and activist praxis in service of the transnational', in Swarr, A. and Nagar, R. (eds), *Critical Transnational Feminist Praxis*, Minneapolis, MN: University of Minnesota Press, 206–218.

Peake, L. and Pratt, G. (forthcoming, 2017), 'Why women in cities matter', in Bain, A. and Peake, L. (eds), *Urbanization in a Global Context*, Toronto: Oxford University Press, 276–294.

Peake, L. and Rieker, M. (eds) (2013), *Rethinking Feminist Interventions into the Urban*, London: Routledge.

Rampton, R. (2015), 'Four waves of feminism', http://www.pacificu.edu/about-us/news-events/four-waves-feminism. Accessed 2 February 2016.

Robinson, J. (2006), *Ordinary Cities: Between Modernity and Development*, London: Routledge.

Robinson, J. (2011), 'Cities in a world of cities: the comparative gesture', *International Journal of Urban and Regional Research*, **35** (1), 1–23.

Robinson, J. (2016), 'Comparative urbanism: new geographies and cultures of theorizing the urban', *International Journal of Urban and Regional Research*, **40** (1), 187–199.

Rottenberg, C. (2014), 'The rise of neoliberal feminism', *Cultural Studies*, **28** (3), 418–437.

Roy, A. (2003), *City Requiem, Calcutta: Gender and the Politics of Poverty*. Minneapolis, MN: University of Minnesota Press.

Roy, A. (2010), *Poverty Capital: Microfinance and the Making of Development*, London: Routledge.

Roy, A. (2016), 'What is urban about critical urban theory?', *Urban Geography*, **37** (6), 810–823.

Sen, G. and Durano, M. (2014), *The Remaking of Social Contracts: Feminists in a Fierce New World*, London: Zed Books.

Sen, G. and Mukherjee, A. (2014), 'No empowerment without rights, no rights without politics: gender-equality, MDGs and the post-2015 development agenda', *Journal of Human Development and Capabilities*, **15** (2–3), 188–202.

Smith, N. (2004), 'Scale bending and the fate of the national', in Sheppard, E. and McMaster, R.B. (eds), *Scale and Geographic Inquiry*, Oxford: Blackwell, 192–212.

United Nations Population Division (UNDP) (2015), *World Urbanization Prospects: The 2014 Revision* (ST/ESA/SER.A/366), Department of Economic and Social Affairs, UNDP.

Wilson, E. (1991), *The Sphinx in the City: Urban Life, the Control of Disorder, and Women*, Berkeley, CA: University of California Press.

World Forum of Women (2004), *Charter for Women's Right to the City*, www.hic-al.org/documento. cfm?id_documento=1274. Accessed 8 March 2016.

8 Urban foodways: a research agenda

James Farrer

The fishball revolution: food in the Asian metropolis

Over 50 people were arrested, 100 injured, and shots fired in the air by police during the 2016 Chinese New Year celebrations in Hong Kong. The *casus belli* was the police removal of unlicensed mobile street vendors peddling fishballs, meat skewers, and other traditional Chinese snacks in the canyon-like alleyways of Mongkok, the most densely populated neighborhood in the world. Naturally, more than fishballs were at stake, as the protests could also be seen as a continuation of the 2015 "umbrella revolution" that brought thousands of young people to the streets in protest against the Chinese central government's undemocratic election law proposal. Seen differently, the feared loss of the fishball, in its sensual materiality, represented a material threat to urban lifestyles, an issue that could bring people to streets despite a general despair at achieving larger political changes. As explained by one restaurateur to a reporter:

> It is the quintessential Hong Kong street food and – culturally – it represents the Hong Kong working class like no other institutions can. Street food, and the fishball represent the values of entrepreneurship. Of capitalism. Of liberal democracy. Anthropologically, they mean more than a $5 skewer with curry satay sauce. (Moss 2016)

If fishballs mean something more than a snack to people in Hong Kong, how do they mean it? More broadly, what can urban foodways teach us about cities and how people imagine and experience their lives in them? Also, we must not forget that a fishball or skewer actually does represent a cheap meal in one of the most expensive and economically stratified cities in Asia. Cities require affordable food. The daily quest for food animates the city streets, and the city itself can be metaphorically understood as a hungry body consuming resources and spewing wastes on a global scale. The question of what food means for city dwellers thus calls for a multi-scalar approach to urban foodways, from the space of the consuming body itself up to global flows feeding the hungry metropolis (Bell and Valentine 1997).

The term "foodways" encompasses the economic, cultural and social organization of food production and consumption. This chapter explores existing research on urban foodways and aims to show how food studies may uniquely contribute to urban studies. It focuses on East Asian global cities because this is where I have lived and done my research for over 20 years. East Asia is also experiencing the most dramatic urbanization of any world region (ESCAP 2011). By 2010, East Asia alone had 869 urban areas with more than 100,000 inhabitants, 600 of which were in China. If the region's new urban population from 2000 to 2010, nearly 200 million people, were a country unto itself, it would be the world's sixth largest (World Bank 2015). Issues surrounding feeding Asian cities thus should be central to urban studies.

The body in the city: urban experiences of good and bad eating

No other social activity, with the possible exception of sexuality, intertwines the bodily and social aspects of the human being as does eating (Bell and Valentine 1997, 21–56). However, as Krishnendu Ray points out, while the "body" has been widely celebrated within the social sciences, less obvious progress has been made in capturing corporeal experiences of food (Ray 2012). The 1990s scholarly "turn to the body" ironically remained largely focused on discourse (heavily influenced by Foucault). Studying embodied acts of eating, like sexual activity, has remained methodologically tricky for urban ethnographers. Specialized perceptual, emotional, and cognitive mechanisms are active in taste and smell. As embodied sensations, these are difficult for the social scientist to access and to convey, yet central to the everyday experience of the city. A mixed methods approach may be necessary, melding insights from neuroscience to ethnographic perspectives.

We can start with the commonly evoked example of the "Proust phenomenon," after French writer Marcel Proust. In the novel *In Search of Lost Time*, Proust's narrator dips a madeleine cookie into a cup of tea, and long-forgotten memories of his childhood come flooding back into his consciousness. Food, with its emotionally charged associations, becomes the perfect vehicle for conveying urban nostalgia. Indeed, neurological research shows that odors are especially more evocative of emotions rather than cues from sights or sounds (Chu and Downes 2000; Herz et al. 2004). It is thus not surprising that food is often associated with and deliberately used to invoke nostalgia for specific places, in ways that would fall flat in purely verbal messages. As the ethnographic urban studies literature shows, culinary nostalgia is employed by Asian immigrants recalling ties to home (Mannur 2007), by Singaporeans marketing rapidly changing urban places as still embodying the spirit of old neighborhoods (Duruz 2016; Eng 2016) or by Shanghainese constructing a Shanghai urban identity in which the national narratives are downplayed in favor of local ones (Farrer 2014; Swislocki 2009). Culinary nostalgia is a political and social process that borrows the physiological mechanism of olfactory memory to connect people to the concrete places and times in the city. Olfactory childhood memories anchor people to the physical spaces of the city, as well as allowing culinary marketers a direct entry point into the psyche.

The embodied politics of food is not only about manipulating good tastes and happy memories. Food may also be a vehicle for expressing visceral feelings of revulsion and disgust. Food safety scares in urban China, for example, have become powerful foci of public disgust at economic corruption and a lack of public trust (Yan 2012). The icon of culinary revulsion is "gutter oil," cooking oil that is recycled from food restaurant refuse, boiled, filtered, and resold. According to Chinese informants, it is everywhere, even in many "good" restaurants. Indeed, some claim that one in ten meals in China may be prepared with some form of gutter oil (Barboza 2010). Disgust, like culinary nostalgia, has a social as well as physiological dimension. Among urbanites, the culinary revulsion towards gutter oil is directed particularly at migrant street vendors. As the overwhelming majority of vendors, cooks, and servers, migrant culinary workers are central to food production in Chinese cities such as Shanghai. Given their own reluctance to become waiters, chefs, or busboys, Shanghainese urbanites are now faced with a situation not unlike the urban USA, in which migrant laborers completely dominate the food service sector. In essence, what is polluting about "gutter oil" seems to lie less in the oil itself but in the people who make it. Culinary politics therefore may not only be targeted at the state, as in the case of Hong Kong fishball protests, but may be a diffuse form of blame directed at both migrant workers *and* the state for the societal ills felt viscerally in adulterated food. As Upton Sinclair's polemic novel *The Jungle*, about harsh labor conditions in unsanitary meat markets, showed Americans a century ago, we cannot understand the urban experience without reference to this gastronomic politics, often aimed at a moral "heart," but conveyed through our collective "stomachs" (Kantor 1976).

Beyond nostalgia and revulsion, city foodways present the urban dweller with a heterotopia of olfactory indulgence and savory adventure, ranging from grazing in urban food fairs to the cultivation of culinary capital in five-star restaurants. Across Asia, for example, we see an explosion in sweet shops targeting the young female consumer, peddling gourmet chocolates, traditional Asian rice-based desserts, or storefront cooking schools offering quickie cake-baking classes. Beyond such liminal spaces of sugary conviviality, however, city living is organized through well-timed bodily routines centered largely on food. These repetitive "techniques of the body" create the temporalities and rhythms of urban life from regular lunch times to seasonal meals (Appadurai 1997). We cannot understand these everyday routines nor broader understandings of "good living" without reference to dietary practices that mark time in space.

Life in the Asian city is also increasingly organized by regimens of bodily discipline, often centering on dieting and weight control. As with the feminized marketing of chocolates and cake-baking classes, these disciplinary practices are gendered and tied to sexuality (Bell and Valentine 1997, 25–42). They are also globalized. In Tokyo and Shanghai, for example, we see an expansive growth in fitness centers, marketing body-shaping regimens to urban women (Spielvogel 2003). These are often linked to particular diets. Sproutworks, a fast-growing vegetarian restaurant chain I studied in Shanghai, specializes in salads and quick healthy meals for young female office workers, who are the majority of patrons. The manager said that the company deliberately locates new branches near major fitness centers so that they can become part of these urban women's daily routines of body-maintenance.

Overall, we can see urban foodways as not only sustaining bodies but shaping minds, from the erotic pungency of a durian pudding to the purifying rituals of hot yoga. These ritualized practices of release and regulation are deeply emotional, producing pleasure and pride, anxiety and disgust. These bodily practices connect people to the city through the stomach and heart (or *xin* in Chinese). Connected to this idea, I have been working as part of a team identifying the social rituals and symbolic practices associated with happiness and well-being in China (see Swanson 2016). Though embracing the recent social science emphasis on subjective well-being, we believe this research is over-reliant on a few disembodied survey questions. In my ongoing research I identify food practices as part of everyday rituals embodying the good life in urban China, while showing that the language of food also is used to describe the dystopias of alienated living. As described above, these practices and discourses are imbued with deep emotional contents (Farrer 2016a). An urban sociology of food that relates carefully to emotions, and contextualizes these in culturally specific notions of the good life, can be an effective way of representing the embodied experiences of life in the city.

The city as body: the global urban metabolism

When we move up the geographic scale to the level of the city as a whole we can envision the city as itself a "body" consuming resources and producing wastes. In a pioneering discussion of the "urban metabolism," Abel Wolman estimated that a one-million-person US city in the 1960s had daily inputs of 625,000 tons of water, 9,500 tons of fuel, and 2,000 tons of food (Wolman 1965). A more recent review of the changing urban metabolisms of several major cities shows that rates of both input and waste outputs have largely increased throughout the world. Because of public transportation, dense Asian cities such as Hong Kong are generally more efficient than New World cities. However, a Hong Kong study showed that per capita food, water, and materials consumption had increased by 20 percent, 40 percent, and 149 percent, respectively, from 1971 to 1997 (Warren-Rhodes and Koenig 2001, cited in Kennedy et al. 2007). The urban metabolism model shows that cities are dependent on vast inputs of resources involving systems that are global in scope.

Food system studies show that cities have an ecological and economic footprint far beyond their immediate hinterland. For example, 81 percent of London's 6.9 million tons of annual food is imported from outside the UK, with an average distance of more than 5,000 kilometers (Kennedy et al. 2007). In a Singapore supermarket we find fresh vegetables from five continents arrayed in adjacent display cases, vividly illustrating the global supply chains that enable a diverse diet in this wealthy city state.

Concerns over costs, food safety, strategic vulnerability, and the ecological impact of long-distance supply chains have prompted locavore and urban farming movements all over Asia, including Japan, advocating eating local products (though sometimes only as a thinly disguised form of agricultural protectionism) (Assmann 2010). Community farms and small-scale urban farming have long been part of the Japanese cityscape. Researchers, however, debate the feasibility of urban farming as a large-scale solution. Southern African cities in particular have been held up as examples of successful cases of high-volume urban farming, but careful quantitative studies have cast doubt on the widespread efficacy of urban farming even there (Crush et al. 2011). Asian cities such as Shanghai have traditionally depended very heavily on farming in the immediate suburban area, but with development of farmland for residential and industrial use, these areas are decreasing. Nonetheless, there is a movement, especially among wealthy entrepreneurs and government officials, to secure suburban land for private farms to ensure a safe supply of foods not available on the open market (Yan 2012). In this case urban farming has a distinctive class and political bias.

Still, urban studies should not return to the classical view of cities as giant mouths consuming the countryside. Cities are also the markets that distribute foodstuffs outward to the world. Ted Bestor's study of Tokyo's Tsukiji fish market shows how it acts as a global nexus for the movement of fresh fish and seafood to and from points all over the world (Bestor 2004).

When energy for transportation, consumption, and the innumerable activities of urbanites earning their "daily bread" are taken into account, food is central to the urban metabolism, and food waste and wasted energy in the production of food become urgent issues for urban studies. Leiden University's new project on "Garbage matters: A comparative history of waste in East Asia" promises to merge historical and ethnographic approaches to this topic in East Asia, a region where total food consumption, food waste, and food packaging have exploded in quantity (Cwiertka 2015).

Embodied cosmopolitanism: eating the other in Asian cities

The global culinary flows in and out of the city ultimately converge at the level of the individual consumer. City dwellers of all economic levels eagerly pursue the varied tastes available in the city and use these experiences to construct a sense of the self as cosmopolitan and worldly. In Western critical race theory, this ubiquitous "eating the other" has been questioned as a form of cultural appropriation in which the foods of the other consumed by the white majority serve merely to "spice up" white lives, who then can claim multicultural authenticity without actually materially engaging with the other (Hooks 2000). Australian anthropologist Ghasan Hage describes this kind of culinary cosmopolitanism as "multiculturalism without ethnics" in which sampling of the foodways of others is abstracted from history, colonialism, and inequalities (Hage 1997). Rick Flowers and Elaine Swan, however, question this critique as static and one-dimensional, using the study of foodways in intercultural families to show how culinary sharing can be fluid, complex, and meaningful (Flowers and Swan 2012). This debate suggests that the ubiquitous practice of urban culinary cosmopolitanism – of eating the other – cannot be divorced from claims about class, national, and identity politics. Indeed, food is one of the most common ways of claiming (and transforming) social identity, including the cosmopolitan identities of global city dwellers, distinguishing themselves from more insular culinary localists.

Up until now, scholarly discussions of culinary cosmopolitanism have focused largely on the "food adventuring" of white diners exploring the exotic foods of non-white others (Heldke 2003). In the twenty-first century, however, Asian cities have emerged as cosmopolitan culinary capitals in their own right, and culinary adventuring is now common among Asian city residents. Already, by 1998, close to 40 percent of restaurants in Singapore served Western or International cuisine while around 56 percent offered "Oriental" cuisine (Leung et al. 2001, cited in Kong 2016). Tokyo now boasts more Michelin stars than Paris and Japan's most popular dining website, tabelog, lists 127,465 restaurants in Tokyo, including 9,420 Chinese, 5,725 Italian, 2,904 French, and 719 Thai. There were also 4,646 generic "curry" restaurants, a category that includes Japanese-style curry rice restaurants and South Asian-style curries (from tabelog.co.jp, Feb. 13, 2016).

Even Shanghai, from which international cuisine had all but disappeared under the Maoist program of culinary nationalism and socialist austerity in the 1960s and 1970s, now boasts thousands of international eateries, including over 3,000 Japanese restaurants (Farrer 2015). In all these cities, some foreign restaurants remained pricey luxuries, but cheap versions can be found even as fast food or in hawker centers and street stalls. Moreover, over a hundred million Asian tourists yearly engage in the same types of culinary "adventuring" that characterize Western tourists in Asia, with social media making a culinary journalist of everyone.

Do Asian consumers therefore simply repeat the same patterns of culinary exoticism described above, with simply a role reversal between "East" and "West"? Historical and anthropological research points to striking points of similarity and divergence. In the most important difference, Western foodways were introduced to Asian cities in the nineteenth century as an embodied symbol of Western civilization and colonial power. In Japan, the Meiji Emperor, wearing a Western military uniform and eating French cuisine, showed his subjects that Western gastronomy, and meat eating in particular, was essential to national revival. Nineteenth-century imports of Western foodways into both Japan and China focused on consuming Western food as a source of power, both corporeal and political, not mere culinary exoticism (Cwiertke 2006; Swislocki 2009).

This form of culinary Occidentalism has clear echoes in Asian cities today (Farrer 2010). Michelin stars lend restaurants and chefs in Hong Kong and Tokyo instant status and attention that is not always wanted but cannot be ignored. Even before the Michelin guide was published in Shanghai in September 2016, customers flocked to any restaurant run by a chef with a Michelin pedigree. After the guide was published, starred restaurants were booked months in advance, even while the list of awardees was contested (Farrer 2016b). And, despite Singapore's multiple Asian food traditions, Singaporean food writer Sheere Ng points out that innovation in fine dining restaurants is still measured by its approximation to Western culinary standards (interview Jan. 1, 2016). In the global circulation of culinary capital, only Japanese cuisine has achieved a status comparable to the French culinary tradition and its various spin-offs as nouvelle cuisine, molecular gastronomy, the new Nordic cuisine, and so on. Moreover, in Japan, the term "ethnic" (*esunikku*) food refers largely to lower-priced "spicy" Southeast Asian, Latin, and African cuisines, closely reproducing the culinary hierarchies in Western cities.

At the same time Western foodways are not simply seen as foreign in these Asian global cities. Tokyo, Singapore, Hong Kong, and Shanghai all have their own versions of indigenized Western foods. In Japan, *yoshoku*, or localized Western cuisine, represents some of the most popular everyday meals, such as hamburger steak, curry rice, and rice omelets (Cwiertke 2006). In Singapore, the ubiquitous *kopitiam*, or local coffee shops, specialize in serving a highly localized version of an English breakfast of toast smothered in butter and coconut jam (*kaya*) with a sweetened coffee (*kopi*) (Duruz 2016; Eng 2016). In Shanghai and Hong Kong, localized Western dishes include a cabbage soup derived from Russian borscht and fried pork chops (*dapai*) seasoned with a local version of Worcestershire Sauce (*lajiangyou*) (Farrer 2014). All of these are understood, not as exotic imports, but as nostalgic urban foods that form part of the cosmopolitan heritage of these cities.

Across East Asia, this type of culinary post-colonial nostalgia is combined with a civic pride in their rise as cosmopolitan cities that rival New York and Paris economically as well as culturally. Eating the "other" in Asia is thus about confronting, and reinterpreting the colonial past, as well as about forms of food adventuring and exoticism that are common in the West. Cosmopolitan identities constructed through hybrid urban foodways may thus be simultaneously nationalistic statements about arrival on the world stage. In East Asia, we thus find many parallels to the West, but also differences that relate in part to a not-so-distant colonial past.

Culinary place making: authentic foodways and culinary non-places

Cities do more than feed people: they provide meals in social spaces that either support or deny meaningful relationships and identifications. Sharon Zukin has written eloquently on the struggle over "authentic" urban spaces, often characterized by small-scale purveyors of food who make neighborhoods affordable, livable, heterogeneous spaces on a "human scale" (Zukin 2011, Zukin et al. 2015).

As the example of Hong Kong's fishball riots above shows, threats to (perceived) authentic urban spaces can become a flashpoint for political contest. In a city in which a handful of billionaire developers are accused of steadily eroding access to public spaces with the support of the state, Hong Kong's mobile food vendors represent the counter-claims of communities and individuals to city streets. Similarly, across the People's Republic of China, illicit street food vendors represent a point of resistance against the developmental priorities of city governments eager for land-use fees, and hence willing to cooperate with private developers to sanitize and privatize public spaces. Heavy-handed *chengguan*, urban para-police, are known for violently removing vendors and confiscating their goods. A police report issued in 2009 reported that yearly there were 600 violent incidents involving *chengguan* and street vendors in Guangzhou alone (Human Rights Watch 2012, 21–22). Across East Asia, including China, we see the rise of shopping-mall cities, in which foods are purveyed in air-conditioned food courts operated exclusively by large food corporations. However, in all these cities, small-scale eateries, including mobile vendors, survive and thrive in the interstices of modern infrastructure, and around Asia's cities these street-level foodscapes are most closely associated with authentic eating and a good city life.

If we understand this as simply a David and Goliath struggle between small vendors facing a developmental state, however, we would fail to appreciate the considerable role of the state in shaping "authentic" urban culinary spaces. Especially in the case of Singapore, the government was central to banning street vendors but also to preserving their characteristic cooking in multistory, open-air concrete towers. Between 1974 and 1979, 54 such "hawker centers" were built to house vendors relocated from neighborhood streets. By 1986 there were 113 hawker centers housing 6,000 cooked-food stalls, selling myriad specialties, including localized and hybridized versions of Chinese, Indian, Malay, but also Western and Japanese foods (Kong 2007, 41).

A shared love of this multi-ethnic and low-market hawker center food is a singular marker of contemporary Singaporean urban identity, one that is celebrated by the government in exhibitions such as a photographic history of hawker centers shown in December 2015 in the Clementi Public Library (itself in a shopping mall adjacent to a lively hawker center). Singapore food bloggers devote themselves to finding the best *char kwey teow* (flat rice noodles stir-fried with a heavy soy-sauce with lard, chives, cockles, or other ingredients). Families travel across the city to queue for a famous vendor. The future of hawker center cuisine even has become a national concern, as aging hawkers retire and are not replaced by young cooks. Ironically, for a hybrid cuisine that was created by migrant vendors in the early twentieth century, Singaporeans are largely opposed to the entry of recent migrant culinary workers into hawker centers and (privately owned) food courts, out of fear that "authentic" Singaporean flavors would be lost (interview with Sheere Ng, Jan. 1, 2016). A hybridized migrant cuisine thus runs a risk of being "heritaged" out of existence.

City governments in Japan have also had a complex relationship with small-scale eateries and street vendors. Recently there has been a boom in back-alley (*roji*) eateries, with some of the most celebrated examples developing in former black markets (*yami-ichi*) adjacent to commuter stations. In the immediate postwar period, cities closed most of these markets and supported the development of modern department stores featuring sanitized restaurants for the rising middle classes. However, in the past two decades local governments have come to recognize the nostalgic and touristic appeal of the remaining ramshackle blocks of two-story bars and eateries. For example, Harmonica-Yokocho in suburban Tokyo's Kichijoji neighborhood is a flourishing patchwork of tiny bars and restaurants squeezed into the shells of the former black market. Although an alcoholic watering hole for workers and "salarymen" for decades, the area was discovered by young people, particularly women, in the 2000s (partly because clean toilet facilities for women were installed). Many of the more popular eateries are actually operated by a single company, VIC Corp., started by a former videographer with an eye for matching the nostalgic maze of a postwar black market with a cosmopolitan vibe, serving global foods, wines, and craft beers, and hiring many international students as servers. Whether owner-operated or with a larger enterprise lurking in the background, such small-scale, open-air venues create spaces of conviviality among strangers (Inoue 2015). Such carefully staged "authentic" urban food scenes are one of the reasons the Kichijoji consistently tops the list of the most desirable neighborhoods to live in Japan.

Of course, contemporary cityscapes also contain many forgettable culinary non-places, with generic options and thin sociability. In the USA and UK, there are even discussions of "food deserts" or entire inner-city areas in which healthy food is unobtainable, too expensive, or limited to fast-food chains, though some researchers dispute their existence, at least in the UK (Cummins 2014). In Asian cities, which are denser and also less class-stratified than US cities, food deserts do not seem to exist, but there are many spaces in which meaningful sociability over food is limited either out of choice or lack of options. All over Asia, we find increasing numbers of people living apart from families and regularly eating alone. One of the most important institutions serving them is the convenience store, which has probably passed the fast-food outlet as the most common purveyor of convenience meals in cities from Taipei to Tokyo. Convenience store eating is – rightly or wrongly – associated with a lack of social ties, irregular employment, and the decline of dating and marriage among Asian young people (see Whitelaw 2006). Studies of culinary place making should document not only spaces of authenticity and sociability, but also these culinary non-spaces frequented by the growing urban precariat.

Conclusions: new directions

This chapter has reviewed some research on urban foodways with an eye to pointing out new directions in research, including a focus on tastes, emotions, and the urban body, food, and energy waste in the urban metabolism; the embodied cosmopolitanism of culinary consumption; and the notions of good and bad living expressed through different forms of culinary place making. This chapter asks the

Anglophone researchers to think more about regions outside North America and Northwest Europe, especially Asia, where most of the world's large cities will soon be (and many already are). Finally, I also implicitly make connections to established traditions of urban ethnography. Ethnographic research brings to bear the full-bodied experiences of the researcher and the creativity and imagination of the writer. Indeed, the primary message of my brief chapter here may be that much exciting ethnographic research is being conducted on urban foodways in East Asia, but much more could be done.

References

Appadurai, Arjun (1997), 'Consumption, duration, and history', in David Palumbo-Liu and Hans Ulrich Gumbrecht (eds), *Streams of Cultural Capital: Transnational Cultural Studies*, Stanford, CA: Stanford University Press, pp. 23–46.

Assmann, Stephanie (2010), 'Food Action Nippon and Slow Food Japan: The role of two citizen movements in the rediscovery of local foodways', in James Farrer (ed.), *Globalization, Food and Social Identities in the Asia Pacific Region*, Tokyo: Sophia University Institute of Comparative Culture, accessed Feb. 3, 2016 at http://icc.fla.sophia.ac.jp/global%20food%20papers/pdf/2_2_ASSMANN.pdf.

Barboza, David (2010), 'Recycled cooking oil found to be latest hazard in China', *New York Times*, Mar. 31, accessed Feb. 11, 2016 at http://nyti.ms/1KCxhL3.

Bell, David, and Gill Valentine (1997), *Consuming Geographies: We Are Where We Eat*, Hove, UK: Psychology Press.

Bestor, Theodore C. (2004), *Tsukiji: The Fish Market at the Center of the World*, Berkeley, CA: University of California Press.

Chu, Simon, and John J. Downes (2000), 'Odour-evoked autobiographical memories: Psychological investigations of Proustian phenomena', *Chemical Senses*, **25**, 111–116.

Crush, Jonathan, Alice Hovorka, and Daniel Tevera (2011), 'Food security in Southern African cities: The place of urban agriculture', *Progress in Development Studies*, **11**(4), 285–305.

Cummins, Steven (2014), 'Food deserts', in William C. Cockerham, Robert Dingwall, and Stella R. Quah (eds), *The Wiley-Blackwell Encyclopedia of Health, Illness, Behavior, and Society*, pp. 436–438.

Cwiertka, Katarzyna (2006), *Modern Japanese Cuisine: Food, Power and National Identity*, London: Reaktion Books.

Cwiertka, Katarzyna (2015), 'Garbage matters: A comparative history of waste in East Asia', accessed Feb. 14, 2016 at http://www.universiteitleiden.nl/en/research/research-projects/humanities/garbage-matters-a-comparative-history-of-waste-in-east-asia.

Duruz, Jean (2016), 'The taste of retro: Nostalgia, sensory landscapes and cosmopolitanism in Singapore', in Lily Kong and Vineeta Sinha (eds), *Food, Foodways and Foodscapes: Culture, Community and Consumption in Post-Colonial Singapore*, Singapore: World Scientific Publishing, pp. 207–241.

Eng, Lai Ah (2016), 'The *Kopitiam* in Singapore: An evolving story about cultural diversity and cultural politics', in Lily Kong and Vineeta Sinha (eds), *Food, Foodways and Foodscapes: Culture, Community and Consumption in Post-Colonial Singapore*, Singapore: World Scientific Publishing, pp. 103–132.

ESCAP (2011), *Statistical Yearbook for Asia and Pacific*, accessed Feb. 10, 2016 at http://www.unescap.org/stat/data/syb2011/I-People/Urbanization.asp.

Farrer, James (2010), 'Eating the West and beating the rest: Culinary occidentalism and urban soft power in Asia's global food cities', in James Farrer (ed.), *Globalization, Food and Social Identities in the Asia Pacific Region*, Tokyo: Sophia University Institute of Comparative Culture, accessed Feb. 3, 2016 at http://icc.fla.sophia.ac.jp/global%20food%20papers/pdf/2_3_FARRER.pdf.

Farrer, James (2014), 'Imported culinary heritage: The case of localized Western cuisine in Shanghai', in Sidney Cheung (ed.), *Rethinking Asian Food Heritage*, Taipei: The Foundation of Chinese Dietary Culture, pp. 75–104.

Farrer, James (2015), 'Shanghai's Western restaurants as culinary contact zones in a transnational culinary field', in James Farrer (ed.), *Globalization and Asian Cuisines: Transnational Networks and Contact Zones*, New York: Palgrave Macmillan, pp. 103–124.

Farrer, James (2016a), 'Happy and unhappy meals: Culinary approaches to the good life in Shanghai', paper presented at Conference on Blessed Happiness: Visions of the Good Life in Urban China, Georgetown University, Washington DC, Jan. 21, 2016.

Farrer, James (2016b), 'Michelin stars over China: French cuisine in Shanghai's culinary contact zones', *Chinese Food Culture in Europe: French Food Culture in Asia*, Tours, France: Université François-Rabelais Tours/ Foundation of Chinese Dietary Culture.

Flowers, Rick, and Elaine Swan (2012), 'Eating the Asian other? Pedagogies of food multiculturalism in Australia', *PORTAL Journal of Multidisciplinary International Studies*, 9(2), accessed Feb. 3, 2016 at http://epress.lib.uts.edu.au/ojs/index.php/portal.

Hage, Ghasan (1997), 'At home in the entrails of the West: Multiculturalism, ethnic food and migrant home-building', in Helen Grace, Ghassan Hage, Lesley Johnson, Julie Langsworth, and Michael Symonds (eds), *Home/World: Space, Community and Marginality in Sydney's West*, Annandale, NSW, Australia: Pluto, pp. 99–153.

Heldke, Lisa (2003), *Exotic Appetites: Ruminations of a Food Adventurer*, Abingdon, UK: Routledge.

Herz, Rachel S., James Eliassen, Sophia Beland, and Timothy Souza (2004), 'Neuroimaging evidence for the emotional potency of odor-evoked memory', *Neuropsychologia*, 42, 371–378.

Hooks, Bell (2000), 'Eating the other: Desire and resistance', in Juliet Schor and Douglas B. Holt (eds), *The Consumer Society Reader*, New York: The New Press, pp. 343–359.

Human Rights Watch (2012), '"Beat him, take everything away" abuses by China's *Chengguan* para-police', accessed Feb. 3, 2016 at https://www.hrw.org/sites/default/files/reports/china0512ForUpload_1.pdf.

Inoue, Kenichiro (2015), *Kichijoji 'Hamonica Yokocho' Monogatari*, Tokyo: Kokusho.

Kantor, Arlene F. (1976), 'Upton Sinclair and the Pure Food and Drugs Act of 1906: "I aimed at the public's heart and by accident I hit it in the stomach"', *American Journal of Public Health*, 66(12), 1202–1205.

Kennedy, Christopher, John Cuddihy, and Joshua Engel-Yan (2007), 'The changing metabolism of cities', *Journal of Industrial Ecology*, 11(2), 43–59.

Kong, Lily (2007), *Singapore Hawker Centres: People, Places, Food*, Singapore: National Environment Agency.

Kong, Lily (2016), 'From *sushi* in Singapore to *laksa* in London: Globalising foodways and the production of economy and identity', in Lily Kong and Vineeta Sinha (eds), *Food, Foodways and Foodscapes: Culture, Community and Consumption in Post-Colonial Singapore*, Singapore: World Scientific Publishing, pp. 207–241.

Leung, Roberta Wong, Zalar U. Ahmed, and Shubhasree Seshanna (2001), 'A study of ethnic restaurants in Singapore', *International Area Studies Review*, 4(1), 51–61.

Mannur, Anita (2007), 'Culinary nostalgia: Authenticity, nationalism, and diaspora', *Melus*, 32(4), 11–31.

Moss, Stephen (2016), 'Is Hong Kong really rioting over fishball stands?', *The Guardian*, Feb. 9, accessed Feb. 9, 2016 at http://www.theguardian.com/lifeandstyle/shortcuts/2016/feb/09/hong-kong-fish-ball-revolution-china-riot?CMP=fb_gu.

Ray, Krishnendu (2012), 'Global flows, local bodies: Dreams of Pakistani grill in Manhattan', in Krishnendu Ray (ed.), *Curried Cultures: Globalization, Food, and South Asia*, pp. 175–195.

Spielvogel, Laura (2003), *Working Out in Japan: Shaping the Female Body in Tokyo Fitness Clubs*, Durham, NC: Duke University Press.

Swanson, Ana (2016), 'What people around the world mean when they say they're happy', *Washington*

Post, Feb. 3, accessed Feb. 3, 2016 at https://www.washingtonpost.com/news/wonk/wp/2016/02/03/what-english-speakers-dont-get-about-the-meaning-of-happiness/.

Swislocki, Mark (2009), *Culinary Nostalgia: Regional Food Culture and the Urban Experience in Shanghai*, Stanford, CA: Stanford University Press.

Warren-Rhodes, Kimberley, and Albert Koenig (2001), 'Escalating trends in the urban metabolism of Hong Kong: 1971–1997', *AMBIO: A Journal of the Human Environment*, **30**(7), 429–438.

Whitelaw, Gavin Hamilton (2006), 'Rice ball rivalries: Japanese convenience stores and the appetite of late capitalism', in Richard Wilk (ed.), *Fast Food/Slow Food: The Cultural Economy of the Global Food System*, Lanham, MD: Rowman Altamira, pp. 131–144.

Wolman, Abel (1965), 'The metabolism of cities', *Scientific American*, **213**(3), 179–190.

World Bank (2015), *East Asia's Changing Urban Landscape: Measuring a Decade of Spatial Growth*, Washington, DC: World Bank.

Yan, Yunxiang (2012), 'Food safety and social risk in contemporary China', *Journal of Asian Studies*, **71**(3), 705–729.

Zukin, Sharon (2011), *Naked City: The Death and Life of Authentic Urban Places*, Oxford: Oxford University Press.

Zukin, Sharon, Philip Kasinitz, and Xiangming Chen (2015), *Global Cities, Local Streets: Everyday Diversity from New York to Shanghai*, Abingdon, UK: Routledge.

Part III

Changes in the city

9 Gentrification

Elvin Wyly

Vancouver, Silicon Valley, Oxford, and Nanjing

If average home sales prices are compared to average local incomes, the City of Vancouver, in British Columbia on the West Coast of North America, is often tied with Sydney, Australia, as the world's second most expensive real estate market after Hong Kong. The latest record-setting Vancouver real estate transaction involved a mansion sold by Don Mattrick, CEO of the social media company Zynga, for C$51.8 million; the private sale in the city's elite West Point Grey neighborhood might well have been "the biggest residential transaction ever conducted in Canada" (Young, 2015), perhaps unsurprising in light of the fact that CNBC had ranked Mattrick as the second highest paid CEO in the San Francisco Bay Area. But if it was a farming simulation social networking game (Farmville) that put Zynga on the path to success with a suite of games that eventually reached more than 260 million monthly active users, the company's headquarters were quintessentially urban. "The last time I was in San Francisco," reports the journalist Samantha Allen (2014),

> I saw an entire family living in a tent underneath the highway overpass across the street from Zynga's offices. This image of abject poverty set against the headquarters of the social gaming giant . . . is a painfully apt reminder of the social and economic forces that are currently turning San Francisco into a shadow of its former self: Silicon Valley capitalism, gentrification, and the widening income inequality that results from their mutual interaction.

Wall Street capitalism cheered with a 10.4 percent jump in Zynga shares (and another 5.9 percent boost in after-hours action) on the news of recruiting Mattrick, who had been running Microsoft's Xbox division (Rusli and Ovide, 2013). Mattrick, a native Vancouverite "who lives like a Saudi prince and jets to work" (LaPorte, 2013) and boasts of being friends with Wayne Gretsky and Steven Spielberg (Young, 2015), moved quickly to reposition Zynga towards games played on smartphones and tablets. The company's shares "soared the most since its initial public offering" (Edwards, 2014) when Mattrick fired 314 people on the same day he sealed a US$527 million deal to buy NaturalMotion, an Oxford University spinoff developed by a neuroscientist pursuing a PhD in Complex Systems and Zoology before he "decided to go in a totally different direction" (Cutler, 2014). Biological

113

expertise yielded advanced 3D animation and a cutting-edge "middleware" enterprise that rendered the stunningly realistic action in the *Grand Theft Auto* series and the *Lord of the Rings* trilogy. Oxford got a 10 percent cut of the NaturalMotion acquisition – part of a wave of innovation that generated more than US$200 million in venture capital raised by Oxford-based startups in 2015.

The Zynga–NaturalMotion–Oxford narrative was then featured prominently in coverage of the advice offered by Professor Andrew Hamilton, outgoing vice-chancellor of Oxford, on how to achieve the full potential of a twenty-first-century university. Part of Oxford's success, we are told, comes from being "one of the most international universities in the world," and part comes from being "at the centre of a 'knowledge spine,' embracing scientific and entrepreneurial establishments" from a vast regional urban network (Rafferty, 2015). Similar "corridors of knowledge" are also fundamental to the success of other "world-class universities, including Cambridge, Stanford, and Harvard-MIT," we learn from a journalist's report of Hamilton's remarks, published as a commentary in the *South China Morning Post*. The commentary is presented as a defense of academic freedom and the "clash of ideas" that "add to the richness of human knowledge" as opposed to Xi Jinping's apparent vision of "universities as teaching machines that preach the party line, didactic Confucianism at work" (Rafferty, 2015).

Within the Chinese People's Political Consultative Conference, though, the Nanjing City representative is a former farmer – a real one, not a Farmville simulation – who worked his way up to create a "skyscraper-building conglomerate" while, according to his corporate website, "pursuing the goal of achieving economic, social, and environmental efficiency and giving back to communities" (quoted in Young, 2015). This is Chen Mailin, who bought that C$52 million Vancouver home from Don Mattrick. "I love Vancouver. It's a very beautiful city," the media-shy Chen told CBC News (2015) in a rare interview: "They have the best education for kids."

In this story, what urban process is at work? Is this about knowledge corridors, creative cities, and Silicon Valley disruptive innovation? Twenty-first century universities? Transnationalism? The rise of China? To be sure, all of these are involved. But in this chapter I suggest that vignettes like these help us gain a fresh perspective on gentrification. There's an enormous academic literature on gentrification, and the keyword is a widely recognized battle cry among policy elites, developers, investors, journalists, and activists. Yet no matter how eloquent and sophisticated it has become over the years, all of this research and debate has reinforced a view of gentrification as a localized, neighborhood-scale process that takes place within the bounds of cities as discrete spatial containers. This way of thinking invariably descends into endless empirical tedium. The family living in a tent next to Zynga's headquarters is a sign of inequality, critics say, but nobody was directly displaced as the new social media giants moved into the patchwork of old industrial buildings, parking lots, and elevated freeways of San Francisco's South of Market (SoMa) district – so how can this be gentrification? Likewise, the Don Mattrick–Chen Mailin transaction may be an interesting case of globalizing real estate markets, but critics will note that

Mattrick is hardly a poor renter facing eviction like those constantly on the edge of homelessness in Vancouver's infamous Downtown Eastside, and the elite enclave of West Point Grey is not the downgraded inner-city poor or working-class community that everyone envisions when the word "gentrification" is used.

I suggest that we need to rethink our understandings of gentrification. At the precise moment when gentrification is becoming thoroughly pervasive, transnational, and spatially contingent – manifest in multiple kinds of localized yet often fast-moving spatial contexts – our tradition-bound definitions are blinding us to the true urban significance of contemporary planetary urbanization. "Gentrification" is and should be central to our research agenda on cities, but not in the ways we've been led to believe. We need to stop obsessing over the empirics of precise, neighborhood-level details of *where* urban class succession takes place; instead we must place greater emphasis on *how* class relations evolve. We must see the entire networked constellation of individuals, institutions, and competitive processes as a clear manifestation of contemporary gentrification. Moreover, I argue that while many of the details of today's postcolonial planetary urbanization are new, there is absolutely nothing novel about a cosmopolitan, networked understanding of gentrification: this is an excavation of a forgotten history. Put simply, most discussions of gentrification over the past half century (including my own scribblings on the subject) have been misguided. From the very beginning, we have misunderstood the process that the word "gentrification" tried to capture.

To explain what I mean, I'll reconsider the theoretical and political history of the word and the concept before returning to today's more cosmopolitan forms of planetary gentrification.

What is gentrification?

Everyone who studies gentrification eventually gets around to mentioning that the word was coined by Ruth Glass in the early 1960s, to describe changes underway in parts of post-World War II London. Here's the full paragraph where Glass (1964, pp. xviii–xix) describes what's happening:

> One by one, many of the working-class quarters of London have been invaded by the middle classes – upper and lower. Shabby, modest mews and cottages – two rooms up and two rooms down – have been taken over, when their leases have expired, and have become elegant, expensive residences. Larger Victorian houses, downgraded in an earlier or recent period – which were used as lodging houses or were otherwise in multiple occupation – have been upgraded once again. Nowadays, many of these houses are being subdivided into costly flats or "houselets" (in terms of the new real estate snob jargon). The current social status and value of such dwellings are frequently in inverse relation to previous levels in their neighbourhoods. Once this process of "gentrification" starts in a district, it goes on rapidly until all or most of the original working-class occupiers are displaced, and the whole social character of the district is changed. There is very little left

of the poorer enclaves of Hampstead and Chelsea: in those boroughs, the upper-middle-class takeover was consolidated some time ago. The invasion has since spread to Islington, Paddington, North Kensington – even to the 'shady' parts of Notting Hill – to Battersea, and to several other districts, north and south of the river. The East End has so far been exempt, although before long some of its districts, too, are likely to be affected. And this is an inevitable development, in view of the demographic, economic and political pressures to which London, and especially central London, has been subjected.

An enormous scholarly literature, rich with empirical detail and theoretical debate, has developed in the half century since Glass wrote these words (for samples, see Lees et al., 2010, 2015). If we had to summarize a "consensus" definition, it might look like this: gentrification is a transformation of 1) inner-city neighborhoods, where 2) poor and working-class residents are replaced or displaced by middle- or upper-class residents, through 3) the combined effects of wider societal changes that alter the socio-cultural meanings of urban living, and the land-market economics that can make reinvestment into "downgraded" inner-city districts extremely profitable.

Consensus, however, has always been tenuous and contested. Many who study (or fight) the process define the process broadly to include the upscaling of suburbs, rural areas, commercial/retail spaces, the construction of luxury condos on old waterfront, industrial, and railway lands, and even what Lees calls the "supergentrification" displacement of the rich by the super-rich. Others question the "meaningless terminological entrepreneurship" (Palen and London, 1984, p. 6) of expanding definitions that conflate "many diverse if interrelated" events and causal processes into a singular and thus fatally "chaotic" concept (Beauregard, 1986, p. 40). At the extreme, the "far broader meaning of gentrification" developed by the "new scholarship" (Sassen, 1991, p. 255) is attacked as "definitional overload." Liz Bondi (1999, p. 255) is the most explicit:

> Ruth Glass's (1964) coining of the term "gentrification" opened up new questions about urban change. But the more researchers have attempted to pin it down the more burdens the concept has had to carry. Maybe the loss of momentum around gentrification reflects its inability to open up new insights, and maybe it is time to allow it to disintegrate under the weight of these burdens.

Recently, more serious criticisms have emerged. Thomas Maloutas (2011, p. 34) argues that gentrification is "highly dependent on contextual causality," and that any attempt to apply a concept that is so deeply enmeshed in the "Anglo-American metropolis" to the different circumstances of cities elsewhere in the world is nothing short of intellectual colonialism. Others warn against a "diffusionist" tendency to see gentrification spreading from the Global North to the Global South (Lees, 2012), and remind us that the language and processes of urban change take very different forms in the developmental states of East Asia (Ley and Teo, 2013; Ong, 2011). Asher Ghertner (2015, p. 552) argues that the concept of gentrification "renders unthinkable and invisible" the legal and regulatory causes of the most violent forms of displacement in societies with legacies of public land ownership, informality, and common property – China, post-socialist Europe, many parts of Southeast Asia and sub-Saharan Africa – and thus gentrification theory "fails in much of the world." In a recent commentary, Matthias Bernt (2016, p. 1) summarizes where the literature now stands:

> While conceptual quarrels over the question whether gentrification as a concept is overstretched are not brand new … the intensity with which gentrification is challenged as a concept has changed considerably in the last couple of years. Echoing the call of postcolonial thinkers to "provincialize" Western theories, today more and more scholars tend to see gentrification as an urban phenomenon rooted in rather specific experiences made in a handful of Western metropolises in the last century.

Gentrification has always inspired heated debate, but today's controversies are globally divisive binaries. Either gentrification is a globalizing process, or this assertion is itself a Northern/Western neocolonial imposition. Either the process is what Atkinson and Bridge (2005) label "the new urban colonialism," or the label is itself the product of enduring neocolonial structures in knowledge production. The intensity of this debate makes it clear that the top priority for a research agenda on gentrification involves sustained, comparative, multi-lingual, cross-cultural ethnographic fieldwork to reconcile the standpoint-epistemological divides of positionality and power between theories and experiences of urbanism across the North/South divide. Sadly, I am pathetically unqualified to offer guidance on how to do this (but I am inspired by the valuable but divergent perspectives we get by juxtaposing Smith, 2011, Slater, 2015, and Schafran, 2014, with Roy, forthcoming, Ley and Teo, 2013, Harris, 2008, Ghertner, 2015, Ren, 2015, and Lees et al., 2015). What I offer here is more modest, albeit for certain post-Reaganite American Christians a bit more offensive (Witham, 2002) with insufficient time or space for nuance (Healy, 2016). I offer a reminder that we will never understand today's global gentrification debates if we misunderstand the "contextual causality" of the Global North setting in which gentrification was first diagnosed. Today's debates are flawed insofar as they assume that 1) gentrification theory began with concerns about a neighborhood-scale process that was 2) focused on the particular circumstances of London, and that 3) subsequent researchers "expanded" this original definition.

These assumptions collapse when we stop treating Ruth Glass's (1964) definition as scripture. Everyone cites the eloquent words about shabby mews and cottages being taken over and upgraded, and everyone delights in exploring the contemptuous connotations of the etymology of the English "gentry." But if we actually read the essay – a lengthy introduction to an edited collection of research papers analyzing the results of the Third Survey of London Life and Labour – a very different set of meanings appears. Yes, it's about London. But it's a situated, transitional London at a dramatic historical post-war, post-colonializing moment. The entire purpose of the Centre for Urban Studies that Glass directed was to be deeply critical and cosmopolitan – scrutinizing the cultural and planning histories of urbanism in Britain in the context of what was happening in Asia, Africa, and Latin America (see Glass, 1963). Glass's use of the word "gentrification" appears a few pages into an extraordinary, wide-ranging analysis. She examines regional industrial restructuring, commuting and transportation networks, the consolidation and upscaling of retail and consumption spaces, and the kaleidoscope of occupational, educational, aesthetic, and class subcultures. She analyzes the legacy of imperial rule abroad that now brings the descendants of slaves and indentured servants from the far reaches of the Commonwealth. She analyzes how the segregation, racism, and economic oppression of the empire's racialized citizens expose the flaws of British society – and its reluctance to adapt to "the postcolonial world of today." Glass, who died in 1990, would be a passionate advocate of today's postcolonial calls to provincialize the Global North, the West, and the "developed" world; this was exactly what she was trying to do in the early 1960s (see also Glass, 1962). Every sentence shines with brilliant analytical rigor and unforgiving, mischievous sabotage of an arrogant, frayed imperial hegemony poised between a history of inherited class privilege and the mindless modernism of technological worship, commodified mass communication, and intensified consumption.

Reading Glass's entire essay makes it clear that gentrification is far more than a neighborhood-scale process. While the term is introduced amidst a description of a specific set of sites in central London, the word and the concept are utterly meaningless without an appreciation of the wider context – the newfound post-war affluence of London, the public debates over its creeping "Americanization," and its precarious position as the primate city of a planetary Commonwealth on the edge of decolonization. Over the years, the best work on gentrification has always considered the interdependencies between local and extra-local processes – this is a common theme uniting the otherwise contrasting approaches of David Ley's sociocultural postindustrial society analysis and Neil Smith's work on circuits of capital, for instance (cf. Lees et al., 2015, pp. 449–450). Yet we must go further, to look past all the details of neighborhoods, housing conditions, occupational groupings, consumption preferences, and even the legal and institutional specifics of displacement, rent, tenure, and property. All of these things matter. But they are all manifestations of a much deeper essence in the ontology – the nature of being – in an urban world: *competition*. Glass repeatedly emphasizes the "competition for space" that has become "more and more intense." She describes many different subcultures of migrants – from other parts of Britain and from all over the world – who have one thing in common: the intense competition for a place to live that renders them targets for ever-worsening exploitation. She describes how spiraling central land values force firms to allocate scarce commercial space to ever-higher tiers of the managerial and executive workforce – amidst a regional suburbanization that stretches journeys-to-work so far that highly paid workers take tiny *pied-à-terre* second homes near their financial-district workplaces (fueling a further spiral of locational competition).

Again and again Glass documents the intensification of competition in urban life, and she makes it clear that upscale "invasions" are by no means *natural*, but they are *inevitable* given certain theories and decisions. The problem lies in the dangerous perversions of how urban thought and planning understood "human nature." Glass sees rising competition as inevitable given the interaction between two factors. First, the Great Depression reinforced deeply entrenched "neo-Malthusian" hopes and fears of population decline, leading to assumptions of a stationary economy and culture that were embedded into Patrick Abercrombie's (1945) *Greater London Plan 1944*. Second, in the early 1950s the first post-war Conservative Government began a series of drastic amendments that transformed the Town and Country Planning Act 1947 into "anti-planning" legislation. Through the 1950s, amendments "de-nationalised" development rights, relaxed rent controls, required local authorities undertaking public-purpose redevelopment to pay full market price for land assessed at full development potential, and thus "liberated" market speculation. "In such circumstances," Glass (1964, p. xx) observed,

> any district in or near London, however dingy or unfashionable before, is likely to become expensive; and London may quite soon be a city which illustrates the principle of the survival of the fittest – the financially fittest, who can still afford to work and live there. (Not long ago, the then Housing Minister advised those who cannot pay the price to move out.)

For the study of gentrification, Ruth Glass is undisputably what Foucault (1969, p. 387) called a "founder of discursivity." While the gentrification process has a much longer history (and has changed in all sorts of ways in the last 50 years), her essay established certain possibilities conditioning the formation of other texts – setting the parameters in which later generations refine and challenge a discourse and what it seeks to represent and produce. My purpose in undertaking this "return to the origin" (Foucault, 1969) is to excavate the forgotten histories of the time and place in which Glass was writing. That time and place – the first decades after World War II in England – was shaped by the combination of newfound affluence, a collapsing global colonial empire, the new modernist possibilities of Karl Pearson's (1927) statistical innovations as applied to human populations as envisioned by Francis Galton (1869), and the first Orwellian echos of the "liberating markets" language we now call neoliberalism.

Considering that context makes it clear that the essence of gentrification is the urban evolution of human competition. Glass chose her words carefully, and the evolutionary references are not simply casual metaphors. Elsewhere she wrote of "incessant competition" of land uses, the "takeover" of poor districts by "prosperous colonists," and other aspects of "the process of Social Darwinism in the displacement and succession of population groups." (Glass, 1970, p. 100). Glass was dubious of how "displacement and succession" naturalized inequality in the human-ecological tradition of the Chicago School of Sociology, with its curious theoretical strains of "cognitive Darwinism" (Entrikin, 1980). And even as she narrated the public debates over the "Americanization" of London's post-war society of consumption, communications, and advertising – and how the reorganization of London's "zone in transition" was different from the "urban renewal" bulldozing of US cities – she coyly channeled other American mutations by writing of the "survival of the fittest." Glass and her readers fully understood that this wasn't the wording of the

Englishman Charles Darwin; it was the catchphrase of the most influential conservative philosopher of nineteenth-century America, Herbert Spencer. Spencer, who pissed in the gene pool as he built a bizarre precursor of "Intelligent Design" that allowed America's political and religious leaders to avoid the worst implications of the Darwinian revolution for Christian doctrine, became the favored philosophical mouthpiece for America's robber-baron billionaire class. John D. Rockefeller once told children in a Sunday-School class that Spencer's "survival of the fittest" doctrine was a "law of nature and a law of God" justifying the wealth and power he and his peers controlled in the giant corporate trusts of the day.

Today the labels "Social Darwinism" and "survival of the fittest" sound like strange relics from a distant time and place. Perhaps. But that is the time and place where the turnover of shabby mews and cottages to the gentry could only be understood in relation to wider struggles for space throughout the metropolis amidst a dying global colonial order. That colonial empire had been built and defended not just by military force, but also by the cognitive terrorism of Malthusian theological political economy and racist Social Darwinism – and early post-war London was the pivot between the progressive-collective intentions of "managerial" evolutionary thought, from Patrick Geddes to John Maynard Keynes, to a new kind of marketized econometric eugenics promising a world of choice and freedom. It was Keynes, after all, who gave a speech to the British Eugenics Society introducing Sir Alexander Carr-Saunders, the winner of the Society's 1946 Gold Medal. Keynes (1946, p. 40) reminded his fellow eugenicists that Darwin had developed his theories by reading Malthus, but that "Carr-Saunders was led to Malthus through Darwin." Carr-Saunders had achieved fame with a neo-Malthusian treatise on the "quantity and quality" of population, and as Director of the London School of Economics from 1937 to 1957 he paid very close attention to "quality" people. One of them was Friedrich von Hayek, whom he had met during the War at Cambridge, and in later years nearly every aspect of Hayek's theory of human competition and cultural evolution was derived from Carr-Saunders's thesis that "selection operates on acquired habits and tradition" (Angner, 2007, p. 81).

"Acquired habits and traditions" is, of course, the old flawed pre-Darwinian Lamarckianism of Father Malthus's era – but bad science often makes for brilliant politics. In her 1993 autobiography, Margaret Thatcher credits Hayek as the key intellectual figure of the neoliberal revolution that became the new global colonial project – which, like "gentrification," has now evolved to the point where those in the Global North/West who apply the *critique of neoliberalism* to understand urbanization in the Global South are themselves attacked as a new generation of colonizers. Let me be clear. I am inspired by the invigorating plurality of today's postcolonial urban voices "From the South" (Parnell and Oldfield, 2014) – a collective cry of "Our society is unique, our culture is our own" – but the real enemies are not the *critics* of neoliberalism, but those who are working to build, profit from, or encode Thatcher's "There's no such thing as society" sourcecode into the networked, digitized, Android acceleration of competition in today's urban world. Glass (1989) predicted all of this shortly before she died. The Thatcherites dreamed of a "high-tech Britain" with a "miniaturized robotic labour force" as the working classes of all erstwhile industrial societies become "an expendable, even a dying species." While the rich continue to "annex territories of the poor for gentrification," the poor and working classes are sifted and sorted into entrepreneurial "goodies" versus welfare-dependent "baddies," the latter herded into "segregated colonies" and stigmatized as "undesirable, feckless species." A previous century's social divisions of morbidity and mortality reappear with a vengeance, while privatization transforms public education into "programming" of the next generation – forcing a coercive competition among schools for "sponsorships and donations" under the happy banner of "parental choice" and a recrudescence of the systematic "pre-selection of children" for different kinds and "classes" of schools.

The evolution of gentrification, and the gentrification of evolution

Let's return to our opening story. A family is living in a tent underneath a highway overpass. Zynga's stock price surges after Don Mattrick fires a few hundred people and buys an Oxford neuroscience-software spinoff. And today's reincarnation of John D. Rockefeller, Chen Mailin, buys the largest house in British Columbia, 9,000 kilometers away from his corporate headquarters in a city that he praises as having the best education for kids. If we look for "gentrification" as conventionally understood in the separate urban locales featured in this story, we'll certainly find enormous contextual contrasts in housing markets, land development practices, histories of colonization and dispossession, ethnoracial and class relations, and roles of the state in Vancouver, San Francisco, Oxford, and Nanjing. Most obviously, the experience in Nanjing is "different from Western countries," because the "evolutionary mechanisms" of the post-reform People's Republic of China (PRC) are driven by a powerful nation-state urban growth machine built for "capital appreciation realized through spatial reproduction"; still, a distinctively non-Western process yields social exclusion, segregation, and marginalization of low-income people – creating a "hindrance to harmonious society" which is "necessary for the state and scholars to seriously consider" (Song and Wu, 2010, pp. 569, 574, 575).

When we look beyond the empiricist spatial details of localized urban change, all of these contrasts – important as they are for people and institutions embedded in particular sites – are irrelevant to the question of whether this constitutes gentrification. Can there be any doubt? Properly understood, as Glass meant it, as the urbanization of intensified competition for the needs of urban life in an unequal world of colonization and capital, every aspect of this story documents the evolutionary essence of gentrification. Rising competition is pervasive. People compete with other people to find and keep a place to live: some wind up living in tents; some wind up living in 25,000-square-foot homes with ten-car garages and commuting by private jet; some live, a few blocks from where I write these words, on a tiny social assistance housing allowance in a dilapidated single room occupancy hotel (SRO) on the verge of collapse, under constant threat of eviction by a slum-landlord family that embodies the very best Canadian multicultural promises of non-European, non-White upward mobility: the family's real estate holdings are assessed at more than C$130 million (Colebourn, 2016), all of it, like all property in this city, built on the stolen, unceded ancestral territories of the Musqueam, Squamish, and Tsleil-Waututh peoples. People compete with other people to succeed, to get a spot on the *Forbes World Billionaires* ranking, or the *Hurun Rich List*: Chen Mailin dropped out of high school and failed in his first venture, a duck farm, but he worked to achieve success in construction and development – his Nanjing Dingye Investment Group is a hybrid of the molecular *neoliberalism* and state-capitalist *neo-dirigisme* that Lefebvre (1970, pp. 78ff.) analyzed in the fields, levels, and dimensions of the production of urban space, and a relational place-making approach now helps us understand the multiple epistemologies of overlapping transnational fields of urban social space (Pierce and Martin, 2015). People compete for jobs, and people must also compete with investors pushing CEOs to cut the "headcount" and with non-human algorithms as Silicon Valley's evolutionary artificial-intelligence "singularity" obsessions (Bostrom, 2014) gradually fulfill Thatcher's dreams of an obedient, miniaturized robotic workforce. And Chen Mailin's praise for Vancouver's "best education for kids" only makes sense when we appreciate how the next generation of people are forced into ever more intense competition in an increasingly competitive transnational educational field (Ley, 2010, pp. 207–213). "Western decay" has become a powerful postcolonial meme to inspire entrepreneurs and tiger-parents, and the PRC's *gaokao* is ruthlessly effective in producing *you xiu ren* ("excellent people"): "Raising the quality of the population was important if China were to catch up to the West and possibly even surpass the United States," an informant tells the anthropologist Susanne Bregnbaek; yet "decay" has its humanistic merits compared to the proliferation of suicides at elite Mainland universities that has become a "public secret" (Bregnbaek, 2011, p. 20). As I read Glass's warnings of Social Darwinist urbanism and Keynes's praise for Carr-Saunders's production of "quality" people like Hayek, I think of the kind, brilliant undergraduate who showed me across campus on my way to deliver a lecture at a university in Shanghai; as we strolled through the crowds chatting about student life, she casually pointed out the tall building on campus where students who couldn't cope with the pressure jumped to their deaths during exam season.

Eugenicist thought and policy is now transnational and cosmopolitan, from the evolutionary justifications for Western neoliberalism peddled by the Hayek-Prize-winning Matt Ridley (2010), to the variegated fusions of Social Darwinism with non-Western cultural histories and nationalist projects in Asia (Chung, 2014). As it was 50 years ago, gentrification is the urbanization of colonialist Social Darwinist competition, and our research agenda must be to expose and challenge the implicit eugenicist logics of urban economics and politics – which today mask a machinery of accelerating competition behind the sunny promises of creativity, diversity, and multicultural meritocracy. We need to continue Smith's (1982, 2011) unfinished project, to integrate Clark and Clark's (2012) insights on participation in our own evolution with Harvey's (2011) comprehensive model of "coevolutionary" capitalism, to advance Boggs and Boggs's (1974) evolutionary humanist project of becoming more kind, compassionate, and egalitarian.

References

Abercrombie, Patrick (1945). *Greater London Plan 1944: A Report Prepared on Behalf of the Standing Conference on London Regional Planning*. London: HMSO.

Allen, Samantha (2014). "San Francisco's Gay Culture Is Dying." *The Daily Dot*, 31 October.

Angner, Erik (2007). *Hayek and Natural Law*. New York: Routledge.

Atkinson, Rowland, and Gary Bridge, eds (2005). *The New Urban Colonialism: Gentrification in a Global Context*. London: Routledge.

Beauregard, Robert A. (1986). "The Chaos and Complexity of Gentrification." In Neil Smith and Peter Williams, eds, *Gentrification of the City*. London: Allen & Unwin, 35–55.

Bernt, Matthias (2016). "Very Particular, or Rather Universal? Gentrification through the Lenses of Ghertner and Lopez-Morales." *City*, 7 April, advance online publication.

Bondi, Liz (1999). "Between the Woof and the Weft: A Response to Loretta Lees." *Environment and Planning D: Society and Space* 17(3), 253–255.

Boggs, James, and Grace Lee Boggs (1974). *Revolution and Evolution in the Twentieth Century*. New York: Monthly Review Press.

Bostrom, Nick (2014). *Superintelligence: Paths, Dangers, Strategies*. Oxford: Oxford University Press.

Bregnbaek, Susanne (2011). "A Public Secret: Education for Quality and Suicide among Chinese Elite University Students." *Learning and Teaching* 4(3), 18–36.

CBC News (2015). "Vancouver Mansion Sells for More than $51M." *CBC News*, 10 March.

Chung, Yuehtsen Juliette (2014). "Better Science and Better Race? Social Darwinism and Chinese Eugenics." *Isis* 105(4), 793–802.

Clark, Thomas L., and Eric Clark (2012). "Participation in Evolution and Sustainability." *Transactions of the Institute of British Geographers* NS37, 563–577.

Colebourn, John (2016). "They Thought I Was Going to Back Down and Leave: Tenant Who's Owed $1,675 by His Multimillionaire Landlord Stands Up for His Rights." *The Province*, 10 July, 10–12.

Cutler, Kim-Mai (2014). "Zynga Buys NaturalMotion for $527M, Signaling a New Tack for the Gaming Giant." *Techcrunch*, 30 January.

Edwards, Cliff (2014). "Zynga Buys NaturalMotion to Bolster Mobile, Cut Staff." *Bloomberg*, 31 January.

Entrikin, J. Nicholas (1980). "Robert Park's Human Ecology and Human Geography." *Annals of the Association of American Geographers* 70(1), 43–58.

Foucault, Michel (1969). "What Is an Author?" In Paul Rabinow and Nikolas Rose, eds (2003), *The Essential Foucault*. New York: New Press, 377–391.

Galton, Francis (1869). *Hereditary Genius: An Inquiry Into its Laws and Consequences*. London: Richard Clay and Sons.

Ghertner, D. Asher (2015). "Why Gentrification Theory Fails 'In Much of the World.'" *City* 19(4), 552–563.

Glass, Ruth (1962). "Insiders/Outsiders: The Position of Minorities." *New Left Review* I/17, Winter, 34–45.

Glass, Ruth (1963). "Centre for Urban Studies." *Town Planning Review* 34(3), 169–184.

Glass, Ruth (1964). "Introduction." In Centre for Urban Studies, ed., *London: Aspects of Change*. London: McKibben & Gee, xii–xlii.

Glass, Ruth (1970). "Changing Urban Problems in Developed Countries." Discussion paper for WHO meeting on "Health Effects of Urbanization." Reprinted in Ruth Glass (1989). *Clichés of Urban Doom*. Oxford: Basil Blackwell, 98–105.

Glass, Ruth (1989). "Introduction." In *Clichés of Urban Doom*. Oxford: Basil Blackwell, vii–xxii.

Harris, Andrew (2008). "From London to Mumbai and Back Again: Gentrification and Public Policy in Comparative Perspective." *Urban Studies* 45(12), 2407–2428.

Harvey, David (2011). *The Enigma of Capital and the Crises of Capitalism*. Oxford: Oxford University Press.

Healy, Kieran (2016). "Fuck Nuance." *Sociological Theory*, January, early online publication.

Keynes, John Maynard (1946). "The Galton Lecture, 1946: Presentation of the Society's Gold Medal." *Eugenics Review* 38(1), 39–42.

LaPorte, Nicole (2013). "Meet Former Xbox Boss Don Mattrick, Who Just Left Microsoft to Turn around Zynga." *Fast Company*, July 2.

Lees, Loretta (2012). "The Geography of Gentrification: Thinking through Comparative Urbanism." *Progress in Human Geography* 36(2), 155–171.

Lees, Loretta, Hyun Bang Shin, and Ernesto Lopez-Morales, eds. (2015). *Global Gentrifications: Uneven Development and Displacement*. Bristol: Policy Press.

Lees, Loretta, Tom Slater, and Elvin Wyly, eds. (2010). *The Gentrification Reader*. New York: Routledge.

Lefebvre, Henri (1970). *The Urban Revolution*. Translated by Robert Bononno, 2003 edition. Minneapolis, MN: University of Minnesota Press.

Ley, David (2010). *Millionaire Migrants: Trans-Pacific Life Lines*. Chichester, UK: Wiley-Blackwell.

Ley, David, and Sin-Yih Teo (2013). "Gentrification in Hong Kong? Epistemology vs. Ontology." *International Journal of Urban and Regional Research* 38(4), 1286–1303.

Maloutas, Thomas (2011). "Contextual Diversity in Gentrification Research." *Critical Sociology* 38(1), 33–48.

Ong, Aihwa (2011). "Introduction: Worlding Cities, or the Art of Being Global." In Ananya Roy and Aihwa Ong, eds., *Worlding Cities: Asian Experiments and the Art of Being Global*. Chichester, UK: Wiley-Blackwell, 1–26.

Palen, John, and Bruce London, eds. (1984). *Gentrification, Displacement, and Neighborhood Revitalization*. Albany, NY: State University of New York Press.

Parnell, Susan, and Sophie Oldfield (2014). "From the South." In Parnell and Oldfield, eds., *The Routledge Handbook on Cities of the Global South*. New York: Routledge, 1–4.

Pearson, Karl, and Margaret Moul (1927). "The Mathematics of Intelligence: The Sampling Errors in the Theory of a Generalised Factor." *Biometrika* 19(3/4), 246–291.

Pierce, Joseph, and Deborah Martin (2015). "Placing Lefebvre." *Antipode* 47(5), 1279–1299.

Rafferty, Kevin (2015). "What Universities in Hong Kong and the Rest of China Can Learn from Oxford." *South China Morning Post*, 28 December.

Ren, Julie (2015). "Gentrification in China?" In Loretta Lees, Hyun Bang Shin, and Ernesto Lopez-Morales, eds., *Global Gentrifications: Uneven Development and Displacement*. Bristol: Policy Press, 329–347.

Ridley, Matt (2010). *The Rational Optimist: How Prosperity Evolves*. New York: HarperCollins.

Roy, Ananya (forthcoming). "Dis/Possessive Collectivism: Property and Personhood at City's End." *Geoforum*.

Rusli, Evelyn M., and Shira Ovide (2013). "Zynga Founder Mark Pincus Hands CEO Job to Don Mattrick." *Wall Street Journal*, July 1.

Sassen, Saskia (1991). *The Global City: New York, London, and Tokyo*. Princeton, NJ: Princeton University Press.

Schafran, Alex (2014). "Debating Urban Studies in 23 Steps." *City* 18(3), 321–330.

Slater, Tom (2015). "Planetary Rent Gaps." *Antipode*, DOI:10.1111/anti.12185.

Smith, Neil (1982). "Gentrification and Uneven Development." *Economic Geography* 58(2), 139–155.

Smith, Neil (2011). "The Evolution of Gentrification." In J. Berg, T. Kaminer, M. Schoonerbeek, and J. Zonneveld, eds, *Houses in Transformation: Interventions in European Gentrification*. Rotterdam: NAi Publishers, 15–26.

Song, Weixuan, and Qiyan Wu (2010). "Gentrification and Residential Differentiation in Nanjing, China." *Chinese Geographical Science* 20(6), 568–576.

Witham, Larry (2002). *Where Darwin Meets the Bible: Creationists and Evolutionists in America*. Oxford: Oxford University Press.

Young, Ian (2015). "Former Duck Farmer Revealed as Buyer of US$40 Million Vancouver Mansion." *South China Morning Post*, 19 March.

10 Suburbs

Bernadette Hanlon

World population growth in upcoming decades will take place in urban regions of all sizes (Hardoy, Mitlin and Satterthwaite, 2001). Future urban population growth will also occur in the metropolitan periphery due, in part, to rural-to-urban migration but also because of the annexation and reclassification of peripheral land as part of the urban (Cohen, 2004; Forsyth, 2014). Recent research examines the metropolitan periphery by taking stock of suburban spaces across a variety of global urban regions (e.g. Clapson and Hutchison, 2010; Hamel and Keil, 2015). Examinations of global suburbs and processes of global suburbanization have both empirical and theoretical significance to our understanding of urban life around the world.

The recent global reach of suburban studies includes an examination of the suburban experience in nations of Africa (e.g. Buire, 2014a), Latin America (e.g. Audirac et al., 2012; Herzog, 2014) and Asia (e.g. Wu and Phelps, 2008) as well as within the North American and European contexts (e.g. Hanlon, Short and Vicino, 2010; Harris, 2015; Phelps, 2015). This literature informs us about the varied forms of global suburbanisms, and the more recent emergence of new landscapes of profound socio-spatial differentiation in peripheral parts of the urban world.

In this chapter, I outline three specific areas for the future study of global suburbs. The first concerns the measurement and processes of suburban sprawl and its associated challenges. The visible aspects of urban growth focus on the dramatic expansion across the globe of the built environment far out into the peripheral reaches of urban areas. Suburbanization as low-density and sprawling is a signature feature. The second concerns the transformation and evolution of the American suburb in ways that call into question the use of the U.S. suburban model as, in the words of Ekers, Hamel and Keil (2012, p. 409), "the paradigmatic case . . . that other cases must be measured against." Global suburbs are defined many times as American exportations, and yet the American suburban experience has itself changed dramatically in the past 40 years. Third, this latter point leads to a discussion about the need to recognize and further investigate the ways in which global suburban transformations undermine the typical "city versus suburbs" model of urban regions. This traditional metropolitan model is increasingly challenged by recent shifts in suburban conditions across the globe. We need to understand this process.

Measurement and processes of suburban sprawl

When defining the global suburb, scholars have suggested a few common attributes with one of the most prominent concerning the physical feature of density. Suburbs are typically defined by their low-density development. In an excellent chapter in the book *Suburbanization in Global Society*, Richard Harris (2010, p.29) states that, "suburbs usually display residential densities that are intermediate between those of the city and the country." Certainly in the United States, Australia and parts of Latin America this is the case with much low-density residential development spreading for many miles outside of much denser cities. Yet, as Harris recognizes, suburban tower block housing in Western and Eastern European countries as well as Russia means density can be reversed, with suburbs expressing higher housing densities than their city counterparts. In France, the massive suburban concrete apartment complexes in certain *banlieues* outside Paris, for instance, tower above the city core (Cupers, 2014). Housing densities in the suburbs can vary from nation to nation. I will come back to this question of density later.

Another physical characteristic scholars apply to suburbs is their newness. Ann Forsyth (2014, p.261) suggests that, "[suburbs] are new in the sense of most of their fabric having been built since widespread use of automobiles, motorcycles, motorized buses, and trucks." The newness, in many respects, stems from the ability of the suburban landscape to continuously expand spatially and shift outward to the metropolitan edge (Keil, 2013), in part because of the use of motorized vehicles. Certainly an element of this story is the sheer extent of urban limits.

Sprawl is often characterized as a worldwide condition synonymous with the suburbanization process. Yet, it is important to note that much of the empirical research on sprawl and its impacts is focused on the U.S. context. With U.S. metropolitan regions as the backdrop, this research examines the negative environmental impacts of sprawl (Johnson, 2001), its public health effects (Frumkin, Frank and Jackson, 2004), the social and public costs of this type of development, the processes that lead to sprawl (Squires, 2002), and how best to measure it. On this last point, density is seen as one way to gauge sprawl, often measured using population, households or residential development per square mile. However, in recent years researchers have employed much more sophisticated multidimensional frameworks to depict various dimensions of sprawl in the U.S. context including, beyond density, such measures as the degree to which development is close to the central business district (CBD) or the degree to which development is continuous rather than broken up (e.g. Cutsinger et al., 2005; Galster et al., 2001).

Sprawl indices rank metropolitan areas in the United States from the most compact to the most sprawling. One example combines a number of variables into a few factors representing density, land use mix, the degree of centrality or strength of activity centers and downtown, and street connectedness (Ewing, Pendall and Chen, 2003). Later work added walkability data (Ewing and Hamidi, 2014). Surprisingly, in these studies, scholars found that Los Angeles, often described as a quintessential sprawling region, is actually reasonably compact. Measuring sprawl is complicated, and sophisticated calculations can bring surprising results.

Suburbs of different city regions across the globe vary in density; so it seems necessary to investigate what suburban sprawl might be like in different contexts, how we ought to measure it, what its effects are on the environment and people of different global regions, and why it is happening. Let us consider the measurement issue. Accurately measuring sprawl in a variety of city regions across the globe is a difficult task. First, there are definitional problems. Measuring sprawl begins with delineating urban areas. As Cohen (2004, p. 25) notes, the definition of what constitutes the urban varies from country to country, challenging comparative work. Brenner and Schmid (2014) describe in detail the somewhat arbitrary nature of empirical measures of the urban, and note that many countries frequently change their official urban classifications in ways that make it difficult to determine the urban population. Second, there is a lack of reliable demographic data for cities, within the global urban system (Short et al., 1996), and particularly for those smaller cities with less than 750,000 residents (Cohen, 2004) and located in low-income countries (Montgomery, 2010).

In recent decades, there have been some exciting developments in the use of remote sensing data to more accurately measure suburban sprawl across a range of urban regions, with the potential to make comparisons and better understand the impacts. Remote sensing data can avoid the problem of relying on changing classification systems or inadequate demographic data in certain urban regions by instead measuring the percentage of impervious surfaces in a given area. Through these measurements, comparisons can be made and impacts measured, albeit with a degree to understanding the intensity of land use in a given location.

Using remote sensing data on land cover, Schneider and Woodcock (2008), for example, examined sprawl in 25 cities across different parts of the world including North America, Latin America, Europe, Africa and Asia, investigating specifically the size of the built-up areas within these cities, the rate of change in the built-up areas, the density of built land, the fragmentation of built land, and the population per square kilometer of built land, and how this has changed over time. Their study period was from 1990 to 2000. Focusing, for instance, on the rate of spatial expansion, this research found that two Chinese cities in the sample experienced between a 36 percent and 50 percent increase in their built environment during the 1990s. In addition, a rather diverse set of cities including Bangalore, Brasilia, Ankara and Chengdu experienced the most rapid change.

Among the 25 cities, Schneider and Woodcock (2008, p. 682) found four possible "city types." These types include *frantic-growth cities, high-growth cities, low-growth cities* and *expansive-growth cities*. The *frantic-growth* cities, as the name suggests, experienced rapid land conversion and fragmented patterns of urban development. *High-growth cities* similar, only the speed of change was not as intense. The *low-growth cities* experienced more infill development than other cities, keeping these cities compact by comparison to other cities. Schneider and Woodcock categorized the U.S. cities as *expansive-growth cities*, impressive in size with nearly three times the spatial extent than other cities in the study. They (2008, p.683) state, "expansive-growth cities show sustained increases in urban land in both the periphery and hinterland rings (the two outermost rings), a trend which is not apparent in the majority of the sample cities." Sprawl maybe a bigger problem in the United States than other nations.

Accurate measures of sprawl can determine the exact extent and nature of sprawl in different city regions and identify its effects on the environment, people and economies. In China, for instance, cities like Beijing have witnessed intense urban growth, some in the form of peripheral development that is low-density, occurring in a fragmented piecemeal fashion, and consuming agricultural land at a rapid pace (Jiang et al., 2007). Some research suggests that suburban sprawl in Beijing has led to the increased use of automobiles and trip distance (Zhao, 2010). There is much concern that an emerging auto-centric lifestyle in China will continue to greatly impact CO_2 emissions (Yan and Crookes, 2009) and, as a result, global climate. Recognizing the problem of climate change, we need to investigate and conduct meta-analyses to determine the effects across a broad range of global city regions.

In addition, we need to determine the reasons for sprawl. In a recent review article, Mabin, Butcher and Bloch (2013, p.171) note that one of the aspects of contemporary suburbanization in Africa is what they refer to as "the moving urban frontier," largely in the form of suburban sprawl, with some African cities (e.g. Ado-Ekiti in Nigeria) better able to contain edge development than others (e.g. Dar es Salaam with its high levels of car ownership). In a recent article on suburbanization around Durban in South Africa, Todes (2014) suggests that development in Durban's eThekwini municipality is contained and controlled by one large landowner while growth is much more fragmented and rapid in nearby KwaDukuza because land has multiple owners each seeking to profit from sprawl. Different patterns of sprawl are driven, in part, by differences in local landowning structures.

Explanations of sprawl in the United States often emphasize people's rejection of the city for the suburbs, and there is an assumption that suburban living is a personal choice (Harris, 2010). This differs, say, from the Chinese case. As Zhou and Logan (2008, p.156) note, two-thirds of all moves from the city to the suburbs in China were involuntary. In addition, as scholars of African suburbanism note, the emphasis is on approaching the city from the periphery rather than moving from the city to the periphery. In many parts of the world, suburban settlers come from the countryside with the goal of ending their journey in the city (Harris, 2010). Measuring and explaining the ways in which suburban expansion occurs (or does not occur) in different urban regions should be part of a suburban research agenda that raises more general questions: Are there universal forces causing peripheral urban expansion across the globe? What are the particularities that can create different types of suburban expansion in different global city regions, and can they be classified into meaningful comparisons?

It is necessary to investigate both universal forces shaping suburban sprawl and the particularities of this process.

Beyond the American-style suburb

Historically, the American suburbs have oscillated from their characterization during the turn of the nineteenth into the twentieth century as bourgeois utopias (Fishman, 1989) and arcadian solutions to the malaise of the industrial city to, by the 1950s and 1960s, being portrayed as bland, homogenous, soulless places (see Modarres and Kirby, 2010). The latest version of suburban dystopia focuses on global suburbs as American-style creations. This has some purchase in reality since so-called U.S.-style suburbia has been exported to different parts of the world (Fishman, 2002; Leichenko and Solecki, 2005). In a recent book, *Global Suburbs: Urban Sprawl from the Rio Grande to Rio de Janeiro*, Lawrence Herzog (2014, p.129) describes the "nature of the new periphery" forming at the edge of Latin American cities, for instance, as a form of American-style suburbanization "driven by a set of values that include: social exclusivity, an increasing desire for private over public space, fear of crime, a preference for predictable, homogenous built environments, and a greater emphasis on consumerism and shopping within artificially constructed spaces." In his work, Herzog (2014) defines the suburbs by certain sociocultural characteristics, critically assessed as conformist, consumer-driven and isolated in ways that are peculiarly American.

Yet, there are two problems with defining global suburbs by an American prototype. First, the U.S. suburban experience itself has changed dramatically in the past 40 years and, in fact, there has been much recent research exploring both the historic and contemporary heterogeneity of the American suburbs (e.g. Kruse and Sugrue, 2006; Mikelbank, 2004). Within the U.S. metropolitan experience, there is a need to recognize that, in reality, there is no traditional American suburban model but rather the remnants of a postwar suburban ideal where, at a point in time, white middle-class Americans were secure and comfortable in ways they deemed entitled to (Lassiter, 2006). In many respects, the traditional American suburb is an imagined space, a moment, if you like, in the constantly evolving and restless suburban landscape (Knox, 1991). Suburbs in the U.S. are highly diverse.

The second problem with defining global suburbs by a U.S. model is that the term "suburb" has different meanings in different places. Yes, in the Anglo-American world, suburbs might conjure up images of middle-class residential neighborhoods. But, in France, for instance, suburbs – *les banlieues* – denote dense working-class and state-planned immigrant Muslim communities (Harris, 2010). In Brazil, *subúrbio* acts as an "imprecise expression used everywhere to indicate the quarters (*bairros*) which do not appear on maps and are usually forgotten by public authorities" (see Mabin, Butcher and Bloch, 2013, p.169). In colonial parts of Africa, *subúrbios* typify white-planned "cement city" juxtaposed against informal African settlements on the periphery (Jenkins, 2009, p.90). In China, "suburb" can mean an exclusive gated community, distinguished from the *danwei* work-unit developments on the metropolitan fringe (Harris, 2010). The terms themselves denote and stress the social division and complexity of peripheral space.

When we think about the periphery in the Global South, we tend to think of haphazard squatter settlements. As Harris (2010) points out, squatter settlements are rarely described as suburbs. Should we reconsider this characterization? It could be argued that these places are part of a self-built suburban space. Roger Keil (2013, p. 9), in his book *Suburban Constellations*, advocates for the use of "a simple definition of suburbanization as the combination of an increase in non-central city population and economic activity, as well as urban spatial expansion." A flexible and broad definition enables the addition of many different elements of suburban development into the discussion. As Ann Forsyth (2012, p. 277) suggests, the global reality of "suburban public housing estates, industrial worker suburbs, and self-built suburbs (including squatter settlements, shanty towns, mobile home parks, and low-cost subdivisions) . . . make it hard to defend a view of suburbs as essentially white and affluent." The complexity of global suburbanisms undermines the traditional view of the global suburb as merely a middle-class, American-style creation.

Undermining the traditional metropolitan model

The traditional U.S. model of a homogenous ring of suburbs juxtaposed against an ever-depressed core city has been undermined by changing demographics, recent evidence of suburban poverty, continued expansion of economic activities in the metropolitan fringe, and gentrification of the city (Hanlon, Vicino and Short, 2006). In their recent article on the Miami suburbs, Nijman and Clery (2015, p. 86) suggest that, "dichotomous thinking that pervades much work on suburbanization (suburb versus central city, rich versus poor, White versus Black, sparse versus dense, residential versus mixed functions) is out of sync with evolving metropolitan constellations." Typical dichotomous thinking in the context of metropolitan areas in the Global South (city versus periphery, rich versus poor, planned versus unplanned, mixed functions versus residential) is similarly out of step with emerging realities. In this section, I focus on two processes that undermine the traditional model of the suburban realm. The first concerns the juxtaposition between zones of wealth and places of poverty. The second considers shifts in the suburban economy.

The outer reaches of metropolitan areas of the Global South are often defined by squatter settlements, a "planet of slums" (Davis, 2007). Yet, evidence of contestation has emerged in the periphery as the demand for land for more affluent and luxurious suburbs has increased. An important dimension of growing suburban affluence is the emergence of gated communities. In their work on suburban governance, Ekers, Hamel and Keil (2012, p. 416) refer to these gated communities as "privatized authoritarian forms of governance." As scholars have documented, gating is a global phenomenon, long established as an important urban form in

Latin America and South Africa, but since the 1990s growing in prominence in North America, Europe, China and South Asia. Atkinson and Blandy (2006) suggest that the rise of gated communities reinforces a trend toward a more polarized metropolis, particularly as the middle-classes withdraw from the public realm and embrace more privatized forms of governance and a growing privatized security infrastructure. The rise of gated suburban communities highlights a differentiated global suburban landscape.

In the periphery, then, there is a mix of poor settlements alongside more prosperous places. This is not necessarily a recent occurrence. As in other colonized cities, in Nairobi in Kenya, for example, suburban tract housing was laid out for the privileged white settlers. Many early planned suburban settlements had long-lasting effects as adjacent squatter settlements emerged around them to create a "land use mosaic" of planned and unplanned areas that continues to shape many African cities today (Kironde, 2007, p. 115). Colonial suburbanization in the form of "pseudo-suburban" South African townships was built on an Anglo-model of detached or semi-detached houses and a yard, with reliance on motorized vehicles as the form of transportation (Freund, 2007, p. 126). These places helped in the rise of an African home-owning middle-class (Freund, 2007).

In recent times in certain city regions, a suburban dichotomy arises with the insertion of suburban affluence in an otherwise poor periphery. In the context of other regions, particularly in the Anglo-American context, variegation occurs because of the rise of suburban poverty. In the United States, for example, there is increasing evidence that poverty is now more decentralized than in the past. According to a recent study by Brookings Institution scholars Elizabeth Kneebone and Alan Berube (2014), the largest and fastest-growing poor population in the United States is located in suburbs. In their work, they found that more than half the metropolitan poor lived in suburban rather than urban communities in 2005. In a recent study, Paul Hunter (2014) found that between 2001 and 2011 there was an increase in the number of suburban areas in England and Wales that experienced greater than average poverty concentrations. This study found that in a number of cities including Liverpool, London, Manchester, Sheffield and others, the suburbs became poorer relative to the inner city over the same time period. In a separate study for Scotland, Kavanagh, Lee and Pryce (2014) also found a growing prevalence of suburban poverty in the outskirts of the cities of Glasgow and Clyde.

In the case of the United States, immigration, changes in housing policy aimed at deconcentrating poverty in the inner city, the foreclosure crisis, and the overall effects of the Great Recession are explained as possible reasons for poverty shifts (Kneebone and Berube, 2014) but there is little empirical work to identify more specifically the causes of increased suburban poverty. For instance, are some suburbs experiencing increased poverty because poor people from gentrifying inner-city neighborhoods are being displaced to declining inner-ring suburbs? The dynamics between city gentrification and suburban poverty is an area ripe for future research.

In some instances, suburbs have become poorer places as a result of deindustrialization. Within the urban studies literature, much research considers the impact of deindustrialization on the economic health of cities. Far less work examines the impact on suburbs. The traditional model emphasizes a residential suburbia when in fact the suburbs are sites for much economic activity. Heavy industry was located in the suburbs of many cities in the United States and Europe from at least the nineteenth century. Two industrial suburbs of Dundalk and Edgemere outside Baltimore City are classic examples. They are traditional working-class neighborhoods that grew around the Bethlehem Steel plant built close by in the 1850s. Beginning about the 1970s, both industrial suburbs witnessed increased poverty and overall disinvestment as a result of the loss of manufacturing jobs (Hanlon and Vicino, 2007).

Industrial suburbs in a variety of regions of the world have been similarly impacted. A comparative study of industrial suburbs of Europe and Latin America found similar dynamics to those found in Baltimore. Examining Govan outside Glasgow, Saint Denis outside Paris, Sao Caetano do Sol outside Sao Paulo and Guadalajar in Mexico, Audirac et al. (2012) describe the impacts of post-Fordist economic restructuring on industrial suburbs of very different parts of the world. The European suburbs, like their North American counterparts, lost out to newly industrializing spaces in the Global South. In the Latin American context, newly industrial countries such as Brazil and Mexico have abandoned their Fordist Import Substitution Industrialization (ISI) for urban peripheries that are receiving offshore or outsourced manufacturing. In the article, the emphasis is on the growth of manufacturing in China. Audriac et al. (2012, p.239) state:

> from the earliest Parisian steel and textile suburb of Saint Denis and Glasgow's shipyard burgh of Govan, to São Paulo's São Caetano automobile industrial suburb and El Salto, Guadalajara's first industrial suburban corridor, one can see many similarities: varying levels of shrinkage and growth spurred by competition for foreign investment; resultant gentrification and displacement from the pressure to redevelop the most profitable sites; unemployment from deindustrialization with dwindling public welfare safety net; declining support for public housing and provision of affordable housing; and relatively large populations of poor immigrants attracted by cheap or dilapidated housing.

In city regions of the Global South, suburbs are sites for the concentration of new economic activities (Mabin, Butcher and Bloch, 2013). Expansive decentralization of service-based economic functions to the periphery of city regions has occurred in various countries across the globe, since at least the 1980s. Multiple business districts alongside large-scale shopping malls outside of cities in Africa and Asia, for instance, stand out as similar exemplars of edge cities. In Johannesburg, consider the massive growth of the edge city of Sandton. In Tanzania, consider the large-scale mall in Mlimani City outside Dar es Saleem, or in the case of Kuala Lumpur in Malaysia, the suburban city of Subang Jaya. In a European context, think of Croydon outside London or Sandyford Industrial Estate in the suburbs of Dublin. In every continent, service-based economic activity has shifted outward from the city to create new suburban cities and towns.

Lawrence Herzog (2014) examines the ways in which high profile corporate and residential developments were planned and built in Mexico and Brazil largely in the 1980s and 1990s. He highlights Santa Fe outside Mexico City as an example. This suburban city is home to the headquarters of such transnational companies as Hewlett Packard, General Motors, IBM, Goodyear, Pepsi, Federal Express and Kraft. Mexico's own corporate giants such as Cuervo, Sauza, Televisa and Bimbo have also moved there. Architects such as Ricardo Legorreta were brought in to develop a master plan, and others to design key buildings (Herzog, 2014, p. 140). In the context of the Global South, the traditional metropolitan model compares "planned areas to spontaneous developments, urbanised core to non-serviced peripheries" (Buire, 2014b, p. 242). The evolution of highly planned edge cities and suburban towns in the Global South undermines the notion of the periphery as an unplanned and spontaneous space with few services relative to the city core.

In his book *Postmetropolis*, Edward Soja (2000) noted that the contemporary U.S. city had become highly complex and polarized. Using Los Angeles as an example, he described it as a fractal city with intense inequalities or "metropolarities," focusing on the sharp ethnic divisions and segregated city spaces. The traditional model is undermined by the emergence of a sharp social division of suburban space in city regions of both the Global North and the Global South. In the context of the United States, for example, suburban poverty is on the rise, undermining the notion of the suburbs as sites of success. In other contexts, suburban affluence has emerged in a poor periphery.

A research agenda for suburbs

There are a number of themes within the global suburban literature that pinpoint great changes occurring in the metropolis. First, sprawl, or what Mabin, Butcher and Bloch (2013, p. 171) refer to as "the moving urban frontier," is a global phenomenon. Suburban growth in the form of low-density, car dependent development is evident in many nations across the globe. Yet, there is the need for a more comprehensive examination of the extent and nature of sprawl in different contexts, particularly in light of varied classifications of the urban and challenges with acquiring accurate demographic data to truly measure this form of urban expansion. There is also the need to subsequently determine the environmental, social and political impacts of sprawl in different contexts and under different regimes. This is an important research agenda for suburbs.

Second, global suburbs have been defined as American-style creations. Yet the notion of an American suburban prototype is being undermined by profound changes in the U.S. metropolis. As much recent work suggests, the American suburbs are highly diverse. There is a need to move beyond a definition of the global suburb against an imagined American suburban ideal. Research aimed at building a deeper understanding of the diversity of global suburbs is a step in this direction. There is a major international research collaboration entitled *Global*

Suburbanisms: Governance, Land and Infrastructure in the 21st Century housed in the City Institute of York University in Toronto, Canada that brings together some fifty researchers from around the world to investigate processes of suburbanization. Such collaborations can help understand as well as move beyond the American suburban experience.

Third, the changes taking place in different city regions across the globe call into question the traditional model of metropolitan areas. As we proceed with global suburban investigations, it will be increasingly necessary to determine how we might characterize suburbs, and what ways they are changing and why. The periphery of urban regions across the globe is now divided between places of affluence and places of poverty. There are certainly middle-class suburbs across the globe, but they exist alongside much poorer constellations. I suggest that we need to further define suburban space and investigate the processes underlying recent suburban transformations, particularly in light of profound social segregation and shifting functional aspects of the suburban realm within the metropolitan economy.

References

Atkinson, Rowland and Sarah Blandy (eds.) (2006), *Gated Communities: International Perspectives*, London and New York: Routledge.

Audirac, I., E. Cunningham-Sabot, S. Fol and S. Torres Moraes (2012), 'Declining suburbs in Europe and Latin America', *International Journal of Urban and Regional Research*, **36** (2), 226–244.

Brenner, N. and C. Schmid (2014), 'The "urban age" in question', *International Journal of Urban and Regional Research*, **38** (3), 731–755.

Buire, C. (2014a), 'The dream and the ordinary: an ethnographic investigation of suburbanisation in Luanda', *African Studies*, **73** (2), 290–312.

Buire, C. (2014b), 'Suburbanisms in Africa? Spatial growth and social transformation in new urban peripheries: introduction to the cluster', *African Studies*, **73** (2), 241–244.

Clapson, Mark and Ray Hutchison (eds.) (2010), *Suburbanization in Global Society*, Bingley, U.K.: Emerald Group Publishing.

Cohen, B. (2004), 'Urban growth in developing countries: a review of current trends and a caution regarding existing forecasts', *World Development*, **32** (1), 23–51.

Cupers, Kenny (2014), *The Social Project: Postwar Housing in France*, Boston, MA: MIT Press.

Cutsinger, J., G. Galster, H. Wolman, R. Hanson and D. Towns (2005), 'Verifying the multi-dimensional nature of metropolitan land use: advancing the understanding and measurement of sprawl', *Journal of Urban Affairs*, **27** (3), 235–259.

Davis, Mike (2007), *Planet of Slums*, New York: Verso.

Ekers, M., P. Hamel and R. Keil (2012), 'Governing suburbia: modalities and mechanisms of suburban governance', *Regional Studies*, **46** (3), 405–422.

Ewing, R. and S. Hamidi (2014), 'Smart growth America: measuring sprawl 2014', accessed February 21, 2016 at http://gis.cancer.gov/tools/urban-sprawl/.

Ewing, R., R. Pendall and D. Chen (2003), 'Measuring sprawl and its transportation impacts', *Transportation Research Record*, **1831**, 175–183.

Fishman, R. (1989), *Bourgeois Utopias: The Rise and Fall of Suburbia*, New York: Basic Books.

Fishman, R. (2002), 'Global suburbs', accessed February 9, 2016 at http://www-personal.umich.edu/~sdcamp/up540/Fishmanglobalsuburb.pdf.

Forsyth, A. (2012), 'Defining suburbs', *Journal of Planning Literature*, **27** (3), 270–281.

Forsyth, A. (2014), 'Global suburbia and the transition century: physical suburbs in the long term', *Urban Design International*, **19** (4), 259–273.

Freund, Bill (2007), *The African City: A History*, Cambridge: Cambridge University Press.

Frumkin, Howard, Lawrence Frank and Richard E. Jackson (2004), *Urban Sprawl and Public Health*, Washington, DC: Island Press.

Galster, G., R. Hanson, M. R. Ratcliffe, H. Wolman, S. Coleman and J. Freihage (2001), 'Wrestling sprawl to the ground: defining and measuring an elusive concept', *Housing Policy Debate*, **12** (4), 681–717.

Hamel, Pierre and Roger Keil (eds.) (2015), *Suburban Governance: A Global View*, Toronto, Canada: Toronto University Press.

Hanlon, B., and T. J. Vicino (2007), 'The fate of inner suburbs: evidence from metropolitan Baltimore', *Urban Geography*, **28** (3), 249–275.

Hanlon, Bernadette, John Rennie Short and Thomas J. Vicino (2010), *Cities and Suburbs: New Metropolitan Realities in the U.S.*, New York: Routledge.

Hanlon, B., T. Vicino and J. R. Short (2006), 'The new metropolitan reality in the US: rethinking the traditional model', *Urban Studies*, **43** (12), 2129–2143.

Hardoy, Jorge, Diana Mitlin and David Satterthwaite (2001), *Environmental Problems in an Urbanizing World: Finding Solutions for Cities in Africa, Asia, and Latin America*, London: Earthscan.

Harris, Richard (2010), 'Meaningful types in a world of suburbs', in Mark Clapson and Ray Hutchison (eds.), *Suburbanization in Global Society*, Bingley, UK: Emerald Group Publishing, pp. 15–47.

Harris, R. (2015), 'Using Toronto to explore three suburban stereotypes, and vice versa', *Environment and Planning A*, **47** (1), 30–49.

Herzog, Lawrence (2014), *Global Suburbs: Urban Sprawl from the Rio Grande to Rio de Janeiro*, New York: Routledge.

Hunter, P. (2014), 'Poverty in suburbia: a Smith Institute study into the growth of poverty in the suburbs of England and Wales', accessed March 4, 2016 at https://smithinstitutethinktank.files.wordpress.com/2014/09/poverty-in-suburbia.pdf.

Jenkins, Paul (2009), 'African cities: competing claims on urban land', in Francesa Locatelli and Paul Nugent (eds.), *African Cities: Competing Claims on Urban Spaces*, Leiden, The Netherlands: Brill, pp. 81–108.

Jiang, F., S. Liu, H. Yuan and Q. Zhang (2007), 'Measuring urban sprawl in Beijing with geo-spatial indices', *Journal of Geographical Sciences*, **17** (4), 469–478.

Johnson, M. P. (2001), 'Environmental impacts of urban sprawl: a survey of the literature and proposed research agenda', *Environment and Planning A*, **33** (4), 717–735.

Kavanagh, L., D. Lee and G. Pryce (2014), 'Poverty in suburbia: has Glasgow gone the way of American cities', accessed March 4, 2016 at https://www.aqmen.ac.uk/sites/default/files/RB5-poverty-suburbia.pdf.

Keil, Roger (ed.) (2013), *Suburban Constellations*, Berlin, Germany: Jovis Verlag GmbH.

Kironde, J. M. Lusugga (2007), 'Race, class and housing in Dar es Salaam: the colonial impact on land use structure, 1891–1961', in James Brennan, Yus Lawi and Andrew Burton (eds.), *Dar es Salaam: Histories from an Emerging African Metropolis*, Dar es Salaam: Mkuki na Nyota, pp. 97–117.

Kneebone, Elizabeth and Alan Berube (2014), *Confronting Suburban Poverty*, Washington, DC: Brookings Institution Press.

Knox, P. L. (1991), 'The restless urban landscape: economic and sociocultural change and the transformation of metropolitan Washington, DC', *Annals of the Association of American Geographers*, **81** (2), 181–209.

Kruse, Kevin and Thomas Sugrue (eds.) (2006), *The New Suburban History*, Chicago: University of Chicago Press.

Lassiter, Matthew (2006), *The Silent Majority: Suburban Politics in the Sunbelt South*, Princeton, NJ: Princeton University Press.

Leichenko, R. M. and W. D. Solecki (2005), 'Critical surveys', *Regional Studies*, **39**, 241–253.

Mabin, A., S. Butcher and R. Bloch (2013), 'Peripheries, suburbanisms and change in sub-Saharan African cities', *Social Dynamics*, **39** (2), 167–190.

Mikelbank, B. A. (2004), 'A typology of US suburban places', *Housing Policy Debate*, **15** (4), 935–964.

Modarres, A. and A. Kirby (2010), 'The suburban question: notes for a research program', *Cities*, **27** (2), 114–121.

Montgomery, Mark (2010), 'The demography of the urban transition: what we know and don't know', in George Martine, Gordon McGranahan, Mark Montgomery and Rogelio Fernandez-Castilla (eds.), *The New Global Frontier*, London: Earthscan, pp. 17–34.

Nijman, J. and T. Clery (2015), 'Rethinking suburbia: a case study of metropolitan Miami', *Environment and Planning A*, **47** (1), 69–88.

Phelps, Nicholas (2015), *Sequel to Suburbia: Glimpses of America's Postsuburban Future*, Cambridge, MA: MIT Press.

Schneider, A. and C. E. Woodcock (2008), 'Compact, dispersed, fragmented, extensive? A comparison of urban growth in twenty-five global cities using remotely sensed data, pattern metrics and census information', *Urban Studies*, **45** (3), 659–692.

Short, J. R., Y. Kim, M. Kuus and H. Wells (1996), 'The dirty little secret of world cities research: data problems in comparative analysis', *International Journal of Urban and Regional Research*, **20** (4), 697–717.

Soja, Edward (2000), *Postmetropolis: Critical Studies of Cities and Regions*, Hoboken, NJ: Wiley-Blackwell.

Squires, Gregory (2002), *Urban Sprawl: Causes, Consequences and Policy Responses*, Washington, DC: Urban Institute.

Todes, A. (2014), 'New African suburbanisation? Exploring the growth of the Northern Corridor of eThekwini/KwaDukuza', *African Studies*, **73** (2), 245–270.

Wu, F. and N. S. Phelps (2008), 'From suburbia to post-suburbia in China? Aspects of the transformation of the Beijing and Shanghai global city regions', *Built Environment*, **34** (4), 464–481.

Yan, X. and R. J. Crookes (2009), 'Reduction potentials of energy demand and GHG emissions in China's road transport sector', *Energy Policy*, **37** (2), 658–668.

Zhao, P. (2010), 'Sustainable urban expansion and transportation in a growing megacity: consequences of urban sprawl for mobility on the urban fringe of Beijing', *Habitat International*, **34** (2), 236–243.

Zhou, Yixing and John R. Logan (2008), 'Growth on the edge: the new Chinese metropolis', in John R. Logan (ed.), *Urban China in Transition*, Hoboken, NJ: Wiley-Blackwell, pp. 140–160.

11 The creative city

Tom Hutton

Introduction: interrogating the creative city discourse

In the present century the idea of the 'creative city' has risen to prominence within the discourses of urban studies, city planning and community development, across diverse sub-disciplines and fields. A markedly positivist interpretation celebrates the emergence of the 'creative city' as an altogether more vibrant successor to the intermediate services economy and sterile office landscapes of the late-twentieth-century 'postindustrial city', a view enunciated by writers such as Charles Landry, Franco Bianchini (Landry and Bianchini 1995) and most of all Richard Florida, with the last's *The Rise of the Creative Class* (2002) still regarded by some urbanists as a prescription for successful cities, despite its deeply problematic features (Peck 2005; Markusen 2006; Krätke 2011). In this ebullient reading of contemporary urbanism an injection of 'creativity' not only transforms the architecture, design values and built environment of the city, but also generates rewarding employment opportunities, animates the social spaces of the city, gives recognition to the city's cultural assets and identity, and inspires lively imaginaries for the purposes of place-making and marketing. There is a substantial literature that addresses the lead roles assigned to culture and creativity in urban regeneration strategies, not least in the revitalization of cities which have experienced deep industrial restructuring and decline (Evans 2001; Hutton 2008; Pratt 2009; Grodach and Silver 2013).

Creativity in its diverse forms represents an important feature of many twenty-first-century cities, exemplified by the inclusion of creative workers and cultural industries and institutions within the repertoire of global cities such as Paris, New York and London (GLA 2012). Peter Hall notably inserted a place for 'creative and cultural' industries in his model of 'major service clusters in the polycentric global city', along with the established specializations of 'finance and business services' and 'power and influence' (Hall 2000; 2006). In this reading 'culture' is part and parcel of the competitive advantage of global (or globalizing) cities: another element of external 'power projection' as well as comprising a key element of the internal space-economy of the metropolis.

For many individuals, creative work offers a rewarding and satisfying opportunity for securing livelihood as well as self-actualization, while entrepreneurs are active agents in the proliferation of creative business start-ups. The 'state' in its central and local government settings is increasingly engaged in promoting 'creativity' for a variety of symbolic purposes and more instrumental intentions, while non-governmental organizations (NGOs) among both 'advanced' and 'transitional' societies have in many cases brought 'culture' and 'creativity' to the foreground of community development. But far from offering a panacea to cities searching for a new economic vocation in an era of insistent competition and restructuring, a closer inspection of cultural economy programmes discloses a very mixed set of outcomes, replete with uneven development, dislocations and other negative externalities. And indeed the creative city as a trope of progressive urbanism is deeply imbued with conflicts and contradictions.

In this chapter I offer a selective review of the creative cities discourse, emphasizing the saliency of key arguments and debates, and including an acknowledgement of where culture intersects with the extended theorization of cities in the late modern era. In my view this approach takes in a broader set of concepts than the 'cultural economy', 'creative labour', and affiliated class connotations, although it assuredly encompasses features of each. This concise review sets up a deconstruction of the creative cities model, with focus on three signifying elements: first, the cultural economy of the city and its relations with the 'creative city' script; second, the qualities of space, landscape and the built environment as comprising the field (after Bourdieu) or habitus of creativity; and third, creativity as expressed at the neighbourhood level, including reference to recent work on the richness of 'everyday globalization' which reframes (and remixes) the 'local' in globalizing cities. I then offer some promising research directions for creative cities, including prospective theory-building as well as normative issues and policy directions.

Urban change and the creative city script: engagement with theory

Over the past quarter-century a cultural economy comprising a dynamic mélange of industries, institutions, labour and production networks has emerged as a key feature of urban-regional economies among both 'advanced' and 'transitional' societies. The emergence of the cultural economy and its apparent centrality to the fortunes of 'creative cities' suggests to more exuberant urbanists the rise of a 'creative class' exerting both cultural saliency and political influence as well as a high-level economic development opportunity which aligns with the pursuit of competitive advantage in attracting high-value labour, enterprise and investment capital (Florida 2002). Relatedly, a number of scholars have endorsed a culture-infused resurgence of the 'consumer city' (Glaeser, Kolko and Saiz 2001) – a successor to the industrial city of manufacturing and services production. In this view the classic advantages of the city as a locus of production have been swept away by a toxic mix of cost factors, destructive labour relations, industrial obsolescence and the alleged 'death of distance' produced by advances in digital communications, undermining the advantages of agglomeration economies for cities within national urban systems and circuits of trade and capital.

Taking the narrative further, the collapse of traditional manufacturing and allied industries, and the labour-shedding effects of competition and substitution of capital for labour in many service industries, combined with a rise of digitally infused cultural production industries and allied 'creative consumption', paves the way for the emergence of cities as 'entertainment machine' (Clark and Lloyd 2004), and contributes in ways large and small to what Harvard economist Edward Glaeser confidently proclaims as the 'triumph of the city' (Glaeser 2011). What these ebullient proclamations have in common is a selective reading of narratives which exalt the more positive features of growth and change which undoubtedly form part of the storyline, while underplaying the more trenchant social costs and dislocations.

To be sure, consumption and spectacle form important features of creative cities and the cultural economy. Performative features of cultural expression constitute important elements of the cultural economy, along with the myriad consumption industries and activities that serve locals, cultural tourists and other visitors, contributing to the idea of the 'convivial city'. But I contend that production constitutes the axial principle of the cultural economy of the city, as all expressions of creativity must be 'produced' in some way: within formal industrial production systems and enterprise systems (Hutton 2008); within informal networks of artists and other workers (Arthurs 2013); within temporary 'project ecologies' of creative professionals (Grabher 2001); within novel arrangements between architects and other élite creatives and their super-wealthy clients in the 'serial' production of the built environment, often bypassing established local design cultures and processes (Kaika 2011; Knox 2011); and increasingly within digital circuits of outsourcing and cultural co-production (Hesmondalgh and Baker 2013). In many cases cultural production occurs as a personal expression of the creative impulse, not directed toward any market or monetized form of exchange, but serving nonetheless to enrich individual and community life.

The cultural economy of the city has also been problematic for urban theorists seeking to advance robust propositions which account for the place of creativity within the larger development trajectories of cities. One difficulty is the complex temporality of culture and creative industry formation within the development pathway of the city. Allen Scott observed in an influential essay (1997) the saliency of cultural assets, product specialization and creative work practices within classical, renaissance and early modern periods, as well as continuities of cultural production in signifying urban-regional networks, including those which characterize the 'third Italy' between Milan and Rome, based on trust, skills and social capital. As another demonstration, Kazuko Goto (2012) has written about seven centuries of craft production in Kyoto, including the observation that the 'cultural depth' of the city in terms of skills, traditions and practices has provided a platform for sustaining the cultural economy amid periods of war, civil disturbance and economic shocks. Thus the cultural economy of the city represents not simply another discrete process of innovation, growth, maturity and eventual decline, along the lines of the 'industrial city' (c. 1830–1970), or 'postindustrial' city (c. 1970–2000), but rather takes the form of an extended historical storyline replete with continuity as well as disjuncture.

Neither is the development of the cultural economy of the city a process of pure succession, as many of the older/traditional underpinnings of culture in the city (theatres and amphitheatres, galleries, museums and other institutions, restaurants and cafes, and forms of artistic and artisanal work; see Ocejo 2010) co-exist with contemporary industries, complex production systems and labour, increasingly infused with digital production and communications technologies. These traditional and contemporary cultural activities together comprise the cultural economy of the creative city. But there can be conflicts between established and newer cultural industries, workers and markets in the city, owing to behavioural frictions among cohorts of cultural consumers among other factors, as Pedro Costa has shown in the case of Lisbon (Costa 2004). There is also contestation associated with the intrusion of high-margin IT businesses within the terrains of the cultural economy.

In recognition of these complex features which make up the trajectory of the cultural economy over time, it seems essential that explanatory models incorporate sufficient robustness to provide traction across diverse cities and urban systems. This clearly is a challenge, notably in light of urgent claims asserting the diversity of urban experience represented by the 'ordinary cities' discourse (Robinson 2006) and the postcolonial cities and societies problematic (Jacobs 1996), which touch down within local communities, landscapes and social memory of place (Crinson 2005). These represent major challenges to theory, and imply the need to open up the dialogue.

A progressive form of political economy can offer useful perspectives on culture, and more specifically the place of the cultural economy within the creative cities discourse. Theoretical propositions advanced by Allen Scott (2008) and Stefan Krätke (2011) reassert the saliency of capital, agglomeration and labour markets in the formation of cultural industries, while Michael Storper (2013) presses for a deeper consideration of institutional factors in the networked new economy. These critical stocks and systems are infused by technological innovation and knowledge which takes in Scott's amalgam of the 'cognitive-cultural economy' (2008), together with an appreciation of the centrality of both material and semiotic values of space, place and landscape which assuredly comprise foundations of 'cultural industries' as well as the ecology of 'creative cities'.

Creative cities: space and place in the metropolis

There is a more complex spatiality of creativity and cultural production in the city which may serve to occlude (or alternatively stimulate) the contours of new theory. I interpret 'space' here not simply as a plane surface which serves to accommodate activity, but rather as a historically layered complex of development experiences, past and present; as a field of human activity, encounter, interaction and conflict; as the complex territory for urban development, replete with upgrading tendencies and dislocations; and as 'territories of governance', which embody aspirations of political bodies, policies for regulation, and a potential resource for the (re)construction of the urban imaginary.

The spatial correlates of the classic industrial city of the nineteenth and early twentieth centuries comprised industrial districts of manufacturing and allied warehousing, distribution and transportation, together with the extensive working-class communities proximate to industrial districts. These districts also encompassed in important cases specializations based on skilled labour and craft-based practices, exemplified by electronics in Berlin, gun manufacture in Birmingham, and precision instruments (Clerkenwell) and tailoring (Shoreditch) in London. These spaces were replete with complex social relations, dense and mostly low-quality housing, and generally insalubrious environmental conditions (Bell and Jayne 2004). Next, the hallmark features of the 'postindustrial' city included the growth of segmented office labour (executives, managers, sales, clerical and technical workers) concentrated within the high-rise office complex of the central business district (CBD) – the largest agglomeration in the late-twentieth-century city – with secondary service industry clusters in the educational, health services, and government sectors, and large retail centres in the city and suburbs. Defining social correlates took the form of new high-density housing and an insidious gentrification process, in which members of an ascendant 'new middle class' (Ley 1996) infiltrated low-income communities, while the growth of service employment is also associated with the formation of new residential development in the suburbs, exacerbating the journey-to-work problem for regional and city planners.

At first glance there is a distinctive spatiality to the defining constitutive features of the creative city, including in many cases concentrations of principal cultural institutions such as museums, galleries, exhibition space, studios and arts and design schools in the central city, and, second, clusters of cultural production firms and workers within the postindustrial terrains of the CBD fringe and inner city, with revealed preferences for the adaptive re-use of heritage buildings (Ley 2003). Clustering of creative enterprise in these areas has been facilitated since the 1970s by a mix of factors including affordable rents, proximate supply of skilled labour and housing, educational and training facilities, consumption amenity, and not least by the resonant semiotic value and distinctive material qualities of the heritage built environment (Hutton 2006). Apex-level global cities such as London, New York, Chicago, Singapore and Shanghai, while clearly following quite different urban histories and development trajectories, each encompass extensive ensembles of cultural industries and creative enterprise within postindustrial and/or inner-city heritage conservation districts.

But rather than providing a stable platform for cultural innovation, production and consumption, and thus by extension a spatial frame for new theory of the creative city, processes of capital relayering, upgrading and dislocation have dislodged artists, designers and other creatives from the CBD fringe and inner districts of globalizing cities. At one level there are the inflationary tendencies of revalorization common to cities within global circuits of capital, and the ever-expanding reach of development within the spaces of the metropolis. There are emergent experiences of social upgrading to account for, as exemplified by the 'new' and 'super' gentrifiers (Butler and Lees 2006) who increasingly include cohorts of transnational élites, facilitated by the aggressive machinations of property markets and development corporations. At the same time other cities are in the throes of prolonged disinvestment, such as Detroit and Cleveland, setting up conditions within urban systems which increasingly feature inequality, deprivation and socio-spatial polarization.

In global metropolises such as London and New York, the demand for upscale housing imbued with symbolic values of 'place' (Zukin 1995) serves to destabilize the tenure of cultural firms in the city – a phenomenon observed as well in small cities such as Vancouver which act for the most part as passive receptors of transnational capital. The insidious social upgrading of the postindustrial era, within which aspirational members of the 'new middle class' infiltrated the modest residential habitus of the working class, has been supplanted by a far more insistent set of related processes which incorporates the ever-more extensive redevelopment of urban neighbourhoods and districts for the super-wealthy. The familiar experiences of social class succession and upgrading of residential areas have been augmented by the pressures of the market to rezone and redevelop former industrial districts for upscale housing, imbued with real or reconstructed historical imaginaries in places like Clerkenwell in London, Brooklyn in New York, Suzhou Creek in Shanghai, the South of Market Area (SOMA) in San Francisco, Southeast False Creek in Vancouver and Liberty Village in Toronto (Catungal, Leslie and Hii 2009).

To these structural processes of capital relayering and social upgrading seen as forces inimical to the tenure of cultural activity in the creative city, we must now add the direct dislocation pressures of 'industrial gentrification' (Pratt 2009). Urban districts which initially provided an attractive ecology for artists and designers, including myriad start-ups, independent creatives, and low-margin firms which in many cases survived as sub-contractors for corporations keen to reduce costs through outsourcing, have now in many cases attracted larger and more profitable creative corporations, as well as start-ups in the IT, financial and business services sectors.

Of course there is a place for creative production infused by digital technology, since the early days of the so-called dot.coms (Lloyd 2006), and for the use of e-retailing to facilitate cultural consumption within spatially extended markets. But there are tensions as well as complements in the co-existence of advanced-technology firms and creative enterprise in the city. The generally greater profitability and higher returns accruing to financial, IT and professional services firms tends to place competitive pressure for space resources on many firms in the cultural sector, as observed in the Northeast Mission in San Francisco, and Fremont in Seattle, undermining the tenure of arts-based enterprises key to the 'creative city' agenda.

A case in point is Shoreditch, formerly a bastion of the extensive industrial terrain of inner northeast London, which specialized in furniture production and tailoring for over a century, then accommodated a world-scale cultural district over the 1980s and 1990s, and more recently has been recast as site of technological innovation, IT start-ups and mainstream business services. Andrew Harris (2012) has written about the illusory aspects of artists and other creatives pursuing the 'urban pastoral' imaginary in Shoreditch, while Edward Jones of University College London has chronicled the shifting governance values which have facilitated change in the district since the 1980s, including the recent insertion of a central government narrative enunciated by former Prime Minister David Cameron. In this latest episode, the messaging of '*creativity* is great' proclaimed in official signage throughout the district has been accompanied and to an extent dislodged by the insistent signalling of '*technology* is great' along prominent streetscapes (Jones 2014; see also Hutton 2015: 245–255).

Another resonant example of insistent industrial upgrading is the SOMA in San Francisco. Historically SOMA encompassed much of the Bay Area's industrial economy, comprising manufacturing, machine shops, wholesaling and warehousing, as well as working-class communities, immigrant neighbourhoods and low-income rental housing. Over the 1990s SOMA became a principal bastion of the global 'new economy', defined by the dot.coms and their social correlates, live–work housing (Solnit 2000; Hutton 2008: 178–221). Much of this capacity was lost in the tech-crash of 2000 and afterwards.

But over the last decade SOMA has emerged as a site of emergent tech-based corporations, inflected with creative impulses and cultural content, including producers of 'apps' for various digital technologies, and social media corporations such as LinkedIn (on Second Street in SOMA). At a strategic scale SOMA now comprises an important element of the global powerhouse of San Francisco and the Bay Area (Storper 2015). San Francisco assuredly remains one of America's established 'creative cities', encompassing many artists and professionals within the fields of the visual and performing arts, important museums and galleries and related educational institutions, creativity in architecture, the built environment, and food and beverages production and consumption. But arguably much of the old Bohemian spirit (and charm) of San Francisco as a city of artists has been dislodged by the scale of recent industrial upgrading which at some level represents an inflection of the 'creative city' narrative.

Creative cities: illustrative research frontiers

I now turn to a discussion of what I see as particularly rich opportunities both for research and for policy development for creative cities, with examples drawn from 'advanced' and 'transitional' city types, and also across space and territory within the metropolis, encompassing social as well as economic realms.

The 'creative city': links to cosmopolis and transnationalism

The creative city script tends to emphasize the economic dimensions of culture in the formation of new industries, emergent production modalities, and a diverse consumption sector which animates conviviality within the urban landscape. Certainly it seems clear that this instrumental deployment (or appropriation) of 'creativity' for economic development purposes has effectively dislodged other applications and meanings, notably in the community life of the city, in the nature of social relations in neighbourhoods, and in the sustainability of cultural diversity in the city at large (Appadurai 1996). There is a parallel (and in many ways related) discourse on the ideals of 'cosmopolis', a spirit of tolerance and openness to cultural diversity shaped by the increasingly multicultural quality of cities and urban neighbourhoods (Vertovec and Cohen 2002), which includes aspects of 'everyday globalization' shaped by immigration, new community formation and persistent localism in cities such as Paris and New York (Shortell 2014).

Cultural diversity inarguably contributes in many ways to the creative economy. And to be sure, the most culturally diverse cities, exemplified by London, Paris, New York and Los Angeles, rank among the most important metropolitan cities of culture and creativity, in terms of scale, specialization and external projection. But there is more subtlety, contradiction and tension in the relations between culture(s) and the creative city than those implied within the comforting nostrums of Richard Florida's prescriptions for economic revival in the city (2002). Neither should the richness of the multicultural city be assigned exclusively an instrumental role in the urban economy, a persistent form of reductionism rightly critiqued by Michael Peter Smith (2001), Edward Soja (2000) and others. 'Creativity' can be observed in social relations, in the 'exchange value' of discourse at the levels of the community and the neighbourhood, in the local animation of beliefs and practices, and in multilevel layering of cultural expression and experience in the spaces of the city.

The 'creative city' beyond the Atlantic sphere

Much of the creative cities discourse has privileged cases situated within the broadly defined Atlantic realm, and more particularly the deep cultural societies and cities of Western Europe and North America. Thus we can readily locate thick narratives of cultural development and their centrality to the storylines of Paris, London, Milan, Barcelona, New York and Chicago, to cite some of the prominent cases.

But the creative city script must now take in a far wider set of cities and urban realms across global space, including the rich but often deeply polarized cities of Latin America, South Asia and Africa. And even an overview perspective needs to avoid the pitfalls of essentialism and over-generalization. Thus I start with cases drawn from the 'growth economies of east Asia' (Routledge monograph series), nomenclature which takes in some of the lead cities of the developmental state including Japan, South Korea, Taiwan, Singapore and China, as well as exemplary and instructive case studies in Southeast Asia, including Malaysia, Vietnam and

Thailand. Each exhibits aspects of national exceptionalism and singularity, together with classic features of the state-directed, export-led and capital-intensive developmental state.

Historically 'culture' and creativity have been deployed instrumentally by the state in East Asia in expressions of national identity, symbolisms of national values, and of course as expression of the power of the state. An important treatment of 'culture and the city in East Asia' is included in a collection of essays edited by Won Bae Kim, Mike Douglass, Sang-Chuel Choe and Kong Chong Ho for Oxford University Press (1997). Historical features and continuities of the use of culture include principal thematics of 'function, symbolism, and power' (pp. 7ff), exemplified by Tiananmen Square in Beijing, while the more recent, postwar record in the East Asian developmental state underscores the centrality of culture in the production of 'the city in a new global order' (pp. 9ff). While the field is rife with complexity, Kim et al. suggest that cultural tensions between global and local interests, and between 'traditional' and 'modern' values, is more acute in 'orthogenetic cities' shaped by ancient traditions and practices, such as Beijing, Hanoi and Seoul, than in 'heterogenetic' cities such as Hong Kong and Singapore (Kim et al. 1997: 4).

The evolution of cities shaped by diverse and often conflicting cultural values also forms a large part of the influential discourse on the postcolonial city (Abbas 1997). This necessarily entails stringent critique of the overt (and covert) practices of racism and oppression, and attendant cultural displacement, observed in the forceful segregation of racial and ethnic groups in colonial cities. An example is Singapore, where the ethnic division of the city was shaped by the British colonial authorities, and where this spatial segregation has been redeployed in cultural terms as part of the marketing of Singapore as a tourism destination. But Brenda Yeoh and Lily Kong (1995), among others, are critical of the government-directed conservation programme which frames not only the boundaries and built environment of Chinatown, Little India and Kampong Glam, but also the national master cultural narrative, producing rupture in cultural-historical stories and social memory among state, corporate and community actors. But the state has nonetheless promoted 'creativity' in the Floridian sense as an important feature of the policy rubrics of the contemporary developmental programme, including clusters of creative industries in each of the heritage conservation districts (Ho 2009).

While Singapore represents an instructive case study of the transference of the 'creative city' script and the 'policy mobilities' of cultural programme assemblages (Prince 2010), Shanghai constitutes an altogether more spectacular exemplar of the conflation of culture and global city formation – conforming in all respects to Hall's schematic of the twenty-first-century global city. Centrepieces of Shanghai's global projection include the Lujiazui World Financial Centre in the Pudong mega-project site. 'Culture' comprises a multi-layered expression of landscape and history, not least the residual features of the British, French, German and American 'concessions' along the Bund, and the old Hong Kong and Shanghai

Banking Corporation building, as well as the numerous statuary and other memorials to Mao, and the extensive industrial districts which underpinned Shanghai's twentieth-century experience of growth and development. A significant portion of this industrial era legacy has been deployed in culture-led regeneration, including the important M50 project along Suzhou Creek and the Red Town redevelopment (Zhong 2012a and 2012b).

Over the past decade the number of designated cultural districts and creative zones has risen from a few to 30, then 60 and now a scarcely credible 100 – implying an official acceptance on the part of the Shanghai Municipal Government that the cultural economy and creative clusters comprise important ensembles of global cities. Established cultural districts present a varying mix of artists' studios, galleries and bars and cafes, while private sector graphic designers, architects and other professional design firms have infiltrated the spaces of an increasing sample of districts. There is also the larger policy reality that for many of these designated cultural districts, an arts-based imagery and land use plan represents mostly a temporary status until a more profitable development opportunity is presented – an upgrading tendency familiar to those studying the fungibility of space in the contemporary globalizing city.

Emergent frontiers of the creative city: suburban/exurban cultures

The institutional set-pieces of the cultural economy (museums, galleries, colleges and art schools), principal cultural production industries (architecture, advertising and corporate branding, new media, film and video industries) and sites of consumption (public markets, restaurants, cafes, bars) all tend to be concentrated within the city proper and indeed exhibit a marked propensity for the central and inner city. But there are also important representations of culture and creativity within the suburbs and in smaller cities and communities that need to be acknowledged.

At first glance suburban communities and smaller cities lack the agglomeration economies and 'creative capital' of cities identified by Stefan Krätke as underpinning growth factors of the contemporary cultural economy. But there are in fact significant representations of culture and creativity within the suburbs, including 'indie' music (sub)cultures operating within the suburban terrains of the metropolis. In this regard Brian Hracs (2009) has written about the robust quality of the indie music scene in suburban Toronto, where successful musicians find ways to obtain the necessary inputs (technical, business and marketing) for performance and production, while avoiding the increasingly high costs of practice and rehearsal space characteristic of the revalorized terrains of the central city. Increasing international immigration to the suburbs from diverse source societies also opens up new possibilities of cultural expression throughout the larger metropolis in an era of 'global suburbanisms' (Roger Keil 2015).

Conclusion: culture and creativity in the city – development and discontents

At one level the cultural economy – an amalgam of production modalities, industries and institutions, labour and work practices, and importantly cultural clusters as a contemporary spatial expression of the 'new industrial district' in the metropolis – shapes the contours of the 'creative city', and represents a corner-stone of the global (or globalizing) city. These include the historic urban centres of culture in Europe, with origins in classical or at least pre-modern times, as well as the great cities of America in which creativity is central to the production of architecture, landscapes and a range of what Allen Scott terms high-value 'cultural products' (Scott 1997; 2008).

As important as creativity is to modern urban economies, though, the 'cultural economy' doesn't replicate the totalizing experience of the classic industrial city of the nineteenth and mid-twentieth centuries, in terms of production modalities, labour formation and class representation, but instead comprises a complex subla-tion of trajectories and tendencies, including artisanal (and neo-artisanal) craft industries and labour; design industries and professions which formed a central axis of the 'flexible specialization' production modalities of late-twentieth-century post-Fordism; contemporary industries, corporations and enterprises in the fields of software innovation, digital knowledge production, broadcasting and commu-nities, social media, and e-retailing; and the 'experiential' forms of culture and creativity as exemplified by cultural tourism, performance and spectacle, and other forms of consumption.

Further, the emergence of the cultural economy of the city is associated with other critical signifiers of contemporary urbanization and urbanism. In policy and gov-ernance terms, increasingly assertive urban programmes designed to promote cul-tural industries represent a vivid expression of the pursuit of competitive advantage for globalizing cities under neo-liberalism, and more specifically an exemplar of assemblages of 'fast policy' mimicry as critiqued by Jamie Peck and Nick Theodore (2015), Kate Shaw (2005) and other critical scholars.

But creativity as urban impulse also demonstrates effects of rescaling and disloca-tion, as the capital (financial, social and human) of cultural development 'touches down' within the spaces (and places) of the city. While (as we saw earlier) the territorialization of creativity encompasses a range of scales, it is the case that much of the machinery of cultural production is arrayed within clusters within or adjacent to vulnerable, low-income and formerly marginalized communities. The cultural capital generated by these activities is also successfully appropriated by developers, property firms and marketing agencies to expedite the revalorization of urban space, facilitating in turn a potent upgrading process which produces both direct social displacement and dislocation. Evidence from a number of jurisdictions including London, Manchester, San Francisco and Chicago demonstrate that it is difficult to control for these externalities in culture-led regeneration programmes.

This observation leads to consideration of what else (and who else) is left out of the creative city script. The industrial city privileged holders of capital and the managerial class in the urban factory world, producing mostly male labour cohorts, and livelihoods on the whole better than those associated with the rural economy, but also pervasive inequality, deprivation and oppression, as elucidated by Marx, Dickens and others. Fordism produced new social realities along with production innovation, including a generally well-paid and relatively secure unionized labour force. The postindustrial city comprising intermediate service industries and a segmented labour force generated a prosperous new middle class of executives, managers and professionals, as well as less well-remunerated clerical labour of mostly women, and sales staff within retail and personal services. But each production era also created a highly gendered work structure, as critiqued by (notably) Doreen Massey (1994), Angela McRobbie (1997) and Linda McDowell (2015).

The contemporary cultural economy privileges what Florida calls the 'supercreatives', together with mostly younger cultural workers, many of whom gain entry through a mix of creative talents and technological prowess: producing what K.C. Ho acknowledges as a pyramid structure of employment, including a very large contingent labour segment. Males, especially young men with advanced technological expertise as well as cultural capital, are over-represented within the most highly remunerated creative industries. The cultural economy is rife with inequality and precarity, producing in turn exclusion and marginality in the revalorized city and within urban systems within which cultural capital is by no means evenly distributed, disclosing darker hues of the ebullient creative city script and imagery.

References

Abbas, A. (1997) *Hong Kong and the Politics of Disappearance*. Minneapolis, MN: University of Minnesota Press.

Appadurai, A. (1996) *Modernity at Large: cultural dimensions of globalization*. Minneapolis, MN: University of Minnesota Press.

Arthurs, K. (2013) *Creative Cities, Creative Spaces, and Urban Policy: the impact of regulations on artist-run centres and independent art spaces in Vancouver, British Columbia*. Unpub. MA Thesis, Centre for Human Settlements, School of Community & Regional Planning, University of British Columbia: Vancouver.

Bell, D. and Jayne, M. (2004) 'Conceptualizing the City of Quarters', in: Bell and Jayne (eds) *City of Quarters: urban villages in the contemporary city* (pp. 1–12). Aldershot, UK: Ashgate.

Butler, T. and Lees, L. (2006) 'Supergentrification in Barnsbury, London: globalization and gentrifying global elites at the neighbourhood level', *Transactions of the Institute of British Geographers* 31: 467–487.

Catungal, J.-P., Leslie, D. and Hii, Y. (2009) 'Geographies of Displacement in the Creative City: the case of Liberty Village, Toronto', *Urban Studies* 46: 1095–1114.

Clark, T.N. and Lloyd, R. (2004) *The City as an Entertainment Machine*. Amsterdam and Boston: Elsevier.

Costa, P. (2004) 'Milieu Effects and Sustainable Development in a Cultural Quarter: the "Bairro Alto –

Chiado" area in Lisbon', paper presented to the Annual Meeting of the Association of American Geographers, Philadelphia, PA (March).

Crinson, M. (ed.)(2005) *Urban Memory: history and amnesia in the modern city*. Abingdon (Oxon) and New York: Routledge.

Evans, G. (2001) *Cultural Planning: an urban renaissance?* London: Routledge.

Florida, R. (2002) *The Rise of the Creative Class: and how it's transforming work, leisure, community and everyday life*. New York: Basic Books.

Glaeser, E. (2011) *Triumph of the City: how our greatest invention makes us richer, smarter, happier and healthier*. New York: Penguin.

Glaeser, E.L, Kolko, J. and Saiz, A. (2001) 'Consumer City', *Journal of Economic Geography* 1: 27–50.

Goto, K. (2012) 'Craft and Creativity: new economic spaces in Kyoto', Chapter 6 in: P.W. Daniels, K.C. Ho and T.A. Hutton (eds) *New Economic Spaces in Asian Cities: from industrial restructuring to the cultural turn* (pp. 87–101). Abingdon (Oxon) and New York: Routledge.

Grabher, G. (2001) 'Ecologies of Creativity: the Village, the Group, and the heterarchic organisation of the British advertising industry', *Environment and Planning A* 33: 351–374.

Greater London Authority (GLA) (2012) *World Cities Cultural Report*. London: GLA and the Office of the Mayor.

Grodach, C. and Silver, D. (eds) (2013) *The Politics of Urban Cultural Planning*. Abingdon (Oxon) and New York: Routledge.

Hall, P.G. (2000) 'Creative Cities and Economic Development', *Urban Studies* 37: 639–651.

Hall, P.G. (2006) 'The Polycentric City', PowerPoint presentation. London: The Bartlett School, University College London.

Harris, A. (2012) 'Art and Gentrification: pursuing the urban pastoral in Hoxton, London', *Transactions of the Institute of British Geographers* 37: 226–241.

Hesmondalgh, D. and Baker, S. (2013) *Creative Labour: media work in three industries*. Abingdon (Oxon) and New York: Routledge.

Ho, K.C. (2009) 'The Neighbourhood in the Creative Economy: policy, practice and place in Singapore', *Urban Studies* 46: 1187–1202.

Hracs, B. (2009) 'Beyond Bohemia: geographies of everyday creativity for musicians in Toronto', Chapter 6 in: T. Edensor, D. Leslie, S. Millington and N. Rantisi (eds) *Spaces of Vernacular Creativity: rethinking the cultural economy* (pp. 75–88). London and New York: Routledge.

Hutton, T.A. (2006) 'Spatiality, Built Form and Creative Industry Development in the Inner City', *Environment and Planning A* 38: 1819–1841.

Hutton, T.A. (2008) *The New Economy of the Inner City: restructuring, regeneration and dislocation in the twenty-first-century city*. London and New York: Routledge.

Hutton, T.A. (2015) *Cities and the Cultural Economy*. Abingdon (Oxon) and New York: Routledge.

Jacobs, J.M. (1996) *Edge of Empire: postcolonialism and the city*. London: Routledge.

Jones, E. (2014) 'Governing Creative Economies in Inner East London', presentation to the Annual Meeting of the Association of American Geographers, Tampa: 8–12 April.

Kaika, M. (2011) 'Autistic Architecture: the fall of the icon and the rise of the serial object of architecture', *Environment and Planning D* 29: 968–992.

Keil, R. (with P. Hamel) (2015) *Suburban Governance: a global view*. Toronto: University of Toronto Press.

Kim, W.B., Douglass, M., Choe, S.-C. and Ho, K.C. (eds) (1997) *Culture and the City in East Asia*. Oxford: Oxford University Press.

Knox, P. (2011) *Cities and Design*. Abingdon (Oxon) and New York: Routledge.

Krätke, S. (2011) *The Creative Capital of Cities: interactive knowledge creation and the urbanization economies of innovation*. Malden, MA and London: Wiley-Blackwell.

Landry, C. and Bianchini, F. (1995) *The Creative City*. London: Demos.

Ley, D.F. (1996) *The New Middle Class and the Remaking of the Central City*. Oxford: Geographical and Environmental Studies, Oxford University Press.

Ley, D.F. (2003) 'Artists, Aestheticization and the Field of Gentrification', *Urban Studies* 40: 2527–2544.

Lloyd, R. (2006) *Neo-Bohemia: art and commerce in the postindustrial city*. Abingdon (Oxon) and New York: Routledge.

Massey, D. (1994) *Space, Place and Gender*. Minneapolis, MN: University of Minnesota Press.

Markusen, A. (2006) 'Urban Development and the Politics of a Creative Class: evidence from a study of artists', *Environment and Planning A* 38: 1921–1940.

McRobbie, A. (1997) 'Bridging the Gap: Feminism, Fashion and Consumption', *Feminist Studies* 55: 73–89.

McDowell, L. (2015) 'The Lives of Others: Bodywork, the Production of Difference, and Labor Geographies', *Economic Geography* 91: 1–23.

Ocejo, R.E. (2010) 'What'll It Be? Cocktail bartenders and the redefinition of services in the creative economy', *City, Culture and Society* 1: 179–184.

Peck, J. (2005) 'Struggling with the Creative Class', *International Journal of Urban and Regional Research* 29: 740–770.

Peck, J. and Theodore, N. (2015) *Fast Policy: Experimental Statecraft at the Threshold of Neoliberlism*. Minneapolis, MN: University of Minnesota Press.

Pratt, A.C. (2009) 'Urban Regeneration: from the arts "feel food" factor to the cultural economy: a case study of Hoxton, London', *Urban Studies* 46: 1041–1062.

Prince, R. (2010) 'Policy Transfer as Policy Assemblage: making policy for the creative industries in New Zealand', *Environment and Planning A* 42: 169–186.

Robinson, J. (2006) *Ordinary Cities: between modernity and development*. London: Routledge.

Scott, A.J. (1997) 'The Cultural Economy of the City', *International Journal of Urban and Regional Research* 21: 323–339.

Scott, A.J. (2008) *Social Economy of the Metropolis: cognitive-cultural capitalism and the global resurgence of cities*. Oxford: Oxford University Press.

Shaw, K. (2005) 'The Place of Alternative Cultures and the Politics of its Protection in Berlin, Amsterdam and Melbourne', *Planning Theory and Practice* 6: 151–170.

Shortell, T. (2014) *Everyday Globalization: a spatial semiotics of immigrant neighbourhoods in Brooklyn and Paris*. Abingdon (Oxon) and New York: Routledge.

Smith, M.P. (2001) *Transnational Urbanism: locating globalization*. Oxford: Blackwell.

Soja, E. (2000) *Postmetropolis: critical studies of cities and regions*. Oxford: Blackwell.

Solnit, R. (with S. Schwartzenberg) (2000) *Hollow City: the siege of San Francisco and the crisis of American urbanism*. London and New York: Verso.

Storper, M. (2013) *The Keys to the City: how economics, institutions, social interaction, and politics shape development*. Princeton, NJ: Princeton University Press.

Storper, M. (2015) *The Rise and Fall of Urban Economies: lessons from San Francisco and Los Angeles*. Palo Alto, CA: Stanford University Press.

Vertovic, S. and Cohen, R. (2002) 'Introduction: conceiving cosmopolitanism', Chapter 1 in: S. Vertovec and R. Cohen (eds) *Conceiving Cosmopolitanism: theory, context and practice* (pp. 1–22). Oxford: Oxford University Press.

Yeoh, B. and Kong, L. (eds) (1995) *Portraits of Places: history, community and identity in Singapore*. Singapore: Times Editions.

Zhong, S. (2012a) 'New Economy Space, New Social Relations: M50 and Shanghai's new art world in the making', Chapter 11 in: P.W. Daniels, K.C. Ho and T.A. Hutton (eds) *New Economic Spaces in Asian Cities: from industrial restructuring to the cultural turn* (pp. 166–183). Abingdon (Oxon) and New York: Routledge.

Zhong, S. (2012b) 'Production, Creative Firms and Urban Space in Shanghai', *Culture Unbound* 4: 169–191.

Zukin, S. (1995) *The Cultures of Cities*. Oxford: Blackwell.

12 Towards more sustainable cities

Lisa Benton-Short and Melissa Keeley

In September of 2015 world leaders, heads of global financial institutions and other dignitaries met in New York to formally adopt the newest framework for sustainability, the 2030 Agenda for Sustainable Development. The new Sustainable Development Goals (SDGs) are 17 goals and 169 targets to eliminate poverty, fight inequality and tackle climate change over the next 15 years. Of particular note is Goal #11 which seeks to make cities "inclusive, safe, resilient and sustainable." This goal is in response to the new urban reality of 50 percent of the world's 7.3 billion people living in urban areas and that cities account for most of the world's consumption of energy and greenhouse gas emissions. Now more than ever, cities are challenged to move towards sustainability (Portney, 2003; Tang et al., 2011).

Urban researchers have long recognized that the city scale can be a beneficial starting point for local activism and community involvement around sustainability (Boone and Moddares, 2006; Gandy, 2002; Robbins, 2012; Short, 1989). Kent Portney notes that local "governance mechanisms in cities are most likely to be responsive to the environmental concerns of their citizens," both because of their direct control over sustainability mechanisms and because a degraded environment is most apparent at the local level (Portney, 2003, p. 16). Indeed, cities have primary control over land use, public education and economic development, meaning local policy can have a significant impact (Wheeler, 2013). In the U.S., as federal leadership in the creation of environmental policies has faltered, there has been growing support for local initiatives, often referred to as "new localism" (Parker and Rowlands, 2007; Portney, 2003).

City governments also have their own incentives for voluntarily committing to a sustainability agenda. Local governments often see sustainability as a way to help their cities economically, by raising the value of land, improving the health of the population and even directly saving money by implementing sustainability policies (Portney, 2003; Zeemering, 2009). Cities are more likely to voluntarily commit to greenhouse gas reduction if they perceive themselves more environmentally, socially or economically vulnerable to climate change. In addition, cities have discovered that being identified as green and sustainable may attract investment, residents and tourists (Zahran et al., 2008).

A range of established networks at various scales encourage cities to move towards sustainability and facilitate the sharing of information and best practices. For example, Freiburg, Germany, created the Freiburg Charter for Sustainable Urbanism. Regionally, in Europe the Aalborg Charter connects cities and provides information about sustainability initiatives. This organization also honors outstanding cities with the annual European Sustainability City Award, which is coveted and valued by politicians and city officials. In the U.S. many cities have supported action for climate change at the local level through the 2005 U.S. Mayors Climate Protection Agreement – a document in which cities pledge to meet the targets outlined in the Kyoto protocol, despite the U.S. not ratifying it (U.S. Mayors, 2005). This agreement commits mayors to create a greenhouse gas reduction plan, and in turn this has often become the starting point or inspiration for the creation of a more comprehensive sustainability plan (U.S. Mayors, 2005). At the global scale, ICLEI (http://icleiusa.org/), or Local Governments for Sustainability, organizes conferences and webinars and provides reports on a range of sustainability efforts. Today, more than 1,000 cities in 84 countries are members of ICLEI.

As a result of emerging issues, better networks and calls for action, many cities around the world have developed sustainability plans. Municipal sustainability plans are comprehensive visions and goals set forth by a government or other civic organization covering environmental, economic and social equity issues. In addressing steps for sustainability, these tend to be holistic and multi-departmental documents that outline goals, visions and priorities for the future. Examples of topics often found within sustainability plans are:

- Climate (mitigation and adaptation)
- Tree canopy
- Green spaces (parks)
- Green jobs
- Resource conservation (energy use, water use)
- Brownfields/land use redevelopment
- Housing
- Human health (reduction of asthma and obesity)
- Infrastructure (water, sanitation, energy)
- Air quality
- Water quality
- Transportation and congestion
- Solid waste/zero waste programs
- Green buildings
- Flood risk reduction
- Environmental justice.

These plans generally inventory current problems and standings, identify solutions and priorities and set indicators for measuring progress (Evenson et al., 2009). Paris, Freiburg, Helsinki, Oslo and London are pioneers in the area of sustainability plans. Malmö and Copenhagen often rank among the top of many "green cities" lists. Many European cities have initiated innovations in bike sharing and car sharing and climate action plans. But sustainability planning has not been limited to Europe. Many cities including Singapore, Seoul, Bangkok, Rio and Mexico City have all recently developed sustainability plans (Benton-Short and Short, 2013).

Despite increasing environmental concerns and growing citizen support, the U.S. government has lagged behind many European countries and some developing countries in crafting progressive sustainability legislation (Beatley, 2003; Rabinovitch and Leitman, 1996). However, that has been changing. Since 2010 many U.S. cities have begun crafting comprehensive sustainability plans. Today numerous U.S. cities have sustainability plans, including large cities like New York City and Chicago, medium-sized cities like Cincinnati, Chattanooga, Portland and Salt Lake City and small cities like Topeka and Burlington.

It is clear that urban sustainability planning is a growing and important trend. The newly launched 2030 SDGs call for a substantial increase in the number of cities and human settlements adopting and implementing integrated policies and plans towards inclusion, resource efficiency, mitigation and adaptation to climate change, and resilience to disasters. We know that many cities will undertake sustainability planning in the next five to ten years; many cities that created plans in 2000 or 2005 will certainly revise and update their plans.

It is also apparent that urban sustainability plans are incipient and varied. Because there is no global or national standard for sustainability plans and because priorities can be so varied across different cities and geographies, the plans tend to differ in the way they are created and organized, the topic areas they contain or omit, and the regional and local-specific problems they aim to solve. Some plans focus on the issue of climate change, while others may focus more on local environmental, economic or equity issues, or broad community goals (Portney, 2003; Saha, 2009). For example, PlaNYC, New York City's sustainability plan, is more than 160 pages long and covers numerous issues including housing, open space, brownfields, water, transportation, energy and climate change (City of New York, 2011). London's 2012 *Blueprint for Change* is also large at 118 pages and addresses issues such as biodiversity, climate change, inclusion and the legacy of the 2012 Olympic Games (City of London, 2012). On the other end of the spectrum is Austin, Texas, whose plan is about 16 pages long and focuses mostly on water (City of Austin, 2008). Finally, many city sustainability plans are more vision statements than a set of articulated goals and targets, perhaps evidence of their nascency.

Because municipal sustainability plans are relatively new phenomena, the literature has only recently begun to analyze the planning and implementation process. In this chapter, we identify four opportunities for urban scholars to advance and support urban sustainability planning and implementation. They are 1) governance and integration; 2) setting priorities; 3) benchmarking, measuring and mapping; and 4) equity and access.

Governance, integration and prioritization

Sustainability challenges traditional urban governance and the mechanisms prioritize projects and investments (Adger and Jordan, 2009). It demands integration of both a wide variety of stakeholders and objectives in decision-making and requires the integration of multiple concerns – environment, economics, equity – in all undertakings. By extension, many of the most sustainable municipal practices will be conceived, vetted, and maybe even implemented by actors with diverse perspectives and backgrounds, likely from different city agencies and the public. This differs from traditional planning which tended to be led by a single municipal agency.

Integration, then, is a significant challenge given that urban governance is traditionally stove-piped. Moving towards sustainability may require the endorsement and implementation of multisector cooperation. The change required is structural and necessitates alterations in traditional portfolios, threatens existing power structures, must transcend political boundaries and elected official's term limits, and requires continual commitments to maintain communication and collaboration between agencies.

Scholarly work in this area is just emerging. Scholars Dimitri Devuyst and Luc Hens (2000) have looked at how municipalities manage and measure sustainable development initiatives and visions. We highlight, for instance, the choices that municipalities make in where to "house" offices of sustainability. While sustainability initiatives based in the offices of a mayor might have better success in getting their calls returned and more success in holding various agencies accountable to sustainability targets than those housed, for instance, in a department of the environment, the latter situation might bring long-term advantages through political transitions (Benton-Short, Keeley and Rowland, in press).

Another related challenge is public involvement and education and awareness of issues of sustainability within the community. Research on sustainability and governance is just beginning to look at governance and how best to promote sustainability through public participation (Adger and Jordan, 2009; Conroy and Berke, 2004). Many sustainability plans were created with public involvement but also set goals and targets acknowledging that these will only be reached when actions are taken by the public. However, in our contemporary culture, the public's awareness of the natural processes and systems supporting us is weak, and this limits effective engagement in civic processes on issues of sustainability. Greater education at the community level can be empowering to community members and enhance our collective ability to reach sustainability objectives.

Prioritization and decision-making

Both the development and implementation of sustainability plans are exercises in priority setting. Cities face the emerging challenge of paying for all of the community benefits that can result from sustainable development. Cities cannot assume there will be national or state subsidies to make sustainable development happen. Scholars can help as cities think creatively about how to pay for individual projects as well as at the place-level for the local jurisdiction.

Under conditions of resource constraint (not just money, but also manpower, time and goodwill), how should a city decide what its sustainability goals should be? Which issues are the most pressing? How should a city weigh concerns that are immediate, like protecting the water quality in the local river or lake, as opposed to those connected to global citizenship, like climate change? Which of the many "apples and oranges" of possible programs will have the most impact, at the least political and real cost? How are these issues resolved when agencies with differential power and diverse perspectives and portfolios disagree? The field of urban political ecology can help to clarify how these decisions are currently being made and contribute to the body of knowledge necessary for more informed and transparent planning practice. This is because urban political ecologists analyze the city as a place in which power is revealed, contested and enforced (Gandy, 2008; Swyngedouw, 2004). Such a perspective can be valuable in examining how cities set goals and priorities and illuminating the planning process and the politics that underlie this process.

The comprehensive, integrated nature of sustainability plans together with the required changes in governance practices contribute to both action and implementation challenges. Tang et al. (2011) discuss cities' strong ability to conceptualize climate change, but lower capabilities for action and implementation. Because many sustainability plans are recent, leadership and implementation are in the early stages. Some cities regularly and thoroughly report on progress towards sustainability goals while others do not. Progress is hard to measure – as will be discussed later – but it is also possible that progress is seen on goals that for a variety of reasons are relatively easy, low-hanging fruit while harder, longer-term goals and objectives lag behind.

While most of the questions raised above have to do with process and inclusion, they also rely upon technical information. Cities face information deficits as they decide which steps they will take to make their region more sustainable and prioritize these investments. Specifically, sustainability calls for cities to explore new policy options and engage in planning and goal setting in new areas. For many topics, there is lack of empirical evidence to support proposed goals or specific interventions. Below, we highlight two examples that expose the need cities have for empirical evidence and improved decision-making tools in light of global change.

A number of U.S. cities raise public health issues, including obesity, as areas of focus within their sustainability plans. For example, Washington D.C. aims to "cut the citywide obesity rate by 50%," an ambitious goal (City of Washington D.C., 2012, p 10). But the actual strategy they suggest to achieve this goal is vague: the city will "encourage residents to be more active, eat more nutritiously, and be healthier through an awareness campaign" (City of Washington D.C., 2012, p. 14). Like many cities, Washington D.C. links reducing obesity with increasing access to parks and recreation areas. However, within the literature, there is little evidence to support the association between increasing green space in a city and overall obesity reduction (Cleary, 2016). Thus, there is a clear need for research that helps to document the effectiveness of strategies to achieve the goals that cities have set for themselves in sustainable planning exercises.

A second information deficit centers on the impacts of climate change and how these affect urban planning decisions. Traditionally, engineered systems like bridges, sewer systems and power systems are designed assuming "stationarity" in climate systems, which means that "natural systems fluctuate within an unchanging envelope of variability" (Milly et al., 2008). However, many human disturbances – with climate change at the forefront – have compromised this assumption of stationarity. Extreme events such as heat waves, droughts or floods may be related to non-stationarity in the underlying climatic systems and can stress engineered systems beyond their designed capacities. This occurs because the mathematical tools used to prioritize investments under uncertainty in engineered systems are not valid if the statistical processes to which they are subjected will change over time. Underscoring the fundamental change that humans must make within planning, Milly et al. (2008) provocatively title their piece on water management: "Stationarity is dead." Thus, urban planners and engineers need new models that will allow these investments to be made while acknowledging limited economic resources. Therefore, measurement of infrastructure resilience is important for sustaining community functions by adapting to climate change risks.

Benchmarking, measuring and mapping

A clear challenge within sustainability planning is moving from theoretical visions to develop concrete goals and targets for the future, and envisioning the steps needed to achieve these. Challenges associated with this type of planning are many and should not be underestimated.

The first step for many cities should be benchmarking exercises, used to understand where they are currently in order to set achievable goals and targets. There are many elements to sustainability that can be measured or mapped, such as tree canopy, access to parks and recreation, greenhouse gas emissions, energy and water use, and biodiversity. It is critical to develop baseline data and trends in order to design effective management programs. We utilize three examples – urban tree canopy, greenhouse gas emissions and green space connectivity – to highlight the need for better measurement, mapping and analysis.

One prominent example is the urban tree canopy. Many factors, not the least their ubiquitousness in some cities, make assessments of the distribution of trees within cities a particular challenge. This warrants further discussion here because of the important role that geographic tools such as geographic information systems (GIS) and remote sensing bring to urban tree canopy planning, distribution and measurement.

Many municipal sustainability plans have goals related to tree canopy. New York City's 2007 One Million Trees program to plant 1 million new trees by 2020 is perhaps the most well-known of these goals (City of New York, 2011), although Washington D.C. has a similar goal to "plant 8,600 new trees citywide per year until 2032" (City of Washington D.C., 2012, p.76). Many cities, however, set a general goal increasing the tree canopy coverage (sometimes by a certain percent) yet often do not include benchmarking or specific measurement plans. It is clear that measuring the urban tree canopy – for the purposes of establishing a baseline number of trees or tracking progress towards a set goal – poses particular problems.

While municipal departments of parks and recreation often try to create inventories of parks and open spaces through field observation, the decentralized nature of street trees means that other methods, including remote sensing and GIS, are typically necessary (Huang et al., 2013).

Thus, tree canopy is measured quite differently than other forms of green space and much research and methods development on this front has been done in the realm of urban forestry measurement. Currently, there are two popular and well-established technical ways to measure urban tree canopy: 1) using measures of field-based visual estimations with the U.S. Department of Agriculture (USDA) Forest Services' i-Tree program and 2) the use of GIS and high-resolution land cover data (King and Locke, 2013). In remote sensing, the V-I-S model defines the urban landscape as the sum of Vegetation, Impervious surfaces and Soil (Ridd, 1995). Although this model has its limitations (it does not discriminate well between trees and other forms of vegetation), it remains widely used. Remotely sensed images are data recorded from a distance and include aerial photos and satellite images. The process can also be time-consuming and becomes less accurate with the more types of green space that one attempts to classify (Shin and Lee, 2005). Another problem has been that some methods assume tree cover as a static component of urban areas and cannot evaluate interannual tree cover variability at the city or neighborhood scale (Johnston, 2013; Nowak and Greenfield, 2012). Urban geographers have already been at the leading edge, and will play a critical role in refining this method of measurement and analysis.

A second example is greenhouse gas emissions. Many sustainability plans pledge to cut greenhouse gas emissions. Seoul says it will reduce emissions by 40 percent by 2030. Amsterdam pledges to cut emissions by 75 percent by 2040. Seattle aims to eliminate all emissions by 2050. And yet, the inventory methods that cities have used to date vary significantly, raising questions around data quality, and limiting the ability to aggregate local and subnational greenhouse gas emissions data. Cities use all kinds of different methods of measuring and reporting their emissions – there is still no single accepted standard for measurement (Swope, 2014). And yet creating a reliable greenhouse gas emissions inventory enables city leaders to better manage their emissions reduction efforts and allocate resources. One challenge has been that measuring emissions is a complex science, even more so at the geographic scale of a city than across a whole country (Swope, 2014). Calculating accurate and meaningful greenhouse gas emissions is still in its formative stages, although there have been recent attempts to harmonize methodologies. In early 2015 the World Resources Institute, the C40 Cities Climate Change Leadership Group and ICLEI (Local Governments for Sustainability) launched the first widely endorsed standard for cities to measure and report their greenhouse gas emissions at the 20th yearly meeting, The United Nations Climate Change Conference, featuring mayors and officials from cities around the world (http://www.ghgprotocol.org/Release/GPC_launch). Scholars should continue research to verify this methodology, or to suggest alternative ones and be sensitive to scale to ensure that inventory and measurements are "scaled" from metro region down to neighborhoods.

A third example where measurement and mapping is needed to establish benchmarks is in the area of the distribution of environmental features and land use. Green space connectivity within cities is emerging as an important goal in many sustainability plans, and one that contributes not only to the habitat value of these systems and utility as transit and recreation corridors for humans but also to system stability and benefits in other ways as well. We see examples of these aspirations in the city of Madison's goal to connect parks, bike trails and stormwater management systems. Specifically, their aim is to "link all parks and open spaces to the maximum extent possible" (City of Madison, 2011, p. 16).

However, there remain significant barriers to increasing green space connectivity. The complexity of the mapping, inventorying and analyzing of existing and potential green spaces to increase connectivity should not be underestimated. The complexity of this type of analysis fits with the expertise of urban geographers who can bring sensitivity to scale and assessment using tools such as GIS and remote sensing. It can also assist in connecting green spaces and open spaces in wider planning efforts (Erickson, 2006). Complexities also arise when one considers the extent to which private and unprotected areas can or could constitute an important component of network planning. In some cities the extent of private green space can be larger than that of public green space. And these private green spaces might be composed of relatively few large parcels or be the sum of very small run-of-the-mill backyards (Pauleit, 2003). Further, many cities have little or no information on private green space, despite its potential importance (Huang et. al., 2013). Geographic techniques have the potential to permit overarching assessments of green spaces, including privately owned ones. In this way, municipalities can address this information gap and allow better analysis of access, quality and the level of connectivity.

Equity and access

Equity is often the least defined and operationalized of sustainability's three "E's" (environment, economics and equity) and frequently takes a back seat in both planning and politics (Wheeler, 2013). Indeed, scholars have noticed the lack of inclusion of equity goals and actions, particularly among U.S. sustainability efforts (Portney, 2003; Saha, 2009). While cities are increasingly addressing equity, the conceptualization and implementation of the concept remains highly constrained. The ways equity is discussed indicates that it may "be primarily symbolic and indicative of [it] ... being a low-priority concern" (Pearsall and Pierce, 2010, p. 571).

Geographers Hamil Pearsall and Joseph Pierce (2010) argue there are two core elements of environmental justice: distributional and procedural justice. Distributional justice refers to the distribution or maldistribution of environmental consequences on traditionally disadvantaged groups in American society (Pearsall and Pierce, 2010). The procedural element refers to the "meaningful involvement" aspect of the definition and focuses on the right of all people to participate in environmental decision-making (Pearsall and Pierce, 2010). Both distributional and procedural inequity challenge sustainability planning in cities and remain topics for further applied geographic research.

Distributional equity

Consider the issue of green space (parks, trails, open space, etc.). Green space inequity is a complex issue. Literature on the topic of green space inequity often concludes that areas with lower socioeconomic status and/or a higher minority population contain fewer green space resources than their higher socioeconomic and lower minority population counterparts (Vaughan et al., 2013). These sorts of inequities in the amounts and distribution of green space can lead to "reproduced uneven social space" due to the disproportionate distribution of the benefits associated with green spaces (Benton-Short and Short, 2013, p. 242).

Some cities are working to increase access to green space. For instance, New York City states that each neighborhood should provide 1.5 acres of open space per 1,000 people (City of New York, 2011). Rather than aiming for equity, Dunn (2010) specifies that green infrastructure policies should be concentrated in areas to best provide the urban poor with environmental services. Along these lines, Washington D.C.'s plan calls for a unique solution to address accessibility challenges with plans to create small parks and green spaces in areas with inadequate open space as well as investing in "mobile parklets" (City of Washington D.C., 2012). Green space goals that are measured by neighborhood are another move towards equitable distribution of these resources. Chicago and New York set goals to make sure that every resident in these cities lives within a 10 minute walk of a park, recreation area or open space (City of Chicago, 2012, p. 27; City of New York, 2011). This means the measuring green space accessibility is more closely tied to the lived experience of residents, and thus reflects accessibility differentials that could exist between neighborhoods.

Equity in process

Scholars familiar with working in urban development at the neighborhood or local scale are attuned to the importance of process. Green space improvement or creation should include deliberative and inclusionary processes and procedures to actively engage the public in decision-making related to green space location, desired amenities or safety (Seymour, 2012). Such community involvement in revitalization projects serves an important role in ensuring community needs are met and that new or improved "spaces are not perceived as inferior," unwanted or unsafe (Wright et al., 2011, p. 6731). For instance, communities with different age, gender or ethnic compositions may wish to tailor their green space plans to local needs and preferences (Payne, 2002). However, many cities' sustainability plans do not have explicit goals to include local residents in decision-making about desired amenities or safety related to green space and green infrastructure.

Lessons could perhaps be drawn from efforts to engage residents in care for street trees, which was one community engagement effort featured in a number of sustainability plans. For example, Austin, Texas, has two related goals: first, to "coordinate a campaign to encourage citizens to help plant trees and care for the urban forest" and, second, to "continue tree planting programs in partnership with community organizations" (City of Austin, 2008, p. 3). Such efforts could help engage residents with horticulture and sustainability, foster a connection with nature and the local environment, and provide an avenue for multilateral communication about local needs, priorities and values.

Another reason the cultivation of partnerships is important is that in many cases non-profit organizations and community groups are in charge of local programs. In Washington D.C., for example, the non-profit Casey Trees is primarily responsible for all public space tree plantings; they work directly with the community to organize tree planting events. In addition, this non-profit has a GIS expert on its staff, and it was their research on the tree canopy that the city relied on in developing their goals for tree canopy increase. Community partners can provide information about safety, traffic and walkability at a local scale.

There remains much room for work on participatory equity as there is still a gulf between the frequency with which equity is "mentioned and the depth with which it is explored" (Steele et al., 2012, p. 77). We have identified three areas where more research is needed:

1.   Increased comprehensive mapping of amenities and disamenities

Mapping of both amenities such as parks or open space and disamenities such as hazardous facilities is critical to understanding issues of equity and development.

GIS has tremendous potential to inform analysis around environmental amenities and infrastructure distribution and equity. It also allows planners the ability to prioritize interventions and expand on goals based on the power of visualizing disparity (Bell et al., 2007). A combination of geographic techniques and critical analysis allows us to investigate historical land use patterns, examine policies around parks and recreation, and consider the politics of funding of public amenities. These are important roles in the larger picture of sustainable urbanism.

The example of "food deserts" is a topic much discussed these days. It is a term that refers to areas of the city with limited access to fresh and affordable food. Geographer Neil Wrigley's work on food deserts in British cities shows that these deserts reflect social exclusions and contribute to health inequalities (Wrigley, 2002). Work on food deserts has continued to advance; the tools and the approaches used can be employed to examine a range of equity issues. Scholars who employ such approaches also allow us to re-envision the city as more equitable (Haughton, 1999; Stefanovic and Scharper, 2012).

But just mapping alone does not always explain the amenity or disamenity. For example, recent studies have shown that the assumptions about the inequality paradigm of green space distribution are not always correct (Vaughan et al., 2013). Nik Heynen and colleagues found inequitable distribution of urban trees in the U.S. city of Milwaukee (Heynen et al., 2006, p. 12) and Christopher Boone and colleagues investigated the distribution of parks in Baltimore, Maryland (Boone et al., 2009). Their research found that a simple look at the distribution of parks shows that African Americans were located closer to parks. However, more in-depth historical research showed a more complex picture. Whites had once lived in such areas, but after white middle-class flight in the 1960s and 1970s, African Americans moved into those areas with greater access to parks. Geographic research that combines amenities maps with more in-depth socio-ecological analysis can reveal that inequity (and equity) has deep historical patterns of unequal treatment (Benton-Short and Short, 2013). As mentioned previously, the sub-field of urban political ecology can make important contributions to advancing urban sustainability by looking at the city as a place in which power is revealed, contested and enforced (Cooke and Lewis, 2010; Swyngedouw, 2004). This research has revealed the interconnections between the physical and the social, and can be a useful lens through which to examine politics behind such issues as green infrastructure distribution and benefits. The combination of mapping with a deeper analysis can yield important insights into environmental justice.

2.   Analysis of quality of amenities

As cities work to improve the quality of their environment – green space, rivers, parks, etc. – it is not merely the distribution of these that is important, but also the quality. The quality of environmental amenities is important because it reveals factors such as desirability, accessibility and safety. Considerations of green space quality are further complicated by tensions between conflicting social and ecological priorities. For example, green space that has multi-level vegetation (tree canopy, lower-level shrubs) provides better habitat value for animals, but may be perceived by some in the community as being a safety hazard.

Scholars have much to contribute on this front. For instance, both in practice and scholarly research, we must move beyond citywide goals and analysis, and think about access and amenity quality and accessibility at smaller scales such as neighborhoods and wards, or perhaps even individuals. Working more locally may, for instance, provide historic and contemporary perspectives on the local context and community needs (Pauleit, 2003). Such critical analysis can also help assess the level of community participation in sustainability efforts.

3. Spatializing social equity

Increasingly, researchers are examining uneven urban development. The concentration of poverty and wealth, racial segregation/inequality, and gentrification continue to be critical issues and provide spatial evidence of social inequity. While cities are revitalizing their waterfronts and downtowns as part of sustainable efforts, it is critical that we not build "golden ghettos." The valuation premiums that many so-called sustainable development projects and places are now achieving has also created a social equity challenge that threatens to derail sustainable development. Urban scholars are researching the impact and the potential of community banks and other innovative financial methods to address issues of social equity and affordable housing. There is much work to be done to evaluate the "value capture" or "value sharing" of mixed-income residential developments. In brief, there is much work to be done on spatializing social equity.

Conclusion

As cities move towards sustainability they are confronted with numerous and diverse challenges as varied as climate change, air and water quality, human health, affordable housing, energy, transportation and recreation. Equity and inclusion will likely remain central challenges on which cities must concentrate; these issues further problematize and inflect how each of the above challenges will be addressed. At the same time, there are many positive developments: cities around the world are discussing sustainability and creating sustainability plans; networks and resources now exist for cities to share best practices and innovations. Urban scholars are poised to contribute in meaningful ways through their research in the thematic areas of sustainability planning (for example climate mitigation or green space connectivity) as well as the broader processes – both physical and human – that facilitate implementation and advancement. There is much to be done to move cities towards a more sustainable future, and urban scholars need to roll up their sleeves and get going.

References

Adger, W. N. and A. Jordan (eds) (2009) *Governing Sustainability*. Cambridge: Cambridge University Press.

Beatley, T. (2003) "Planning for sustainability in European cities: a review of practices in leading cities," in Stephen M. Wheeler and Timothy Beatley (eds), *The Sustainable Urban Development Reader*, 2nd edn. New York: Routledge.

Bell, S., A. Montarzino and P. Travlou (2007) "Mapping research priorities for green and public urban space in the UK," *Journal of Urban Forestry and Greening*, **6**, 103–115.

Benton-Short, L., M. Keeley and J. Rowland In press. "Green space in urban sustainability plans: trends and best practices," in Kevin Archer and Kris Bezdecny (eds), *Handbook of Cities and the Environment*. Cheltenham, UK and Northampton, MA, USA: Edward Elgar Publishing.

Benton-Short, L. and J. R. Short (2013) *Cities and Nature*, 2nd edn. New York: Routledge.

Boone, C. G., G. L. Buckley, J. M. Grove and C. Sister (2009) "Parks and people: an environmental justice inquiry in Baltimore, Maryland," *Annals of the Association of American Geographers*, **99**, 767–787.

Boone, C. and A. Moddares (2006) *City and Environment*. Philadelphia, PA: Temple University Press.

City of Austin (2008) *Rethink Austin*. Accessed 18 August 2015 at http://austintexas.gov/sites/default/files/files/Sustainability/Rethink_-_SAA/Rethink_%26_Sustainability_Action_Agenda.pdf.

City of Chicago (2012) *2015 Sustainable Chicago Action Agenda*. Accessed 18 August 2015 at http://www.cityofchicago.org/content/dam/city/progs/env/SustainableChicago2015.pdf.

City of London (2012) *A Blueprint for Change*. Accessed 8 January 2016 at http://learninglegacy.independent.gov.uk/documents/pdfs/sustainability/2-london-2012-sustainability-report-a-blueprint-for-change.pdf.

City of Madison (2011) *The Madison Sustainability Plan: Fostering Environmental, Economic and Social Resilience*. Accessed 18 August 2015 at http://www.cityofmadison.com/sustainability/documents/SustainPlan2011.pdf.

City of New York (2011) *PlaNYC: A Greener, Greater New York*. Accessed 18 August 2015 at http://www.nyc.gov/html/planyc/downloads/pdf/publications/planyc_2011_planyc_full_report.pdf.

City of Washington, D.C. (2012) *Sustainable DC*. Accessed 18 August 2015 at http://sustainable.dc.gov/sites/default/files/dc/sites/sustainable/page_content/attachments/DCS-008%20Report%20508.3j.pdf.

Cleary, S. D. (2016) Personal communication. Dr. Cleary is an Epidemiologist with the GW School of Public Health.

Conroy, M. M. and P. R. Berke (2004) "What makes a good sustainable development plan? An analysis of factors that influence principles of sustainable development," *Environment and Planning A*, **36** (8), 1381–1396.

Cooke, J. and R. Lewis (2010) "The nature of circulation: the urban political ecology of Chicago's Michigan Avenue Bridge, 1909–1930," *Urban Geography*, **31**, 348–368.

Devuyst, D. and L. Hens (2000) "Introducing and measuring sustainable development initiatives by local authorities in Canada and Flanders (Belgium): a comparative study," *Environment, Development and Sustainability*, June 2000, **2** (2), 81–105.

Dunn, A. D. (2010) "Siting green infrastructure: legal and policy solutions to alleviate urban poverty and promote healthy communities," *Boston College Environmental Affairs Law Review*, **37** (1). Accessed 8 January 2016 at http://lawdigitalcommons.bc.edu/ealr/vol37/iss1/3/.

Erickson, D. (2006) *Metrogreen: Connecting Open Space in North American Cities*. Washington, DC: Island Press.

Evenson, K., S. Aytur, S. Rodriguez and D. Salvesen (2009) "Involvement of parks and recreation professionals in pedestrian plans," *Journal of Park and Recreation Administration*, **27** (3), 132–142.

Gandy, M. (2002) *Concrete and Clay: Reworking Nature in New York City*. Cambridge, MA: MIT Press.

Gandy, M. (2008) "Landscapes of disaster: water, modernity and urban fragmentation in Mumbai," *Environment and Planning A*, **40**, 108–130.

Haughton, G. (1999) "Environmental justice and the sustainable city," *Journal of Planning Education and Research*, **18**, 233–243.

Heynen, N., H. A. Perkins and P. Roy (2006) "The political ecology of uneven urban green space," *Urban Affairs Review*, **42**, 3–25.

Huang, Y., Y. Bailang, Z. Janhuan, H. Chunlin, T. Wenqi, H. Zhiming and H. Jianping (2013) "Toward automatic estimation of urban green volume using airborne LiDAR data and high resolution Remote Sensing images," *Frontiers of Earth Science*, **7** (1), 43–54.

Johnston, A. (2013) *Tree Cover Variability in the District of Columbia*. Unpublished Doctoral Dissertation, College Park Maryland, University of Maryland.

King, K., and D. Locke (2013) "A comparison of three methods for measuring local urban tree canopy cover," *Arboriculture and Urban Forestry*, **39** (2), 62–67.

Milly, P. D. C., J. Betancourt, M. Falkenmark, R. Hirsch, Z. Kundzewicz, D. Lettenmaier and R. Stouffer (2008) "Stationarity is dead: whither water management?" *Science*, **319** (5863), 573–574.

Nowak, D. J. and E. J. Greenfield (2012) "Tree and impervious cover change in U.S. cities," *Urban Forestry and Urban Greening*, **11** (1), 21–30.

Parker, P. and I. Rowlands (2007) "City partners maintain climate change action despite national cuts: residential energy efficiency programme valued at local level," *Local Environment*, **12** (5), 505–517.

Pauleit, S. (2003) "Perspectives on urban greenspace in Europe," *Built Environment*, **29** (2), 89–93.

Payne, K. (2002) "Graph theory and open-space network design," *Landscape Research*, **27** (2), 167–179.

Pearsall, H. and J. Pierce (2010) "Urban sustainability and environmental justice: evaluating the linkages in public planning/policy discourse," *Local Environment*, **15** (6), 569–580.

Portney, K. (2003) *Taking Sustainable Cities Seriously: Economic Development, the Environment and Quality of Life in American Cities*. Cambridge, MA: MIT Press.

Rabinovitch, J. and J. Leitman (1996) "Urban planning in Curitiba," in Stephen M. Wheeler and Timothy Beatley (eds), *The Sustainable Urban Development Reader*, 2nd edn. New York: Routledge.

Ridd, M. K. (1995) "Exploring a V-I-S (vegetation-impervious surface-soil) model for urban ecosystem analysis through remote sensing: comparative anatomy for cities," *International Journal of Remote Sensing*, **16** (12), 2165–2185.

Robbins, P. (2012) *Political Ecology: A Critical Introduction*, 2nd edn. Chichester, UK: Wiley-Blackwell.

Saha, D. (2009) "Empirical research on local government sustainability efforts in the USA: gaps in the current literature," *Local Environment*, **14** (1), 17–30.

Seymour, M. (2012) "Just sustainability in urban parks," *Local Environment*, **17** (2), 167–185.

Shin, D. and K. Lee (2005) "Use of remote sensing and geographical information systems to estimate green space surface temperature change as a result of urban expansion," *Landscape Ecology Engineering*, **1**, 169–176.

Short, J. R. (1989) *The Humane City*. Oxford: Blackwell.

Steele, W., D. MacCallum, J. Byrne and D. Houston (2012) "Planning the climate-just city," *International Planning Studies*, **17** (1), 67–83.

Stefanovic, I. G. and S. B. Scharper (2012) *The Natural City: Re-envisioning the Built Environment*. Toronto: University of Toronto Press.

Swope, C. (2014) "Two forward leaps in how cities measure greenhouse-gas emissions." Accessed 10 January 2016 at http://citiscope.org/story/2014/two-forward-leaps-how-cities-measure-greenhouse-gas-emissions#sthash.UHHJeD1l.dpuf.

Swyngedouw, E. (2004) *Social Power and the Urbanization of Water*. Oxford: Oxford University Press.

Tang, Z., S. Brody, C. Quinn, L. Chang and T. Wei (2011) "Moving from agenda to action: evaluating local climate change action plans," *Journal of Environmental Planning and Management*, **53** (1), 41–62.

U.S. Mayors (2005) *The U.S. Mayors Climate Protection Agreement*. Accessed 18 August 2015 at http://www.usmayors.org/climateprotection/documents/mcpAgreement.pdf.

Vaughan, K., A. T. Kaczynski, S. Wilehlm, A. Sonja, G. Besenyi, R. Bergstron and K. Heinrich (2013)

"Exploring the distribution of park availability, features and quality across Kansas City, Missouri by income and race/ethnicity: an environmental justice investigation," *Annals of Behavioral Medicine,* **45** (1), S28–S38.

Wheeler, S. M. (2013) *Planning for Sustainability: Creating Livable, Equitable, and Ecological Communities,* 2nd edn. New York: Routledge Press.

Wright Wendel, H. E., J. Downs and J. Mihelcic (2011) "Assessing equitable access to urban green space: the role of engineered water infrastructure," *Environmental Science and Technology,* **45,** 6728–6734.

Wrigley, N. (2002) "Food deserts in British cities: policy context and research practice," *Urban Studies,* **39,** 2029–2040.

Zahran S., S. D. Brody, A. Vedlitz, H. Grover and C. Miller (2008) "Vulnerability and capacity: explaining local commitment to climate-change policy," *Environment and Planning C: Government and Policy,* **26** (3), 544–562.

Zeemering, E. S. (2009) "What does sustainability mean to city officials?" *Urban Affairs Review.* Accessed 10 January 2016 at http://uar.sagepub.com/content/early/2009/05/28/1078087409337297.full.pdf.

PART IV

Cities in place

13 The urban pulse of the global South: the case of Cali, Colombia

Lina Martínez

Introduction

This chapter provides an insight into life in a traumatized city. It documents changes in Cali, Colombia as an example from the research frontier of cities of the global South and especially cities in the traumatized South.

The chapter highlights and aims to fill at least two gaps. The first is the lack of studies on large metropolitan areas in South America; the lack of data to conduct academic studies on city development is a major issue. Governments invest little into research on urban problems, and most academics do not have the resources to undertake studies of this magnitude. The data available in most of the cases is aggregated, and micro-analysis at a city level is rare. In this study, information combining different sources is presented to provide a detailed picture of a traumatized city that has been trying to overcome a history of violence and drug-trafficking.

Second, the study provides a combination of objective and subjective data that is an uncommon mix. In this analysis, objective data is used to show how the quality of life in Cali has changed over the last years, and comparisons are made with Bogotá and Medellín, the other major cities in Colombia. The analysis also helps one to understand the evolution of two cities that have been heavily impacted by crime and drug-trafficking. During the 1980s and 1990s, Cali and Medellín were famous for their cartel wars, high rates of homicide and the brutality of the drug business. This chapter of recent Colombian history has been portrayed in countless documentaries, books, movies and series. The other story, the one of the evolution of quality of life after such a high rate of violence is less well known to the public.

The analysis also uses subjective data. The main focus here is to portray the levels of life satisfaction or happiness of three distinctive segments of Cali's population. Original – and very uncommon – data are used to show that in Cali every strata of the population, no matter how poor, register happy and satisfied lives. Happiness in Cali contrasts with high levels of crime, poverty and questionable public administration. It seems counterintuitive to expect to have a content population with all the odds against a happy life. This case calls for a revision of our understanding of happiness in traumatized cities.

Searching for heaven's outpost

Glaeser (2011) affirms that cities are the safest, greenest and most attractive places to live in. This was not true in Cali during the 1990s. In one decade, the city had to confront the largest mortgage crisis in the country, economic liberalization and drug-trafficking violence. All these factors combined to weaken local governments and institutions, spread violence to nearby municipalities and make the city incapable of confronting social issues like poverty and equality (Otero, 2012).

Violence was the most serious problem in the city. Generally speaking, in Colombia there are two sources of violence: drug-trafficking, which occurs mostly in urban contexts, and civil armed conflict, which is heavily concentrated in rural areas. Cali has had to deal with both. During the 1990s Cali was amongst the ten most violent cities in the world, with an urban homicide rate of more than 90 per 100,000 habitants per year. This was the result of drug-related violence (Otero, 2012; World Bank, 2002). The armed conflict violence penetrated the city through the permanent influx of displaced populations from the Pacific region. In 1990 the city had about 1.7 million habitants, and by 2015 the population had grown to about 2.4 million. Almost half of the population growth is due to the resettlement of large population groups affected by conflict in rural areas. These migration flows have created social tensions and have widened inequality in the city, as economic opportunities, already scarce, became a privilege for a few. Newcomers had to access the informal economy to earn a living (Poveda, 2011).

During the decades of the 1990s and 2000s, local authorities were unable to manage the city. Three elected majors were recalled due to allegations of corruption or irregularities in the election process. The absence of leadership meant there was little progress towards economic growth and poverty alleviation (World Bank, 2002). On top of this, the 1998 financial crisis hit Colombia hard, and Cali suffered the most. Central government lacked resources to overcome the crisis; then international creditors imposed an austerity plan on the city (Echavarría et al., 2002; World Bank, 2002).

Cali is now overcoming some of these problems. Violence is down to historical lows, public administration has strengthened, and there are important investments in poverty alleviation policies. The economy in the region has also been reactivated (Escobar et al., 2013). In terms of city panning, several revitalization plans, including a mass transit transportation system, territories for social inclusion (*Territorios de Inclusión y Oportunidades*, TIOS) implemented in the most impoverished districts of the city, environmental programs and parks and renovation, are in place (Plan de desarrollo municipal, 2012–2015 – see Alcaldía de Cali, 2012).

Cultural industries are emerging and playing a central role in the reconstruction of a broader identity of the city. Cali, is the "world capital of salsa music" and no other city in Colombia has being able to create as distinctive a characteristic as the salsa culture. Through this cultural identity Cali has been able position itself as cultural hub within a modern and globalized society (Wade, 1995; Waxer, 2010). With tropical weather and countless cultural venues for salsa music there is a new economic resurgence, an increase in security and urban renovation. Cali is being rebranded as "heaven's outpost" in the global South.

Improving quality of life

Seventy-six percent of the population of Colombia live in urban areas (World Bank, 2014). Bogotá, Medellín and Cali are the three major cities and their combined population is more than 12 million habitants (DANE, 2015). Over 34 percent of the total urban population live in these cities.

Bogotá is the capital and largest city in the country. Twenty-four percent of total GDP in 2012 was produced in the capital (Banco de la República, 2013) and 38 percent of the working population resides there (DANE, 2015). Cali and Medellín are similar in size and economic activity. Both cities have a population of about 2.4 million habitants. In 2012, the regions where Cali and Medellín are the capitals (Valle del Cauca and Antioquia) contributed to 4.1 and 4.3 percent of total GDP, respectively. Besides sharing similar economic and demographic characteristics, Cali and Medellín suffered the drug trade violence of the 1980s and 1990s. The cartel wars created high homicides rates, unemployment, poverty and weak institutions (Rocha, 2000; Vargas, 2005).

The decade of the 2000s provided the opportunity for Cali and Medellín to overcome a deep economic crisis and rebuild the cities to make them more equitable and livable. During this time there was an uneven resurgence of both cities despite their similar conditions. Three dimensions provide a picture of how these cities have advanced (or stagnated) in institutional strengthening and quality of life over the years: security, social investment and fiscal performance. The numbers show that urban development is not a homogenous story across the country.

Security

Cali and Medellín are the most violent cities in Colombia. During the decade of the 1990s and the early 2000s they were amongst the most violent places in the world (Llorente, 2005; Restrepo and Osorio, 2011). Even though security has significantly improved due to the interventions of central and local governments, it has proved challenging to reducing crime to the average levels of cities with similar characteristics in the South. Two factors explain this difficulty. On the one hand, the competition for control over drug markets generates high homicide rates in urban areas. On the other hand, the growth of criminal activity (related with drug-trafficking) has taxed the limits and abilities of law enforcement institutions (Gaviria and Vélez, 2001).

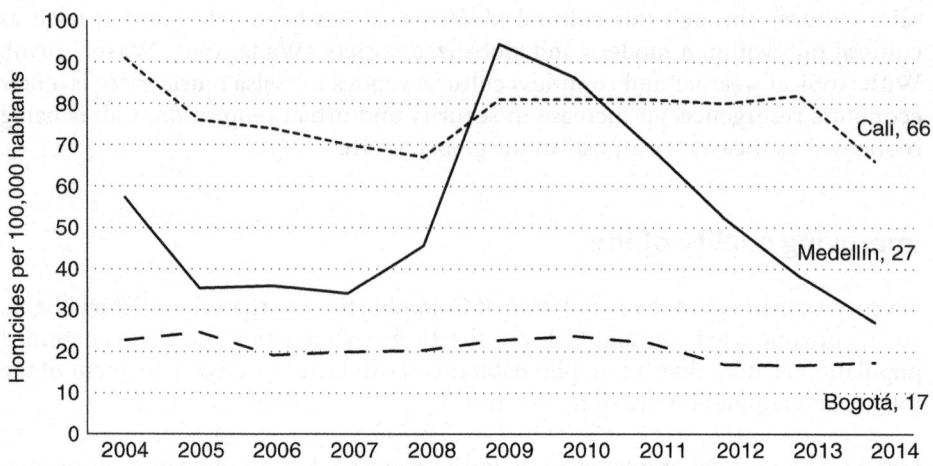

Sources: Cali Cómo Vamos (2014), Medellín Cómo Vamos (2014), Bogotá Cómo Vamos (2014).

Figure 13.1   Homicides rate per 100,000 habitants, 2004–2014

Figure 13.1 shows the trend of homicide rates. During the past decade Cali was the most violent city in the country, with an average of 77 homicides per 100,000 habitants every year. From 2009 to 2013, the trend has remained stable. Medellín also reported high rates, but the average over the same period is lower, 52 homicides per 100,000 habitants per year. During the period 2008–2010 Medellín experienced a serious increase of violence due to wars within illegal armed groups fighting to control territory for drug-trafficking (Cotte, 2011; Medina et al., 2011). Bogotá presents homicide rates similar to other major cities in the region, averaging 21 homicides per 100,000 habitants per year (Cotte, 2011). In all cases 2014 was a year of historically low homicide rates.

Homicide rates have declined over the past years. Nevertheless, streets assaults and thefts have increased in all major metropolitan areas in the country. In Bogotá petty crime is soaring: between 2008 and 2014 this indicator increased by 40 percent. Cali and Medellín also present a similar but less accentuated trend. Street assaults and petty crime have become the most sensitive issue in major cities. During the past years, the perception of unsafety has increased and citizens declare themselves to feel more insecure walking in the streets (Bogotá Cómo Vamos, 2014; Cali Cómo Vamos, 2014; Medellín Cómo Vamos, 2014). In Cali, 31 percent of individuals surveyed declared that one family member or friend of the interviewed was assaulted or was a victim of street theft during the past year (CaliBRANDO, 2015).

Given the dimension of crime activity, local governments have to divert an important share of public resources into making cities safer, particularly in Cali, a much more violent and unsafe city than Medellín and Bogotá. Despite all the efforts and resources invested in security, the improvement over the years has been modest, at least when compared to Medellín.

Social investment and progress

Poverty, lack of accumulation of human capital, stagnated economic growth and scarce employment opportunities are amongst a larger list of factors associated with violence in urban settings (Fajnzylber et al., 1998; Tadjoeddin and Murshed, 2007). Crime and violence are identified as the major public policy topics in Colombia. Central government and, particularly, local governments in Medellín and Cali have had to incur many public costs related to policing, prevention, criminal justice and prison systems. This has a direct effect on what government is able to do on other fronts like city planning, economic growth and social intervention (Soares and Naritomi, 2010). Scarce resources are diverted to security.

Although Cali and Medellín have, generally speaking, similar characteristics and problems, Medellín invests a higher proportion (and with better outcomes) on social policies than Cali. Figure 13.2 presents the evolution of the index of society progress, which is a composite measure of how cities are doing in terms of education, poverty reduction, health and wellbeing, affordable housing, safety, environment, social inclusion, water, sanitation and democracy. This index classifies cities from low to high. Compared to Medellín and Bogotá, Cali has stagnated, and the progress made over the past years is minimal.

Compared to Bogotá and Medellín, Cali has the highest rates of poverty (19%), informal economy (46%) and unemployment (11%) for 2014.

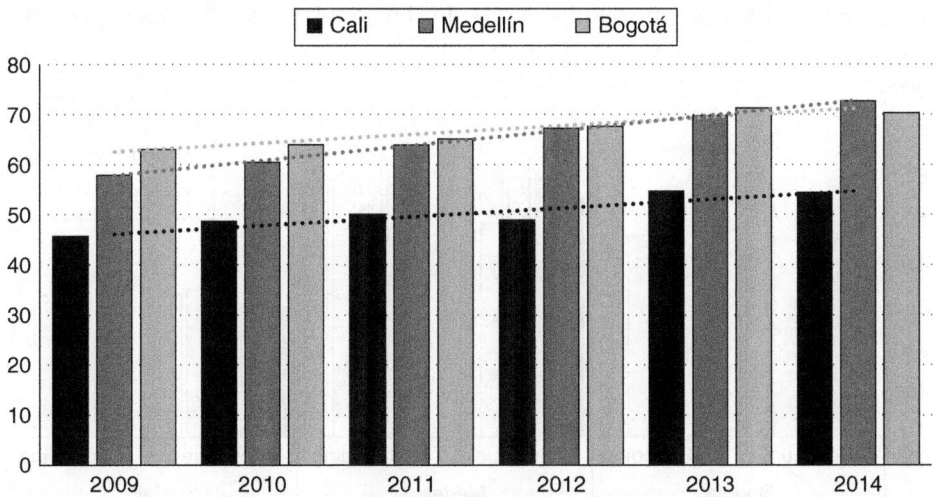

Source: Aranibar et al. (2015). Índice de Progreso Social.

Figure 13.2   Index of society progress, 2009–2014

Fiscal performance

In 2002 the World Bank provided technical assistance to Cali's local government aimed at designing a "city development strategy." One of the major conclusions of this assistance was that Cali lacked the fiscal and human resources to execute many of its policies (World Bank, 2002). One of the reasons for this claim was the inability of the city to collect local taxes and profit from public companies such as sanitation, water supply and telecommunication companies, which are one of the main sources of revenue for local investment. Figure 13.3 presents data on government per habitant revenue and spending during the period 2007–2011. Surprisingly, Medellín is the city with the highest revenue per habitant amongst major cities in Colombia, even above Bogotá. Spending per habitant is also the highest, amounting to US$660 per habitant during 2007–2011. Likewise, Medellín is the city with major investment in poverty reduction, education and urban development, which reflects a responsible fiscal policy as well as the ability to capture central government resources for developing projects (Muñoz, 2013).

It is important to stress that Cali and Medellín are very similar in terms of size and economic dynamic. Moreover, they share a similar history of the violence and institutional corruption that made Colombia infamous during the 1990s. The important differences between Cali and Medellín on fiscal performance and social investment are an issue understudied in the literature.

Cali reports the lowest per habitant revenue and spending, even lower than mid-size cities (fewer than 400,000 habitants) in the country. Two factors explain the

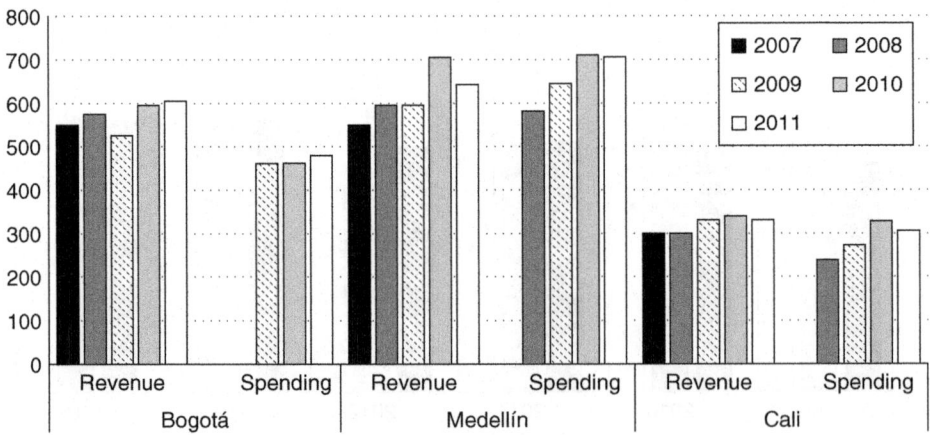

Note: *Calculated on an exchange rate of 2000 pesos Colombian to 1US$.

Sources: Revenue per habitant: Muñoz (2013, Figure 1). Spending per habitant: Redes ciudades como vamos, informes de calidad de vida Bogotá, Medellín y Cali.

Figure 13.3 Revenue and spending per capita in US dollars,* 2007–2011

poor fiscal performance of the city. First, one of the revoked elected majors out-sourced local taxes collection in 2005 to a third party. This contract became a permanent basis for corruption claims (El Tiempo, 2012). Second, Emcali, the public services company (which is the main source of local revenue), came close to bankruptcy in 2000 and central government intervened for 13 years (El País, 2013). By 2013, a new administration tried to recover public finances. Collection of local taxes and control of Emcali allowed the city to improve fiscal performance (El País, 2015).

Poor and rich equally happy?

The objective data presented in this analysis shows that Cali has stagnated com-pared to the two other large cities in the country. Lack of improvements made over the past years in safety, social investment and fiscal performance indicate that the city is struggling to catch up with the demands of modern cities. There have been some improvements over the last administration, but it is too early to detect a major change. Cali has not being able to overcome its violent past as Medellín has done, despite sharing similar problems and economic dynamics.

Objective data only allows the presentation of a partial picture of societal progress. An important dimension of urban policy is how satisfied or happy are the people who inhabit the space (Florida et al., 2013; Goldberg et al., 2012). Cali may not come first in terms of government performance, but its habitants are as happy and satisfied with their lives as residents of Bogotá and Medellín. The national quality of life survey showed that in 2014 a large share of Cali's residents declared that they were satisfied or very satisfied with their lives (85 percent); in Medellín and Bogotá the proportion is very similar, 89 percent and 86 percent, respectively (DANE – ECV, 2014).

To portray happiness and life satisfaction in Cali, data from three distinctive groups in the city was used, waste pickers, street vendors and the general population, who were asked to rate, on a scale of 1 to 10, how satisfied they were with their lives. Results show that in Cali, socioeconomic conditions, even for the poorest, are not determinants of living a happy and satisfied life.

Data for the general population comes from CaliBRANDO (2015), a population survey statistically representative for gender and socioeconomic strata of the city (n = 1,206). Information for street vendors comes from a direct survey of infor-mal vendors in downtown Cali in 2014 (n = 527). The numbers for waste pickers comes from census data on trash collectors in 2015 (n = 3,109). Information on these three groups was collected for different purposes, but the question of life satisfaction was formulated in the same way. To capture the levels of life satis-faction the following question was asked of the three groups: "on a scale of 1 to 10 how satisfied are you with your life?" When the score was lower than 10, the survey inquired "what do you need to have a completely satisfied life?" Table 13.1

Table 13.1   Characteristics of waste pickers, street vendors and the general population

	Waste pickers	Street vendors	General population
Age (years)	44.0	41.9	38.2
Educational level – higher education (%)	1.5	6	41.9
Lower SES (%)	97.5	82.7	51.0
Married or living with a partner (%)	44.2	51.9	43.5
Number of children	3.1	2.9	2.2
Age first child	21.0	21.1	23.1
Income – less than minimum wage* (%)	87.3	40.8	24.2
Observations	3,109	527	1,204

Note: *Less than US$322,175.

Sources: General population: CaliBRANDO, 2015 database; Street vendors: socioeconomic profile of street vendors of Cali, 2014 database; Waste pickers: census of waste pickers of Cali, 2015 database.

presents socioeconomic information. Waste pickers are poorest. Eighty-seven percent earn less than the minimum wage, 97 percent live in the most deprived and violent areas of the city[1] and only 1.5 percent have been able to study any type of post-secondary education.

Despite clear differences between them in terms of income, education and the quality of the neighborhood where they live (measured through SES), all of them report living happy and satisfied lives. Figure 13.4 shows the results. For all groups, people declared being very happy with their lives. As expected, waste pickers are the least satisfied, but more than 50 percent of them rate their life satisfaction over 8 (on a 1–10 scale). There are no differences between street sellers and the average Caleño, despite the clear gap in several other domains of urban life.

The bourgeoning literature on happiness and life satisfaction (Alesina et al., 2004; Bok, 2010; David et al., 2013; Delle Fave, 2013; Easterlin, 2001; Layard and Layard, 2011; Van Praag and Ferrer-i-Carbonell, 2008) has led to three main conclusions: 1) rich people are, generally speaking, happier than poor people; 2) people tend to declare that more money would make them happier; and 3) individuals tend to be less happy when inequality is high.

In Cali a different pattern is found for at least one of these findings. Generally speaking, the data on life satisfaction shows that there is a linear relationship with income and life satisfaction, which adheres to the body of research that claims that people get happier as their income increases. However, a caveat is necessary: all of them report high levels of satisfaction, at least higher than levels reported in developed countries.

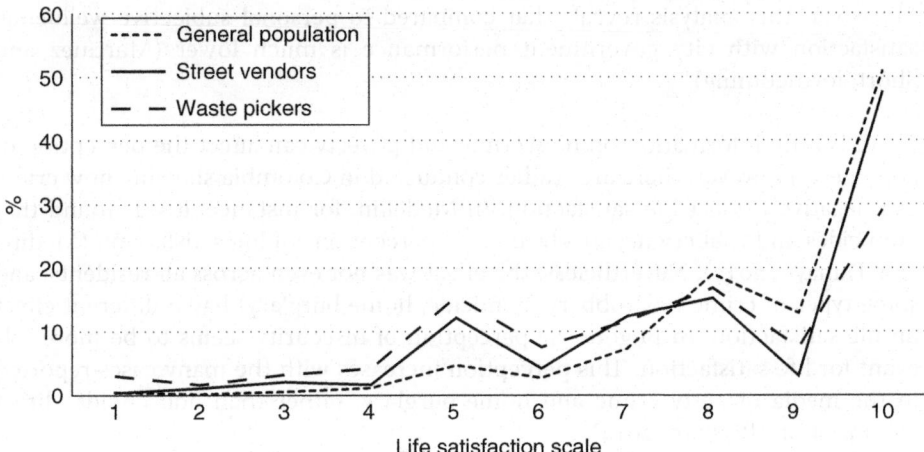

Sources: General population: CaliBRANDO, 2015 database; Street vendors: socioeconomic profile of street vendors of Cali, 2014 database; Waste pickers: census of waste pickers of Cali, 2015 database.

Figure 13.4   Life satisfaction for general population, street vendors and waste pickers in Cali

People tend to declare that more money will make them happier (Bok, 2010). This is also true in Cali for all groups. To the question "what do you need to be completely satisfied with your life" it is found that money, or the things money can buy, is the missing piece to be completely happy. Twenty-five percent of waste pickers declared that they will be completely happy if they own a house, 17 percent consider that they need a stable job and 11 percent would like to have better health conditions. Street vendors have similar preferences: 20 percent would like to have more money, 11 percent want a better job and 5 percent want to improve their health. The average Caleño looks for more money (11 percent), better employment (5 percent) and house ownership (5 percent). Is very interesting to find that preferences are quite similar despite their conditions. This may suggest that in Cali, rich and poor are stuck on a hedonic treadmill (Bok, 2010).

One major finding in the literature of life satisfaction is that individuals tend to be less happy when inequality is high (Alesina et al., 2004; Graham and Felton, 2006). Cali is a very unequal city and the opportunities are not equally distributed within the population. If even the poorest declare themselves happy, it is due to other types of factors different from income and the consumption of durable goods. It could be that social relations, family and personal factors may be more relevant when explaining what makes people happy (Rojas, 2011).

On the surface, it seems that everyone is getting a high share of happiness in Cali. However, there is a limit. A recent analysis conducted in the city shows that behind the general perception of content there are important differences by gender. Women, at a much higher rate than males, are negatively affected by several issues like mental health, perception of poverty and job instability.

Moreover, this analysis reveals that compared to personal subjective wellbeing, satisfaction with city government performance is much lower (Martínez and Short, forthcoming).

There is little information on how crime and poverty can affect the perception of happiness. However, there are studies conducted in Colombia showing how crime can negatively affect life satisfaction. In Medellín, for instance, it was found that homicides and robbery negatively affected perceptions of life satisfaction (Medina and Tamayo, 2012). Nevertheless, the effect was not even across all residents, and some types of crime (i.e. robbery, homicide, home burglary) had a different effect on life satisfaction. In Bogotá the perception of insecurity seems to be more relevant for life satisfaction. This perception increases with the many cases reported in the media of petty crime and home burglary, rather than households' direct victimization (Romero, 2014).

Life satisfaction has been extensively studied, and the literature on developed countries abounds. However, little is known of this dimension in the global South, particularly in terms of its connections with crime and victimization given that Latin America is one of most violent regions in the world (Luhnow, 2014).

Development in this area is necessary. The increase of criminal activity in the global South and the limits that violence imposes on government performance call for a more active research agenda in the region.

Conclusions

Colombia as a whole is a very violent country. More than 50 murders per 100,000 inhabitants per year have been reported during most of the last 25 years. In other countries in the region the rate is below 10 homicides (Gaviria et al., 2010). Cali is the most violent city in a violent country. During the 1980s and 1990s Cali and Medellín were quite similar; in both cities the drug-trafficking, and violence related to this business, penetrated and corrupted all social and political institutions. Nowadays, Medellín has been able to manage building a better place to live for their habitants, while Cali has stagnated.

Objective data presented in this chapter shows how the quality of life of the three largest cities in the country has evolved in the recent past. Compared to Medellín (a similar city), Cali has shown shallow progress. Nevertheless, Cali is trying to become a global city. There is a new coherence in the city that constructs new narratives, including greener spaces, better urban planning and better governance.

The people in the city are happy, no matter how poor they are. Waste pickers, street vendors and average individuals show similar levels of life satisfaction. On the surface it seems that happiness is equally distributed.

This work attempts to start building a body of research on urban life in the global South. There are so many issues that make cities in this region unique cases: violence, poverty, informal jobs and happy people. Cali fits in this profile. The analysis presented is original in different ways. It combines objective and subjective data at a city level. Most of the literature focuses only on objective or subjective data and analyses are conducted at country level.

NOTE

1 Socioeconomic strata (SES) is calculated using geographical information. Cities in Colombia are divided into 6 socioeconomic strata, 1 is the poorest, 6 is the richest. Lower SES comprises people living in neighborhoods in 1 and 2 of the socioeconomic strata.

References

Alcaldía de Cali (2012). Plan de desarrollo municipal 2012–2015. Cali, Valle del Cauca. http://www.cali.gov.co/publicaciones/plan_de_desarrollo_municipal_2012_2015_pub. Accessed September 10, 2015.

Alesina, A., Di Tella, R. and MacCulloch, R. (2004). Inequality and happiness: are Europeans and Americans different? *Journal of Public Economics*, 88(9), 2009–2042.

Aranibar, A., Maldonado, D., García, J., Jiménez, O. and Caro, P. (2015). Índice de progreso social 2015. Red de progreso social Colombia.

Banco de la República (2013). Informe de Coyuntura económica regional. Banco de la República, Bogotá, DC.

Bogotá Cómo Vamos (2014). Informe de calidad de vida 2014.

Bok, Derek (2010). *The Politics of Happiness: What Government Can Learn from the New Research on Well-Being*. Princeton, NJ: Princeton University Press.

Cali Cómo Vamos (2014). Informe de calidad de vida 2014.

CaliBRANDO (2015). Boletín POLIS N. 15. ISSN: 1909-7964.

Cotte, A. (2011). Socio-economic development and violence: an empirical application for seven metropolitan areas in Colombia. *Peace Economics, Peace Science and Public Policy*, 17(1): 1–23.

DANE (2015). Estadísticas por tema. Demografía y población. http://www.dane.gov.co/index.php/estadisticas-por-tema/demografia-y-poblacion. Accessed October 6, 2015.

DANE – ECV (2014). Encuesta de calidad de Vida. Bogotá.

David, Susan A., Boniwell, I. and Ayers, Amanda C. (eds.) (2013). *Oxford Handbook of Happiness*. Oxford: Oxford University Press.

Delle Fave, Antonella (ed.) (2013). *The Exploration of Happiness*. Dordrecht, The Netherlands: Springer.

Easterlin, R. A. (2001). Income and happiness: towards a unified theory. *Economic Journal*, 111: 465–484.

Echavarría, J. J., Fainboim, I. and Zuleta, L. A. (2002). Explicaciones de la crisis de la economía vallecaucana y posibles elementos para su recuperación. Bogotá: Fedesarrollo.

El País (2013). Hoy el presidente Santos pone fin a 13 años de intervención de Emcali. http://www.elpais.com.co/elpais/cali/noticias/hoy-cumple-hora-cero-para-devolucion-emcali-municipio. Accessed October 10, 2015.

El País (2015). Cali volvió a hacer bien la tarea en materia de impuestos. http://www.elpais.com.co/elpais/cali/noticias/cali-volvio-hacer-bien-tarea-recaudo-impuestos. Accessed October 10, 2015.

El Tiempo (2012). Alcaldía de Cali terminó contrato con concesionaria de Hacienda. http://www.eltiempo.com/archivo/documento/CMS-12123821. Accessed September 15, 2015.

Escobar, J., Moreno, S. and Collazos, J. (2013). *Composición de la economía de la región suroccidente de Colombia*. Ensayos sobre economía regional No. 52. Banco de la República.

Fajnzylber, P., Lederman, D. and Loayza, N. V. (1998). *Determinants of Crime Rates in Latin America and the World: An Empirical Assessment.* Washington, DC: World Bank.

Florida, R., Mellander, C. and Rentfrow, P. J. (2013). The happiness of cities. *Regional Studies,* 47(4), 613–627.

Gaviria, A., Medina, C. and Tamayo, J. A. (2010). Assessing the link between adolescent fertility and urban crime. *Borradores de Economía,* 594.

Gaviria, A. and Vélez, C. (2001). Who bears the burden of crime and violence in Colombia? Working paper. Fedesarrollo and World Bank.

Glaeser, E. (2011). *Triumph of the City: How Our Greatest Invention Makes Us Richer, Smarter, Greener, Healthier and Happier.* London: Pan Macmillan.

Goldberg, A., Leyden, K. M. and Scotto, T. J. (2012). Untangling what makes cities liveable: happiness in five cities. *Proceedings of the ICE-Urban Design and Planning,* 165(3), 127–136.

Graham, C. and Felton, A. (2006). Inequality and happiness: insights from Latin America. *Journal of Economic Inequality,* 4(1), 107–122.

Layard, P. R. G. and Layard, R. (2011). *Happiness: Lessons from a New Science.* London: Penguin.

Llorente, M. (2005). Another perspective for security experience and coexistence in Bogotá, *Revista Quórum,* 12, 1–15.

Luhnow, D. (2014). Latin America is world's most violent region. *The Wall Street Journal,* April 11. http://www.wsj.com/articles/SB10001424052702303603904579495863883782316. Accessed November 1, 2015.

Martínez, L. and Short, J. R. (forthcoming). Life Satisfaction in Cali, Colombia: Behind the Happiness Syndrome.

Medellín Cómo Vamos (2014). Informe de calidad de vida 2014.

Medina, C., Posso, C. and Tamayo, J. A. (2011). *Costos de la violencia urbana y políticas públicas: algunas lecciones de Medellín* (No. 009076). Banco de la República.

Medina, C. and Tamayo, J. A. (2012). An assessment of how urban crime and victimization affects life satisfaction. In D. Webb and E. Wills-Herrera (eds.), *Subjective Well-Being and Security* (pp. 91–147). The Netherlands: Springer.

Muñoz, A. (2013). Evolución de las cifras fiscales entre 2007 y 2011. Gobiernos centrales de las principales 6 ciudades Colombianas (Num. 773). Banco de la República.

Otero, Andrea (2012). Cali a comienzos del Siglo XXI: ¿Crisis o recuperación? *Banco de la República, Economía Regional* (No. 009903).

Poveda, A. C. (2011). Economic development, inequality and poverty: an analysis of urban violence in Colombia. *Oxford Development Studies,* 39(4), 453–468.

Restrepo, A. and Osorio, C. (2011). Behaviour of homicides 2007–2009 in the Colombian cities (Cali, Bogotá and Medellín). www.medicinalegal.gov.co/images/stories/root/CRNV/boletinesregionales/Comportamientodeloshomicidios20072009.pdf. Accessed November 7, 2015.

Rocha, R. (2000). *La economía colombiana tras 25 años de narcotráfico.* Siglo del Hombre Editores.

Rojas, M. (2011). Happiness, income, and beyond. *Applied Research in Quality of Life,* 6, 265–276.

Romero, D. (2014). Insecurity or perception of insecurity? Urban crime and dissatisfaction with life: evidence from the case of Bogotá. *Peace Economics, Peace Science and Public Policy,* 20(1), 169–208.

Soares, R. and Naritomi, J. (2010). Understanding high crime rates in Latin America: the role of social and policy factors. In R. Di Tella, S. Edwards and E. Schargrodsky (eds.), *The Economics of Crime: Lessons for and from Latin America* (pp. 19–55). Cambridge, MA: National Bureau of Economic Research.

Tadjoeddin, M. and Murshed, S. (2007). Socio-economic determinants of everyday violence in Indonesia: an empirical investigation of Javanese districts, 1994–2003. *Journal of Peace Research,* 44(6), 689–709.

Van Praag, B. M. and Ferrer-i-Carbonell, A. (2008). *Happiness Quantified: A Satisfaction Calculus Approach.* Oxford: Oxford University Press.

THE URBAN PULSE OF THE GLOBAL SOUTH: THE CASE OF CALI, COLOMBIA   181

Vargas, R. (2005). Narcotráfico, guerra y política antidrogas. *Acción Andina. Bogotá.* Junio.

Wade, P. (1995). *Blackness and Race Mixture: The Dynamics of Racial Identity in Colombia.* Baltimore, MD: JHU Press.

Waxer, L. A. (2010). *The City of Musical Memory: Salsa, Record Grooves and Popular Culture in Cali, Colombia.* Middletown, CT: Wesleyan University Press.

World Bank (2002). *Cali, Colombia. Toward a City Development Strategy.* World Bank Country Study.

World Bank (2014). Data. Urban population in the world. http://datos.bancomundial.org/indicador/SP.URB.TOTL.IN.ZS. Accessed September 8, 2015.

14 The city in Brazil

Thomas J. Vicino

In 2009, the cover of *The Economist* depicted Rio de Janeiro's iconic Christ the Redeemer statue as a rocket taking off into the sky, declaring, "Brazil takes off" (Economist, 2009). Indeed, Brazil's global moment had arrived. After decades of stagnation, its population and economy has boomed for a decade. The ultimate symbol of Brazil's arrival on the world stage was the award to host the FIFA World Cup in 2014 and the Olympic Summer Games in 2016. Only four years later (2013), Brazil's same statue reappeared on the cover falling out of the sky with the headline, "has Brazil blown it?" This short period of unprecedented growth and decline reflects the enduring impacts of urbanization and globalization. Cities across Brazil are the sites of large-scale changes in society, the economy, and politics.

Brazil conjures up many iconic images of the city: breathtaking landscapes, concrete jungles, and favelas. From the Marvelous City of Rio de Janeiro to the Cosmopolitan City of São Paulo, the city in Brazil is defined by contrasts (Rohter, 2012). It is home to one of the world's largest multiethnic societies, yet it is one of the most segregated. While it is one of the world's largest democracies with over 200 million inhabitants, its political history is turbulent. The environmental landscape offers a vast array of diverse—yet vulnerable—ecosystems, but Brazil's cities and urban growth outpace most others in the world. These defining characteristics, including demographic shifts, economic transition, political change, and landscape transformation, shape the pattern of growth of Brazil's cities (Baer, 2013). The goal of this chapter is to better understand the complexities of the production of urban space in Brazil.

In this chapter, I consider the evolution of the city in Brazil. The chapter is divided into four sections. First, I review the history of the Brazilian tradition of urbanism, and then I examine the characteristics of urbanization in Brazil. Next, I turn to a critical analysis of the issues facing cities in twenty-first-century Brazil, and I conclude by offering future research directions on, and lessons from, the urban experience in Brazil.

The Brazilian tradition of urbanism

Urbanism informs our understanding about how "civilisations have chosen to represent themselves in spatial form, and the processes through which specific urban forms come about" (Cuthbert, 2006, p. 1). In this vein, Brazilian urbanism can be best understood as the social production of the built environment of cities. The city emerges as a multifaceted symbol of modernism: the economic growth of a developing country, the social inequality of rapid growth, and the political struggle for liberty. Brazil is one of the only countries in the world where the movement to democracy ushered in an era of planning and policymaking to create inclusive urban space as a form of citizenship (Jones, 2004). Let us then consider how the roles of architecture, modernism, and geographic thought played in the evolution of urban thinking in Brazil. It is from these perspectives that we can understand the Brazilian tradition of urbanism.

Architecture and modernism

Whereas the field of urban studies in the United States is closely aligned with the social sciences, the study of the city in Brazil is deeply rooted in the field of architecture and urbanism. Architects such as Lúcio Costa, Alfred Agache, and Oscar Niemeyer laid the foundation for the spatial dimensions of the modern city. Let us review each of their contributions in turn.

On April 21, 1960, President Juscelino Kubitschek mandated that the capital of Brazil be moved from Rio de Janeiro to Brasília. In the late 1950s, famed architect Lúcio Costa collaborated with the federal government to design a master planned city that today planners herald as a model city. The public rationale for relocating the capital was to populate the interior of the nation and build a more accessible capital city. However, the goal was also to harness urbanism to move the country forward, a symbolic step toward the modernization of a growing country. Anthropologist James Holston (1989) notes that, "Brasília was built to be more than merely the symbol of this new age. Rather, its design and construction were intended as means to *create* it by transforming Brazilian society" (p. 3, emphasis in original). Costa's plan, known as the Pilot Plan, emerged as a national symbol of progress. The plan transformed the hinterlands of Brazil into a polynucleated metropolis that contained the infrastructure for a new utopian city and a nascent capital—clean modern buildings, dense housing stock, and large swaths of public space. Today Brasília stands as a symbol of Brazil's future.

Brazil's most widely known architect, Oscar Niemeyer, collaborated with Lúcio Costa to develop Brasília. In designing the new capital city, Niemeyer instilled his bold, modernist principles into many of Brasília's new buildings. He was often quoted as stating that, "form follows beauty." This notion is expressed in the structures he designed such as the National Congress, the National Cathedral, the National Library, and the Palácio do Planalto, the president's official place of work. Niemeyer left his imprint on many cities throughout Brazil, including Belo

Horizonte, São Paulo, and Rio de Janeiro. In his obituary, the *New York Times* reflected that, "his curvaceous, lyrical, hedonistic forms helped shape a distinct national architecture and a modern identity for Brazil that broke with its colonial and baroque past" (Ouroussoff, 2012). This identity further helped to define Brazilian urbanism.

Similarly, French architect Alfred Agache was commissioned to formulate urban plans for four of Brazil's great cities: Curitiba, Porto Alegre, Recife, and Rio de Janeiro. Co-founding the French Society for Urban Studies, Agache was grounded in the Beaux-Arts architectural movement. Agache viewed the goal of urbanism as a way to "express plastically the social program of the city while clarifying the ideas that are scattered and unformulated in his social milieu" (Underwood, 1991, p. 130). In his plan for Rio de Janeiro, Agache imagined the city as a tropical Paris— above all else, it was a beautification plan that involved public health reforms, demolitions, slum clearance, grandiose buildings, and stately boulevards. Agache later turned his attention to Curitiba and is perhaps most associated with the urban design of this region. As a planned urban center for the southern tier of Brazil, Agache turned to Ebenezer Howard's garden city concept to formulate a series of neighborhoods connected by greenways and transportation routes. This plan led Jaime Lerner (2014), former mayor of Curitiba, to develop a rapid transit system that is widely viewed as making the city one of the most livable and sustainable in the world. Agache (1930, p. 4) captures the essence of Brazilian urbanism, noting that it:

> is a Science and an Art and, above all, a Social Philosophy. By urbanism we mean the set of rules applied to the improvement of buildings, street systems, circulations, and decongestion of public arteries. It is the remodeling, extension, and beautification of a city executed by means of a methodological study of the human geography and urban typography, without ignoring financial considerations.

The modernism movement came to define Brazil's aspirations. The novelist Stefan Zweig (1941) fondly observed the vibrant growth and progress of Rio de Janeiro and called Brazil "a country of the future"—a phrase that has become ubiquitous among Brazilians. This tradition of urbanism symbolized the idea of growth and positivity, and, ultimately, it facilitated the transition to democracy. However, the modernization of Brazil was far from fulfilled. Efforts to modernize Brazil's cities through large industrial complexes, tall buildings, and public spaces were not accompanied by improvements in the socioeconomic condition of urban residents. Thus, Brazilian urbanism remains largely symbolic and idealist in nature.

Geographic thought

Geographers, sociologists, and other social scientists with similar interests have shaped our thinking on the city. In the early twentieth century, pioneers like Robert Park, Ernest Burgess, and Roderick McKenzie (1925) and Louis Wirth (1938), among others, contributed significant works on the form and evolution of the city.

The theories of the Chicago School dominated the discourse on the city until the later part of the twentieth century. Challenging the Chicago School's focus on modernism and nuclear urban form, scholars like Michael Dear (2001), Allen Scott and Edward Soja (1996), and Mike Davis (1990), among others, became affiliated with the Los Angeles School, arguing that the postmodern city is much more decentralized than the Chicago School. For the Los Angeles School, competing economic forces of neoliberalism and globalization shape the city.

While the Chicago and Los Angeles Schools influenced our thinking about cities, they did little to further our understanding about urbanism and spatial processes in the developing world, particularly in Latin America. In the mid-twentieth century, several geographers in the United States such as James Preston (1946), Kempton Webb (1974), and Hilgard O'Reilly Sternberg (1959) made noteworthy contributions to a broad body of work about the physical landscape and human geography of Brazil. Yet a deep knowledge about the urbanization of Brazil was still lacking in the English language. To fill the void, it is necessary to consider some of the leading voices on the urbanization of Brazil including Nestor Goulart Reis Filho and Milton Santos.

Nestor Goulart Reis Filho is a prominent urbanist in Brazil. Since 1967, he has served on the faculty of the School of Architecture and Urbanism at the University of São Paulo. Goulart's seminal work is *Urban Evolution of Brazil 1500–1720* (Reis Filho, 1968). His central thesis posits that urbanization in Brazil was a social process embedded in the nation's colonial history. The urban network evolved based on the Portuguese's mercantile economy and feudal regime. Brazil's early cities were divided and governed autonomously by noble captains. The cities functioned as major ports for the trading of goods: slaves, agriculture products, and natural resources. Increased economic activity and migration to cities led to the rapid development of early urban centers such as Salvador, Recife, and Rio de Janeiro. The growth of cities results in the social division of labor and the establishment of an urban market. Goulart's later works included *Notes About Urban Sprawl* (Reis Filho, 2006) and *São Paulo: Village, City, Metropolis* (Reis Filho, 2004). Ultimately, Goulart's work demonstrates that rapid urban growth is characterized by the formulation of many spatial agglomerations of human activity that are rooted in the colonization of Brazil.

The work of Milton Santos provides us with innovative conceptualizations of urban space. Santos was interested in better understanding the urban processes that shape social change, economic development, and political power. In 1979, he published his seminal book *Shared Space* (Santos, 1979), which explains that urban growth is a function of two circuits in the economy. Santos argues that the first circuit consists of the formal economy and is composed of private firms in finance, banking, insurance, and real estate. This produces wealthy residents. The second circuit consists of the informal economy and is composed of street vendors, laborers, and other undocumented work. This produces poor residents. Thus, the urban economy, as it grows, tends to produce an unequal society. Santos referred to this phenomenon as the development of the "third world" metropolis and analyzed the metropolis as a site of globalization and modernization. The processes were inherently urban: globalization facilitates the flow of information, and modernization provides the tools for a command and control economy and a globalized society. Santos (1993) argues that the metropolis in Brazil must be analyzed on two levels: 1) as a part of a global network of cities connected by geographic flows of people and economic activities; and 2) as a part of local histories of place that produce the political economy of growth. Without a doubt, this corpus of work influenced future generations of social scientists around the world and shaped our collective understanding about the causes and consequences of urbanization in Brazil. In 1994, Santos was recognized with the *Vautrin Lud Prize*, the highest award in the discipline of geography (akin to the Nobel Prize), for his lifelong achievements in the field of urban geography in the developing world.

In summary, the contributions that geographers and architects made to understanding and creating Brazilian urbanism cannot be understated. Architects like Niemeyer, Costa, and Agache as well as social scientists like Nestor Goulart Reis Filho and Milton Santos, plus the many who followed in their paths, influenced the ways in which we understand urbanism in Brazil.

The urbanization of Brazil

Brazil's cities are a reflection of its society—Brazil is an urban nation. It is the fifth largest country in the world by land area and population. The nation includes over 3 million square miles of land, spanning a variety of physical geographies. In 1900, Brazil's population was approximately 17 million. It topped 50 million in 1950, and only 25 years later, it reached 100 million. In the following three decades, the population doubled, reaching 200 million in 2014. By 2050, the national population is estimated to level off at 250 million. Table 14.1 displays the population change of the top ten largest cities by key periods in the twentieth and twenty-first centuries in Brazil. Collectively, these ten largest cities grew from 1.6 million residents in 1900 to over 36 million residents in 2015. However, while these cities experienced marked population growth, it was not until 1920 that Brazil had a city, Rio de Janeiro, with a population of at least one million. A decade later, São Paulo reached one million residents. In 1970, Salvador, Belo Horizonte, and Recife joined; and by 1985, all of Brazil's ten largest cities had over one million residents. From the 1950s through the 1980s, Brazil's largest cities experienced the most growth, averaging a growth rate of 65 percent. Few other places, if any, in the western hemisphere witnessed such dramatic changes in the population of urban areas.

Brazil's cities are among some of the largest in the world. The coastal megalopolis region of São Paulo–Rio de Janeiro is composed of 450 cities and over 45 million residents. In 1973, these regions had approximately 15 million residents. Greater São Paulo grew from 8 million residents to a region of 20 million; similarly, greater Rio de Janeiro grew from 6 million residents to a region of 12 million. The

Table 14.1 Population change in the ten largest municipalities in Brazil (%)

City	State	1900–1920	1920–1940	1940–1950	1950–1960	1960–1970	1970–1980	1980–1991	1991–2000	2000–2010	2010–2015
São Paulo	São Paulo	142	129	66	27	113	43	14	8	8	6
Rio de Janeiro	Rio de Janeiro	43	52	35	39	30	20	6	7	8	2
Salvador	Bahia	38	2	44	56	55	49	37	19	10	8
Brasília	Distrito Federal	–	–	–	–	285	120	33	28	26	13
Fortaleza	Ceará	62	130	49	91	64	55	35	21	14	5
Belo Horizonte	Minas Gerais	312	280	67	97	78	44	13	11	6	5
Manaus	Amazonas	143	52	3	15	47	95	10	33	34	12
Curitiba	Paraná	59	78	28	98	80	60	26	23	10	7
Recife	Pernambuco	111	46	51	52	36	14	5	10	8	5
Porto Alegre	Rio Grande do Sul	143	52	45	61	39	27	12	8	4	4
Average		117	91	43	59	83	53	19	17	13	7

Source: IBGE, Census, Brazil.

megalopolis of southeastern Brazil is now an interconnected web of development where people and capital flow freely.

The "Brazilian people"

The nature and distinctiveness of urbanization in Brazil is rooted in the long history of colonization of this nation (Fausto and Fausto, 2014; Skidmore, 2009). Three historical points shaped the formation of cities and their people in Brazil, including the Portuguese colonization of Brazil, the legacy of slavery, and formation of Brazilian identity. The people of colonial and modern Brazil were influenced by the arrival of the Portuguese. The legacy of slavery changed the structure of cities in important ways (Freyre, 1986). Between 1501 and 1888, nearly five million slaves had been imported from the west coast of Africa to Brazil, which resulted in a long tradition of miscegenation between all groups of people, including slaves and native Indians. Today, cities in Brazil reflect this phenomenon—there is no majority racial or ethnic group. In the census, approximately 47 percent of population is white; 43 percent is *pardo*, or mixed; 8 percent is black; 1 percent is yellow; and 0.5 percent is indigenous, which makes Brazil one of the most diverse societies in the world (Nobles, 2000). Thus, Brazilian identity is a noteworthy social construction that shaped the growth of cities. To be Brazilian is to be part of a national ethnicity based on the multiplicity of people, cultures, and territories. Society and culture have been influenced by very different civilizations of Western European whites, African blacks, and indigenous American Indians. Brazil's people are defined by their own distinct histories and characteristics that led to the growth and development of a new society, an urban society. Ribeiro (2000, p. 3) best summarizes this notion as "Brazilians have come to know themselves, to feel themselves, and to act as a single people, belonging to one and the same ethnicity."

The urban economy

The rapid growth of cities in Brazil can be attributed to two processes: dependent development and industrialization. Urbanization was fueled by the national government's public investment in infrastructure, transportation, and firms. The Brazilian model of dependent development was led by the military authoritarian regime. It forged a triple alliance between the state, private, and foreign capital to develop the country during the 1960s and 1970s. Evans (1979, p. 51) notes that this model featured "capital accumulation at the local level accompanied by increasing differentiation of the economy, which is to say by some degree of industrialization." This approach had several effects, including the integration of the economy under the central control of the government, the provision of technological and management opportunity to private firms, and the legitimacy of local economic development. This created an environment that stimulated substantial growth, something that led observers to call it the "Brazilian miracle" of the generation.

Sociologist and former president of Brazil Henrique Fernando Cardoso and his colleague Enzo Faletto (1979) published an influential book *Dependency and*

Development in Latin America, which traces the socioeconomic evolution of this region. They argue that the capitalist expansion of Western Europe and the United States left economies in Latin America dependent on them for development. In Brazil, this phenomenon was manifest in the nationalization of many industries including those of natural resources (i.e., electricity, water, gas, mining, etc.), transportation (i.e., aviation, buses, trains, etc.), and financial services (i.e., banking, finance, etc.). This created a demand to specialize the economy and led to a division of the labor force. The urban economy blossomed as new factories were built on the periphery of major metropolitan areas in the southeastern industrial part of Brazil. This spurred a large migration from the underdeveloped, poor northern states to the developed, wealthier southern states. Forty percent of the population in southern Brazil migrated from the north between 1930 and 1980. Simultaneously, Brazil grew from 35 percent urbanized in 1930 to 75 percent in 1980 (Saunders, 2011). Thus, the state played a large role in developing not only the urban economy but also cities themselves.

Urbanism in twenty-first-century Brazil

The new millennium ushered in a new era of urbanism in Brazil—an era shaped by the challenges that urbanization presents to developing societies. Cities are plagued by issues such as growing sprawl and inequality, the lack of a strong public infrastructure, urban violence, corruption, and questions about social justice. The following review of these urban issues demonstrates the challenges that face Brazilian cities.

Sprawl, inequality, and infrastructure

Brazil is a highly urbanized society, and its cities are sprawling (Misra and Dung, 1983). Today the nation is 85 percent urbanized, and the São Paulo–Rio de Janeiro megalopolis is among the largest in the world. In 1995, shortly after Fernando Henrique Cardoso was elected president, he astutely observed that, "Brazil is no longer an underdeveloped country. It is an unjust country" (Purcell and Roett, 1997). Urbanization often results in inequality. The Gini coefficient, a common measure of inequality, remains staggeringly high at 52.7. Table 14.2 shows the distribution of income by five economic classes in Brazil. The lowest quintile, known as Class E, is composed of residents living in extreme poverty. In 2002, there were 25 million residents, or 14 percent of the population, living in extreme poverty. By 2013, more than two-thirds fewer residents lived in extreme poverty. Similar progress is noteworthy in the middle class, the Class C. The number of residents of the middle class doubled during this time period, from 57 million to 108 million, which is more than half of the country. While significant economic gains were realized during the 2000s, Brazil remains one of the most unequal countries in the world.

Uncontrolled, rapid urbanization creates many challenges for residents; housing, infrastructure, and security are chief among them. According to the Brazilian

Table 14.2 Income distribution in Brazil, 2002–2013

	Annual Household Income (USD)		2002		2009		2013	
	Min.	Max.	Percent	Population	Percent	Population	Percent	Population
Class A	57,237	N/A	2	2,880,000	1	2,283,300	1	2,204,400
Class B	28,618	57,237	12	21,600,000	15	29,025,000	15	30,060,000
Class C	11,447	28,618	32	57,600,000	43	83,205,000	54	108,216,000
Class D	5,724	11,447	40	72,000,000	34	65,790,000	25	50,100,000
Class E	0	5,724	14	25,200,000	7	13,545,000	5	10,020,000

Source: IBGE, Census, Brazil. Author's calculation.

Institute of Geography, the agency responsible for maintaining the country's census, approximately 12 million residents live in informal, slum settlements. These places are commonly known as favelas, and nearly one in four residents of Rio de Janeiro call them home (Davis, 1996; Perlman, 2010). Similarly, public infrastructure in Brazil is failing. Roads need paving. Sanitation systems need upgrading. Mass transit needs substantial investment. Airports are over-capacity with passengers and aircraft squished into every corner of Brazil's aging facilities. Meanwhile, schools are overcrowded and hospitals suffer from a lack of beds and adequate services.

Violence and corruption

Brazil is one of the most violent countries in the world (Graham, 2009). Violence threatens residents on a daily basis, and it paralyzes the economy. Since the 1990s, firearms have killed about 35,000 people annually, which is approximately four times the rate of the United States. Daily robberies on public transport and kidnappings instill fear in all Brazilians, rich and poor alike. As a result, many middle class residents live in walled fortresses, and lower class residents live in militarized communities in the favelas (Caldeira, 2000; Fahlberg and Vicino, 2016). Likewise, the political and economic systems in Brazil have long suffered from corruption. The country faces its largest scandal, which threatens political and economic institutions throughout society. Over $3.5 billion dollars was laundered from Petrobras, the state oil company. An entire class of politicians and businesses are under investigation.

Social justice and economic development

These sobering issues shape the public discourse about the state of cities in Brazil. The most riveting accounts draw our attention to the conditions of favelas, urban violence, and sprawl. They expose the roots of corruption and structural inequality in Brazil. The need for social justice and sustainable economic development is paramount. The disenfranchised have a long tradition of protest in Brazil. From the days of protesting the military dictatorship to economic reforms, they have long taken to the streets to fight for social equality, economic security, and democracy. For example, the "March on Rio de Janeiro" in 1968 drew some 100,000 Cariocas to the streets to protest abuses by the military police. Similarly, during the 1980s, the Diretas Já movement (Direct Elections Now) sent millions of Brazilians to the streets for years, which ultimately ushered in a transition to re-democratize Brazil in 1985 (McCann, 2014).

It has now been a half-century since the authoritarian military regime came to power by ousting President João Goulart in a coup d'état. While Brazil's democratization was accompanied by unprecedented economic growth, the country's public infrastructure and welfare state did not keep pace (McCann, 2008). In 2013, a proposal to increase the bus fare by ten cents sparked a revolution in Brazil. Over 1 million Brazilians poured into the city streets to demonstrate their widespread anger about the abysmal state of social services and political graft. Many said that

"Brazil woke up" last year. The Brazilian Spring resonated with the masses. Indeed, public opinion polls showed that three-quarters of Brazilians supported the protests and their cause: to improve the urban condition.

The national strategy to improve these conditions has focused on mega-events like the World Cup and the Olympics. Typically, such events foster nationalistic pride and civic culture. However, this has not happened in Brazil. The anger about urban decline, inequality, failing infrastructure, and corruption has united Brazilians, from slum dwellers to the middle class, to oppose Brazil's huge public investment in these mega-events. The promise of a new Brazil is still unfulfilled. Lula, the popular former president, said upon winning the bid to host the Olympics, "Today is the day that Brazil gained its international citizenship." Now, the world waits for Brazil to live up to it.

Learning from the Brazilian urban experience

There is much to learn from the urban experience of Brazil. Reflecting on the Brazilian tradition of urbanism, the architecture, modernist, and geographic movements shaped our understanding about cities in Brazil. The characteristics of the urban process define the distinct nature of the Brazilian people and the urban economy through national industrialization and migration. Modern cities are faced with a host of urban issues that threaten their sustainability, such as uncontrolled sprawl, growing inequality, failing public infrastructure, urban violence, and political corruption. Cities become the contested spaces for seeking justice for these issues.

William Siembieda (2009) puts forth some useful lessons about contemporary urbanism in Brazil. He uses a "spatial political economy approach" to distill urbanism in Brazil today (p. 291). The first lesson is that the development and growth of the city is a tool for social justice. The second lesson is that regions with a variety of urban forms strengthen the public voice and build forms of accessibility to the city. The third lesson is that a participatory democracy leads to inclusionary planning and design processes. These lessons serve to remind us that urbanization is a social, economic, and political process that constantly reshapes the spatial realms of people and place.

Indeed, these lessons remind us that there is a need to further develop urban theory from a comparative perspective. Theories of urban development tend to be centered on the urban experience of cities like Chicago and Los Angeles. The process of urbanization in Brazil, as well as its causes and consequences, offers novel opportunities to inform theories that seek to explain the urban condition. While research questions abound, let us focus on three primary themes. First, the interplay between urbanization and globalization needs to be better understood. Economic restructuring and large-scale urbanization has created a new international division of labor, and the migration of people to cities has changed their landscapes in dramatic ways. Second, the factors that cause the production of poverty and inequality need further examination. Internal differentiation and neighbor-hood studies should focus on uncovering these factors. Third, social structure and demographic change on the urban periphery is changing the shape and scale of metropolitan regions. The causes and consequences of this form of development need to be further studied.

Brazil and its cities stand at a crossroads (Reid, 2014). Many observers of Brazil have noted that it is a country of the future, always looking forward. Indeed, Brazilian optimism is contagious. One only needs to glance at the nation's flag to be reminded of this. The words "Order and Progress" showcase the national motto at the flag's center. But the burden of uneven urbanization and the forces of globaliza-tion have tested Brazil's devotion to order and progress. Cities and their residents are divided. The future will depend on a nation's willingness to confront these big urban issues.

References

Agache, A. (1930), *Cidade do Rio de Janeiro: Extensão, Remodelacão, Embellezamento*, Paris: Foyer Brésilien.
Baer, W. (2013), *The Brazilian Economy: Growth and Development, 7th Ed.*, Boulder, CO: Lynne Rienner Publishers.
Caldeira, T.P.R. (2000), *City of Walls: Crime, Segregation, and Citizenship in São Paulo*, Berkeley, CA: University of California Press.
Cardoso, F.H. and F. Enzo (1979), *Dependency and Development in Latin America*, Berkeley, CA: University of California Press.
Cuthbert, A.R. (2006), *The Form of Cities: Political Economy and Urban Design*, Malden, MA: Blackwell.
Davis, M. (1990), *City of Quartz: Excavating the Future in Los Angeles*, New York, NY: Verso.
Davis, M. (1996), *Planet of Slums*, New York, NY: Verso.
Dear, M. (2001), *The Postmodern Urban Condition*, Malden, MA: Wiley-Blackwell.
Economist (2009), "Brazil takes off," *The Economist*, 14 November 2009.
Evans, P. (1979), *Dependent Development: The Alliance of Multinational, State, and Local Capital in Brazil*, Princeton, NJ: Princeton University Press.
Fahlberg, A. and T.J. Vicino (2016), "Breaking the city: militarization and segregation in Rio de Janeiro," *Habitat International*, **54** (Part 1), 10–17.
Fausto, B. and S. Fausto (2014), *A Concise History of Brazil, 2nd Ed.*, New York, NY: Cambridge University Press.
Freyre, G. (1986), *The Masters and the Slaves: A Study in the Development of Brazilian Civilization*, Berkeley, CA: University of California Press.
Graham, S. (2009), "Cities as battlespace: the new military urbanism," *City*, **13** (4), 383–402.
Holston, J. (1989), *The Modernist City: An Anthropological Critique of Brasília*, Chicago, IL: University of Chicago Press.
Jones, G.A. (2004), "The Geo-politics of democracy and citizenship in Latin America." In Clive Barnett and Murray Low (eds) *Spaces of Democracy: Geographical Perspectives on Citizenship, Participation, and Representation*, Thousand Oaks, CA: Sage, pp. 161–184.
Lerner, J. (2014), *Urban Acupuncture*, Washington, DC: Island Press.
McCann, B. (2008), *The Throes of Democracy: Brazil since 1989*, New York, NY: Zed Books.

McCann, B. (2014), *Hard Times in the Marvelous City: From Dictatorship to Democracy in the favelas of Rio de Janeiro*, Durham, NC: Duke University Press.

Misra, R.P. and N.T. Dung (1983), "Large cities: growth dynamics and emerging problems," *Habitat International*, **7** (5–6), 47–65.

Nobles, M. (2000), *Shades of Citizenship: Race and the Census in Modern Politics*, Stanford, CA: Stanford University Press.

Ouroussoff, N. (2012), "Oscar Niemeyer, architect who gave Brasília its flair, dies at 104," *The New York Times*, 5 December.

Park, R.E., E. Burgess, and R. McKenzie (1925), *The City*, Chicago, IL: University of Chicago Press.

Perlman, J. (2010), *Favela: Four Decades of Living on the Edge in Rio de Janeiro*, New York, NY: Oxford University Press.

Preston, J.E. (1946), *Brazil*, New York, NY: Odyssey Press.

Purcell, S. and R. Roett, eds. (1997), *Brazil under Cardoso*, Boulder, CO: Lynne Rienner Publishers.

Reid, M. (2014), *Brazil: The Troubled Rise of a Global Power*, New Haven, CT: Yale University Press.

Reis Filho, N.G. (1968), *Evolução urbana do Brasil 1500–1799*. São Paulo, SP: Livraria Pioneira Editora.

Reis Filho, N.G. (2004), *Notas sobre Urbanização Dispersa e Novas Formas de Tecido Urbano*. São Paulo, SP: Via das Artes.

Reis Filho, N.G. (2006), *São Paulo: Vila, Cidade, Metrópole*. São Paulo, SP: Via das Artes.

Ribeiro. D. (2000), *The Brazilian People: The Formation and Meaning of Brazil*, Gainesville, FL: University Press of Florida.

Rohter, L. (2012), *Brazil on the Rise: The Story of a Country Transformed*, New York, NY: Palgrave Macmillan.

Santos, M. (1979), *The Shared Space: The Two Circuits of the Urban Economy in Underdeveloped Countries*, New York, NY: Methuen.

Santos, M. (1993), *A Urbanização Brasileira*, São Paulo: Hucitec.

Saunders, D. (2011), *Arrival City: How the Largest Migration in History Is Reshaping Our World*, New York, NY: Vintage.

Scott, A. and E.W. Soja, eds. (1996), *The City: Los Angeles and Urban Theory at the End of the Twentieth Century*, Berkeley, CA: University of California Press.

Siembieda, W. (2009), "Conclusion: lessons from Brazilian contemporary urbanism." In Vicente del Rio and William Siembieda (eds) *Contemporary Urbanism in Brazil: Beyond Brasília*, Gainesville, FL: University Press of Florida, pp. 291–302.

Skidmore, T.E. (2009), *Brazil: Five Centuries of Change, 2nd Ed.*, New York, NY: Oxford University Press.

Sternberg, H.O. (1959), "Geographic thought and development in Brazil," *Professional Geographer*, **11** (6), 12–17.

Underwood, D.K. (1991), "Alfred Agache, French sociology, and modern urbanism in France and Brazil," *Journal of the Society of Architectural Historians*, **50** (2), 130–160.

Webb, K.E. (1974), *The Changing Face of Northeast Brazil*, New York, NY: Columbia University Press.

Wirth, L. (1938), "Urbanism as a way of life: the city and contemporary civilization," *American Journal of Sociology*, **44** (1), 1–24.

Zweig, S. (1941), *Brasilien, Ein Land der Zukunft*, Stockholm, Sweden: Bermann-Fischer.

15 Cities in China and India: disjuncture, master-concepts, and comparison

Xuefei Ren

China and India are epicenters of the world's urbanization. India's urbanization rate has been rising steadily over the second half of the twentieth century, as people started moving from the countryside to the cities. In India, about one-third of the population lives in urban areas. The urban population growth in China is more recent—spurred in the 1980s by the relaxation of the *hukou* system that restricted country-to-urban migration. Driven mostly by migration, China's urban population spiked by more than 200 million in the single decade between 2001 and 2010. In 2011, China's urbanization rate tipped over 50 percent, and the central government wants to push the urbanization rate to 75 percent by 2020.

The massive-scale urbanization in China and India presents daunting challenges for local governments in sectors such as housing, land-use planning, health care, education, and environmental protection. These challenges have proven intractable for both countries' urban governance systems. These systems take on different configurations in the two countries. Urban governance in China is characterized by powerful territorial actors such as city mayors and institutions such as the *hukou* system, which distributes rights, benefits, and resources unevenly across groups. By comparison, urban governance in India is characterized by weak municipal authorities and a high degree of fragmentation among different government bureaucracies, often in poor coordination with one another.

The scale of urban growth and the associated social problems have made cities in China and India laboratories for research. For urban China studies, the empirical focus of the scholarship has evolved around the market reforms unleashed in the 1980s that accelerated major urban restructuring and changes in urban governance (Ren, 2013). Examples include housing reform that shuttered public housing held over from the socialist era and replaced it with privatized housing (Huang and Li, 2014); land reform that subjected urban land-use rights to market transactions (Lin and Ho, 2005; Lin 2009); *hukou* reform that spurred the largest-scale domestic migration in history, with close to 300 million migrant workers fleeing the countryside for opportunities in the cities (Fan, 2008; Chan, 2009); and reform of State Owned Enterprises (SOEs) that resulted in mass layoffs of state-sector workers and the collapse of the socialist welfare system (Lee, 2007).

The dominant theoretical frameworks are largely borrowed from the West, with master-concepts such as "urban entrepreneurialism" (Harvey, 1989) and "neoliberal urbanism" (Brenner and Theodore, 2002a). A consensus has been reached that urban governance in post-market reform China exhibits neoliberal and entrepreneurial features, as local governments employ alternative strategies, policies, and programs to enhance the competitive position of their cities to attract investment and promote economic growth. Such master-concepts can explain certain features of urban governance in post-reform China, but they cannot capture everything. One obvious deviation is the role of the Chinese state—at the central, provincial, and municipal levels. The state's strategy of promoting urbanization has been unprecedented and is supported by a large web of formal policies, laws, institutions, and time-bound quotas, such as reaching a 75 percent urbanization rate by 2020. In no other country is the state so deeply involved in setting the pace of and target for urban growth. Such deviations are often buried under labels such as "actually existing neoliberalism" (Brenner and Theodore, 2002b) or "neoliberalism with Chinese characteristics" (Harvey, 2005). The variations are acknowledged, but not theorized.

Similarly, an outpouring of scholarship has tracked India's rapid urbanization. The focus of urban social inquiry is centered on slums and housing inequality (Appadurai, 2000), access to water and politics of infrastructure (Anand, 2015; Bjorkman, 2015), emergent dynamics in the land market (Chakravorty, 2013), new economic policies such as special economic zones (Jenkins et al., 2014), and changing citizenship rights (Desai and Sanyal, 2012; Shatkin, 2014). The theoretical framework in the urban India scholarship oscillates between two perspectives: neoliberalism and post-colonialism (Shatkin and Vidyarthi, 2014). The neoliberal framework focuses on entrepreneurial forms of governance, such as policies and projects sponsored by the state, the private sector, and international institutions to make Indian cities more competitive for investment in the international marketplace (Banerjee-Guha, 2002; Nijman, 2008; Goldman, 2011). The post-colonial perspective emphasizes the incompleteness of neoliberal and entrepreneurial approaches, often attributing the failure or blockage of "world-class" city-making projects to subaltern contestations (Benjamin, 2008). As in the Chinese case, the two perspectives only partially capture the trends of urban restructuring in Indian cities. The meta-narrative of neoliberalism cannot explain why some localities are more resilient to neoliberal redevelopment drives while others are less so (Weinstein, 2014). Similarly, the post-colonial perspective often fails to acknowledge other operative factors—beyond subaltern contestations—that erode world-city making projects, such as the fragmented state power prevalent throughout urban India.

The field of urban China and India studies is now at a crossroads. Its publication output has been prolific but not theoretically innovative. It needs a new vocabulary to better explain how inherited modes of governance collide with the modern economy (market reforms in China and liberalization programs in India) and how constellations of urban governance are produced.

This chapter will propose three approaches as a modest attempt to develop a theoretical vocabulary for the next generation of urban China and India scholarship. The scholarship needs to grapple with (1) historical patterns of continuity and change in urban policies; (2) master-concepts derived in post-industrial cities in the West; and (3) comparative experiences of cities from elsewhere.

Continuity and change: urban renewal from Shanghai to Guangzhou

My first proposal is that more attention be paid to identifying patterns of continuity and change in urban processes, as well as turning points that mark the emergence of new phases of urban development. Urban renewal policies and practices in China present an excellent example in this regard. The predominant narrative to date is "strong state vs. weak civil society": since the early 1990s, local governments initiated many large-scale demolition drives, and in the process displaced millions of urban residents who had to relocate to the urban periphery. This narrative, however, no longer appears clear-cut today, as most cities encounter difficulty implementing ambitious urban renewal programs due to strong opposition from property owners. How can we explain this new situation in non-democratic China, where demolitions have become politically infeasible and local officials are now reluctant to push through urban renewal programs? In other words, what has changed, what has not, and how should we adapt our analytical strategies to interpret the change and continuity?

Beginning in the late 1990s, many top-tier cities in China initiated large-scale "urban renewal" programs to attract investment in inner-city districts. Called *jiucheng gaizao* (i.e., remaking the old city), such programs were highly disruptive by design—city governments would mark neighborhoods for "renewal" and grant real estate developers permission to carry out demolitions without even seeking consent from residents. In 1990, Beijing's municipal government began an ambitious urban renewal program that aimed to redevelop three million square meters of old urban housing stock by 2005. During the program, many historical *hutong* neighborhoods were demolished despite opposition from residents and preservationists (Wang, 2003; Johnson, 2004; Zhang and Fang, 2004). The evicted residents had to relocate to the urban fringe poorly connected to the city and far away from work. Shanghai pushed through its urban renewal program even more forcefully. In 1992, its municipal government announced the "365 plan," declaring that by 2000 the city would demolish 365 hectares of housing stock in dangerous conditions (i.e., *weifang*, in Chinese), and the plan was accomplished in 1999 with heavy government subsidies extended to developers. As a result of this effort, more than one million households were evicted (Ren, 2008; Shao, 2013).

The urban renewal programs and demolition drives are well documented in the scholarship (Zhang, 2002; He and Wu, 2005; Chen, 2009), and the dominant narrative is that pro-growth coalitions formed by local governments and developers undertake large-scale urban demolitions that dispossess and marginalize residents in the process. The narrative, however, no longer captures developments on the ground, especially in the Pearl River Delta in south China. In Guangzhou, for example, the local government in 2009 announced an ambitious "three old" program that proposed to redevelop three types of old places—old neighborhoods, old villages, and old factories—in preparation for the 2011 Asian Games. But after six years, progress has stalled. There are few redevelopment projects for old neighborhoods, where residents object to such proposals. There also are few completed projects for redeveloping old villages—also called "urban villages"—because property owners demand expensive compensation packages that developers cannot afford.

The redevelopment of urban villages in Guangzhou presents a good example to illustrate the changing trends in state policies and popular resistance against urban renewal. Urban villages are a type of informal settlements widely observed in cities in south China, where villagers built apartment buildings to rent rooms to migrant workers. Due to the lack of other affordable housing options, and cheaper rent, many migrant workers choose to stay in these urban villages. The land on which urban villages stand is rural land belonging to village collectives. The city government is eager to acquire land from villages and convert it to urban land—all urban land in China belongs to the state—and then lease it out for developers for substantial fees. But unlike north China, villagers in south China are more organized—often drawing upon traditional clan networks and folk associations—and have become a powerful interest group that negotiates hard with the local government and developers. From 2009 to 2016, only two out of the 138 urban villages marked by the city government for renewal have been redeveloped, and in both cases villagers—the only beneficiaries for compensation—have been enriched, some even becoming millionaires. By contrast, the majority of the tenant population of migrant workers has no voice in negotiations, and they have no recourse but to search for another residence further away from the city center.

The above example of Guangzhou's recent urban renewal program raises many research questions. For example, how can we explain the rise of villagers as a new propertied-class? How do we characterize the changing growth coalition between local governments and developers? These questions suggest that new forms of urban governance are in the making, qualitatively different from the previous Shanghai model of demolitions and evictions. Moreover, in the current phase of urban renewal, how can one meaningfully theorize urban citizenship for migrant workers? In Guangzhou's urban villages, they form the majority of the population, but have no representation at the negotiating table. They develop little attachment to their urban villages, and can be displaced easily when redevelopment takes place. These developments suggest continuity of institutional effects and policy practices. In spite of the widely publicized *hukou* reforms, designed to extend more social security benefits to migrant workers, the reality of urban village redevelopment in Guangzhou demonstrates that *hukou* is still the most powerful institutional device used by the local state to exclude the migrant population.

Now that China's market reform has entered its fourth decade, the time is ripe to examine both continuity and change, and to revise previously dominant narratives to better explain today's urban policies, programs, and practices.

Questioning master-concepts: fragile entrepreneurialism in Mumbai

Scholars routinely borrow concepts developed in post-industrial cities in the West to interpret urban social change in China and India. The most widely adopted theoretical frameworks are urban entrepreneurialism (Harvey, 1989) and neoliberalism (Brenner and Theodore, 2002a). Both have immense explanatory power for interpreting urban structuring in North America and Western Europe since the 1970s, as local governments employ market-oriented strategies to enhance the positions of their cities as sites to attract investment. To a certain degree, urban governance in Chinese and Indian cities exhibits tendencies of urban entrepreneurialism and neoliberalism. However, overall, Chinese and Indian cities, such as Mumbai, Delhi, Shanghai, and Guangzhou, have never experienced high Fordism and post-industrialization. Therefore, their "entrepreneurial" and "neoliberal" tendencies have to be explained by factors other than post-industrial urban restructuring. Urban entrepreneurialism and neoliberalism take quite different forms in these cities, compared with post-industrial cities in the West such as Detroit, Chicago, and Manchester.

Writing more than two decades ago, David Harvey described the transition of urban governance in the West as a shift from managerialism to entrepreneurialism (Harvey, 1989). After the collapse of the Keynesian welfare state in the 1970s, policy makers in post-industrial cities in West Europe and North America reached a consensus regarding the position of local governments: instead of being merely service providers (i.e., as managers), local governments had to be more competitive, innovative, and experimental with new policies and programs in order to alleviate the stressed fiscal conditions of their cities (i.e., as entrepreneurs). As for how to be innovative and entrepreneurial, Harvey discussed four alternative strategies: to create particular advantages for the production of goods and services, to promote consumption, to build command-and-control functions, and to compete for subsidies from the federal government with other localities. These strategies should cultivate a favorable climate for investment, even if they spawn uneven development between and within cities. What distinguishes entrepreneurial urban governance from conventional managerial modes of governance, as argued by Harvey, is a public–private partnership in which local state power is combined with private capital to promote projects oriented for competition and capital accumulation. Urban entrepreneurialism is also characterized by speculation in project design and execution, as well as selective targeting of specific localities, projects, and places as opposed to the metropolitan territory as a whole.

One example of Harvey's entrepreneurial strategies might be the largest ongoing slum redevelopment project in Mumbai—the airport slum project. The Mumbai international airport is surrounded by a spectacular sprawl of slum settlements that house more than 400,000 people. Many are long-time residents who settled there half a century ago and who over time transformed the marshy land into habitable living quarters. Under an ambitious plan approved by the State Government of Maharashtra, they will have to be resettled elsewhere so that airport facilities can be modernized and shopping malls and luxury hotels built. In 2014, a new terminal flung open its doors for business. Designed by the American architectural firm Skidmore, Owings & Merrill, the striking new terminal towering above the slums showcases the immense polarization in India's built environment between global architecture and the informal city.

The airport slum redevelopment project seems to be no different from the profit-driven, entrepreneurial projects led by public–private partnerships in post-industrial cities in the West, as described by Harvey. But Indian cities present a different political and institutional context from post-industrial cities in the West. State power is highly fragmented at the local level. Who is being entrepreneurial and about what is often unclear. To resettle residents, the government had to conduct a survey to determine the current population and their tenure status. Residents blocked the survey because not everybody is eligible for compensation. Meanwhile, the airport company contracted out the resettlement to a private developer, who has constructed resettlement buildings for eligible slum dwellers. But without the survey to determine eligibility, nobody can be resettled and the project has fallen apart at the very beginning stage of its execution. In 2014, the developer took all other parties to the court—various state agencies and the airport company—and it is demanding the loss of its investment in constructing resettlement housing, which today stands empty.

Thus in the Indian context, urban entrepreneurialism has taken a highly fragile and contingent form. Coalition-building for large-scale, complex redevelopment projects has proved to be especially precarious and difficult to achieve. Entrepreneurialism, in this case, might be useful to explain the "urban imagination" of government agencies and the private sector—to make a world-class, slum-free Mumbai. But it cannot explain the execution of entrepreneurial policies and projects, which are often undermined by the fragmentation of the governance apparatus. In the airport slum case, there is no coalition of private–public partnerships to speak of and, instead, decision-making power is fragmented among various federal and state agencies in poor coordination with one another and with actors in the private sector.

The example above raises more questions. How and why does entrepreneurialism operate differently in urban India than in the West or other countries? What characterizes coalition-building and private–public partnerships in slum redevelopment in Mumbai? Who is being entrepreneurial and about what? And what explains the blockage of entrepreneurial visions for the city held by state and private elites? The investigations into these questions would require digging deeper under master-concepts such as entrepreneurialism and neoliberalism. Answers to these questions can shed light on the complex constellations of urban governance in contemporary India.

Moving beyond exceptionalism: doing comparisons

In addition to wrestling with emergent trends and questioning master-concepts, the fields of urban studies in China and India can also benefit by undertaking comparative analyses. Notwithstanding a surge in publications on each country, urban China and India studies have developed along parallel tracks with little exchange between them. Comparative studies engaging Chinese and Indian cities are rare— this is rather surprising considering the ubiquitous media discourse on the rise of China and India as economic superpowers and the explosive urban growth in the two countries (McKinsey Global Institute, 2009, 2010). The lack of comparative studies on China and India can be attributed to a set of tendencies observed in these intellectual fields—introversion in the urban China scholarship and self-imposed exile among urban India specialists. In the urban China field, scholars mostly write for each other and rarely pursue comparative angles of inquiry. This has to do with commonly shared assumptions that the Chinese urban experience is too unique to be compared, as well as with more practical matters, such as the lack of funding for international and comparative work. For the urban India field, which is heavily influenced by the subaltern studies tradition, scholars are more inclined to do single-city studies and in general are skeptical of transporting theoretical insights from one locality—especially from outside—to others.

Such self-imposed exceptionalism has to be overcome in the next generation of urban scholarship on China and India. Critical comparisons with each other, and with other countries, can help develop a new vocabulary with which to theorize Chinese and Indian urbanism. Tilly (1984) articulates the theoretical payoff of engaging in comparisons, and he identifies four types of comparisons—individualizing, universalizing, variation finding, and encompassing—all of which can be achieved with a carefully designed comparative study on urban governance in China and India. Individualizing comparisons focus on the uniqueness of a case by comparing that case with others; universalizing comparisons focus on identifying common patterns present in all cases; variation-finding comparisons seek variations across cases; and encompassing comparisons focus on the structural positions of different cases in the larger world-system (Tilly, 1984). These are very constructive ways to think about the next generation of urban studies of China and India. Chinese and Indian urbanism is not as unique as specialists assume, and by opening up the fields to comparisons, we can better understand the unique features characterizing urban governance in each country, commonalities and variations, and also the positions Chinese and Indian cities occupy in the larger system of global capitalism.

I use the examples of urban renewal in China and slum redevelopment in India to illustrate how a comparative study can be designed. First, one can pursue similarities, such as by comparing municipal policies regarding informal settlements in Guangzhou and Mumbai. Here, a set of research questions arises: what explains the turn in housing policies toward market-led redevelopment in both countries? Is Mumbai's vision of becoming slum-free, or Guangzhou's declaration of eliminating urban villages, inspired by best practices elsewhere, such as Shanghai or Singapore? Can we generalize, from these similarities, a trend in slum housing policies toward more market participation?

Second, researchers can also investigate differences. For both Guangzhou and Mumbai, their ambitious slum redevelopment programs have been interrupted, but the project delay is caused by different mechanisms and processes. In Guangzhou, as explained earlier, villager-landlords have become a powerful new interest group engaging in intense negotiations with developers, and no project can go forward unless all property owners have agreed to the compensation and relocation. In Mumbai, power is dispersed among various agencies, and private–public partnerships are often too precarious to carry out any large-scale slum redevelopment project. Variation-finding comparisons, as illustrated here, can help us better understand the different modes of urban governance in China and India, as well as their diverging implications on citizenship rights.

Lastly, not only should urban China and India be compared with one another, they should also be compared with cities in other countries. Robinson (2011) critiques the methodological closure in urban studies, that is, the assumption that only certain kinds of cities can be compared. She argues, instead, that scholars should embrace methodological openness and compare cities within and between categories, such as global South vs. global North, rich countries vs. poor countries. The slum housing policies in China and India can be compared to those in Brazil, another country that has been wrestling with the issue of integrating informal settlements (Perlman, 2010). Also, urban renewal and displacement in Guangzhou, Mumbai, and Rio de Janeiro can be compared with demolitions of public housing projects in Chicago dating back to the 1990s. In spite of the vast differences across these localities—democracy vs. non-democracy, richer vs. poorer cities, global South vs. global North—striking similarities emerge in how local governments deal with the urban poor, and dispossession predictably results from pro-market housing policies that try to recover the market value of centrally located land occupied by Mumbai's slums, Guangzhou's urban villages, Rio de Janeiro's favelas, or Chicago's public housing projects. By juxtaposing different cases, new pathways will open up for us to theorize both similarities and variations in the modes of urban governance.

Conclusion

As one out of seven people today lives in Chinese or Indian cities, urban China and India present privileged sites to study urban structures and processes. The intellectual output of urban studies in China and India has been tremendous over the past two decades, as the fast-paced urban transformations supply endless topics for urban researchers. Casting a sharp contrast with the flourishing empirical work is the lack of a new conceptual vocabulary with which to better capture urban social change in China and India. The predominant theoretical frameworks in the fields are still "urban entrepreneurialism" and "neoliberalism," which no doubt have immense explanatory power in post-industrial cities, but they only capture certain elements of urban processes in China and India. Also, narratives developed from a prior era are still used to describe urban transformations today, such as strong state vs. weak civil society in China. Moreover, both urban China and urban India fields are turned inward with little comparative sensibility.

This chapter proposes that the next generation of scholarship must grapple with historical patterns of continuity and change, master-concepts borrowed from the West, and the comparative experiences of cities from elsewhere. I have used informal housing redevelopment in Guangzhou and Mumbai as examples to illustrate the three proposals. First, emergent trends in housing policies in Guangzhou signal a turning point in the history of urban renewal from the late 1990s: different from demolitions and removal, the current policy adopts a more conciliatory approach that creates space for the rise of a new propertied-class. These new trends do not fit the narrative of strong state vs. weak civil society, and they need to be better theorized. Second, there are limitations in using master-concepts derived in post-industrial cities in the West. Urban entrepreneurialism manifests itself in different forms in Chinese and Indian cities than in the West. These differences raise interesting research questions, and they should be theorized, instead of simply labeled as variations of neoliberalism. Finally, I argue that urban scholarship of China and India can greatly benefit from comparisons. Instead of insisting that China or India is too unique to be compared, scholars should embrace methodological openness and experiment with critical comparisons. By so doing, we can better specify similarities and variations across cities and make initial steps toward developing a new vocabulary to capture the urban structures and processes in the global South.

References

Anand, N. (2015), 'Leaky states: Water audits, ignorance and the politics of infrastructure', *Public Culture* **27** (2), 305–330.

Appadurai, A. (2000), 'Spectral housing and urban cleansing: Notes on Millennial Mumbai', *Public Culture* **12** (3), 627–651.

Banerjee-Guha, S. (2002), 'Shifting cities: Urban restructuring in Mumbai', *Economic and Political Weekly* **37** (2), 121–128.

Benjamin, S. (2008), 'Occupancy urbanism: Radicalizing politics and economy beyond policy and programs', *International Journal of Urban and Regional Research* **32** (3), 719–729.

Bjorkman, L. (2015), *Pipe Politics, Contested Waters: Embedded Infrastructures of Millennial Mumbai*, Durham, NC: Duke University Press.

Brenner, N. and N. Theodore (2002a), *Space of Neoliberalism: Urban Restructuring in North America and West Europe*, New York: Oxford University Press.

Brenner, N. and N. Theodore (2002b), 'Cities and the geographies of "actually existing neoliberalism"', *Antipode* **34** (3), 349–379.

Chakravorty, S. (2013), *The Price of Land: Acquisition, Conflict, Consequence*, New Delhi: Oxford University Press.

Chan, K. W. (2009), 'The Chinese *hukou* system at 50', *Eurasian Geography and Economics* **50** (2), 197–221.

Chen, X. (ed.) (2009), *Shanghai Rising: State Power and Local Transformations in a Global Megacity*, Minneapolis, MN: University of Minnesota Press.

Desai, R. and R. Sanyal (2012), *Urbanizing Citizenship: Contested Spaces in Indian Cities*, Thousand Oaks, CA: Sage Publishing.

Fan, C. (2008), *China on the Move*, New York: Routledge.

Goldman, M. (2011), 'Speculative urbanism and the making of the next world city', *International Journal of Urban and Regional Research* **35** (3), 555–581.

Harvey, D. (1989), 'From managerialism to entrepreneurialism: The transformation in urban governance in late capitalism', *Geografiska Annaler. Series B, Human Geography* **71** (1), 3–17.

Harvey, D. (2005), *A Brief History of Neoliberalism*, New York: Oxford University Press.

He, S. and F. Wu (2005), 'Property-led redevelopment in post-reform China: A case study of Xintiandi redevelopment project in Shanghai', *Journal of Urban Affairs* **27** (1), 1–23.

Huang, Y. and S. M. Li (eds) (2014), *Housing Inequality in Chinese Cities*, New York: Routledge.

Jenkins, R., L. Kennedy, and P. Mukhopadhyay (eds) (2014), *Power, Policy and Protest: The Politics of India's Special Economic Zones*, New Delhi: Oxford University Press.

Johnson, I. (2004), *Wild Grass: Three Stories of Change in Modern China*, New York: Pantheon Books.

Lee, C. K. (2007), *Against the Law: Labor Protests in China's Rustbelt and Sunbelt*, Berkeley, CA: University of California Press.

Lin, G. (2009), *Developing Land: Politics and Social Conditions*, London: Routledge.

Lin, G. and P. Ho (2005), 'The state, land system, and land development processes in contemporary China', *Annals of the Association of American Geographers* **95** (2), 411–436.

McKinsey Global Institute (2009), *Preparing for China's Urban Billion*, accessed Feb. 1, 2016 at http://www.mckinsey.com/insights/urbanization/preparing_for_urban_billion_in_china.

McKinsey Global Institute (2010), *India's Urban Awakening: Building Inclusive Cities, Sustaining Economic Growth*, accessed Feb. 1, 2016 at http://www.mckinsey.com/insights/urbanization/urban_awakening_in_india.

Nijman, J. (2008), 'Against the odds: Slum rehabilitation in neoliberal Mumbai', *Cities* **25** (2), 73–85.

Perlman, J. (2010), *Favela: Four Decades of Living on the Edge in Rio de Janeiro*, New York: Oxford University Press.

Ren, X. (2008), 'Forward to the past: Historical preservation in globalizing Shanghai', *City and Community*, **7** (1), 23–43.

Ren, X. (2013), *Urban China*, Cambridge: Polity Press.

Robinson, J. (2011), 'Cities in a world of cities: The comparative gesture', *International Journal of Urban and Regional Research* **35** (1), 1–23.

Shao, Q. (2013), *Shanghai Gone: Domicide and Defiance in a Chinese Megacity*, Lanham, MD: Rowman & Littlefield.

Shatkin, G. (ed.) (2014), *Contesting the Indian City: Global Visions and Politics of the Local*, Malden, MA: Wiley-Blackwell.

Shatkin, G. and S. Vidyarthi (2014), 'Introduction', in Gavin Shatkin and Sanjeev Vidyarthi (eds), *Contesting the Indian City: Global Visions and Politics of the Local*, Malden, MA: Wiley-Blackwell, pp. 1–38.

Tilly, C. (1984), *Big Structures, Large Processes, Huge Comparisons*, New York: Russell Sage Foundation.

Wang, J. (2003), *Beijing Record*, Beijing: Sanlian Press.

Weinstein, L. (2014), *The Durable Slum: Dharavi and the Right to Stay Put in Globalizing Mumbai*, Minneapolis, MN: University of Minnesota Press.

Zhang, T. (2002), 'Urban development and a socialist pro-growth coalition in Shanghai', *Urban Affairs Review* 37 (4), 475–499.

Zhang, Y. and K. Fang (2004), 'Is history repeating itself? From urban renewal in the United States to inner-city redevelopment in China', *Journal of Planning Education and Research* 23 (3), 286–298.

16 Mobile cities, modelling policies: importing/exporting the Singapore 'model' of development

Orlando Woods and Lily Kong

Introduction

We live in what has been termed the 'urban century', and yet 'the urban' – as a physical form; as an assemblage of policies, ideas and networks; and as a category of analysis and understanding – has reached an inflection point in both theory and praxis. Cities are not what they once were, or what they were once thought to be. The integration of the global economy has helped to transform the nature and understanding of urban forms, and has challenged the intellectual underpinnings of urban studies.[1] Such transformations have severely disrupted the discipline, and have cast a question mark over what the future may hold for urban studies, and the scholars and places embroiled therein. In debating the 'new epistemology of the urban' (Brenner and Schmid 2015; see also Walker 2015), scholarship is coming to terms with the 'growing sense of disarticulation, dissipation and fragmentation' (Peck 2015: 162) within which the discipline is embroiled. Simply put, the urban has become such a complex and variegated topic of analysis that the concept of the 'urban' has begun to suffer from 'diminishing explanatory returns' (ibid.), and increasingly runs the risk of becoming neutered by theoretical impasse.

Perhaps the biggest disruption to urban studies is the analytical shift from treating the urban as a fixed category of understanding – one that is static and territorially bounded (and, therefore, distinct) – to one that is more processual and trans-boundary. Such a shift is most clearly evinced in the evolving lexicon of urban studies, which in itself reflects the ever-changing analytical gaze of the discipline. Specifically, the primacy of 'world' or 'global' cities – the 'club class of cities at the top of the global-urban system' (Peck 2015: 163) – has surrendered to a more territorially flexible approach that is now defined by 'neoliberal policy circuits' (Robinson 2011: 1087) and 'traveling models and policy assemblages' (Pow 2014: 287; see also Roy 2009). Scholarship has embraced the fact that 'world' or 'global' cities – and the status bestowed by such a label – are better defined by their embeddedness within boundary-crossing networks and processes than by any sort of form or function inherent to the places that they occupy. As Brenner and Schmid (2015: 151) put it: 'new forms of urbanization are unfolding around the world that challenge inherited conceptions of the urban as a fixed, bounded and universally generalizable settlement type'. Singapore is paradigmatic of such 'new forms', and provides the empirical focus of this chapter.

The 'new forms' of the urban are more inclusivist. They overthrow the traditional hierarchy of urban studies – which has long been weighted in favour of the Anglo-American academy – favouring places that are defined by the relational strength of their networks (whether economic, political, social, cultural or aesthetic), which in turn are recognised as being the creators and conduits of value. Put differently, the foremost cities in the contemporary world are not necessarily bounded sites of economic and cultural production in and of themselves, but globally networked hubs of activity and value creation instead, intricately interwoven with other sites, often not contiguous in the manner of traditional hinterlands, but discrete and even far flung. Importantly, such networks are no longer unidirectional (radiating outwards from the 'West' to the 'rest'), but are much more chaotic in both origin and application. Robinson (2011: 1090) puts it well when she points out that 'these circuits [or networks] are promiscuous, incorporating wealthier and poorer cities, welfare states and post-socialist contexts, as well as East Asian developmentalist states'. The multivalence of such networks mirrors the prominence of postcolonial thought in recent decades, which itself opened up the possibilities for theory to travel in any direction, and from any starting point (Robinson 2006).

Accordingly, a recent focus of research has been the making, mobility and mutations of urban policy. The global circulation of urban models – or exemplars of best practices and values that are deemed to be desirable and achievable – has gained significant traction. Such models are those that are dislocated from their place of origin, and transplanted to an adopted site. This is symptomatic of the more widespread movement beyond the 'territorial orthodoxy' of urban studies (McCann and Ward 2012: 42), and the concomitant refocusing of attention on more relational theorisations (after Massey 1993; Robinson 2006, 2011; Amin 2007). Efforts have begun to heighten visibility and break intellectual impasse. For example, *Urban Geography's* attempts to 'open up knowledge production' (The Editors 2015: 330) through its Urban Pulse initiative, intended to introduce reflections on urban issues from across the globe, thereby making the study of the urban world 'more cosmopolitan'. Decentralisation and disruption are the themes of the moment, and will help to chart out a more equitable future for urban studies.

In particular, the shift towards post-territorialism has fuelled interest in Asian urbanisms. Such urbanisms – of which Singapore is a leading example – have helped to rebalance the orthodoxies of more traditional approaches, and yet have remained stymied by what Perera and Tang (2013: 1) term 'limited visibility and intellectual impasse'. In many respects, Singapore is symptomatic of such stymying effects; it is heralded by policymakers and urban planners from Asia, the Middle East and Africa as a model of urban best practices, but in the same breath, is perceived by some from the Anglo-American academy with 'great ambivalence and [is] often seen as a value-maximising and authoritarian illiberal regime that relentlessly promotes urban growth at all costs' (Pow 2014: 300).

It is important to note that the urban has not become entirely divorced from its territorial anchors. If anything, the idea of territory has proven to be of increasing importance given the new theoretical thrusts of urban studies, which themselves seek a departure from 'the quicksand of metaphysical abstractions' (Walker 2015: 184; after Brenner and Schmid 2015). The notion of 'assemblage', for example, has helped to anchor discourses that explore urban policies that are 'simultaneously mobile and territorial as well as signalling the relational process through which the socio-materiality of cities . . . is being stretched out across time and space and brought together to constitute (contested) urbanism in particular places' (Pow 2014: 288). Urban assemblages collapse ideas of movement and fixity, of networks and places, of the boundless and the bounded into one system of understanding, which in itself has given rise to importable and exportable forms of urban modelling. This chapter focuses on the case of Singapore: one of the most emblematic examples of an importable urban model (or exportable, depending on the perspective, and on the agency of importer or exporter), reflecting a third wave of 'cognitive cultural' (Scott 2011: 309) capitalism which other cities and states have attempted to emulate. In the sections that follow, we first explicate the characteristics and value of the Singapore model of urban development, followed by the problems and challenges associated with its importation/exportation, whilst highlighting avenues for future research.

Defining the Singapore model of urban development

Singapore is a paradigmatic case study that defies easy classification. Like other Asian cities that have experienced accelerated economic growth within a relatively short period of time – notably Hong Kong and Shanghai – Singapore and some other cities have become 'centers to be invoked, envied, and emulated as exemplary sites of a new urban normativity' (Ong 2011b: 14). Its success as a pre-eminent 'model' of urban development stems from the fact that it has solved many of the urban problems that have beleaguered other cities with which it once shared 'developing city' status, and has since become a global icon in its own right. Such problems include, but are not limited to, those associated with the provision of affordable public housing, central city development, pollution, environment protection, sanitation, sustainability, urban heritage, water resource management and so on. As one of the badges of its success, Singapore has become the prototype for 'efficient and growth-oriented urban development' (Shatkin 2014: 116), with 'The Singapore Model' – and the normative and technical plans upon which its growth and management have been based – being the inspiration for many urban innovation projects in Asia and beyond (Ong 2011b). This section and the two that follow explore these themes in more detail, first by defining the Singapore model of urban development, and then by discussing some of the challenges associated with the importation/exportation of 'The Singapore Model'.

Singapore is a small city-state that in 50 years has transformed from a postcolonial trading post to a pre-eminent model of globally networked urbanisation. Since its expulsion from the Federation of Malaya in 1965, the Singapore state – supported by a coterie of private developers – has pursued an aggressive policy of hegemonic entrepreneurialism that has prioritised economic growth. Such economic primacy has since manifested itself in the promotion of workforce and infrastructure development, the encouragement of foreign capital investment, and the establishment of hegemonic state enterprises that operate like private companies (Chua 2011).

Possibly the most decisive factor in ensuring the success of such growth has been the establishment of a political regime often described as authoritarian – pioneered by Lee Kuan Yew and the People's Action Party that has remained in power since independence. Such a stable – if unique – political environment has proven to be conducive to long-term economic planning and execution (Chua 2011). State-directed control over Singapore's urban policies and development has been termed 'state capitalism' (Shatkin 2014), in recognition of the fact that the state is a direct and monopolistic player in the country's public and private real estate markets and landscapes. Notably, the passing of the Land Acquisition Act of 1966 enabled a process of compulsory land acquisition to begin: one that has resulted in approximately 85 per cent of Singapore's landmass being state-owned (Kong 1993), and enabled the state to exert exact control and influence over the city's urban landscape – from land use and zoning, to design and aesthetics – and has also facilitated the production of large-scale, affordable public housing by the Housing Development Board (HDB). Such hegemonic measures are justified by the fact that given Singapore's small size (originally 587km^2, but growing through reclamation towards a desired total landmass of 743km^2 – Marshall 2003), urban development is directly linked to national development, which means that the success of one determines that of the other. Simply put, Singapore's limited and valuable land bank underscores the importance of near-absolute state control over the country's urban development.

Such control serves other economic purposes as well. The prolific state ownership of Singapore's landmass has proven to be a significant source of revenue (through the leasing of land to the private sector), and has enabled the state to exert exacting control over not just Singapore's urban development, but its socio-economic and aesthetic development as well. Unlike almost any other country in the world, 'the marriage of state and corporate power allows the Singaporean state a capacity to manipulate the production of urban space for purposes of social control and economic development' (Shatkin 2014: 117). In addition, Singapore was a forerunner in the development of city branding and the associated 'proliferation of metropolitan spectacles' which in turn 'indexes a new cultural regime' (Ong 2011a: 205) of city planners attempting to build and assert the identity of the nation-state (and to attract international recognition and capital) through the urban landscape (Lash and Lury 2007). Not only has the political economy of state capitalism defined the country's urban development and planning, but it has also 'revolutionize[d] the terms of urban citizenship through its dominance of land economy' (Shatkin 2014: 118). It is such revolutionary effects that have attracted both the admiration and the criticism of non-Singaporean academics, policymakers, planners and publics.

It is these conditions and outcomes that mark the Singapore model as distinct, and which, in the absence of state capitalism, often cause efforts to emulate the Singapore model – of which there have been many (see Chua 2011; Pow 2014) – to result in political corruption and social conflict. As McCann and Ward (2012: 43) posit when speaking of the processes involved in 'assembling urbanism':

> Cities are made coherent through the work of their inhabitants, through the efforts of actors located elsewhere, and through the power-laden and uneven relations among these various actors, all set within larger social and material contexts which tend to complicate straightforward assumptions about causality.

The Singapore case both refutes and supports the idea that assembling urbanism 'complicate[s] straightforward assumptions about causality'. Singapore's cityscape has been sculpted in almost direct accordance with the directives and vision of the state, which refutes the notion posited above that 'people make their own cities and fight over the resources, meanings and the spaces thus created' (Walker 2015: 189; after Brenner and Schmid 2015). Indeed, the success of the Singapore model is as much about development outcomes as it is about the foresight of its government in designing and enacting a series of hegemonic policies aimed to control social, economic and urban development. The city-state has evolved from the top down, and whilst the government has in recent years started to concede some of its decision-making control over the urban environment, its grip remains tight. Efforts to consult the general public, specific communities affected by urban plans, and expert groups support the notion, as the government comes to terms with the on-the-ground realities of application and resistance. Such realities are explored in more detail in the following section.

When viewed as a model of urbanism that can be (and is) leveraged in different, non-Singapore contexts, the assumptions of causality are complicated. Singapore is unique in that the state imposes a clearly defined filter that dictates the city's urban form. To this end, Singapore's networks of urbanity are outwardly neoliberal, but inwardly conservative. Its pre-tested urban policies – specifically, its models of residential, commercial and industrial development – have been imported by and exported to other countries in Asia and the Middle East as models for learning and replication (see Goldman 2011; Hoffman 2011). Yet whilst the Singapore model is highly attractive because of its economic and social successes, it is also flawed (in terms of its importability and exportability) as it draws on a unique (and non-replicable) set of political and territorial circumstances to reach the desired outcomes. These considerations will now be discussed in more detail.

Importing/exporting the Singapore model of urban development

The enviable success of the Singapore model of urban development has caused it to be imported by other countries looking to emulate Singapore's growth trajectory. It is in this sense that Singapore has become a paradigmatic example of 'a site of the production of urban planning knowledge and "best practices" that gets assembled and translated into contemporary circuits of capital' (Pow 2014: 287). Specifically, in recent decades there has been a proliferation of what Shatkin (2011) terms 'urban integrated mega-projects' (UIMs) throughout Asia. Such projects are typically large in scale, profit-driven (and often built and managed by a single developer or group of investors), and self-contained inasmuch as they contain residential, commercial, industrial and social (e.g. schools, hospitals, convention centres) spaces. Importantly, such projects reflect the commodification of contemporary urban forms, and are built on the premise of 'inter-referencing':

> The explicit modeling or urban governance regimes on institutions and practices from elsewhere in Asia . . . and, more abstractly, when the example of 'best practices' in global architecture and urban design from the region . . . are selectively appropriated and interpreted as appropriately 'Asian' models to be emulated through the development of UIMs (Shatkin 2011: 79).

Singapore is an originator of such ideas, with the state actively encouraging and promoting the exportation of the Singapore model of urban development. Notably, this has been through the creation of a township development consultancy called Surbana, which offers the gamut of urban development services: from planning and design, to engineering and consultancy. Surbana's services have gained most traction in China and India, where there is a great demand for tried and tested models of urban planning and development. The demand for urban models of success does, however, go beyond infrastructure alone; as Ong (2011b: 15) recognises, 'urban modeling is . . . not only a technology for building garden cities and knowledge hubs elsewhere; it can become a political tool for changing the built form and social spirit of another urban environment'. It represents the commodification of urban innovation; a product that is packaged and marketed to an international audience of planners, policymakers and politicians looking to leverage the success of countries like Singapore. And, in doing so, 'the Singapore model of corporate and residential planning seems a packaged deal for raising the city profile' (Ong 2011b: 15), helping places like Manila in the Philippines, Surabaya in Indonesia, and Kigali in Rwanda to leapfrog more linear stages of urban progress.

As Shatkin (2011: 94) recognises, however, there are a number of questions that need to be asked and addressed by researchers concerning the exportation and application of urban forms to different contexts. These include:

> How the models . . . respond to local opportunities and constraints, how effective they are in overcoming obstacles to urban redevelopment, and what implications the resulting models of urban governance and design have for social and political change.

Outside of China (where the state owns all urban land, and can therefore – like in Singapore – control all land acquisition and development projects), such projects of urban development and renewal often struggle to meet the developer's objectives. Indeed, the reality is that 'for every UIM that breaks ground, there are several more which have scarcely advanced beyond the concept stage, and in many cases likely never will' (Shatkin 2011: 78). This is most commonly due to political, social and legal obstructions, but also due to problems inherent to the 'modelling' approach to urban development. As Shatkin (2011: 83) argues, whilst the overarching aim of UIMs is to create elite urban spaces that are insulated from the disordered (or, at least, pluralistic) socio-political contexts within which they are located – 'their control by corporate actors and unaccountable government structures provides the political insulation needed to strictly implement zoning and building codes, and to effectively regulate public space' – they are also spaces of resistance to and subversion of the dominant political order. They are islands of urbanity located within a sea of turbulence; a neo-colonial imposition of (successful, ordered, Asian/ Singaporean) urban values to what are often chaotic host-country landscapes. Such contemporary forms of urban development (along with the leapfrogging connotations associated with the term 'hyperdevelopment') have brought about situations whereby

> corporate power and Western technologies are creating a global space that is effacing national identity and undermining the capacity for a nation to control how it wants to be and how it wants to act in the world. Capital here thwarts nation sovereign self-determination by subjecting 'local' spaces to the overarching logic of a capitalist system with translocal or placeless determinations. (Ong 2011a: 206)

Urban modelling is effected and contested at various scales of analysis: from the global (in terms of networks of capital) to the national (policymaking and politics) and the local (community uptake, appropriation and/or resistance). In the contemporary world, there are, therefore, various layers of contestation and negotiation that are entwined with the processes of urban planning. Such layers become increasingly problematic when the urban model to be used as a blueprint is imported from overseas. As Ong (2011a; see also Spencer 2015) suggests, critical analysis is needed to explore the effects of each layer on the other(s); how global capital intersects with sovereign rule and control at the national level; how the everyday practices of local communities shape and are shaped by the determinations of the state; and how each layer in the matrix is constantly evolving and adapting and/or exerting itself in relation to the others within which it is entangled.

Whilst Shatkin's explicit concern is with the sites of application, the sites of origination – in this case Singapore – should not be immune to such critical questioning and analysis. As Brenner and Schmid (2015: 152) observe: 'today, divergent conditions of wealth and poverty, growth and decline, inclusion and exclusion, centrality and marginality, mutually produce one another at all spatial scales'. This is a compelling reminder that critical research and analysis is needed to unearth the negative in the positive (and vice versa), and the politics in the paradigmatic. Both the Singapore case and the countries in which the Singapore model of urban development is applied can bring into acute focus the reality that 'cities are assembled not only by policy actors with a profound command over space, but also by those whose identities condition, but do not necessarily preclude, their involvement in policy decisions' (McCann and Ward 2012: 44; after McCann 2008). Put differently, just because the state can play a determinative role in shaping the urban environment, it does not mean it is the only player, for it is the community that can often determine the relative success of urban planning. Policy transfer is, by definition, an exercise in realising abstraction. Research has so far focused on the policies and the practices of transfer, but has largely overlooked society's responses to such planning predicates. The Singapore brand of urban planning may appeal to planning practitioners worldwide, but the variegated forms of uptake, acceptance and rejection, if not rebellion at the community level, are yet to be explored in detail. It is to these issues that we now turn, highlighting new avenues for research.

The politics of policy transfer

The success of Singapore's urban planning has turned the various facets of its urban development into a set of blueprints that other, less developed countries aspire to. Problems arise, however, when urban models are applied to a new set of material, social and political conditions than those from which they were formulated and gained prominence. The previous section highlights some of the key political and legislative idiosyncrasies of Singapore that have created the right environment for success. Whilst Singapore provides a blueprint for successful Asian urbanism, such an accolade can also run the risk of obfuscating some of the marginalisations that are inherent by-products of growth and 'success'. As Perera and Tang (2013: 14) argue: 'the central question is who and what gets left out . . . Planners and policymakers have a way of focusing on growth and remain[ing] silent about important tensions that emanate from ethnic, religious, and other cultural differences by portraying them as "'low-politics'". The ulterior (and often unintended) effects of policy outcomes – on people, places and the environment – should be given as much attention as the indicators and badges of urban success. In the Singapore case, the tight control of the state can help to engineer specific and intended urban outcomes, but it can also cause a number of unintended consequences. Precluding society from the planning process can strip citizenship of its meaning, and can cause the fomentation of political alienation and apathy (Shatkin 2014). As Pow (2014: 303) notes, the paradox is that 'Singapore's celebrated urban model is increasingly at odds with the reality back home [in Singapore] when income disparity is at its highest . . . [which is] compounded by "urban woes" typically associated with "less esteemed" cities elsewhere'. Such woes have manifested in recent years in the form of growing traffic congestion, an overheated residential property market, a series of unforeseen flash floods within the prime shopping district of Orchard Road from 2010 to 2013, hitherto unprecedented political disenchantment recorded during the 2011 General Election, and questions arising about migrant (and, therefore, community) integration following the Little India riots in 2013.

In a similar vein, research also needs to do more to understand not just the environmental conditions of the country of origin (in this case, Singapore), but the country or region of application as well. As urban studies evolves into an ever-more international discipline – one that is deeply embedded within inter-city connections and comparisons – it becomes increasingly important to sensitise discourse to how

> the moment in neoliberalism's travels when policy is invented, appropriated, contested, imposed, borrowed, refused, or abandoned is the moment when a connected-but-localized politics embedded in the histories and particular assemblages of individual cities is *crucial to any account of policy circulation.* (Robinson 2011: 1095, emphasis added)

Such sentiment reflects the need for the development of an urban studies that is critical of connections, that recognises the malleability of ideas across borders, and is sensitive to the capriciousness of application in different environments around the world. Despite their attractiveness (and, in some instances, success) in catalysing urban development throughout the developing world, the reality is that such models are not a panacea for urban transformation. Instead, they should be recognised for what they are, that is 'socially constructed processes that are deeply embedded in power relations and animated by urban imaginaries of "good places" to live and work' (Pow 2014: 288). As urban models travel from the point of formulation to the point of application, they are (re)territorialised in different ways, and with different outcomes. When it comes to Singapore, Chua (2011: 36) provides a reminder that '"modelling" after Singapore cannot be a process of "cloning" Singapore . . . it is inevitably a process of fragmentary borrowing, mimicking, replication, and other modes of emulation'. This idea of borrowing and reimagining is well captured in the Chinese cities of Shanghai, Beijing, Dalian, Tianjin and Wuhan, all of which have adapted Singapore's low-cost public housing model – that of compact apartment blocks organised around a neighbourhood centre – to develop a series of private residential enclaves that target the privileged upper-middle classes (Pow 2014). In this instance, therefore, ideas that have been developed to provide public (or mass-market) benefits in Singapore, are used to benefit urban elites in China.

In addition, whilst it is often the model that changes form and function when exported/imported, in some instances it can also shape the context in which it is applied as well. In the Chinese city of Shenzhen, for example, Zhang (2012) documents the shift from a Hong Kong-inspired laissez-faire policy landscape, to a more Singapore-styled authoritarian model of urban development. What this shows is that the relationship between model and context is recursive, with each aspect adapting to and shaping the other. In some instances, the very referencing of the Singapore model could be used to help quell domestic opposition to urban planning, with the attraction of the Singapore model (or 'brand Singapore') being as much about the promise of 'success' as it is the promise of the most relevant and convertible practices in urban planning.

Conclusions

The Singapore model of urban development is an extraordinary case that finds great appeal amongst an international audience of urban planners and practitioners. Its economic success and well-ordered society provides a great lure for stakeholders from less developed countries, and yet the fact remains that it is at once a template for and an exception to other cities; a city that has achieved 'extraordinary' status within less than two generations (Amin and Graham 1997; Peck 2015). Whilst the Singapore model is easily (and rightfully) lauded, the unique circumstances within which it has been developed and applied serve to enmesh it not only within contemporary debates surrounding 'smart cities' and 'eco-cities' but also associated projects of socio-political surveillance, social engineering and control (Brenner and Schmid 2015).

The fact remains that work is still needed to better contextualise theory. As Peck (2015: 160) warns: 'the challenge of more worldly, comparative theorization has been unevenly met, often more through difference-finding and deconstructive manoeuvres than through projects of urban-theoretical renewal and reconstruction'. Future research agendas would do well to understand how global forces like post- and neo-colonialism, and social theories like poststructuralism and world systems theory, have helped to unravel old and create new power hierarchies in different parts of the world. Whilst some of the latest research has started to do this – such as Tomba's (2014: 20) study of neighbourhood politics in China, which draws attention to the 'daily practices of power in the production of an idea of legitimacy that might, in turn, result in concrete dividends for the authoritarian rulers'; or Spencer's (2015: 25) advancement of the idea of a 'global urban ecosystem' wherein the focus is on understanding the complexity of natural (human) relationships within a defined space – such questioning remains nascent. There is a particular need to focus on the sites of origination and application of urban models, and of the ways in which social, political, cultural, economic and environmental contexts shape policy transfer – not to mention urban theory – around the world.

NOTE

1 It is arguable whether 'urban studies' constitutes a discipline. Krishnan (2009: 10) suggests that '[i]f a discipline is called "studies", then it usually indicates it is of newer origin . . . and . . . may fall short of one or more of the . . . [disciplinary] characteristics.' Whilst there is clearly a particular object of study (the city), whether there is a 'body of accumulated specialist knowledge . . . which is specific to them and not generally shared with another discipline' (Krishnan 2009: 9) is less clear. Nevertheless, for present purposes, we refer to 'urban studies' as a discipline by virtue of the common object of study.

References

Amin, A. (2007), 'Re-thinking the urban social', *City*, **11**, 100–114.
Amin, A. and S. Graham (1997), 'The ordinary city', *Transactions of the Institute of British Geographers*, **22**, 411–429.
Brenner, N. and C. Schmid (2015), 'Towards a new epistemology of the urban?', *City*, **19** (2–3), 151–182.

Chua, Beng Huat (2011), 'Singapore as model: planning innovations, knowledge experts', in Ananya Roy and Ong Aihwa (eds), *Worlding Cities: Asian Experiments and the Art of Being Global*, Oxford: Wiley-Blackwell, pp. 29–54.

Goldman, Michael (2011), 'Speculating on the next world city', in Ananya Roy and Ong Aihwa (eds), *Worlding Cities: Asian Experiments and the Art of Being Global*, Oxford: Wiley-Blackwell, pp. 229–258.

Hoffman, Lisa (2011), 'Urban modeling and contemporary technologies of city-building in China: the production of regimes of green urbanisms', in Ananya Roy and Ong Aihwa (eds), *Worlding Cities: Asian Experiments and the Art of Being Global*, Oxford: Wiley-Blackwell, pp. 55–76.

Kong, L. (1993), 'Ideological hegemony and the political symbolism of religious buildings in Singapore', *Environment and Planning D: Society and Space*, **11**, 23–45.

Krishnan, Armin (2009), 'What are academic disciplines? Some observations on the disciplinarity versus interdisciplinarity debate', ESRC National Centre for Research Methods (NCRM) Working Series 03/09, UK.

Lash, Scott and Celia Lury (2007), *Global Culture Industry*, Cambridge, UK: Polity Press.

Marshall, Richard (2003), *Emerging Urbanity: Global Urban Projects in the Asia Pacific Rim*, London: Spon Press.

Massey, Doreen (1993), 'Power-geometry and a progressive sense of place', in John Bird, Barry Curtis, Tim Putnam, George Robertson and Lisa Tickner (eds), *Mapping the Futures: Local Cultures, Global Change*, London: Routledge, pp. 59–69.

McCann, E. (2008), 'Expertise, truth, and urban policy mobilities: global circuits of knowledge in the development of Vancouver, Canada's "four pillar" drug strategy', *Environment and Planning A*, **40**, 885–904.

McCann, E. and K. Ward (2012), 'Assembling urbanism: following policies and "studying through" the sites and situations of policy making', *Environment and Planning A*, **44**, 42–51.

Ong, Aihwa (2011a), 'Hyperbuilding: spectacle, speculation, and the hyperspace of sovereignty', in Ananya Roy and Ong Aihwa (eds), *Worlding Cities: Asian Experiments and the Art of Being Global*, Oxford: Wiley-Blackwell, pp. 205–226.

Ong, Aihwa (2011b), 'Introduction: worlding cities, or the art of being global', in Ananya Roy and Ong Aihwa (eds), *Worlding Cities: Asian Experiments and the Art of Being Global*, Oxford: Wiley-Blackwell, pp. 1–26.

Peck, J. (2015), 'Cities beyond compare?', *Regional Studies*, **49** (1), 160–182.

Perera, Nihal and Wing-Shing Tang (2013), 'Introduction: in search of Asian urbanisms: limited visibility and intellectual impasse', in Nihal Perera and Wing-Shing Tang (eds), *Transforming Asian Cities: Intellectual Impasse, Asianizing Space, and Emerging Translocalities*, Oxford and New York: Routledge, pp. 1–19.

Pow, C. (2014), 'License to travel: policy assemblage and the "Singapore model"', *City*, **18** (3), 287–306.

Robinson, Jennifer (2006), *Ordinary Cities: Between Modernity and Development*, London: Routledge.

Robinson, J. (2011), '2010 Urban Geography Plenary Lecture – the travels of urban neoliberalism: taking stock of the internationalization of urban theory', *Urban Geography*, **32** (8), 1087–1109.

Roy, A. (2009), 'The 21st-century metropolis: new geographies of theory', *Regional Studies*, **43** (6), 819–830.

Scott, A. (2011), 'Emerging cities of the third wave', *City*, **15** (3–4), 289–321.

Shatkin, Gavin (2011), 'Planning privatopolis: representation and contestation in the development of urban integrated mega-projects', in Ananya Roy and Ong Aihwa (eds), *Worlding Cities: Asian Experiments and the Art of Being Global*, Oxford: Wiley-Blackwell, pp. 77–97.

Shatkin, G. (2014), 'Reinterpreting the meaning of the "Singapore Model": state capitalism and urban planning', *International Journal of Urban and Regional Research*, **38** (1), 116–137.

Spencer, James (2015), *Globalization and Urbanization: The Global Urban Ecosystem*, London: Rowman & Littlefield.

The Editors (2015), 'New urban geographies', *Urban Geography*, **36** (3), 327–339.

Tomba, Luigi (2014), *The Government Next Door: Neighborhood Politics in Urban China*, Ithaca, NY and London: Cornell University Press.

Walker, R. (2015), 'Building a better theory of the urban: a response to "Towards a new epistemology of the urban?"', *City*, **19** (2–3), 183–191.

Zhang, J. (2012), 'From Hong Kong's capitalist fundamentals to Singapore's authoritarian governance: the policy mobility of neo-liberalising Shenzhen, China', *Urban Studies*, **49**, 2853–2871.

17 The city in sub-Saharan Africa

Edgar Pieterse

Urbanization is unique in Africa because of the compressed time-frame of its unfolding and the predominance of non-formal patterns. The regions that we broadly define as the global North went from predominantly rural to predominantly urban between 1750 and 1950 in lockstep with modernization and industrialization (Satterthwaite 2007). An equivalent demographic and territorial transition will unfold in sub-Saharan Africa between 1950 and 2035 (UN-DESA 2015), but without the economic benefits of imperial extraction enjoyed by the North during its transition. Moreover, the degree of social-cultural dislocation in African societies is much more extreme due to the rolling dynamics of anti-colonial struggles, post-colonial volatility, pilfering and conflict, and, more recently, neoliberal marginalization. The terms of trade and exchange continue to imprison African economies.

In this short chapter I briefly delineate the specificities of African urbanization with an eye on how various traditions of academic research have responded. My central assertion is that we desperately need to advance interdisciplinary research rooted in real-life experiments to find situated responses to the extremities of contemporary urban life. However, the epistemic challenge is to undertake this work with a deep respect for the cultural complexities of everyday life that might hold the political and theoretical clues to make sense of the elusive African city.

Non-formal urbanization

The chapter deliberately elides the concept of informality because it is misleading in contexts where the bulk of urban life and economy does not conform to the taken-for-granted categories of formality. Unfortunately we still do not have a powerful enough concept to both capture and interpret the confluence and interlinkages of the following features of African urbanization elaborated briefly in this section. As a place-holder, "non-formal" seems to do a better job of disrupting self-evident reference points. The unconventional and regionally specific dynamics of African urbanization (See Table 17.1) are best glimpsed through the following five macro characteristics.

Table 17.1   African countries categorized by urbanization, fertility transition and economic transformation

Category	Features
Diversifiers	The urbanization levels of diversifiers range between 40% and 65%. They are also close to completing their fertility transition with total fertility ratios of three or fewer children per woman. These countries are Egypt, Mauritius, Morocco, South Africa and Tunisia. This group has Africa's highest level of income (above USD 10 000 gross national income [GNI] per capita in 2013 with the exception of Morocco) and of human development (with a Human Development Index [HDI] value above 0.60).
Early urbanizers	Nine countries fall into this category distinguished by progress in their urbanization and fertility transition without having been able to diversify their economic base. Mostly found in West Africa, they include Côte d'Ivoire, Ghana and Senegal. These countries are about 35–50% urbanized and have total fertility ratios of about five children per woman. They are typically low- to lower-middle income countries (USD 1000–4000 GNI per capita in 2013), with low-to-medium levels of human development (HDI values between 0.40 and 0.57).
Late urbanizers	The 11 countries that fall into this category are predominantly rural yet have begun their urbanization and fertility transition and structural transformation more recently. In contrast to the early urbanizers, they are located in East Africa and include Ethiopia, Kenya and Tanzania. Less than a third of their population typically lives in urban areas. Their total fertility rates are four to six children per woman. Income levels are low (USD 1000–2200 GNI per capita in 2013), and levels of human development are low-to-medium (HDI values between 0.38 and 0.54). Interestingly, two relatively authoritarian countries, Ethiopia and Rwanda, have demonstrated an impressive capacity to diversify their economic base over the past decade, albeit from a low basis.
Agrarians	This cohort contains predominantly rural countries that are still at a very early stage of their urbanization and fertility transition. Many of the 11 agrarian countries are landlocked, such as Niger, Chad and Malawi. Typically less than a third of the population resides in urban areas, and women have on average at least six children. These countries' income levels did not exceed USD 1600 GNI per capita in 2013, and they have low levels of human development (HDI values between 0.48 and 0.34). Their economies are predominantly agriculture-based: agriculture makes up 25–41% of their GDP and manufacturing 4–12%.
Natural resource-based countries	This group has urbanized with windfalls from natural resources, which have attracted labour out of agriculture. Compared with other countries at similar income levels, these 13 countries show a higher degree of urbanization (40–78%), generally higher fertility rates and a high degree of urban primacy, with the capital usually disproportionally bigger than other cities. The share of GDP in agriculture is low at 3–21%. These countries exhibit huge

Table 17.1   (continued)

Category	Features
Natural resource-based countries	variations in income levels (USD 500–20 000 per capita), in the types of natural resources they produce (e.g. hydrocarbons, minerals and metals) and in their geography (e.g. Libya is predominantly arid while Nigeria is mostly rain-fed). Due to the over-reliance on natural resources they are extremely vulnerable to international market swings, which impact on the investment capacity of the state.

Source: AfDB/OECD/UNDP (2016).

Firstly, 62 per cent of sub-Saharan Africa's housing is slums, the highest figure for any world region (UN-Habitat 2012). It is safe to assume that as urban areas continue to grow at a considerable pace, and concomitant investments in urban services lag behind, the absolute number of people living precariously is likely to increase over the next few decades making an already brutal situation even worse. The speed of urban growth is well beyond the capacity of most African (local) governments. (AfDB/OECD/UNDP 2016). However, amid large-scale deficits in formal service delivery, a rich and multivalent system of compensation pulses to support everyday lives and livelihoods (Jaglin 2014; Myers 2011; Rakodi 2014). Thus, city building is predominantly an organic and non-state affair, embodying vast systems of social organization, exchange, oversight, regulation, violence, reciprocity and continuous recalibration (Myers 2011; Simone 2004, 2010).

Secondly, slum living conditions go hand-in-hand with predominantly informal economic systems (Skinner 2010). Most African economies are lopsided. Owing to colonial determinations, compounded by an asymmetrical global trading regime, most African economies have remained stuck in a commodity-driven export model, rendering them particularly vulnerable to the vagaries of global markets and continuously devoid of investment capital to transition to more diversified economic activities (Jerven 2015; Moghalu 2014). Thus, as the labour force expands, the formal economy is simply not able to grow fast enough to generate sufficient employment opportunities to absorb a rapidly growing youthful population bristling with globalized consumerist aspirations.

Thirdly, due to small tax bases that stem from slight economies, most African cities have by and large failed to invest in critical urban infrastructures for most of the post-colonial era: a failure reinforced by inadequate maintenance of constructed infrastructure (Gutman et al. 2015; Pieterse and Hyman 2014). This creates a crisis of provision and affordability. Two-thirds of urban Africans fall below the $4 per day poverty line. The only (financially) viable infrastructure markets are among the middle classes and business sectors, instantiating an investment regime that worsens spatial and social inequalities. More specifically, almost all new infrastructure investments in African cities go into residential and commercial stock for the (fairly small) middle class, premised on a car-based mobility system. Unsurprisingly there are now a number of speculative bubbles around the concept of new (smart) cities and towns tethered to prodigious highway construction, exacerbating terrible traffic congestion and mobility inefficiencies (Provoost 2010). Considering the perpetuation of urban sprawl, combined with rapid urbanization in vast peri-urban zones, such inefficiencies seem likely to worsen, especially when regulatory systems are by and large ineffective and also rooted in paralegal systems of rule (Berrisford 2014; UN-Habitat 2014).

Fourthly, the combination of urban neglect and inappropriate elite investments accelerates the distorted spatial form of most African cities that derive their fundamental structure from colonial planning and regulation. This produces urban landscapes of inefficient sprawl, stark urban divisions and very poor quality public space (UN-Habitat 2012). This urban form has a particularly debilitating impact on the budgets of poor urban majorities who have to expend up to 40 per cent of their incomes on transport, stifling prospects of social and economic mobility. Paradoxically, in a context of sprawl, slum settlements experience very high densities due to over-crowding and small dwelling units generating all manner of social and safety problems.

Finally, beyond these socio-economic and related infrastructural factors, most African cities are also saddled with ineffective and often unresponsive governments. Sometimes this is due to the lack of devolution of financial resources and legal competencies to lower levels of government (Pieterse and Smit 2014); other times, it is due to deeply entrenched rent-seeking behaviour and patronage (Moss 2007). Importantly, African democracies are being built and tested in cities. Opposition political parties find a footing and springboard in the neglected slums of cities, creating a perverse political incentive for the establishment to further ignore and bypass slum areas (Resnick 2012). In other words, nascent multiparty democracy has as yet no necessary or obvious positive spin-offs for popular neighbourhoods in many African cities. This is just one among many issues lacking systematic research and debate.

The instinctive and understandable response to these observations is a combination of moral outrage and/or political depression. However, it is critical to resist such sentiments. Despite these glaring fault lines of injustice and exclusion, the truth is that we actually know very little about the fine grain of everyday life in the African city. Urban dwellers are nothing if not resilient. Somehow, across diverse urban settings, people are able to find room to hustle, invest, hedge, negotiate, contract, support, extract, deal, consolidate, expand and continuously recalibrate their positions in relation to scarce resources and opportunities. This implies a capacity to read and expertly navigate complex and ever-shifting environments; capacities which have yet to be studied and mined for understanding, insight and innovation.

Africa's urban diversity

However, before we delve into the ways in which the literature addresses African urbanization, another set of statistical markers is of interest because it reinforces the enormous diversity in evidence across 54 African countries.

A report by the African Development Bank (AfDB), Organisation for Economic Co-operation and Development (OECD) and United Nations Development Programme (UNDP) provides a novel typology to categorize African countries in terms of urbanization dynamics, fertility transitions and economic development as expressed in the changing role of agriculture in the economy and by the importance of natural resource extraction in the economy (Table 17.1). This typology illustrates the diversity of conditions and trends across Africa.

The generally high fertility rates across most of Africa contribute to robust projected population growth rates in both rural and urban areas. Figure 17.1, from the same report, compares a disaggregated Africa (sub-Sahara Africa minus South Africa and North Africa) with Latin America to reveal the dramatic patterns.

Urbanization in Africa is most rapid and prevalent in what the OECD calls the urban–rural interface zones, where one can observe a continuum of rural areas, villages, towns and cities of fewer than 500000 inhabitants. This phenomenon is particularly evident in the agrarian and late urbanizer countries. Drawing on United Nations Department of Economic and Social Affairs (UN-DESA) data, the OECD calculates that 83 per cent of Africa's population lives in such a urban–rural interface.

> Across the different regions, the share of the population living in settlements smaller than 500000 inhabitants is as follows: 91% in East Africa, 80% in West Africa, 77% in North Africa, 73% in Central Africa and 65% in Southern Africa. Looking at all of Africa's urban areas, 63% have a population of fewer than 500000 people. Africa's urbanisation has thus to a large extent taken the form of "urban villages", diffusing urban growth in smaller towns. (AfDB/OECD/UNDP 2016: 159)

This does not mean that large cities are not important. In 2010, the rate of growth of cities of fewer than 500000 inhabitants was still second to that of the largest cities.

These macro trends underscore that it is somewhat foolhardy to speak of a singular African urbanization. Instead we need to recognize that the material conditions associated with complex patterns of urbanization are marked by massive deficits which drive the predominantly non-formal basis of everyday life and systems of rule, regulation and social interactions. Since these dynamics do not conform to conventional measures of economic development, state building or modern social cohesion, an extraordinary amount of attention to detail is required to make sense of the adaptive dynamics of African cities.

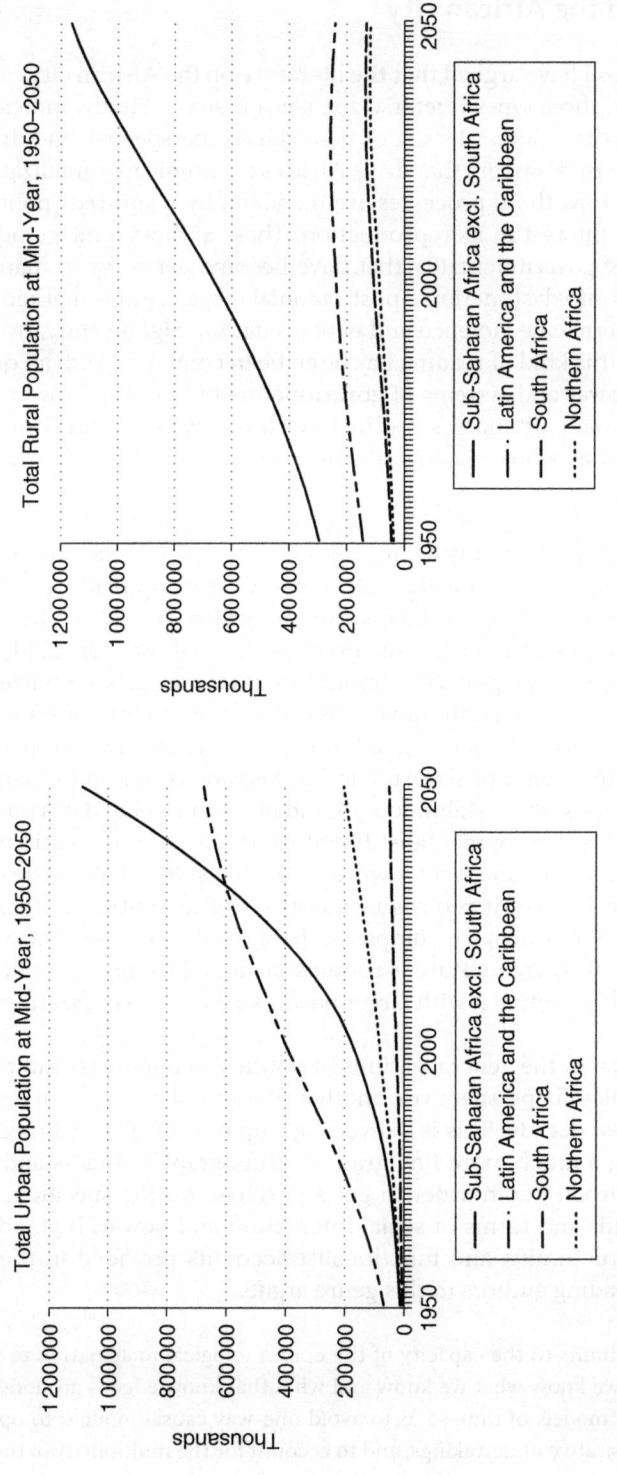

Source: Adapted from UN-DESA (2015).

Figure 17.1 Demographic trends for select regions and South Africa, 1950–2050

Perspectives on the African city

In a series of articles I have argued that the literature on the African city can broadly be categorized into three types (Pieterse 2010, 2011, 2015). Firstly, radical political economists who write from a Marxist or neo-Marxist perspective and draw attention to the big structural factors that drive Africa's economic marginalization in the global system and how these processes are mediated by "captured" political elites who have a vested interest in its reproduction. These authors tend to focus on the neoliberal forms of governmentality that have become pervasive in many African countries, welded onto dysfunctional post-colonial dispensations marked by political corruption, internecine violence and elite predation. Significantly, over the last two decades or so this kind of reading has often been combined with a Foucauldian analysis of state power and systems of governmentality to unveil how progressive-sounding development discourses are in fact clever ways of absolving the state of fundamental duties while making citizens responsible for their own wellbeing (Miraftab 2004).

Secondly, a lot of research stems from what one can call a "policy-fix" genre. This refers to scholarship focused on the vast range of development deficits to provide answers about how these problems can be tackled or solved. Given that the international development industry functions on the basis of perpetually "solving" development dilemmas, a significant amount of resources gets mobilized for this kind of work. Since most African universities have been starved of research funding for most of the post-colonial era, and especially over the last two decades, it is unsurprising that this genre of scholarship has become common in many African universities; a process that Mahmoud Mamdani (2011) elucidates in powerful terms. Typically, this developmentalist literature tends to be thematic or sectoral and changes as the development buzz words morph inside the global development industry. However, a lot of it returns to questions of institutional efficacy of the state to understand and manage complex urbanization processes and manifestations. Unsurprisingly, this literature is roundly critiqued for being apolitical, ameliorative and possibly complicit with larger power structures (Huchzermeyer 2011).

Thirdly, in response to the generalizations of political economists, and the simplifications of the policy-fix perspectives, another literature has grown in importance, especially in the last decade. This is a diverse group of critical social theorists who insist on achieving a much more fine-grained, ethnographic understanding of the lived patterns of urban life in order to get a purchase on the specificities of subjectivities, lifeworlds and forms of social interaction and power. It stands in stark contrast to the structuralist and functionalist accounts provided in the first two literatures. Two leading authors in this genre argue:

> There have been limits to the capacity of the epistemological imagination to pose questions about how we know what we know and what that knowledge is grounded upon; to draw on multiple models of time so as to avoid one-way causal models; to open a space for broader comparative undertakings; and to account for the multiplicity of the pathways

and trajectories of change. Where empirical work and local studies are carried out, generally they are poorly informed theoretically. As fresh questions emerge and new dramas
take shape, the social sciences manifest a surprising lack of openness toward the humanities. Historical and political scholarship is not combined with fundamental philosophical
inquiry, and this has led to a dramatic "thinning" of "the social." The latter is still understood as a matter of *order* and *contract* rather than as the locus of *experiment* and *artifice*.
(Mbembe and Nuttall 2004: 349)

According to Mbembe and Nuttall, taking on the challenge of writing the social
back into our understanding of African "life forms" requires an examination of
everyday practices and imaginaries as they unfold at the nexus of multiple crossings
that constitute urban spatiality. For, like most cities in the world, "the continent
has been and still is a space of flows, of flux, of translocation, with multiple nexuses
of entry and exit points. As evinced by numerous recent studies, the continent
we have in mind exists only as a function of circulation and of circuits" (Mbembe
and Nuttall 2004: 351). This implies a spatiality that is predominantly shaped by
the imperative, desire and tyranny of incessant mobility. This brief summary of
their approach points to the post-structural and post-colonial epistemologies that
inform the critique and the kinds of attentions that it calls for. However, in practice, these literatures on the African city tend to run on separate tracks, and use
caricatures of each other to inform their conceptual certitude or disinterest.

In my own work and the broader epistemic project we are nurturing at the African
Centre for Cities, we adopt a more non-sectarian and experimental approach
(Parnell and Pieterse 2016). It is informed by important critical and exploratory
theoretical efforts to reconsider and redeploy urbanism. For the sake of argument, I
have organized these strands into four categories, which in turn help us understand
the importance of both qualitative and quantitative research, as well as articulate
applied problem-solving questions with more ephemeral concerns that stem from
art, philosophy and literary studies. This is an experimental reading and sensibility
that is meant to stimulate innovation in the fields of urban research and practice.

Broadening urban epistemologies[1]

Urban studies is going through theoretical tumult because of the recognition that
much of the canon is in fact based on very specific historical processes and geographic specificities (Edensor and Jayne 2011; Robinson 2006; Roy 2008; Tonkiss
2011). Yet, this work has tended to function and circulate with universal applicabil-
ity. Recent evidence of this is the explosion of work on neoliberal governmentality
across the global South even though the most elementary governmental and regulatory institutions analysed by the neoliberal critique were never fully in existence
in these societies (Ferguson 2010, 2011). In light of the spirit of greater theoretical
diversity, heterodoxy and openness, I provide a survey of key perspectives from
critical urbanism to inform our approach to the African city (Pieterse 2012). See
Figure 17.2.

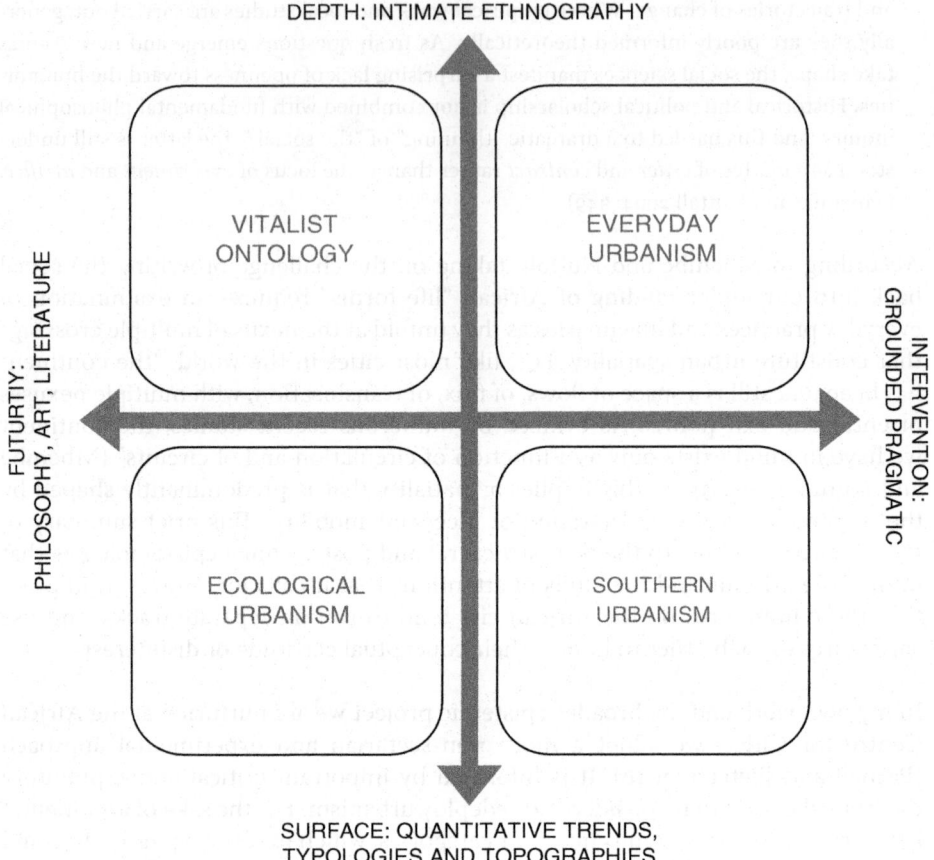

Source: Pieterse (2012: 40).

Figure 17.2 Epistemological fields in urban studies

The survey covers four theoretical fields: southern urbanism, everyday urbanism, vitalist ontology and ecological urbanism. The *southern urbanism* perspective seeks to provide a corrective to mainstream urban theory by foregrounding the demographic weight of the global South alongside a post-colonial re-reading of history, state craft, political identities, hybrid cultural systems and the multiplicity of bases of power, sub-jugation and empowerment. There is an insistence on the incompleteness of power and the capacity of the subaltern to subvert, circumvent and remake formal political intentions. Given the ways in which African cities are too often rendered as simply a product of colonial power and exploitation, or its aftermath, this theoretical field points to an enormous potential to begin to rewrite the history, present and potential futures of African cities on their own cultural, historical and spatial terms. Southern urbanism also reminds scholars to pay attention to the spatial and temporal specific-ity of urbanization processes unfolding in the early 21st century amid globalization, a changing international division of labour and unprecedented environmental risks.

Although epistemologically, *everyday urbanism* as a field of urban theorization shares a great affinity with southern urbanism, in contrast, it is consumed with the molecular dynamics of urbanity. Everyday urbanism seeks to take subjectivity and multiple social assemblages seriously on their own terms without overlaying a normative filter. It is therefore not surprising that a lot of the research in this vein has tended to focus on what some call the informal city (Tonkiss 2011; Varley 2013). Indeed, given the level of slum prevalence and informal economic activity that mark most African cities, this is indeed a central concern in a lot of current research. However, the field extends well beyond informality. Simone (2004, 2010) is a seminal theorist in this epistemic field since his work has for the past three decades painstakingly documented and theorized the centrality of everyday life to a larger appropriation of the urban and cityness. In his oeuvre he has always been less interested in the preoccupation with informality but rather insisted that a more agnostic sensibility was required. So, for Simone,

> the point is to pursue the dogged work of trying to understand the implications of what people do, particularly as it is clear that residents, even in the desperate ways they may talk about their lives, usually think about them as more than survival alone. Yes, survival is the overwhelming preoccupation of many. But the pursuit of survival involves actions, relations, sentiments, and opportunities that are more than survival alone. It is these thousands of small excesses which also act on the city, remaking it ever so slightly into something different than it was before. These changes are not measured by any easily discernable standard that would allow one to say that the city is becoming more just, equal, cutthroat, revolutionary, messianic, or hellish. And thus the important work is perhaps simply to document these efforts on the part of the poor to give rise to a new moral universe, a sense of value, of potential, and of the unexpected to which people's attention, no matter how poor, is also paid. (Simone 2010: 38–39)

Here one can sense Simone's methodological obsession with the infinitesimal pluralism of ordinary life and aspiration, excavated on their own terms, but also with a reluctant normative intent; a recognition that values, (spiritual) practices and mores suture everyday life; but these are also profoundly unstable and malleable and therefore to be understood and projected with great care and provisionality. By definition this approach to urban research demands a commitment to ethnography and painstaking observation and interpretation to make sense of the "thousands of small excesses". This approach also tends to be critical of structural political economy or developmentalist readings of the city (Mbembe and Nuttall 2004).

Approaches to rethink urbanism in the global North have tended to come from scholars who espouse a *vitalist ontology* and non-representational theory (Amin and Thrift 2002). Vitalism can be understood as a "tradition in philosophy that believes in the existence of a life force in material assemblages that cannot be explained through mechanistic approaches. As an ontology, it argues for the immanent emergence of form, rather than the existence of transcendent archetypes" (Lorimer 2009: 334). Amin reminds us that this approach induces an expansive understanding of cities and cityness:

cities might be thought of as machinic entities; engines of order, repetition, and innovation (sparked by the clash of elements and bodies) that drive the urban experience, including what humans make of themselves, others, and their environment. The urban environment is a meshwork of steel, concrete, natural life, wires, wheels, digital codes, and humans placed in close proximity and it is the rhythms of the juxtapositions and associations – coming together in symbolic projections, cultural routines, institutional practices, regulatory norms, physical flows, technological regimes, experience of the landscape, software systems – that surge through the human experience. The machinic rhythms of the city, I would argue, blend together the human and the urban condition, making people subjects of a specific kind, with their demeanor and outlook (compared to that of humans in other time-spaces) formed by their inhabitation of the urban environment and, most importantly, its inhabitation in them, fixed through these rhythms. (Amin 2011: 634)

This relational ontology is coupled to an affective understanding of subjectivity. Again, Lorimer (2009: 334) clarifies that affect "refers to both material, ecological properties of a body and the forces and processes that link them together. It describes prediscursive, embodied experiences that are subsequently codified into subjective emotions." It is clear that this ontology can easily be combined with the theoretical interests of the everyday urbanism. Scholars who adopt vitalist ontology are critical of textually oriented post-structural deconstruction on the one hand, and neo-Marxist structuralist accounts of inert and singular materialities, on the other. Instead, they are attentive in a much deeper and fuller account of how agency is enacted through particular configurations and emergences of both human and non-human actants, in ways that tune into the affective dispositions of people and the atmospheres of places that they inhabit or transit (de Boeck 2015; Larkin 2013). The net effect is an account of cities that emphasizes the fragility of all that seems solid, stable, gargantuan, immutable and taken for granted. Work in this register is just emerging in the African context and seems to be most readily embraced by urban political ecologists (Kaika and Swyngedouw 2011; Lawhon et al. 2014).

In keeping with contemporary concerns about environmental limits, *ecological urbanism* seeks to foreground the longer-term viability of contemporary models of urban development, design and material reproduction. It is consistent with a vitalist ontology and recognizes the variable assemblages of actants (Latour 2005) that support the unremitting social-natural reproduction of the city. By rendering the natural–social–technical interfaces of material infrastructures strange and legible, ecological urbanists also seek out propositional thought: that is, consideration of multiple pathways towards alternative, more resilient and more liveable forms and modalities of habitation (NSFWUS 2000; Swilling and Annecke 2012). Central to this concern is an interest in the natural-social assemblages of the city as mediated by infrastructure networks and the built environment. As Stephen Graham (2010: 1) explains:

energy, water, sewerage, transport, trade, finance, and communication infrastructures allow modern urban life to exist. Their pipes, ducts, servers, wires, conduits, electronic transmissions, and tunnels sustain the flows, connections, and metabolisms that are intrinsic to contemporary cities. Through their endless technological agency, these systems help transform the natural into the cultural, the social, and the urban.

Similar observations can be extended to the role of the built environment as mediators and embodiments of urban functionalities, form, symbolic projection and desires of control (de Boeck 2011; Larkin 2013).

The unique contribution of this perspective is that it offers a powerful and grounded excavation of how urban injustice and inequality is literally wired into the infrastructures and landscapes of the city, but can deploy its analytical purchase to also consider alternative "path dependencies". Thus, Mohsen Mostafavi (2011: 17) argues that new imaginaries of alternative urbanisms can be conjured from a perspective that views "the fragility of the planet and its resources as an opportunity for speculative design innovations rather than as a form of technical legitimation for promoting conventional solutions".

Embracing experimentalism

Figure 17.2 provides a diagrammatic illustration of these four currents in urban theory that can shape a multi-dimensional, open-ended and propositional research agenda on African cities. By putting these approaches in a relational field, it becomes possible to illustrate the methodological and political implications of this heterodox reading. The horizontal axis reflects a vital political sensibility. The urgency of routinized deprivation and exploitation demands a sustained engagement with a politics of intervention to respond to both the manifestations and the deeper structural drivers of uneven development and urban exclusion. This signals where this epistemological approach can draw on the insights of research that is often stuck in a policy-fix mode and combine it with the valuable insights of structuralist scholars about the deeper systems of economic and political power that reproduce the status quo. However, the ontological vantage points of both vitalism and ecological urbanism demand going much further than the structuralist readings of critical theorists while remaining open to a political sensibility that can embrace indeterminacy, futurity and uncertainty through more philosophical, artistic and literary accounts of the world and its multiple becomings (Connolly 2013). Of course, it would be an error to suggest that all these perspective are easily compatible, but it does allow one to engage urban research in highly complex and multivalent settings like the African city with greater provisionality and openness without abandoning an ethical insistence of social and environmental justice.

Finally, Figure 17.2 also hints at the importance of establishing productive complementarities between qualitative and quantitative research methodologies. The different epistemic approaches tend to lean more in one direction than the other. This is the most stylized dimension of the illustration, but it helps to demonstrate why we need to continuously cross-reference and interpolate both kinds of data and exploration. In the case of the African city, quantitative data is often limited and, where it does exist, is problematic (Potts 2012). With the growing influence of post-colonial post-structural readings of everyday urbanism, there has been too much of an emphasis on the particularities of discursive structures, specific places and individuals without sufficient contextualization to provide a sense of the significance of the individual case. In the tenor of the broader argument of this chapter, there is room for both, and more importantly, collaborative research initiatives that seek to expand our understanding of both dimensions of complex and fast changing urban realities.

In conclusion

This chapter has deliberately avoided providing a list of research questions related to the numerous issues that we know little about or understand very poorly in the Africa context. Instead, I seek to locate the unique urbanization dynamics and prospects of the African city within a broader conceptual landscape of shifting epistemologies about contemporary urbanism with a view to provide a rich suggestive account of the fields of knowledge that we need to flesh out and better articulate. It is also important to think questions afresh about the politics of knowledge production, urbanism and methodological priorities to enable an elucidation of the African city both on its own terms and in a dynamic conversation with urbanists everywhere.

ACKNOWLEDGEMENT

I am grateful to the editor, John Rennie Short, for his close reading of the chapter and helping me sharpen the argument. My research is supported by the National Research Foundation of South Africa and Mistra Urban Futures.

NOTE
1 This section draws heavily on Pieterse (2012).

References

AfDB/OECD/UNDP (African Development Bank, Organisation for Economic Co-operation and Development, United Nations Development Programme) (2016) *African Economic Outlook 2016: Sustainable Cities and Structural Transformation*. Paris: OECD Publishing.

Amin, A. (2011) Urban planning in an uncertain world. In: Bridge, G.and Watson, S. (eds) *The New Blackwell Companion to the City*. Oxford: Blackwell Publishing.

Amin, A. and Thrift, N. (2002) *Cities: Reimagining the Urban*. Oxford: Polity.

Berrisford, S. (2014) The challenge of urban planning law reform in Africa. In: Parnell, S. and Pieterse, E. (eds) *Africa's Urban Revolution*. London: Zed Books.

Connolly, W.E. (2013) The "New Materialism" and the Fragility of Things. *Millennium: Journal of International Studies*, 41(3): 399–412.

de Boeck, F. (2011) The modern Titanic. Urban planning and everyday life in Kinshasa. *The Salon*, 4: 76–85.

de Boeck, F. (2015) "Divining" the city: rhythm, amalgamation and knotting as forms of "urbanity". *Social Dynamics*, 41(1): 47–58.

Edensor, T. and Jayne, M. (2011) Introduction: urban theory beyond the West. In: Edensor, T. and Jayne, M. (eds) *Urban Theory beyond the West: A World of Cities*. London and New York: Routledge.

Ferguson, J. (2010) The uses of neoliberalism. *Antipode*, 41(1): 166–184.

Ferguson, J. (2011) Towards a left art of government: from "Foucauldian critique" to Foucauldian politics. *History of the Human Sciences*, 24(4): 61–68.

Graham, S. (2010) When infrastructures fail. In: Graham, S. (ed.) *Disrupted Cities: When Infrastructure Fails*. New York and London: Routledge.

Gutman, J., Sy, A. and Chattopadhyay, S. (2015) *Financing African Infrastructure. Can the World Deliver?* Washington DC: The Brookings Institute.

Huchzermeyer, M. (2011) *Cities without "Slums": From Informal Settlement Eradication to a Right to the City in Africa*. Cape Town: UCT Press.

Jaglin, S. (2014) Regulating service delivery in southern cities: rethinking urban heterogeneity. In: Parnell, S. and Oldfield, S. (eds) *The Routledge Handbook on Cities of the Global South*. London: Routledge.

Jerven, M. (2015) *Africa: Why Economists Get It Wrong*. London: Zed Books.

Kaika, M. and Swyngedouw, E. (2011) The urbanization of nature: great promises, impasse, and new beginnings. In: Bridge, G. and Watson, S. (eds) *The New Blackwell Companion to the City*. Oxford: Wiley-Blackwell.

Larkin, B. (2013) The politics and poetics of infrastructure. *Annual Review of Anthropology*, 42: 327–343.

Latour, B. (2005) *Reassembling the Social: An Introduction to Actor-Network Theory*. Oxford: Oxford University Press.

Lawhon, M., Ernstston, H. and Silver, J. (2014) Provincializing urban political ecology: towards a situated UPE through African urbanism. *Antipode*, 46(2): 497–516.

Lorimer, J. (2009) Posthumanism/posthumanistic geographies. In: Kitchen, R. and Thrift, N. (eds) *International Encyclopedia of Human Geography*. Volume Eight. Amsterdam and Oxford: Elsevier.

Mamdani, M. (2011) The importance of research at the university. Keynote address at Makerere University Research and Innovations Dissemination Conference, Hotel Africana, 11 April 2011. http://www.pambazuka.org/resources/importance-research-university. Downloaded: 20 April 2016.

Mbembe, A. and Nuttall, S. (2004) Writing the world from an African metropolis. *Public Culture*, 16(3): 347–372.

Miraftab, F. (2004) Making neo-liberal governance: the disempowering work of empowerment. *International Planning Studies*, 9(4): 239–259.

Moghalu, K.C. (2014) *Emerging Africa: How the Global Economy's "Last Frontier" Can Prosper and Matter*. Second edition. London: Penguin.

Moss, T.J. (2007) *African Development: Making Sense of the Issues and Actors*. Boulder, CO and London: Lynne Rienner Publishers.

Mostafavi, M. (2011) Why ecological urbanism? Why now? In: Mostafavi, M. and Doherty, G. (eds) *Ecological Urbanism*. Boston, MA: Harvard Graduate School of Design & Lars Müller.

Myers, G. (2011) *African Cities: Alternative Visions of Urban Theory and Practice*. London: Zed Books.

NSFWUS (National Science Foundation Workshop on Urban Sustainability) (2000) *Towards a Comprehensive Geographical Perspective on Urban Sustainability*. Final Report of the 1998: National Science Foundation Workshop on Urban Sustainability. New Brunswick, NJ: Rutgers University.

Parnell, S. and Pieterse, E. (2016) Translational global praxis: rethinking methods and modes of African urban research. *International Journal of Urban and Regional Research*, 40(1): 236–246.

Pieterse, E. (2010) Cityness and African urban development. *Urban Forum*, 21(3): 205–219.

Pieterse, E. (2011) Grasping the unknowable: coming to grips with African urbanisms. *Social Dynamics*, 38(1): 5–23.

Pieterse, E. (2012) High wire acts: knowledge imperatives of southern urbanisms. *The Salon*, 5: 37–50.

Pieterse, E. (2015) Epistemological practices of southern urbanism. In: Ding, W., Graafland, A. and Lu, A. (eds) *Cities in Transition: Power, Environment, Society*. Rotterdam: naio10 Publishers.

Pieterse, E. and Hyman, K. (2014) Disjunctures between urban infrastructure, finance and affordability. In: Parnell, S. and Oldfield, S. (eds) *The Routledge Handbook on Cities of the Global South*. London: Routledge.

Pieterse, E. and Smit, W. (2014) Institutions, decentralisation and urban development. In: Kayizzi-Mugerwa, S., Shimeles, A. and Yeméogo, D. (eds) *Urbanization and Socio-Economic Development in Africa: Challenges and Opportunities*. New York and London: Routledge.

Potts, D. (2012) *Whatever Happened to Africa's Rapid Urbanization?* Counterpoint Series. London: Africa Research Institute.

Provoost, M. (2010) New towns for the 21st century: the planned vs the unplanned city. In: Provoost, M. (ed.) *New Towns for the 21st Century: The Planned vs. the Unplanned City*. Amsterdam: SUN Publishers, 6–27.

Rakodi, C. (2014) Religion and social life in African cities. In: Parnell, S. and Pieterse, E. (eds) *Africa's Urban Revolution*. London: Zed Books.

Resnick, D. (2012) Opposition parties and the urban poor in African democracies. *Comparative Political Studies*, 45(11): 1351–1378.

Robinson, J. (2006) *Ordinary Cities: Between Modernity and Development*. London: Routledge.

Roy, A. (2008) The 21st-century metropolis: new geographies of theory. *Regional Studies*, 43(6): 819–830.

Satterthwaite, D. (2007) The transition to a predominantly urban world and its underpinnings. Human Settlements Discussion Paper. Theme: Urban Change No. 4. London: International Institute for Environment and Development.

Simone, A. (2004) *For the City Yet to Come: Changing African Life in Four Cities*. Durham, NC and London: Duke University Press.

Simone, A. (2010) *City Life from Jakarta to Dakar: Movements at the Crossroads*. London: Routledge.

Skinner, C. (2010) Street trading in Africa: trends in demographics, planning and trader organisation. In: Padayachee, V. (ed.) *The Political Economy of Africa*. London: Routledge.

Swilling, M. and Annecke, E. (2012) *Just Transitions: Explorations of Sustainability in an Unfair World*. Cape Town and Tokyo: UCT Press and United Nations University Press.

Tonkiss, F. (2011) Informality and its discontents. In: Angelil, M. and Hehl, R. (eds) *Informalize! Essays on the Political Economy of Urban Form*. Berlin: Ruby Press.

UN-DESA (United Nations, Department of Economic and Social Affairs, Population Division) (2015) *World Urbanization Prospects: The 2014 Revision* (ST/ESA/SER.A/366). New York: United Nations.

UN-Habitat (2012) *Urban Patterns for a Green Economy: Leveraging Density*. Nairobi: UN-Habitat.

UN-Habitat (2014) *State of African Cities Report 2014. Re-imagining Sustainable Urban Transitions*. Nairobi: UN-Habitat.

Varley, A. (2013) Postcolonialising informality? *Environment and Planning D: Society and Space*, 31(1): 4–22.

18 Main trends in contemporary urban studies of the Middle East and North Africa

Ahmed Kanna

My work for the last decade has focused on the Arab Gulf cities. Because cities in this oil-rich region have so ferociously cycled petrodollars and foreign investment into large urban built projects, I have spent a lot of time looking at, thinking about, and writing on architecture. Architecture, as the visible form of the built environment, is an infrastructure that seems uniquely suited to condense symbolism and evoke or provoke the emotions. Since the 1970s, pursuing a strategy of urban entrepreneurialism (Harvey 1989) in which the look of buildings and urban developments has played a central role in the urban political economy, architecture in Dubai has been photographed, photoshopped, and otherwise circulated in the global economy of urban imagery (Kanna 2011).

One view, perhaps that of an overwhelming majority of foreign instant culture theorists, as well as a sizeable group of United Arab Emirates (UAE) citizens, has it that this is all terrible, cliché architecture that simply imitates the (worst of) Western modernism and postmodernism. Often, this side sees the problem as the supposed disconnection from local vernaculars. Another view, which tends to come from architects based in Dubai or foreign-based architects working on the city, sees twenty-first century Dubai as an exciting experiment in architectural form. Architectural discourse, moreover, is itself often interwoven with cultural discourse, as seen in the frequency with which famous Western architects invoke 'Islamic,' 'Arab,' or 'Bedouin' culture as the inspiration for their Dubai designs. What both views tend to do, as a result, is to deploy a binary, 'Western' versus 'Local' culture, with the former represented as the residence of modernity, experimentation, and insensitivity to history, and the latter as the abode of 'tradition' and 'history.' Both views thus unwittingly pay homage to Max Weber, who is, it is interesting to note, the source of the cultural essentialism of much of the early urban scholarship on the Middle East/North Africa region (MENA).

The 'Islamic city'

For Weber, European towns were one of the main sources of capitalism and therefore modernity (Weber 1978). Emerging in the medieval period and evolving autonomously from the surrounding society, these towns enabled the rise of a bourgeoisie whose interests were mercantile and corporate (Eickelman 2002, pp. 88–89).[1] In no other parts of the world did the same thing occur, according to Weber. Taking these assertions at face value, and not finding an equivalent to the European commune in Muslim-majority societies, early scholars of cities in these societies sought instead the features that made their objects of study distinct from their European counterparts. To do this, they concocted the category of the 'Islamic city,' whose mosques, markets, and public baths supposedly marked this kind of city as, in essence, culturally different from cities of modern Europe (Eickelman 2002, p. 89). As Eickelman points out, however, these early attempts to find the true essence of the so-called Islamic city were largely unsuccessful. Almost all rural communities in the Maghreb, he writes, also have a mosque. My own research in the Levant and the Gulf and that of others in other parts of the MENA confirms this.[2] Similarly, markets in Muslim-majority societies were not necessarily located in cities (Eickelman 2002, p. 89). Eickelman writes that

> urban forms that emerged in the Muslim world in its first four centuries shared no single set of defining features that made them 'Islamic' . . . [I]n general, the urban process of the first four centuries of Islam was one of 'adaptation and accretion rather than creation.' Urban forms generally were adapted from pre-existing Hellenic-Byzantine, Iranian, and other traditions. (Eickelman 2002, p. 89)[3]

Cities in the MENA experienced explosive population growth during the twentieth century. A region whose population was overwhelmingly rural in 1900, with fewer than 10 percent of the population living in cities, was by 2000 approximately 60 percent urban (Eickelman 2002, p. 85). Istanbul, Cairo, Tehran, Baghdad, Riyadh, and Khartoum are among the world's largest cities, each counting more than 5 million people as residents, with Ankara, Casablanca, Dubai, Kuwait, Beirut, Basra, and several others at around or over 2 million. The case of Dubai, though particularly striking for the condensed pace of its population explosion and 'urban revolution' (Lefebvre 2003), parallels the norm for the region: in 1970, a fishing town and remote outpost of the fading British Empire, counting not more than 25 000 people as residents and with a small urban merchant core numbering no more than a few thousand inhabitants, it is today a city of approximately two million people, a regional and global center for finance, real estate development, and retail, boasting in the port and free zone complex of Jebel Ali a major global hub for the transshipment industry (Hvidt 2009, Marchal 2005).

Generalizations about a region as urbanized, populous, diverse, and complex as the MENA are impossible. This applies in particular to the notion of the Islamic city, which reduces this complexity and the unfolding of the urban process to a cultural essence, thus ignoring the various histories and cultures – and not least, the non-Muslim histories and cultures (see Vora 2013) – which have marked the region since antiquity, as well as the issue of power, not least the often brutal, often resisted, sometimes accommodated ways that colonial, imperial, and capitalist forms of power have affected urban processes in the region. Moreover, the

MENA, like other world regions, and perhaps even more so because of its centrality to strategies of capitalism and empire (Hanieh 2011), has undergone what Lefebvre has called an 'urban revolution,' in which the city is not simply a consumption unit, drawing upon and commodifying surpluses from the rural hinterland, but rather a central productive unit in the capitalist accumulation process (Harvey 2008; Lefebvre 2003, p. 47).[4] Therefore, contemporary MENA urban spaces must be seen as spaces of power and, more specifically, following Lefebvre, as produced spaces, crucial parts of class projects producing and reproducing capitalist strategies (Lefebvre 1974).

As I show in the next section, the notion of an 'Islamic city' is unsatisfactory. It cannot withstand the weight of the empirical evidence accumulated on Muslim-majority countries by at least a generation of scholars along with the critical theorization by these scholars. I do, however, rely in this chapter on another problematic term, the 'MENA,' which of course leaves much out, not least Muslim-majority countries outside the traditional map of North Africa and Western Asia. This term also obscures the rich interconnections between Muslim-majority countries and non-Muslim-majority countries. The regionalization of that part of the globe circumscribed by the Atlantic, Sahara, Mediterranean Sea, and Indian Ocean is of course just as arbitrary as the category of the Islamic city, its boundaries since at least Roman times constantly shifting to echo the contours of geopolitical conflict (Lewis and Wigen 1997). None of what I am arguing in this chapter should be taken as a reification of this most recent regionalization of the arena of our inquiry. I have chosen to maintain the conventional terminology of MENA and its referent for simplicity's sake and because, given constraints of space, it efficiently encompasses the literature I am seeking to illuminate. Other regionalizations are entirely possible and probably even better suited to other tasks.[5]

This chapter also does not explicitly discuss conventionally important themes that have been covered in great depth elsewhere. Gender and globalization, in particular, spring readily to mind. Regarding globalization, this is a deliberate choice. As my survey of the literature below shows, most current MENA urban scholarship takes for granted some sort of 'globalized' condition and has indeed moved, theoretically, beyond globalization as an imagined geographic and scalar framing. Instead, this work represents cultural, political-economic, and historical interconnection – which were once often assumed to index the utility of the globalization concept – as operating in ways too complex and multi-scalar to be captured by the nested scalar discourse of globalization.

Regarding gender, as readers will see, many if not most of the studies of MENA urbanism cited below seriously engage issues of gender. One is reminded here of a comment by the Marxist historian Isaac Deutscher, who compared the task of writing Leon Trotsky's biography to dragging his subject out from under 'a mountain of dead dogs, a huge load of calumny and oblivion' (Deutscher 1959, p. v). Though the topic of gender in the MENA suffers no oblivion in the era of Washington's wars in Muslim-majority countries and 24-hour news cycles obediently alert to the

Pentagon's talking points, the task of the contemporary feminist and anti-orientalist scholar of the MENA is similar in so far as the topic of gender in Muslim-majority societies has been buried under mountains of dead dogs and loads of calumny. What struck me in researching this chapter was how the struggle over the ways in which to represent gender has flowed into the urban literature. Some of the studies cited here are more concerned with gender than others, with their useful, sometimes brilliant, analyses and descriptions of urban life a serendipitous byproduct; for other studies, primarily focused on urbanism, gender and gendering, orientalism and its critique seem inevitably to flow from the narrative. Such is life under the hegemony of the aforementioned terror war. In this chapter, I have attempted to highlight how these studies are part of a larger project of counter-hegemony against orientalist gender stereotypes.

In this chapter, I will identify what I see as some of the landmarks on the topography of contemporary MENA urban research, all of which, I show, have moved the conversation far beyond traditional and essentializing Islamic City studies. Because an exhaustive catalogue of contemporary and recent research is not possible here – the literature is too vast – this account will of necessity be partial, reflecting my own biases, the questions and research problems that I find interesting and which I think suggest promising avenues for future research. I expect that other MENA urbanists would come up with a map of current scholarship different to my own, and hope that this chapter forms part of a conversation rather than being seen as a definitive statement on the state of the art in our sprawling multidisciplinary field.

Beyond binaries: tactics, strategies, urbanity as process

Any survey of MENA urban studies, and especially any discussion of the move away from cultural essentialism in this scholarship, must mention Janet Abu-Lughod's *Cairo: 1001 Years of the City Victorious* (Abu-Lughod 1971). So many of the themes that would concern future generations of MENA urbanists are either explicated or suggested by this seminal study. Trained as a sociologist, Abu-Lughod seriously acquainted herself both with the primary historical sources on Cairo and with literature on ecology as she undertook the study, and produced an elegant synthesis of urban sociology and urban history. Abu-Lughod argued that to understand Cairo, the scholar must see the city as a product of a dynamic relation between its inhabitants and their environment. While discussing Cairo's medieval history, the bulk of the book focuses on modern Cairo.[6] What is notable about Abu-Lughod's study is that, while she uses the term 'Islamic City' to refer to the premodern period, she clearly is making a theoretical argument in opposition to cultural essentialism, capturing the process by which the city undergoes historical change. This is especially marked in the section on the modern period, in which Abu-Lughod emphasizes class, urban–rural differences, and knowledge/power differences (as in that between experts such as planners versus everyday people) as the city came under European domination, a domination expressed not least in its mid–late nineteenth century modernist planning. Questions of inclusion and exclusion, the spatialization of poverty and wealth, the politics of planning, and others that anticipate much more recent developments all emerge clearly from Abu-Lughod's remarkably prescient study.

More recently, Rachel Newcomb, in her *Women of Fes: Ambiguities of Urban Life in Morocco* (Newcomb 2009), makes an important and insightful critique of the Islamic city discourse, writing that studies of urban Morocco have ignored the modern(ist) colonial city in favor of the ancient *medina*, representing the latter as the site of authentic Moroccan urbanity. 'Privileging the old *medina* as somehow characteristic of a timeless, essentialized Fes, and disparaging the Ville Nouvelle as that which has been corrupted, is false, and the lie . . . rests the belief that places remain static. The Ville Nouvelle is no less "Islamic," despite the history of its construction' (Newcomb 2009, p. 16). Like Diane Singerman and Farha Ghannam in their field-defining respective books *Avenues of Participation: Family, Politics, and Networks in Urban Quarters of Cairo* (Singerman 1996) and *Remaking the Modern: Space, Relocation, and the Politics of Identity in a Global Cairo* (Ghannam 2002), Newcomb moves away from broad cultural generalizations and the cataloguing of spaces, buildings, and behaviors along binary matrices of 'Islamic – Non-Islamic.' Instead, the work by Singerman, Ghannam, and a younger generation includ-ing Newcomb, reflects a new theoretical sophistication in the growing literature on everyday life in MENA cities (Bou Akar 2012, Collins 2012, Deeb 2006, Deeb and Harb 2013, De Koning 2009, Le Renard 2014, Menoret 2014a, Monroe 2011, Monroe 2016, Osanloo 2009, Sawalha 2010, Vora 2013). More anthropological and sociological in its approach, this work emphasizes issues of power – understood in the anthropological sense as (re)produced in daily practices – along with ideology and cultural identity reinterpreted as processual and situated. For much of this work, De Certeau's distinction between 'strategies' and 'tactics' has represented a powerful theoretical breakthrough enabling this newer work to transcend the aforementioned Weberian ideal-typing (De Certeau 2011). Again Newcomb:

> De Certeau associates strategies with those who hold power, and tactics with the weak, arguing that 'the actual order of things is precisely what popular tactics turn into their own ends, without any illusion that it will change any time soon' . . . I am concerned here with how space is gendered, and how women succeed or fail at manipulating ideologies and transforming the public sphere. (Newcomb 2009, p. 10)

Ghannam's moving ethnography of residents of al-Zawiya al-Hamra, a periph-eral Cairo suburb during the 1990s, is in the same spirit, critical of clichés and binaries about 'Islamic culture,' globalization, and modernity. Ghannam conducted her fieldwork during a time period when the *infitah* or 'liberalization' (literally, 'opening'), a neoliberal project initiated by Anwar Sadat and entrenched by his successor Hosni Mubarak, had become normalized as Cairo's – and arguably all of Egypt's – political horizon. In a move that will strike critics of gentrification worldwide as typical, state authorities moved poor and working class Cairenes to peripheral zones such as al-Zawiya in an attempt to clear central districts of Cairo for capital accumulation. Ghannam's account is of a working class community that, while certainly marginalized, subjected to capitalist violence, and, from the perspective of the neoliberalizing urban officialdom, voiceless, nevertheless enacts refractory tactics that assert their identity, through, among other things, contesting definitions of modernity and the reviving of religious discourses (Ghannam 2002; see also Kuppinger 2014).[7]

Neha Vora's luminous *Impossible Citizens: Dubai's Indian Diaspora*, is another fine example of the move beyond binaries in the newer work, and also reminds us that the equation of MENA with 'Islam' and 'Arab' is mistaken. Vora argues persuasively both that Dubai should be seen not only as a city of the Arab Middle East but also as the westernmost Indian city, its residents of Indian background constituting in some ways its 'quintessential' residents (Vora 2013; see also Gardner 2010 and Longva 2005). Weaving cutting-edge theory on citizenship, political liberalism, and diaspora with detailed ethnography, Vora shows how the deeply multinational urban space of Dubai shapes and is shaped by the ambivalent sense of belonging felt by members of the city's Indian diaspora. Officially excluded from citizenship, diasporic Indians are nevertheless both central to discourses and representations of Emirati nationhood and, as class actors, instrumental in mediating the Emirati state's relationship to its diasporic community (Vora 2013).

Two other recent and notable works are Lara Deeb's *Enchanted Modern: Gender and Public Piety in Shi'i Lebanon* (Deeb 2006) and Arzoo Osanloo's *The Politics of Women's Rights in Iran* (Osanloo 2009), both rich, detailed, superb accounts of women's experiences and political formation in, respectively, Beirut and Tehran. Both anthropologists leverage their theoretically sophisticated and detailed ethnography into persuasive rethinkings of received oppositions between 'religion' and 'modernity,' and move beyond and away from conceptual and imaginary mappings of the 'West' with the former, the '(Middle) East' with the latter. Rather, both Deeb and Osanloo show how in Lebanon and Iran, as in many other societies, the project of advancing women's rights is complexly embedded in local struggles over politics, economics, cultural symbolism, and authoritative religious discourses. To see Islam or the MENA as culturally alien to women's rights is to assume that cultural essence has any explanatory power whatsoever, when in fact women's empowerment, as that of any sociopolitical project, argues Oslanloo, is a product of negotiation and struggle within a field in which various political, social, and economic forces intersect (think of how women in Western societies secured rights: not by passively waiting for a magical emanation of an inherently emancipatory 'Western culture,' but in particular historical circumstances, through active mobilization of forces and deployment of symbols in service of a political project). What is interesting from an urban studies perspective about these texts is their urban setting, a theme subsequently made more explicit by Deeb and her collaborator, the geographer Mona Harb, in their recent work on the urban-geographic constitution of what it means to be a contemporary Lebanese Shi'a. In their book *Leisurely Islam: Negotiating Geography and Morality in Shi'ite South Beirut*, they deploy the concept of the 'Islamic milieu' to capture the complex intersection of urban geography and urban culture among an emergent Beiruti Shi'a middle class (Deeb and

Harb 2013). Mapping the sites of production of consumer leisure, they show how Shi'a notions and *habitus* of piety both inform and are shaped by the production of neoliberal leisure spaces such as cafés, restaurants, and theme parks. For Deeb and Harb, the cultural diversity and complexity favored by an urban geography form a condition of possibility for the emergence of interpretations and practices of Shi'a morality that reconfigure older notions in relation to both the signification of class and of piety.

Infrastructures of experience

Early in her 2006 book *Enchanted Modern*, Lara Deeb presents readers with a remarkable tour of the southern Beirut neighborhood al-Dahiya and its sensorium. Scholars of the urban, Deeb suggests, can not only significantly enrich our understanding of the meaning of place by attending to the appearance of the built environment and its sounds, the spatial grammar and syntax of these visual and aural elements, but also deepen our insight into how spaces and senses are co-constitutive of spatial cultures and worlds (Deeb 2006, pp. 42–66; see also Hirschkind 2006 on Cairo). A year later, in a seminal article in the social scientific study of infrastructures, Dourish and Bell wrote: 'We look on space here as infrastructure – not just a technological infrastructure, but an infrastructure through which we experience the world' (Dourish and Bell 2007, p. 414). Dourish and Bell's invitation to humanists and social scientists to study the 'infrastructure of experience and the experience of infrastructure' has been one of the more promising recent developments in MENA urban scholarship and raises important questions and avenues for future research (Elyachar 2012, Günel 2014, 2016, Ramos 2010; see also Easterling 2014).

Farah Al-Nakib's *Kuwait Transformed* explicates one of the central dilemmas of modern urban development in the MENA (Al-Nakib 2015). Channeling James Scott's (1998) seminal critique of high modernism, Al-Nakib unearths and narrates everyday Kuwaiti experiences of state-led oil-modernity, as manifested in Kuwait City's built environment. As an urban center for a major oil-producing state, Kuwait's modernization since the 1950s has been more intense than in many other parts of the MENA, but its trajectory – transition from a village scale to, first, a high modernist, planned urban condition, and later a complex and contested postmodern/global one – in general parallels that of other parts of the region. Contrary to mid-twentieth-century modernist assumptions about modernist built forms and infrastructures creating the conditions for a more tolerant and cosmopolitan society (high modernists such as Mies van der Rohe would have seen in this the passage from a parochialism to a universality), the suburbanization, planning, and privatization of Kuwait have played an important role in producing a more insular, divided, and, arguably, intolerant society. Al-Nakib's work is analytically persuasive and an often devastating critique of oil modernism. It also avoids nostalgia for the so-called traditional mudbrick and courtyard village of the pre-oil era, instead drawing upon indigenous Kuwaiti repertoires of urbanity to articulate a contemporary Kuwaiti politics of the right to the city.

The recent interest in the sociopolitics of infrastructures, both in MENA studies and more widely in the social sciences, owes a great debt to Asef Bayat's *Street Politics: Poor People's Movements in Iran* (Bayat 1998), which, along with James Holston's *The Modernist City: An Anthropological Critique of Brasilia* (Holston 1989) and Farha Ghannam's aforementioned *Remaking the Modern*, was a path-breaking work rare in the attention it paid to poor people's everyday practices responding, often with ingenuity, to the gaps, lacunae, and even willful neglect of centralized planners, readapting or even creating infrastructures to meet everyday needs (see also Fawaz 2009). The debate on the sociopolitics of technology goes back, at least, to Karl Marx, whose analysis of machinery and the factory space in volume one of *Capital* is worth mentioning. For Marx, machinery and automation are techniques for the appropriation of relative surplus-value, the surplus-value resulting from 'the curtailment of the necessary labor-time' (as opposed to 'absolute surplus-value,' which results by lengthening the working day; Marx [1867] 1976, p. 432). More generally, Marx conceived what he called a 'critical history of technology' as integral to his larger project in *Capital*: in revealing the 'active relation of man to nature . . . [technology] lays bare the process of the production of the social relations of his life, and of the mental conceptions that flow from those relations' (Marx [1867] 1976, p. 493, n. 4).

Recent scholarship on infrastructures in MENA cities has taken seriously Marx's call for a dialectical approach to a 'critical history' of technology. An excellent example is anthropologist Pascal Menoret's *Joyriding in Riyadh: Oil, Urbanism, and Road Revolt* (Menoret 2014a). The dramatis personae of this beautifully written and conceptualized project are diverse: migrants from the countryside to the city, French and Greek urban planners, princes, and joyriders. 'All these characters' expectations about the city were trumped by the logics of urbanization and real estate development' (Menoret 2014b). Taking inspiration from Mike Davis's reading of Los Angeles as a product and ongoing arena of class warfare (Davis 1992), Menoret becomes fascinated by what he calls the 'car riot,' in which young Saudi men go on near-suicidal (and sometimes actually suicidal) car races just out of the reach and eye of the authorities. For casual observers – and I admit to be one of them, having seen a similar phenomenon during my fieldwork in Dubai – such escapades seem irrational if not insane. For Menoret, there is, however, a logic and a politics to joyriding in Riyadh, a form of urban life lived at the extreme limits of sense experience, what Foucault called 'limit experiences,' which 'wrench the subject from itself,' thereby exposing and challenging dominant political and ideological systems (Gutting 2005). Referring to the road system of Saudi modernity, meant to bring development and to discipline the citizen-subjects of the modern Saudi state, Menoret says that his work shows instead 'how western experts, Saudi investors, and Riyadh youth have turned these instruments of authoritarianism into tools of anarchism and disorder' (Menoret 2014b). Infrastructure, Menoret argues, is ambiguous, as it was for Marx, for whom the railway both symbolized the power of the bourgeoisie and was a condition of possibility for the political awakening of the proletariat. 'In a system where the state itself is out of reach, it is roads, cars, and cops that are everyday targets of car riots against infrastructures, commoditization, and trade monopolies. Pedestrian demonstrations may be rare in Riyadh, but for more than three decades, car demonstrations occurred on a daily basis in those very places where financial investments and royal power reshape the cityscape' (ibid.).

With a similar sensitivity to the complexity and ambiguity of urban infrastructures, recent scholars have looked at issues of electrification and lighting, the geographies of nighttime in the city, the politics of 'green' infrastructures, the colonial and class politics and geographies of infrastructural plans and malfunctions, and the contestations over power networks (Günel 2014, 2016, Salamanca 2014, Stadnicki 2003, Verdeil 2013a and b). In his study of Beirut energy networks, for example, geographer Eric Verdeil echoes Menoret's critique of one-dimensional, top-down accounts of the relationship between infrastructures, political centralization, and political power, reframing the topic to highlight:

> The disruptions and reconfigurations of energy circuits and to show that it both reflect(s) existing configurations of power in the city and create(s) new ones ... At a first glance, uneven access to electricity might well be understood as the way to reproduce social and political domination between central Beirut and its suburbs and between the wealthiest and the middle and lower class ... But seen from (Timothy) Mitchell's perspective, the economic arrangements and the technological devices needed to run the system and for the electricity being generated and processed contain in themselves their fragilities that allow such domination to be constantly challenged by the clients-users-citizens or new-comers like informal vendors of alternative electricity devices ... Thus, one might well read the rising protests against the current state of blackness in Beirut as new agencies of power that seek to undermine and derail the symbolical hierarchies of power. (Verdeil 2013a)

The political theorist Mitchell, mentioned in Verdeil's comment, and who did most of his early primary research in the MENA (Egypt to be exact), has been inspirational to this turn toward infrastructures. Mitchell's seminal *Carbon Democracy: Political Power in the Age of Oil* (Mitchell 2011) marks a major shift in the study of the relationship between political power and its material conditions of possibility. Scholars have placed far too much emphasis, he writes, on the ideological dimensions of political power. Democracy, it is said, is an idea or a model that travels to this place or that, conveyed by institutional actors such as nongovernmental organizations (NGOs) or militaries, and is either taken up or rejected ideologically by its intended beneficiaries/targets. This assumption ignores the 'apparatus of oil production' (Mitchell 2011, p. 2).

> The term 'democracy' can have two kinds of meaning. It can refer to a way of making effective claims for a more just and egalitarian world. Or it can refer to a mode of governing populations that employs popular consent as a means of limiting claims for greater equality and justice by dividing up the common world. Such limits are formed by acknowledging certain areas as matters of public concern subject to popular decision while establishing other fields to be administered under alternative methods of control. (Mitchell 2011, p. 9)

Struggles for a more egalitarian social order, as the case of the technopolitics of carbon amply shows, have often been waged not mainly in some sort of idealized Habermasian public sphere, but rather as mobilizations of what Mitchell calls 'effective intransigence,' class conscious seizures or interruptions of power networks (Mitchell 2011, p. 4); while specific political regimes arise 'from particular ways of engineering political relations out of flows of energy' (Mitchell 2011, p. 5).

Oil urbanism

Mitchell's work, along with that of other notable scholars, has, likewise, strongly influenced a related but distinct literature, that on the Middle Eastern oil city (Coronil 1997, Davis and Gavrielides 1991, Fuccaro 2001, 2009, Watts et al. 2014). The work of Nelida Fuccaro and a generation of younger scholars including Reem Alissa, Farah Al-Nakib, Arbella Bet-Shlimon, and Mona Damluji bears special mention here. These scholars have been active in expanding the category of 'oil urbanism' far beyond clichéd images of aircraft carriers, oil installations, and skyscrapers. Indeed, Fuccaro has long been at the forefront of what I call critical Arab/Persian Gulf studies, focusing an anthropologist's and social historian's attention to the daily lives, practices, histories, and ambivalent experiences of modernity in the Gulf's urban societies (Fuccaro 2001). In this way, Fuccaro has moved the scholarly debate beyond the conventional emphases in oil city scholarship on issues of geopolitics, security, and oil state modernization (though these topics, especially the last, have been implicit in her work, which has indeed allowed students of the Gulf to rethink these categories), and toward 'the less tangible qualities of oil, particularly its ability to create both realities and myths about progress and the modern world' (Fuccaro 2013b). Fuccaro et al. have been especially interested in the interdisciplinary study of oil urbanism, as can be seen in a recent issue of *Comparative Studies of South Asia, Africa and the Middle East* (Fuccaro 2013a), guest edited by Fuccaro and to which she and the other mentioned scholars contributed pieces studying cases such as the production of oil-urban space in Ahmadi and Kuwait City, Kuwait (Alissa 2013, Al-Nakib 2013), urban development as politics and ideology in Kirkuk, Iraq in the mid-twentieth century (Bet-Shlimon 2013), and the cinematic representation of Abadan, Iran's main oil processing center (Damluji 2013). As Fuccaro put it in a recent interview, this research represents

> a critical reading of how the oil industry has created modern urban spaces, societies, and cultures . . . the idea that the oil industry was not only about wealth, rent, and state building, but also unleashed a variety of forces that had a profound effect on society, culture, and the environment, including cities. (Fuccaro 2013b)

Fuccaro's comment about the oil industry unleashing complex sociocultural effects, not reducible to issues of wealth and rent, are pertinent to Mandana Limbert's *In the Time of Oil: Piety, Memory, and Social Life in an Omani Town*, another contribution to critical Gulf studies and to the literature on MENA oil urbanism that is essential reading (Limbert 2010). One of the poorest countries in the world on the eve of the discovery of oil in the 1960s, Oman, like its neighbors, used its oil wealth to embark on a major modernization program, encompassing its infrastructure and visible built environment, public education and services, along with its insertion into the Global North-dominated transnational political economy of oil (see also Hanieh 2011), changes that reach and deeply affect Limbert's interlocutors, especially women in the small oasis town of Bahla in the Omani interior. Along with this comes the dramatic transformation of pre-oil social relations, forms of urbanity, and geographic networks and imaginaries, reorienting the country from an East African maritime civilization to a Gulf Arab and Global North/imperial one. While Limbert's study is of a small town community rather than that of a major metropolis, it is nevertheless an illuminating analysis of how the interconnected processes of oil wealth and modern urbanization reshape social relationships and cultural imaginaries, as can be seen in her case study of new forms of piety among a younger generation of Omani women in Bahla, a piety which emphasizes the close reading and autonomous interpretation of Islamic sources. The younger women contrast this to the sociality of an older generation, which they see as too focused on gossip and triviality. There is much else in this thickly described ethnography that goes well beyond issues of urbanism — it is essential reading, for example, for students of African, Middle Eastern, and Indian Ocean interconnection and the rise of nationalisms with alternative imagined geographies in the modern period — but in an indirect way, Limbert's book makes a crucial contribution to our understanding of the meaning of urbanism in the context of rapidly changing living standards with the emergence of the modern Middle Eastern oil state.

Concluding thoughts

The recent and current work on urban life and urbanism in the MENA has taken us well beyond the idea of the Islamic city. Taken collectively, this work calls attention to the inadequacy of culturally reductive or essentialist categories to the task of analyzing urban process in a region of great complexity and diversity. As ethnographic work on MENA cities shows, a better way to approach urban life in the region is by focusing on specificity, context, and process. The work on materiality — infrastructural and geophysical — uncovers the ambivalences of power in MENA urban contexts, as in any other context: centralized plans and projects, as James Scott famously argued, have unintended consequences, vulnerabilities, and can eventuate in spectacular failures (Scott 1998). Yet as Fernando Coronil has pointed out in a critique of Scott, not all plans are equally effective or successful and not all can be so easily dismissed as failures. History supplies examples of state plans that went badly wrong, but also many examples of successful state plans (Coronil 2001). Along with his call in his critique of Scott for more care in social scientific analysis of planning, Coronil warns of a dogmatic insistence on the alleged creativity or agency of individual actors or so-called local cultures in relation to organized concentrated forms of power, specifically, capital, arguing that doing so can inadvertently lend itself to justifying the forms of power, such as neoliberalism, it claims to want to critique. This position can be seen in the repeated assertion, especially within my own discipline of anthropology, that categories such as capitalism, neo-liberalism, or class are inadequate or antiquated concepts when dealing with 'late capitalism.' Thus for example, a group of scholars contributing to a recent issue of the leading disciplinary journal *Cultural Anthropology* on the theme of infra-structures argue that the analytical category of infrastructure is distinct from, and superior to, that of neoliberalism because the latter implies 'a perspective that is too broad and can fail to consider everyday practices in local contexts' (Lockrem and Lugo 2012). As will be clear to readers of this chapter, I share much with Lockrem and Lugo's call to attend to everyday practices, but I think it rash to jettison a radical critique of capitalism, which I believe the rejection of neoliberalism as an analytical and political category inevitably does. Recent work on neoliberalism and MENA cities attempts to take seriously both localized practices and capitalism as a system of organized power (Bogaert 2013, Buckley 2013, Fawaz 2014, Hourani 2012, 2014, Krijnen and Fawaz 2010, Parker 2009). The work of architecture and urban planning scholar Mona Fawaz, who shows how the Lebanese Shi'a political movement Hizbullah emerged in recent years as a major Beirut real estate investor and developer, thereby producing a local, Lebanese and Islamist form of neoliberal-ism that shares much but is distinct from the Global North/Western variant, is an excellent example (Fawaz 2014). So is political scientist Christopher Parker's work on Amman (Parker 2009), in which he shows how 'the government of people and places across the Middle East and North Africa is being transformed by powerful models of pedagogy and practice derived from the laws of the market' (Parker 2009, p. 110). Likewise the work of political scientist and anthropologist Najib Hourani (Hourani 2014), which focuses on Beirut and Amman, and which has shown how, in Lebanon, the post-conflict category of the economy is produced at the intersec-tion of international financial institutions' simplification and rendering 'legible' the complex Lebanese political economy, in the process redefining even war as a mere idiosyncratic shock that may be overcome through the application of conventional development solutions (Hourani 2014, p. 634). This process of reclassification, argues Hourani, in turn becomes a condition of possibility for the class project of the neoliberalization of the Lebanese economy along with Beirut's property regime and its tourism sector. Such work advances and reimagines the Lefebvrian notion of the production of space as class politics while avoiding the pitfalls of a class analysis which reifies class and space, seeing both as *relational* and as *projects*, which often bring together unpredictable formations (such as real estate developers, tourism capitalists, and Islamist political parties). For such projects to succeed they must, in Stuart Hall's words, articulate otherwise disparate (institutional, individual) actors with hegemonic–symbolic systems, in the service of producing capitalist relations (Hall 1988). As Lefebrve has famously said, urbanism is always a class urbanism (Lefebvre 2003). Far from being obvious, class urbanism only reveals itself to a close attention to the local context, to how class urbanism connects to and mediates the translocal, how its alignments are both unpredictable and determinate. In the words of an even more famous critic of capitalism, these alignments and forma-tions are – like another *locus classicus* of capitalist reproduction and production, the working day, highly elastic and protean, both 'determinable' yet 'indeterminate' (Marx [1867]1976).

NOTES

1 Readers wishing to begin their study of the MENA and its urbanism would find not only Eickelman 2002 useful, but also two more recent books, both excellent and up-to-date introductions, respectively, to the scholarship on the region and to its urbanism in a global context: Lucia Volk's *The Middle East in the World* (Volk 2015) and Rivke Jaffe and Anouk de Koning's *Introducing Urban Anthropology* (Jaffe and de Koning 2016). Sharp and Panetta's *Beyond the Square: Urbanism and the Arab Uprisings* is a theoretically sophisticated collection of essays on a wide range of MENA cities, going far beyond traditional approaches both in terms of case study coverage and in its deployment of the concept of the 'sociospatial' to capture sociopolitical process that flow between conceptual and geographic boundaries of urban and non-urban (Sharp and Panetta 2016).

2 Moreover, just what constitutes a 'mosque' in many accounts is not clear. These can range from monumental and splendid architectural gems such as Damascus's Umayyad mosque, the Dome of the Rock in Jerusalem, Istanbul's Hagia Sophia (itself previously a Byzantine cathedral), and many others, all the way down to modest and tiny rooms tucked into the alleys of any place – rural or urban – where Muslims live and worship.

3 See also Wheatley 2001. For a recent and ethnographically informed critique of the concept of the Islamic city, see Newcomb 2009.

4 In the case of entrepot cities such as Dubai or Kuwait, it does not even make sense to talk about a rural hinterland.

5 For critiques of dominant imagined geographies of the MENA, see my essay on the constitution of knowledge about the city in the Arab Gulf (Kanna 2016), along with Abdul Sheriff and Ho 2014, Ho 2007, Onley 2007, Vora 2013, and Willis 2012.

6 i.e., since 1800.

7 Mai Iskander's recent documentary, *Garbage Dreams*, a moving account of the struggles of Christian *zabalin* or garbage collectors in Cairo in the years before the 2011 revolution, strongly resonates with Ghannam 2002 and Kuppinger 2014, subjecting commonplace contrasts between a supposedly efficient neoliberalism and a supposedly inefficient 'traditional' economy to soft-spoken yet devastating critique (Iskander 2009). Jehane Noujaim's *al-Midan (The Square)* is also an ethnographically compelling and richly-textured look at Cairo life, capturing the voices of diverse Cairenes during the extraordinary weeks of the 2011 revolution and overthrow of the Mubarak regime (Noujaim 2013).

References

Abu-Lughod, Janet (1971), *Cairo: 1001 Years of the City Victorious*, Princeton, NJ: Princeton University Press.

Al-Nakib, F. (2013), 'Kuwait's modern spectacle: oil wealth and the making of a new capital city, 1950–90,' *Comparative Studies of South Asia, Africa and the Middle East* **33**(1), 7–25.

Al-Nakib, F. (2015), *Kuwait Transformed: A History of Oil and Urban Life*, Palo Alto, CA: Stanford University Press.

Alissa, R. (2013), 'The oil town of Ahmadi since 1946: from colonial town to nostalgic city,' *Comparative Studies of South Asia, Africa and the Middle East* **33**(1), 41–58.

Bayat, Asef (1998), *Street Politics: Poor People's Movements in Iran*, New York: Columbia University Press.

Bet-Shlimon, A. (2013), 'The politics and ideology of urban development in Iraq's oil city: Kirkut, 1946–58,' *Comparative Studies of South Asia, Africa and the Middle East* **33**(1), 26–40.

Bogaert, K. (2013), 'Contextualizing the Arab revolts: the politics behind three decades of neoliberalism in the Arab world,' *Middle East Critique*, 22 October, accessed February 29, 2016 at https://www.academia.edu/5450182/Contextualizing_the_Arab_revolts_the_politics_behind_three_decades_of_neoliberalism_in_the_Arab_World.

Bou Akar, H. (2012), 'Contesting Beirut's frontiers,' *City and Society* **24**(2), 150–172.

Buckley, M. (2013), 'Locating neoliberalism in Dubai: migrant workers and class struggle in the autocratic city,' *Antipode* **45**(2), 256–274.

Collins, R. (2012), 'Seats of differences: coffeehouses and the geo-economics of gender in contemporary inner-city Tunis,' in Xiangming Chen and Ahmed Kanna (eds), *Rethinking Global Urbanism: Comparative Insights from Secondary Cities*, New York: Routledge, pp. 208–229.

Coronil, Fernando (1997), *The Magical State: Nature, Money, and Modernity in Venezuela*, Chicago: University of Chicago Press.

Coronil, Fernando (2001), 'Smelling like a market,' *American Historical Review* **106**(1), 119–129.

Damluji, M. (2013), 'The oil city in focus: the cinematic spaces of Abadan in the Anglo-Iranian oil company's *Persian story*,' *Comparative Studies of South Asia, Africa and the Middle East* **33**(1), 75–88.

Davis, Eric and Nicolas Gavrielides (1991), *Statecraft in the Middle East: Oil, Historical Memory, and Popular Culture*, Gainesville, FL: University Press of Florida.

Davis, Mike (1992), *City of Quartz: Excavating the Future in Los Angeles*, New York: Vintage.

Deeb, Lara (2006), *An Enchanted Modern: Gender and Public Piety in Shi'i Lebanon*, Princeton, NJ: Princeton University Press.

Deeb, Lara and Mona Harb (2013), *Leisurely Islam: Negotiating Geography and Morality in Shi'ite South Beirut*, Princeton, NJ: Princeton University Press.

De Certeau, Michel (2011), *The Practice of Everyday Life*, trans. Steven F. Rendall, Berkeley, CA: University of California Press.

De Koning, Anouk (2009), *Global Dreams: Class, Gender, and Public Space in Cosmopolitan Cairo*, New York: American University of Cairo Press.

Deeb, Lara (2006), *An Enchanted Modern: Gender and Public Piety in Shi'i Lebanon*, Princeton, NJ: Princeton University Press.

Deeb, Lara and Mona Harb (2013), *Leisurely Islam: Negotiating Geography and Morality in Shi'ite South Beirut*, Princeton, NJ: Princeton University Press.

Deutscher, Isaac (1959), *The Prophet Unarmed: Trotsky 1921–1929*, New York: Oxford University Press.

Dourish, P. and G. Bell (2007), 'The infrastructure of experience and the experience of infrastructure: meaning and structure in everyday encounters with space,' *Environment and Planning B: Planning and Design* **34**, 414–430.

Easterling, Keller (2014), *Extrastatecraft: The Power of Infrastructure Space*, New York: Verso.

Eickelman, Dale (2002), *The Middle East and Central Asia: An Anthropological Approach*, Upper Saddle River, NJ: Prentice Hall.

Elyachar, J. (2012), 'Before (and after) neoliberalism: tacit knowledge, secrets of the trade, and the public sector in Egypt,' *Cultural Anthropology* **27**(1), 76–96.

Fawaz, M. (2009), 'Neoliberal urbanity and the right to the city: a view from Beirut's periphery,' *Development and Change* **40**(5), 827–852.

Fawaz, M. (2014), 'The politics of property in planning: Hezbollah's reconstruction of Haret Hreik (Beirut, Lebanon) as case study,' *International Journal of Urban and Regional Research* **38**(3), 922–934.

Fuccaro, N. (2001), 'Visions of the city: urban studies of the gulf,' *Middle East Studies Association Bulletin* **35**(2), 175–187.

Fuccaro, N. (2009), *Histories of City and State in the Persian Gulf: Manama since 1800*, New York: Cambridge University Press.

Fuccaro, N. (ed.) (2013a), 'Histories of oil and urban modernity in the Middle East,' *Comparative Studies of South Asia, Africa and the Middle East* **33**(1), 1–6.

Fuccaro, N. (2013b), 'New texts out now,' *Jadaliyya*, October 23, accessed February 29, 2016 at http://www.jadaliyya.com/pages/index/14713/new-texts-out-now_nelida-fuccaro-histories-of-oil.

Gardner, Andrew M. (2010), *City of Strangers: Gulf Migration and the Indian Community in Bahrain*, Ithaca, NY: Cornell University Press.

Ghannam, Farha (2002), *Remaking the Modern: Space, Relocation, and the Politics of Identity in a Global Cairo*, Berkeley, CA: University of California Press.

Günel, G. (2014), 'Ergos: a new energy currency,' *Anthropological Quarterly* **87**(2), 359–380.

Günel, G. (2016), 'The infinity of water: climate change adaptation in the Arabian Peninsula,' *Public Culture* **28**(2), 291–315.

Gutting, Gary (2005), *Foucault: A Very Short Introduction*, New York: Oxford University Press.

Hall, Stuart (1988), *The Hard Road to Renewal: Thatcherism and the Crisis of the Left*, London: Verso.

Hanieh, Adam (2011), *Capitalism and Class in the Gulf Arab States*, New York: Palgrave Macmillan.

Harvey, D. (1989), 'From managerialism to entrepreneurialism: the transformation in urban governance in late capitalism,' *Geografiska Annaler. Series B, Human Geography* **7**(1), 3–17.

Harvey, D. (2008), 'The right to the city,' *New Left Review* **53**(September–October), 23–40.

Hirschkind, Charles (2006), *The Ethical Soundscape: Cassette Sermons and Islamic Counterpublics*, New York: Columbia Universith Press.

Ho, Engseng (2007), *The Graves of Tarim: Genealogy and Mobility across the Indian Ocean*, Berkeley, CA: University of California Press.

Holston, James (1989), *The Modernist City: An Anthropological Critique of Brasilia*, Chicago: University of Chicago Press.

Hourani, N. (2012), 'From national utopia to elite enclave: the selling of the Beirut souqs,' in Gary McDonogh and Marina Peterson (eds), *Global Downtowns*, Philadelphia, PA: University of Pennsylvania Press, pp. 136–159.

Hourani, N. (2014), 'Urbanism and neoliberal order: the development and redevelopment of Amman,' *Journal of Urban Affairs* **36**(s2), 634–649.

Hvidt, M. (2009), 'The Dubai model: an outline of key development-process elements in Dubai,' *International Journal of Middle East Studies* **41**, 397–418.

Iskander, Mai (2009), *Garbage Dreams*. DVD. New York: Iskander Films.

Jaffe, Rivke and Anouk de Koning (eds) (2016), *Introducing Urban Anthropology*, New York: Routledge.

Kanna, Ahmed (2011), *Dubai: The City as Corporation*, Minneapolis, MN: University of Minnesota Press.

Kanna, Ahmed (2016), 'Gulf urbanism: the semantic field of a category of space,' in Mehran Kamrava (ed.), *Gateways to the World: Port Cities in the Persian Gulf*, New York: Oxford University Press.

Krijnen, M. and M. Fawaz (2010), 'Exception as the rule: high-end developments in neoliberal Beirut,' *Built Environment* **36**(2), 245–259.

Kuppinger, Petra (2014), 'Crushed? Cairo's garbage collectors and neoliberal urban politics,' special issue on 'Arab Cities,' Najib Hourani and Ahmed Kanna (eds), *Journal of Urban Affairs* **36**(s2), 621–633.

Le Renard, Amelie (2014), *A Society of Young Women: Opportunities of Place, Power, and Reform in Saudi Arabia*, Palo Alto, CA: Stanford University Press.

Lefebvre, Henri (1974), *The Production of Space*, trans. Donald Nicholson-Smith, Malden, MA: Blackwell.

Lefebvre, Henri (2003), *The Urban Revolution*, trans. R. Bononno, Minneapolis, MN: University of Minnesota Press.

Lewis, Martin L. and Kären Wigen (1997), *The Myth of Continents: A Critique of Metageography*, Berkeley, CA: University of California Press.

Limbert, Mandana (2010), *In the Time of Oil: Piety, Memory, and Social Life in an Omani Town*, Palo Alto, CA: Stanford University Press.

Lockrem, Jessica and Adonia Lugo (2012), 'Infrastructure,' *Cultural Anthropology*, curated collections 11, accessed February 29, 2016 at http://www.culanth.org/curated_collections/11-infrastructure.

Longva, Anh Nga (2005), 'Neither autocracy nor democracy but ethnocracy: citizens, expatriates, and the sociopolitical system in Kuwait,' in Paul Dresch and James Piscatori (eds), *Monarchies and Nations: Globalization and Identity in the Arab States of the Gulf*, London: I.B. Tauris, pp. 114–135.

Marchal, R. (2005), 'Dubai: global city and transnational hub,' in Madawi Al Rasheed (ed.), *Transnational Connections and the Arab Gulf*, New York: Routledge, pp. 93–110.

Marx, Karl (1867), *Capital: A Critique of Political Economy*, vol. 1, reprinted 1976, trans. Ben Fowkes, New York: Penguin/New Left Books.

Menoret, Pascal (2014a), *Joyriding in Riyadh: Oil, Urbanism, and Road Revolt*, New York: Cambridge University Press.

Menoret, Pascal (2014b), 'New texts out now', *Jadaliyya*, July 2, 2014, accessed February 26, at http://www.jadaliyya.com/pages/index/18310/new-texts-out-now_pascal-menoret-joyriding-in-riya.

Mitchell, Timothy (2011), *Carbon Democracy: Political Power in the Age of Oil*, New York: Verso.

Monroe, K. (2011), 'Being mobile in Beirut,' *City and Society* **23**(1), 94–111.

Monroe, K. (2016), *The Insecure City: Space, Power, and Mobility in Beirut*, New Brunswick, NJ: Rutgers University Press.

Newcomb, Rachel (2009), *Women of Fes: Ambiguities of Urban Life in Morocco*, Philadelphia, PA: University of Pennsylvania Press.

Noujaim, Jehane (2013), *The Square*. Streamed on Netflix. Los Angeles: Participant Media.

Onley, James (2007), *The Arabian Frontier of the British Raj: Merchants, Rulers, and the British in the Nineteenth-Century Gulf*, Oxford: Oxford University Press.

Osanloo, Arzoo (2009), *The Politics of Women's Rights in Iran*, Princeton, NJ: Princeton University Press.

Parker, C. (2009), 'Tunnel-bypasses and minarets of capitalism: Amman as neoliberal assemblage,' *Political Geography* **28**, 110–120.

Ramos, Stephen (2010), *Dubai Amplified: The Engineering of a Port Geography*, Surrey, UK: Ashgate.

Salamanca, O. (2014), 'Hooked on electricity: the charged political economy of electrification in Palestine,' accessed February 29, 2016 at https://www.academia.edu/11241217/Hooked_on_electricity_the_charged_political_economy_of_electrification_in_Palestine.

Sawalha, Aseel (2010), *Reconstructing Beirut: Memory and Space in a Postwar Arab City*, Austin, TX: University of Texas Press.

Scott, James C. (1998), *Seeing Like a State: How Certain Schemes to Improve the Human Condition Have Failed*, New Haven, CT: Yale University Press.

Sharp, Deen and Claire Panetta (eds) (2016), *Beyond the Square: Urbanism and the Arab Uprisings*, New York: Urban Research.

Sheriff, Abdul and Engseng Ho (eds) (2014), *The Indian Ocean: Oceanic Connections and the Creation of New Societies*, London: Hurst.

Singerman, Diane (1996), *Avenues of Participation: Family, Politics, and Networks in Urban Quarters of Cairo*, Princeton, NJ: Princeton University Press.

Stadnicki, R. (2003), 'Une nuit à Bâb al-Sabâh: emergence de nouveaux rythmes et territoires,' *Arabian Humanities* 11, accessed February 29, 2016 at http://cy.revues.org/161.

Verdeil, E. (2013a), 'Beirut, metropolis of blackness: uneven geographies of electricity supply, protests and private informal electricity suppliers,' accessed February 29, 2016 at http://conference.rgs.org/conference/sessions/View.aspx?heading=Y&session=f0f9cb49-e81d-432e-a9b8-716af894c645.

Verdeil, E. (2013b), 'The geography of public lighting in Arab cities,' *Jadaliyya*, September 30, accessed February 29, 2016 at http://www.jadaliyya.com/pages/index/14378/the-geography-of-public-lighting-in-arab-cities.

Volk, Lucia (ed.) (2015), *The Middle East in the World: An Introduction*, New York: Routledge.

Vora, Neha (2013), *Impossible Citizens: Dubai's Indian Diaspora*, Durham, NC: Duke University Press.

Watts M.J., A. Mason, and H. Appel (eds) (2014), *Oil Talk: The Secret Lives of the Oil and Gas Industry*, Ithaca, NY: Cornell University Press.

Weber, Max (1978), *Economy and Society: An Outline of Interpretive Sociology*, Berkeley, CA: University of California Press.

Wheatley, Paul (2001), *The Places Where Men Pray Together: Cities in Islamic Lands Seventh through the Tenth Centuries*, Chicago: University of Chicago Press.

Willis, John M. (2012), *Unmaking North and South: Cartographies of the Yemeni Past*, London: Hurst.

19 Defining and refining the research agenda for Australian cities

Robert Freestone, Bill Randolph and Andrew Wheeler

Introduction

Australia is among the world's most urbanized countries. In 2014, 89 percent of Australians lived in urban areas, compared to 82 percent in the United Kingdom, 81 percent in the United States, 75 percent in Germany and 54 percent in China (World Bank, 2016). Even more notably, Australian urbanization is characterized by the dominance of its major cities.

It was not until the mid-1960s that formal urban research emerged in Australia in response to problems posed by rapid post-war development. Problem areas in housing, transport, environmental quality and social inclusion endure to this day, although the nature of the city has changed in the twenty-first century, and with it the appropriate research and policy responses. These responses require a more nuanced understanding of the shifting political and institutional settings for urban research, as well as an appreciation of the major social, economic and environmental changes that are currently reshaping people's lives in cities.

This chapter defines and refines the urban research agenda in twenty-first century Australia. The first three sections establish a context for our discussion. Section one identifies the critical developments that have contributed to a distinctively Australian brand of urbanism. Section two examines the key institutional and intellectual events that have defined the evolution of an Australian urban research agenda and influenced federal urban policy since the mid-twentieth century. Section three identifies key research issues that have captured the attention of Australian scholars over the past 15 years. Section four then turns to the future, offering a roadmap for research on Australian cities in response to emerging trends and new challenges in both research and practice. The conclusion grounds this discussion in the realities of contemporary urban research in Australia. While today's researchers must overcome significant institutional and ideological barriers in order to remain relevant and influence policy outcomes, the need for research on Australian cities has never been greater.

The distinctiveness of Australian urbanism

In 1788, an event occurred that has come to define and divide Australia as a nation: the First Fleet arrived on Australian shores with almost 1,500 British convicts and settlers to form a fledgling penal colony. Supported by the legal fiction of *terra nullius* (unclaimed territory), settlement continued into the mid-nineteenth century, progressively dispossessing Indigenous Australians. From these calamitous beginnings, the original British colony at Sydney Cove spread quickly into a network of key coastal settlements: Hobart (1803), Brisbane (1825), Perth (1829), Melbourne (1835) and Adelaide (1836). Knowledge gained from expeditions into a harsh continental interior provided the basis for founding permanent regional towns. Indigenous inhabitants, since they were deemed not to have established a lasting urban imprint, were progressively marginalized into remote "native" reservations or condemned to "fringe dweller" status on the periphery of new townships.

Contemporary urbanism in Australia has strong links to the geography of these colonial foundations. The major coastal towns consolidated their status as colonial capitals and then as state capital cities, becoming the largest centers of the Australian urban system. Key urban DNA regarding form (low-density suburbanization), structure (single centered cities with radial transport networks), governance (institutionalization of state governments as the major metropolitan governments and infrastructure providers) and inequality (haves and have-nots) were inevitably locked in through processes of "path dependency" (Troy, 1995). Even before the turn of the twentieth century, Australian urbanization was declared "most remarkable" because of its "centralization" of one-third of the population "in and around capital cities" (Weber, 1899, p. 1). The fundamental historic role of these cities as entrepôts facilitating the import of British capital and the export of resources for international markets defined them as "pure products of the nineteenth-century expansion of capitalism" (McCarty, 1970, p. 12). This phenomenon of "metropolitan dominance" or "primacy" has endured, reinforced through geography as well as public and private investment (Rowland, 1977). Today, just five cities house more than 60 percent of the national population (Australian Government, 2015) (Figure 19.1). In the future, these cities will continue to attract an increasing proportion of the country's population, especially from immigration, further reinforcing their prominence within both national and global networks (PIA, 2016).

Development patterns and architectural styles in the first Australian cities were informed by the early settlers' British heritage. Surveyors created the blueprints for these cities, often with little concern for long-term growth. In most locations, planning was limited to initial town layout: "formal town planning essentially ended with the physical outline of a very basic plan of development" (Freestone, 2010, p. 11). Sydney, the foundational settlement, eschewed a grand master plan and instead was settled in a high-density, largely uncoordinated fashion typical of what Frost (1991) calls eastern or "Atlantic" urbanism, comparable to Boston in the United States. But thereafter the rolling out of the "urban frontier", as in North

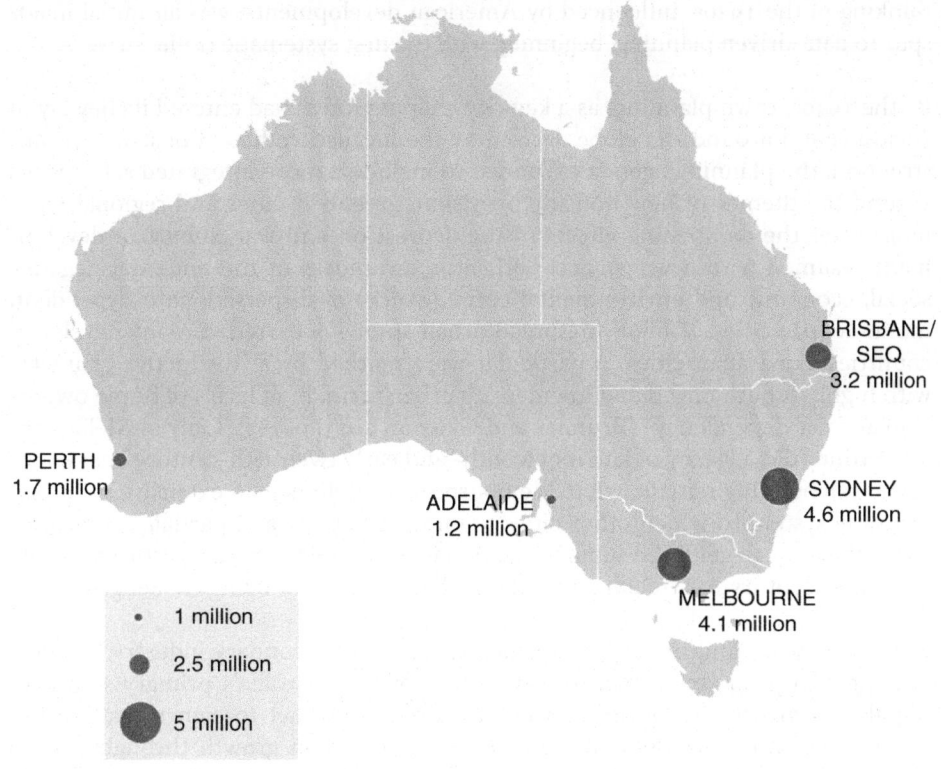

Note: SEQ = South East Queensland.

Source: Authors.

Figure 19.1   Locations and populations of Australia's largest cities

America, tended to follow a standardized gridiron, lower-density template. The planned city of Adelaide, the capital of South Australia, with the grid broken up and adapted to the site and then encased by parklands, is arguably the finest expression of the "grand model" of imperial urban settlement (Home, 2013).

In 1901, Australia became an independent nation when its six self-governing British colonies – New South Wales, Queensland, South Australia, Tasmania, Victoria and Western Australia – united to form the Commonwealth of Australia. Federalism emerged at a time when the town planning profession was beginning to exert increasing influence on Australian towns and cities. The design competition for the planning of Australia's new national capital, Canberra (named 1913), created a focus for much of this idealism. Spurred on by progressive aspirations for urban health, efficiency and beauty, the first town planners championed suburban living, provision of open space, expansion of roads and transit infrastructure, aesthetic guidelines, and new development and zoning regulations. The arrival of "city functional" thinking in the 1920s, influenced by American developments, was an initial major spur to data-driven planning, beginning with the first systematic traffic surveys.

By the 1940s, town planning, as a key city-shaping force, had entered its heyday in Australia and around the globe. Driven by the idealistic ethos of post-war reconstruction, the planning agenda expanded to include a more integrated set of ideas around the themes of new housing provision, greenbelt cities and regional planning. After the dampening effects of the depression and war, suburban development resumed with a vengeance, with little awareness of the potential negative social, economic and environmental consequences of dispersed, auto-dependent, mono-centric cities. While widespread urban sprawl occurred in many developed countries, Australian cities in particular were marked by a "distinctive character with highly suburbanized and low-density urban form, high levels of home ownership and car dependency" (Brunner and Glasson, 2015, p. 383). Only in Melbourne and Sydney did a legacy of late nineteenth- and early twentieth-century heavy suburban rail building remain, while Melbourne alone retained an extensive suburban tramway system to which other cities are now, belatedly and partially, returning. Nevertheless, car-centered suburbanization is the defining characteristic of the late twentieth-century Australian city and one that is only now being challenged.

From the 1950s, and underpinning the expansion of secondary industry, planned immigration programs began to drive city growth. Australia's primary source of population growth is still from overseas. Since 2006, net foreign migration has contributed more to population growth each year than growth through natural increase. The majority of new immigrants settle in major cities, with 85 percent of those born overseas living in a major city in 2011 compared to 64 percent of those born in Australia (ABS, 2014).

Since the 1980s, the global focus on sustainable development has influenced government policy and slowed the outward expansion of Australia's sprawling cities. Governments have actively sought to promote more compact, transit-oriented development. Urban consolidation, for example, has become "an established policy framework within all the capital cities" (Hedgcock and Brunner, 2015, p. 102). The densities of Australian cities have increased through a combination of infill development, urban renewal, smaller lot sizes and requirements for building more medium- and high-density housing in and around major activity centers (Bunker, 2014). Australian cities are, however, still characterized by relatively low densities compared to Asia and Europe (Gleeson, 2006). Nearly 80 percent of the combined population of Australia's 16 largest cities live in communities classifiable as suburban, and it is in these precincts where the vast majority of population growth is occurring (Gordon et al., 2015).

Another distinctive feature of Australian cities globally is their livability.[1] In 2014, Melbourne was named the world's most livable city for the fifth consecutive year, and three other Australian cities – Adelaide, Sydney and Perth – were listed in the top 10 (The Economist Intelligence Unit, 2014). The livability of Australia's major cities, and their attractiveness as centers of social, cultural and economic activity and opportunity, has contributed to significant population growth. In the decade to 2012, population growth placed Australia fourth out of 40 Organisation for Economic Co-operation and Development (OECD) countries and first among OECD countries with a population over 10 million (Krockenberger, 2015). However, Australia's increasing wealth has not been distributed equally, and concentrations of poverty and disadvantage are still present in all Australian cities (Pawson and Herath, 2015; Randolph, 2004). City centers, closely linked to the global economy, are more characteristic of "status and opportunity" while the "sinks of vulnerability and deprivation" have increasingly been suburbanized (Baum, 2008, p. 4).

Australia's tri-level government structure – federal, state/territory and local – and, in particular, the states' role in overseeing urban development, has contributed significantly to an identifiably Australian brand of urbanism (Searle et al., 2011). Through a combination of centralized development powers and extensive land holdings, state governments have long been in a unique position to control and facilitate major city-shaping development. This development has ranged from transport infrastructure such as railways to a more recent proliferation of privately funded motorways and ornaments of the new urban age: large casinos, sporting stadiums and convention centers, usually located on prime, inner-city land. A recent renaissance of political engagement in urban affairs has led to the establishment of a new junior ministerial portfolio of cities at the federal level, its policy brief largely framed within a discourse of partnership and smart land economics (Freestone, 2016).

While Australian cities are a product of the past, critical developments in economic, social, technological and environmental terms have made for "step changes" in their organization. There is evidence of this in the early 1900s, 1940s and 1960s but also since the 1980s, as the interplay of new forces within neo-liberal regimes has driven increasing variation within and between cities. Randolph (2004, p. 492) has demonstrated how the "the turnaround of the inner city, the suburbanization of disadvantage, the new aspirational suburbs, and an increasingly multi-regional city structure with increasingly complex multi-scaling of processes and outcomes all point to new forms of city structure". A new "range of intensifying pressures for change" (p. 481) stretches across just about everything: population growth, household composition, economic restructuring, housing and property dynamics, infrastructure provision, environmental constraints, lifestyle changes and so on. These themes have informed more recent urban research. But before exploring these agendas we will first consider how the genre of urban studies has evolved only comparatively recently in the Australian setting.

An evolving "urban consciousness"

Table 19.1 provides a detailed chronology of key institutional and publication events charting the development of Australian urban research and federal urban

Table 19.1   Chronology of key events in Australian urban research and federal urban policy, 1960–2015

Year	Key event
1960	Robin Boyd, *The Australian Ugliness*
1964	Social Sciences Research Council, 'The Metropolis in Australia', Seminar, ANU
	Planning Research Centre, University of Sydney
1965	Max Neutze, *Economic Policy and the Size of Cities*
	E.G. Whitlam, 'Cities in a Federation', lecture to Royal Australian Planning Institute, Sydney
1966	Australian Institute of Political Science, *Australian Cities: Chaos or Planned Growth*, Summer School, Canberra
	Urban Research Program, ANU
	Don Gazzard (ed.), *Australian Outrage: The Decay of a Visual Environment*, Royal Australian Institute of Architects
1967	Australian Institute of Urban Studies (AIUS)
	Patrick Troy (ed.), *Urban Redevelopment in Australia*
1969	E.G. Whitlam, *An Urban Nation*
1970	Hugh Stretton, *Ideas for Australian Cities*
1971	Centre for Urban Research and Action, Fitzroy, Melbourne
1972	AIUS, *New Cities for Australia*
	National Urban and Regional Development Authority (NURDA) – W. McMahon, PM (Prime Minister)
	Australian Department of Urban and Regional Development (DURD) – E.G. Whitlam, PM
1973	Cities Commission (late NURDA), *Report to the Australian Government*
1974	Frank Stilwell, *Australian Urban and Regional Development*
1975	Leonie Sandercock, *Cities for Sale*
	Mal Logan et al., *Urban and Regional Australia: Analysis and Policy Issues*
	Australian Department of Environment, Housing and Community Development – J.M. Fraser, PM
1976	John Paterson, David Yencken and Graeme Gunn, *A Mansion or No House*
1978	Max Neutze, *Australian Urban Policy*
	House of Representatives Standing Committee on Environment and Conservation, *The Commonwealth Government and the Urban Environment*
	Peter Scott (ed.), *Australian Cities and Public Policy*
1981	Patrick Troy (ed.), *Equity in the City*
1982	*Urban Policy and Research* (new academic and policy journal)
	Joint Venture for More Affordable Housing (JVMAH) – J.M. Fraser, PM
1989	Australian Model Code for Residential Development (AMCORD)
1991	Building Better Cities Program – R.J. Hawke, PM
	Urban Futures: Issues for Australian Cities (new government policy journal), Commonwealth Department of Health, Housing, Local Government and Community Services

Table 19.1   (continued)

Year	Key event
1992	House of Representatives Standing Committee for Long Term Strategies, *Patterns of Urban Settlement*
1993	Robert Freestone (ed.), *Spirited Cities*
1994	Australian Urban and Regional Development Review – P.J. Keating, PM
	Prime Minister's Urban Design Taskforce, *Urban Design in Australia* – P.J. Keating, PM
1996	Patrick Troy, *The Perils of Urban Consolidation*
2001	Australian Housing and Urban Research Institute (AHURI)
2003	Formation of State of Australian Cities Research Network
	1st State of Australian Cities Conference (SOAC), Parramatta
2004	Australian Sustainable Built Environment Council (ASBEC)
2005	House of Representatives Standing Committee on Environment and Heritage, *Sustainable Cities* – J. Howard, PM
2006	Australian Council of New Urbanism, *Australian New Urbanism: A Guide to Projects*
2007	Rowland Atkinson et al., *Urban 45: New Ideas for Australia's Cities*, RMIT
2008	Peter Newton, *Transitions: Pathways towards Sustainable Urban Development in Australia*
2009	Council of Australian Governments (COAG), *National Objective for Capital City Strategic Planning Systems*
2010	Brendan Gleeson, *Lifeboat Cities*
	Infrastructure Australia, *State of Australian Cities 2010* (vol.1)
	Department of Infrastructure and Transport, *Our Cities*, Discussion Paper, and Background and Research Paper – K. Rudd, PM
	Prime Minister's Capital Cities Strategic Planning Panel – K. Rudd, PM
2011	Department of Infrastructure and Transport, *Our Cities, Our Future: A National Urban Policy for a Productive, Sustainable and Liveable Future* – J. Gillard, PM
	Department of Infrastructure and Regional Development, and Australian Sustainable Built Environment Council (ASBEC), *Creating Places for People: An Urban Design Protocol for Australian Cities* – J. Gillard, PM
2012	COAG Reform Council, Review of Capital City Strategic Planning Systems
2013	Australasian Early Career Urban Research Network (AECURN)
2015	Jane-Frances Kelly and Paul Donegan, *City Limits: Why Australia's Cities Are Broken and How We Can Fix Them*, Grattan Institute
	Australian Ministry of Cities and Built Environment – M.B. Turnbull, PM

Source: Authors.

policy from the early 1960s, when urban research emerges as a recognizable transdisciplinary endeavor. There are several key drivers. The first is a growing recognition of the need for research-informed urban policy, a preoccupation to the present day, and of the role of the social sciences in providing authoritative data as the basis for research insights and new policy directions. Civic surveys were a core methodological tool for the town planning movement, although their analytical sophistication and relationship to actual policy recommendations in the immediate post-war reconstruction era were problematic (Rudduck and Grounds, 1955, p. 225). A second driver emerging from this evolution of professional technique was a growing awareness that town planning alone, with its roots in architecture and design, was not a sufficiently holistic paradigm to address the full range of environmental, economic and cultural issues affecting the quality of urban life. A third was the beginnings of legitimate scholarship into Australian urban development with the critical contribution by Noel Butlin of the Australian National University (ANU). His pioneering work identified urbanization as "the outstanding characteristic of Australian economic history" (Butlin, 1964, p. 6).

Butlin established the Urban Research Unit at ANU in 1966. This was arguably the "founding moment" for an Australian urban studies tradition (Davison and Fincher, 1998, p. 184). Max Neutze and then Patrick Troy led this program over the next 30 years. Their eclectic research agenda was responsive to the issues of the day, although inspired primarily by the research interests of individual scholars. Housing, environmental quality, governance, infrastructure, social justice and urban history emerged as strong themes (Troy, 1997). The so-called Joint Urbanization Seminars encouraged a dialogue between academics and practitioners with urban renewal one early focus (Troy, 1967). There were other discussion forums that emphasized the dawn of a new urban era (Clark, 1970; Wilkes, 1966), while Hugh Stretton's *Ideas for Australian Cities*, published in 1970, was the single most influential statement of its day (Hamnett, 2015). The formation of an Australian Institute of Urban Studies in 1967 was a declaration of genuine national concern about the problems of the post-war city, revolving around sprawl, pollution, housing problems, services and aesthetics. This body commissioned its own research reports into various urban issues, launched a drive to establish new cities, and published a series of bibliographies of urban research. The synergies between these various initiatives help explain the taking up of urban problems as a national political issue, most effectively in the programs of the Whitlam Labor Government in 1972–1975 which established a Department of Urban and Regional Development, with Troy a key advisor and seconded bureaucrat.

Davison and Fincher (1998) review subsequent trends up to the turn of the century. By the 1980s, Australian urban studies research was engaging with international scholarly discourse, reflected in the increasing influence of Marxist ideas. They identified a branching into three main strands: environmentalism on the eve of the sustainability turn, feminism in recognition of gender and diversity, and postmodernism to unsettle whatever verities had been established. By the 1990s, the new preoccupations were globalization, social polarization and difference, privatization, and the impact of new communication technologies. A new federal "Better Cities" program, a National Housing Strategy review, and the formation of both the Australian Housing and Urban Research Institute (AHURI) and Australian Research Council (ARC) began to deliver more sustained scholarly and especially competitive research funding (Beer, 1995). Davison and Fincher (1998, p. 194) conclude that by the late 1990s urban studies had been "remarkable in achieving relatively high recognition and influence despite relatively weak institutional expression".

Key research issues since the early 2000s

The new millennium was marked by a resurgence in cross-disciplinary urban research as Australian cities became the focus for increasing research activity. Numerous forums have been utilized to disseminate research findings, the biennial State of Australian Cities (SOAC) Conference series foremost among them. This initiative, launched at Parramatta in western Sydney in 2003, is the major legacy of the bid led by Patrick Troy to establish an ARC-funded national sustainable cities and regions network. Searle et al. (2011, p. 1) note that the conference series has "re-energised Australian urban scholarship by offering what is now the principal venue for communal scholarly debate about Australian cities". In just over a decade, the series has produced close to 1,000 peer-reviewed papers, fostering a more informed exploration of the forces driving Australian cities as well as the reasons for their form and structure.

The SOAC conferences thus provide valuable insights into the key issues that have occupied the Australian urban research landscape since the turn of the twenty-first century. Table 19.2 summarizes these key issues under the six thematic streams on which the SOAC conferences are based.[2] Figure 19.2 details the popularity of these streams across all conferences between 2003 and 2015.[3] Two broad streams, City Governance and City Society, account for nearly half of all the papers presented during this period. Papers grouped under the City Governance theme have focused primarily on public policy formation, metropolitan and regional planning, planning legislation and reform, housing and urban renewal, and climate change mitigation and adaptation. The City Society stream has encompassed research issues ranging from cultural diversity, public participation and human health, to safety and crime prevention, affordable and social housing, and the needs of specific population groups such as children and the elderly.

The City Environment stream, the third most popular, has concentrated on topical environmental issues including climate change and resilience, natural resource management, water, food security, and sustainable development and design. The City Movement stream has been dominated by papers on urban transport and infrastructure provision, with transit-oriented development, the provision of public and active transport infrastructure, and motorway development featuring heavily. This stream has also addressed other dimensions of urban infrastructure provision, including communications and information technology. However, very few papers within this stream, or indeed across all other streams, have examined technological change and its influence on city function in both the short and longer term. Although the topic has not been completely neglected in the broader context of

Table 19.2   Snapshot of urban research issues since the early 2000s

City Governance	City Society	City Environment	City Movement	City Structure	City Economy
– public engagement (incl. emerging use of social media)	– housing supply and affordability	– climate change	– transit-oriented development	– density and urban infill	– infrastructure
– metropolitan and regional planning	– social housing	– resilience	– public transport	– urban con-solidation/ compact	– economic restructuring/ employ-ment shifts/ agglomera-tion effects
– urban renewal	– human health	– water	– active travel	cities and centers	– migration
– housing provi-sion and affordability	– cultural diversity and belonging	– sustainable develop-ment/ design	– IT/ telecom-munications	– city growth	– globalization
– resilience	– public par-ticipation	– growth pressures	– sustainable transport	– infrastruc-ture provision	
– planning legislation and reform	– heritage	– food	– accessibility and transport disadvantage		
– climate change mitigation and adaptation	– safety and crime		– motorway development		
	– ageing		– emissions/pol-lution		
	– children and young people		– autonomous mobility		

Source: Authors, based on SOAC proceedings 2003–2015.

Australian urban studies (see, for example, Troy, 1995), there is now a pressing need for further research in this area.

The penultimate stream, City Structure, was absent from the 2009 and 2011 SOAC conferences, which accounts for the relatively low number of papers. The stream has, nevertheless, proved a popular forum for research on the emerging morphology of the Australian city – particularly in relation to growth and government policies supporting urban consolidation and shifts to higher-density living. However, broader contributions on the national urban "system" have been scarcer; this was a prominent focus in the 1970s, only recently revived in longer-term scenario-based research (Weller and Bolleter, 2013). The sixth and final stream, City Economy, has centered on economic change and labor market outcomes, the economic drivers of growth and urban productivity, the spatial distribution of employment, migration and globalization. Given the economy's primacy in government decision making and policy in Australia, it is somewhat surprising that the City Economy stream has only attracted 102 papers over seven conferences. Perhaps even more perplexing is that there have so far been very few papers on infrastructure funding in Australian cities. This pattern is also evident in other popular research forums, including the

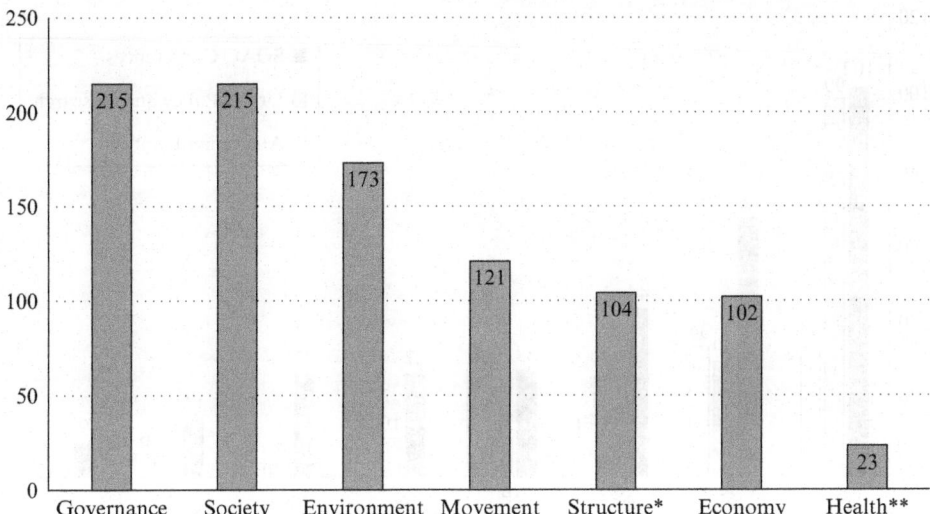

Notes: *"Structure" dropped as a stream in 2009 and 2011; **"Health" only included as a stream in 2009 and 2015.

Source: Authors.

Figure 19.2   Total SOAC conference papers by stream, 2003–2015

two leading Australian urban journals, *Urban Policy and Research* and *Australian Planner* (see Figure 19.3).

This empirical charting of research trends reveals a wide-ranging exploration of urban issues, but also a lack of depth in fundamental issues, notably economic drivers and technological change. In particular, the paucity of serious academic research on infrastructure, finance and the relationship between infrastructure investment, urban economies and land use outcomes emerges as a major lacuna in contemporary urban studies. This is one of the main reasons why academic urban research has had relatively little purchase in contemporary urban policy debates, a theme to which we will return.

Roadmaps for future research

A consensus has emerged in the research community that twenty-first-century Australian cities are qualitatively and quantitatively different to their predecessors (Randolph, 2004). While path-dependent characteristics – the primacy of capital cities, their suburbanism and automobile dependence, the centrality of state governments in their administration, their perceived egalitarianism – undoubtedly persist, significant changes are also evident. Forster (2006) emphasizes falling rates of affordability and thus home ownership, increasing residential densities, worsen-

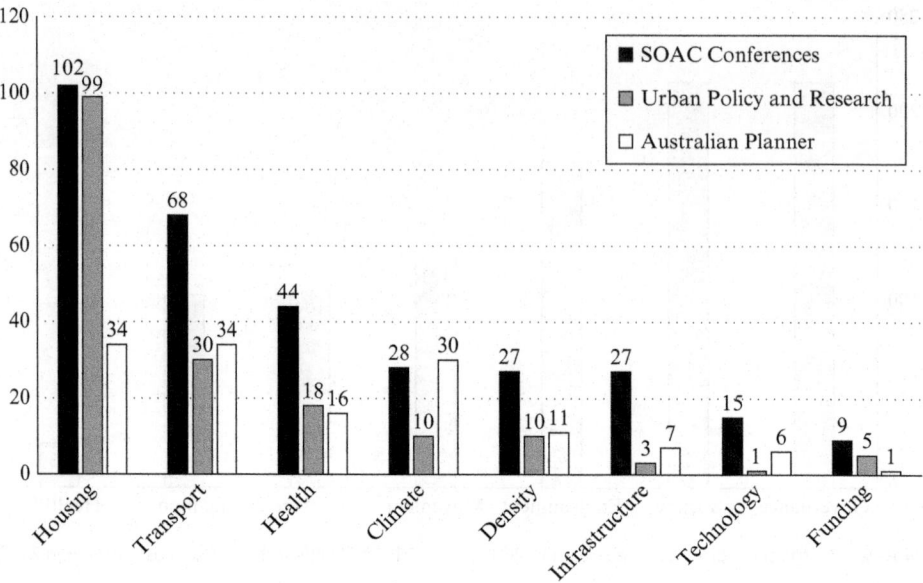

Source: Authors.

Figure 19.3   Frequency of keywords in paper titles, 2000–2015 – *Urban Policy and Research*, *Australian Planner* and SOAC conferences (from 2003)

ing social polarization, and more complex patterns of residential differentiation, population change and employment accessibility; hence, some "taken-for-granted aspects of Australian urban character" are less evident than they once were (Forster, 2006, p. 174). The problems of contemporary Australian cities are well documented: density (the drawbacks of low joined by the challenges of high), transport (the need for greater mass transit connectivity and walkability while reducing car dependency), housing (affordability and variety), inequality (divided by income, health and mobility), the spatial mismatch between jobs and homes, fractured metropolitan governance, limited provision of urban open space, the need for environmental and heritage protection, and poor design standards (Freestone, 2016). Australia's "broken cities" are caught between the three tiers of Australian government, barely registering on the agenda of many politicians (Kelly and Donegan, 2015).

The solutions are even more challenging: the need to connect up critical issues such as housing, employment, environment and infrastructure through both smarter governance and economics is commonly acknowledged. A string of symposia and forums have helped to incrementally recalibrate urban research agendas. A quartet of these is elaborated below.

The *Urban 45* summit brought together "the research experience, thoughts and skills of many Australian academics" to identify three policy proposals each across 15 problem settings: affordable housing, globalization, urban land management, climate change, transport, public health, ageing, social cohesion and multiculturalism, child-friendly cities, Indigenous urban disadvantage, community infrastructure, social exclusion, urban education, culture and crime. The dossier produced from the summit calls for more independent research into these "problem settings" and less ideologically based policy (Atkinson et al., 2007).

The Australia Futures Task Force documented the greater differentiation and complexity in Australia's big cities as well as the challenges faced by coastal environments, regional centers, country towns and Indigenous communities. It identified six issues of national significance through which the urban policy–research nexus could be enhanced: changing demographic balance; labor markets, jobs, incomes and skills; housing choice and affordability; infrastructure deficiencies; resource management and the environment; and institutional dysfunction and reform (The Australia Futures Task Force, 2007). A key implication flowing from this and similar analyses is the need to enhance researcher access to urban datasets – one of the central goals of the recent federally funded Australian Urban Research Information Network (AURIN) initiative (Stimson, 2011).

Since the late twentieth century, Stephen Hamnett has orchestrated a succession of collaborative inquiries which offer a valuable evolving picture of Australian research and policy preoccupations – from the late 1980s (Hamnett, 1985; see also Hamnett and Bunker, 1987), through the early 1990s (Hamnett and Parham, 1992) to the late 2000s (Forster and Hamnett, 2008). The latest compendium, "Australian Cities in the 21st Century: Suburbs and Beyond" (Hamnett and Maginn, 2016) brings together essays addressing edgier, less monolithic issues than three decades earlier, such as the idea of a national suburban policy, housing supply and affordability, planning system reform, climate change, disaster planning, and the regional urban impacts of resource development. Identifying fundamental problems of urban governance and plan-making, there have been calls for policy based on more "rigorous evidence and policy evaluations" and hence on a "more sophisticated, collaborative and integrated urban planning research agenda" (Hamnett and Maginn, 2016, p. 20).

The Planning Institute of Australia (PIA), the peak professional body, has also turned its mind to long-range research and policy needs. *Through the Lens: Megatrends Shaping Our Future* identifies a need for more research on the global forces – or "megatrends" – that will fundamentally shape how Australian cities grow and develop in the face of significant population increases and technological change (PIA, 2016). Economic shifts, including the transition of global power from north to west and south to east, combined with the strengthening of the service economy, present opportunities for new research into how Australian cities can capitalize on their locational advantage in the Asia-Pacific region, and hence become more responsive to changing work patterns and preferences. Environmental shifts, including climate change and the increasing scarcity of natural resources, demand more research on the capacity of cities to reduce their urban footprints and safeguard against extreme weather events. Demographic and social shifts, including an ageing population and increasing overseas migration, will require new research into how cities can better support healthy communities, "ageing in place" and respond to changing cultural preferences (PIA, 2016).

Taking just one of these social shifts – the contemporary epidemic of chronic diseases – enables a sharpened focus around one specific set of research needs. These diseases, which include heart disease, type 2 diabetes, certain cancers and depression, are now the leading cause of death worldwide (WHO, 2011). In Australia, they account for nearly 80 percent of the total morbidity burden and more than two-thirds of all health expenditure (Commonwealth of Australia, 2010). For many years, public health practitioners and bodies such as the World Health Organization (WHO) have been drawing attention to the link between the built environment and human health. However, it is only in the last decade that this link has truly entered the professional consciousness of urban planners (Freestone and Wheeler, 2015).

This realization has contributed to a flurry of research and policy activity into healthy built environments, reflected in special journal issues and conferences on healthy cities, in new research collaborations between health and built environment professionals, and in the inclusion of health objectives in urban policy and planning legislation. In 2009, for example, the Council of Australian Government (COAG) identified "health, liveability and community wellbeing" as one of ten nationally significant policy issues for Australian cities (COAG, 2009, p. 20). And while many cities, both in Australia and abroad, are now aware of the need to plan and design healthier urban places, further research into what built environment interventions will be most effective in combating the growing burden of chronic disease is urgently required. A major scholarly review by Kent and Thompson (2014) has identified key avenues for further research and the need to foster greater interdisciplinary collaboration on healthy cities.

Conclusion

New and unprecedented challenges are redefining and reshaping contemporary notions of city-making in the twenty-first century. At the same time, the very institutional settings for, and priorities of, urban research are shifting. Academic researchers, in particular, are faced with numerous and often conflicting priorities. On the one hand, a wider process of meritocratization in corporatized academic institutions is reinforcing a "publish or perish" mentality and driving researchers to publish in prestigious international journals typically aimed at fellow academics (Freestone, 2011). On the other hand, there is concern that urban research is failing to reach, and therefore influence, practitioners and policy makers because of a proliferation of financial, cultural and institutional hurdles (Bunker, 2015; Taylor and Hurley, 2016; Troy, 2013). However, diminishing government research funding since the early 2000s is perhaps the greatest challenge facing the urban research community today. As noted by Randolph (2013, p. 133): "Without new research funding at scale, we will fail to train the next generation of urban researchers … [and] the forces creating our cities will continue to roll forward without a thoroughgoing understanding of the drivers of urban change and the options for planning and other interventions". In addition to the decline of academic research into key areas such as urban infrastructure, city economic productivity and urban financing, noted above, there has been an increasing tendency for governments at all levels to turn to the private sector as a source of policy-relevant research. This has further undermined the influence of academic research on key decision makers.

The next generation of urban researchers are, nevertheless, well placed to face these challenges. A recent special issue of *Australian Planner* demonstrated that early career urban researchers are "using their scholarship to think through how the research–practice nexus might be differently negotiated and understood to build potential for change" (Legacy et al., 2016, p. 2). This will be crucial in redefining and refining the research agenda for Australian cities, both now and into the twenty-first century.

NOTES

1 Livability is defined as the sum of the factors that add up to a community's quality of life – including the built and natural environments, economic prosperity, social stability and equity, educational opportunity, and cultural, entertainment and recreation possibilities.

2 A seventh thematic area, "Health", was included for the 2009 and 2015 SOAC conferences.

3 The proceedings of all SOAC conferences between 2005 and 2015 have been recently consolidated on the *Australian Policy Online* website: accessed 5 March 2016 at http://apo.org.au/collections/soac-conferences.

References

ABS (Australian Bureau of Statistics) (2014), *4102.0 – Australian Social Trends, 2014*, accessed 12 December 2015 at http://www.abs.gov.au/socialtrends.

Atkinson, R., Dalton, T., Norman, B. and Wood, G., eds (2007), *Urban 45: New Ideas for Australia's Cities*, Melbourne: Royal Melbourne Institute of Technology.

Australian Government, Department of Infrastructure and Regional Development (2015), *State of Australian Cities 2014–2015*, Canberra: Commonwealth of Australia.

Baum, S. (2008), 'Suburban scars: Australian cities and socio-economic deprivation', Research Paper 15, Urban Research Program, Brisbane: Griffith University.

Beer, A. (1995), 'Harlots or heroes? The role of contract research within universities', *Urban Policy and Research*, 13(3), 176–180.

Brunner, J. and Glasson, J. (2015), 'Conclusions: toward the future', in J. Brunner and J. Glasson, eds *Contemporary Issues in Australian Urban and Regional Planning*, London: Routledge, 382–386.

Bunker, R. (2014), 'How is the compact city faring in Australia?', *Planning Practice and Research*, 29(5), 449–460.

Bunker, R. (2015), 'Linking urban research with planning practice', *Urban Policy and Research*, 33(3), 362–369.

Butlin, N.G. (1964), *Investment in Australian Economic Development, 1861–1900*, Cambridge: Cambridge University Press.

Clark, N., ed. (1970), *Analysis of Urban Development: Proceedings of the Tewksbury Symposium*, July 14–16, 1970, Melbourne: Department of Civil Engineering, University of Melbourne.

COAG (Council of Australian Governments) (2009), *Council of Australian Governments' Meeting Communiqué*, 7 December 2009, Canberra: COAG.

Commonwealth of Australia (2010), *Taking Preventative Action. A Response to Australia: The Healthiest Country by 2020. The Report of the National Preventative Health Taskforce*, Canberra: Commonwealth of Australia.

Davison, G. and Fincher, R. (1998), 'Urban studies in Australia: a road map and ways ahead', *Urban Policy and Research*, 16(3), 183–197.

Forster, C. (2006), 'The challenge of change: Australian cities and urban planning in the new millennium', *Geographical Research*, 44(2), 173–182.

Forster, C. and Hamnett, S. (2008), 'The state of Australian cities', *Built Environment*, 34(3).

Freestone, R. (2010), *Urban Nation: Australia's Planning Heritage*, Melbourne: CSIRO Publishing.

Freestone, R. (2011), 'Commentary: ranking planning journals in the Australian research assessment exercise, 2008–2010', *Journal of Planning Education and Research*, 31(1), 88–94.

Freestone, R. (2016), 'Hopes of a new urban age survive minister's fall', *The Conversation*, 14 January 2016, accessed 12 December 2015 at https://theconversation.com/hopes-of-a-new-urban-age-survive-ministers-fall-52975.

Freestone, R. and Wheeler, A. (2015), 'Integrating health into town planning: a history', in H. Barton, S. Thompson, M. Grant and S. Burgess, eds *The Routledge Handbook of Planning for Health and Well-Being*, London: Routledge, 17–36.

Frost, L. (1991), *The New Urban Frontier: Urbanisation and City-Building in Australasia and the American West*, Sydney: UNSW Press.

Gleeson, B. (2006), *Australian Heartlands: Making Space for Hope in the Suburbs*, Sydney: Allen & Unwin.

Gordon, D.L.A., Maginn, P.J., Biermann, S., Sisson, A., Huston, I. and Moniruzzaman, M. (2015), *Estimating the Size of Australia's Suburban Population*, PATREC Perspectives, October. Perth: University of Western Australia.

Hamnett, S. (1985), 'Urban Australia: issues and policies', *Built Environment*, 11(2).

Hamnett, S. (2015), 'Hugh Stretton: ideas for Australian cities', *Built Environment*, 41(3), 419–434.

Hamnett, S. and Bunker, R., eds (1987), *Urban Australia: Planning Issues and Policies*, Melbourne: Nelson Wadsworth.

Hamnett, S. and Maginn, P.J. (2016), 'Australian cities in the 21st century: suburbs and beyond', *Built Environment*, 12(1).

Hamnett, S. and Parham, S., eds (1992), 'Metropolitan Australia in the 1990s', *Built Environment*, 18(3).

Hedgcock, D. and Brunner, J. (2015), 'Planning intervention in metropolitan urban form: the 21st-century challenge of urban consolidation in Australian capital cities', in J. Brunner and J. Glasson, eds *Contemporary Issues in Australian Urban and Regional Planning*, London: Routledge, 95–112.

Home, R. (2013), *Of Planting and Planning: The Making of British Colonial Cities*, 2nd edition, London: Routledge.

Kelly, J-F. and Donegan, P. (2015), *City Limits: Why Australia's cities Are Broken and How We Can Fix Them*, Melbourne: Melbourne University Press and The Grattan Institute.

Kent, J.L. and Thompson, S. (2014), 'The three domains of urban planning for health and well-being', *Journal of Planning Literature*, 29(3), 239–256.

Krockenberger, M. (2015), *Population Growth in Australia*, Canberra: The Australia Institute.

Legacy, C., Lowe, M. and Cole-Hawthorne, R. (2016), '(Re)constituting urban research in a neoliberal planning climate', *Australian Planner*, 43(1), 1–4.

McCarty, J. (1970), 'Australian capital cities in the nineteenth century', *Urbanization in Australia: The Nineteenth Century*, Sydney: Sydney University Press, 9–39.

Pawson, H. and Herath, S. (2015), *Disadvantaged Places in Urban Australia: Residential Mobility, Place Attachment and Social Exclusion*, AHURI Final Report No. 243, Melbourne: Australian Housing and Urban Research Institute.

PIA (Planning Institute of Australia) (2016), *Through the Lens: Megatrends Shaping Our Future*, Canberra: PIA.

Randolph, B. (2004), 'The changing Australian city: new patterns, new policies and new research needs', *Urban Policy and Research*, 22(4), 481–493.

Randolph, B. (2013), 'Wither urban research? Yes, you read it right first time!', *Urban Policy and Research*, 31(2), 130–133.

Rowland, D.T. (1977), 'Theories of urbanization in Australia', *Geographical Review*, 67(2), 167–176.

Rudduck, G. and Grounds, R. (1955), 'The application of the social sciences to town planning in Australia', *International Social Science Bulletin*, 7(2), 220–225.

Searle, G., Dodson, J. and Steele, W. (2011), 'How different are Australian cities?', 5th State of Australian Cities Conference, 30 November–2 December, Melbourne, accessed 2 February 2016 at http://pan dora.nla.gov.au/tep/40669.

Stimson, R.J. (2011), 'The Australian Urban Research Infrastructure Network (AURIN) initiative: a platform offering data and tools for urban and built environment researchers across Australia', 5th State of Australian Cities Conference, 30 November–2 December, Melbourne, accessed 5 March 2016 at http://pandora.nla.gov.au/tep/40669.

Taylor, E.J. and Hurley, J. (2016), '"Not a lot of people read the stuff": Australian urban research in planning practice', *Urban Policy and Research*, 34(2), 116–131.

The Australia Futures Task Force (2007), *Challenges and Directions for Australia's Urban and Regional Future*, Report #1. A Task Force formed by the Australian Research Council Research Network in Spatially Integrated Social Science.

The Economist Intelligence Unit (2014), *A Summary of the Liveability Ranking and Overview*, London.

Troy, P., ed. (1967), *Urban Redevelopment in Australia*, Canberra: URU, Australian National University.

Troy, P., ed. (1995), *Technological Change and the City*, Sydney: Federation Press.

Troy, P. (1997), *The Urban Research Program 1966–1996*, Canberra: URP, Australian National University.

Troy, P. (2013), 'Australian urban research and planning', *Urban Policy and Research*, 31(2), 134–149.

Weber, A.F. (1899), *The Growth of Cities in the Nineteenth Century: A Study in Statistics*, New York: Macmillan.

Weller, R. and Bolleter, J. (2013), *Made in Australia: The Future of Australian Cities*. Perth: UWA Publishing.

WHO (World Health Organization) (2011), *Noncommunicable Disease Country Profiles*, Geneva: WHO.

Wilkes, J., ed. (1966), *Australian Cities: Chaos or Planned Growth?*, Sydney: Angus & Robertson.

World Bank (2016), 'Urban population (% of total)', accessed 5 March 2016 at http://data.worldbank.org/indicator/SP.URB.TOTL.IN.ZS.

20 The post-socialist city: insights from the spaces of radical societal change

Oleg Golubchikov

Introduction

D.M. Smith, who had purposefully integrated insights from cities in Russia and Eastern Europe in his *Geography and Social Justice* (1994), noticed in his later work: 'what might have been learned from the socialism actually practiced, in Eastern Europe and China (and of course Cuba), was largely overlooked by those espousing radical geography' (2000: 1150). Indeed, the position of the former 'Second World' in the conceptual geographical and urban literature, including the one professedly 'international', has always been ambiguous, if not superficial. As the world was split into the two ideological camps, spaces of state socialism were treated as a special category, not easily blended with capitalist narratives, and therefore included in the scholarship on their own terms. What remains less convincing, however, is still a relatively modest conceptual visibility of contemporary cities in ex-socialist Europe – despite their extraordinary experience of radical societal transition.

The intensity, scale, and reach of socio-economic changes in post-socialist Eastern Europe, Russia and ex-Soviet states can only be compared with rapidly developing countries like China. Unlike the latter, however, transition in Eastern Europe has been not so much about development in its traditional sense, but more about 'non-developmentalist' modernization. Nevertheless, it has been similarly far-reaching and rapid as per its effects on the foundations of socio-economic systems. Transition from state socialism to capitalism has involved not simply a handover of ownership over key economic assets, liberalization, welfare state restructuring, and the universalization of the market and globalization imperatives, but more fundamentally deep shifts in the organization of the whole society, including with respect to class transformation, ideological and ethical reorientations, new labor-capital relations, and the redefinition of value and worth.

Of course, cities have not stayed untouched in this spectacular transformation. Here, again, what distinguishes the experiences of the second-world post-socialist cities from rapidly urbanizing third-world developing societies is that, in most cases, the rates of urbanization in the former remain stable and so change has related to the *nature* of urbanization rather than its dimensionality. Cities have been subjected to considerable change and, in many respects, represented the agency of change themselves, providing new material and semiotics framework for the reorganization of the society. As I shall try to show, transition is very much conditioned by the urban experiences, through which it takes its specific narratives and by which it produces new social structures. A proper apprehension of this urban experience, both historical and ongoing, still demands much effort from social scholars.

In what follows, I try to problematize the experience of post-socialist cities. It is not my intention to present a review of urban studies in relation to post-socialism, rather to sketch some questions and vectors demanding further investigation. The rest of this chapter is therefore organized as follows. I will start with problematizing the place of post-socialist cities in international urban scholarship, arguing for the importance of a proper 'worlding' of post-socialist urban experiences for a better understanding of global urbanism today. I then outline how post-socialist cities, through their extraordinary and rapid ideological retrofit, represent a particularly good tool to foreground the nexus of ideology and the city. I also argue that transition itself is a geo-ideological doctrine of planetary reach that makes not only Eastern Europe but the whole world ideologically more one-dimensional – by neutralizing state socialism and allowing the global triumph of neoliberal capitalism. This understanding is critical for studying cities, too, as it reveals the truly totalizing nature of transition and how cities of post-socialism are collectively interwoven in this totality, rather than simply exposing their idiosyncratic and contingent morphological change. I take this forward by unpacking how transition mediates the subsumption of pre-existing spatialities in post-socialist societies. In the final section, I return to the centrality of the urban in the production of post-socialist social relations and, above all, class transformation.

Geographically, I will limit the definition of 'post-socialism' to the ex-communist/ex-socialist countries in Europe and to the former Soviet Union, jointly referring to this very diverse post-socialist continent as 'Eastern Europe', although parts of this region may be designated in literature as Russia, Central Asia, South Caucasus, Central and Eastern Europe, Baltic States, Eurasia, and so on.

Worlding post-socialist city?

Existing research on post-socialist cities parallels any other fields of urban studies in terms of being broad in its ambitions, approaches, subject matters, and conclusions. It also reflects the very diverse experiences and trajectories of East European cities, as well as their host nations and host regions – from East Germany to Russia's Far East, from Tajikistan to Tatarstan, from Estonia to Macedonia, from Suvalkija to Slovakia, from Istria to Transnistria.

The precise understanding of the 'post-socialist' adjective also varies: from a key epistemological framework that expresses continuing urban experience to no more than an area-study descriptor, even an empty signifier, which does not hold much explanatory unity any longer, if it ever did. The latter approach may suggest that, as long as the countries of the ex-socialist sphere have reformed themselves into a market economy and, importantly, as some of them joined the Western signature clubs such as the EU and NATO, while some others slid into resembling the broader Global South categories, there is no longer such a thing as a post-socialist city. There are, rather, individual nation-states and their regionalized families, which experience their individualistic processes of change and which, if necessary, can be classified into the broader rubrics of the West, North, South, or specific regional identities and regimes. This latter attitude already informs the imaginaries of many scholars, especially from outside of the 'post-socialist' region. For example, in the second edition of his *Urban Theory and the Urban Experience*, Parker (2015) places post-Soviet cities 'east of Helsinki' in a chapter on 'the Global South', between China and Latin America, and hardly mentions anything specifically on the wider ex-socialist urban Europe, making it indistinctive as a category from other cities in Europe.

There may be a good reason to do so, as this allows de-territorializing ex-socialist cities from their Second World's area signifier and re-territorializing them perhaps more meaningfully in the contemporary geopolitical partitions of the global processes, thus assigning them new conceptual understandings. However, this also means de-historicizing cities in that region, rejecting the epistemological power of 'state socialism' and 'transition' and in some respect marginalizing post-socialist cities conceptually, because their particular historical experiences become indistinctive from the historical mosaic of the West and are thus simply subsumed by the Euro-American centrism, which tends to over-emphasize the experiences of the West at the cost of the Rest. This centrism thus further asserts its conceptual dominance over the thus silenced experiences of Eastern Europe, while Eastern Europe also continues to fit uneasily into the Procrustean bed of post-colonialism, thus becoming invisible all-round. Ironically, even those who do attempt to decenter ethno-centric models, pay little attention to Eastern Europe. For example, Roy (2009), while directly noting that the 'area study' approach emanates from the Cold War tradition, fails to make any reference to cities in Eastern Europe in her call for the worlding of cities to build new geographies of imagination and epistemology in urban and regional theory, beyond the Euro-American experience.

However, as the experiences of post-socialist cities as a larger group go unaccounted, this provides grounds for protest from some fractions of the urban scholarship community (see Sjöberg, 2014; Tuvikene, 2016). Indeed, what still unites many writings on the subject is the understanding of the shared and distinctive experience of state socialism, which had strong imprints on the urban environment and continues to exert its influences on the contemporary urban processes, as well as similarly distinctive and remarkable experiences of post-socialist transition (also see Stenning and Hörschelmann, 2008). One can argue that it is not that the experience of post-socialist cities cannot offer much new, unique or general to the urban and regional theory; it is rather the lack of attention to post-socialist urban experiences that constitutes a gap in theory production. This brings us to the questions of how to account for the post-socialist city in the wider world; that is, what is the best approach to imagine as well as to 'world' the post-socialist city. Without doubt, this requires much further attentions and debates. What I offer below is just some cursory vectors in that direction.

Articulating with the ideological

Unlike regime change and retrofits in other places and times, the post-socialist momentum has rebuilt the very existential foundations of the affected societies – whose goal was no longer building 'the bright future' of communism, with its aspirations for a classless society, good life and equity for all, but rather embracing the individualistic, entrepreneurial and competition ethos of capitalism, framed politically as a 'market economy'. The change has been underpinned by so-called transition, as a metaphorical and practical framework for the existence of post-socialist societies. Ex-communist societies from now on were all seen as societies in transition, at the core of which was a technocratic package of reforms for the economic and political domains.

This grand societal change – indeed a revolution of sort – is often stylized under the premise of neoliberalization. No doubt, post-socialist transition has been part and parcel of neoliberalism, galvanized by this ideology and allowing this very ideology, through the removal of its state socialism competitor, a *carte blanche* for its planetary triumph. However, being of broad application, the framing of neoliberalism sometimes hides more than it reveals. It is not only that actually experienced neoliberalism demonstrates 'a diversity of positions articulated in response to specific historical circumstances', as Collier (2011: 248) suggests, but also that post-socialism is a very specific geopolitical beast. Indeed, nowhere else recently in the world was the constitution of society so radically and rapidly shaken; nowhere else in the world did white become black and black white so quickly. Stuckler et al. (2012: 949) give an example:

> [In Russia, voucher privatization] helped privatise 80% of the enterprise sector in only two years. Margaret Thatcher, seen by many as the archetypal privatiser, privatised only 31 companies and that took 11 years, in a country with perhaps the most experienced investor class in the world.

Even sophisticated imaginaries about the neoliberal project's mutations, sourced in the experiences of pre-existing capitalist systems, fail to fully account for this revolutionary ontology *en route* from 'mature socialism'.

Having a specific context at play (the communist ideology alternative to capitalism), transition has been by far more far-reaching and dogmatic than the operations of neoliberalism elsewhere. It is even naïve to assume that the neoclassical thought and pro-growth competitive agenda, underpinning the execution of neoliberalism elsewhere, were the only imperatives for designing and implementing the project of transition. Gowan (1995) argued that transition was not so much an economic mission as a chance to reorganize the geopolitical balance of power in favor of the hegemony of Western capital. Burawoy and Verdery (1999) add that neoclassical economics only happened to exhibit the right excuse of this morality by insisting that markets could spontaneously create a good world once the old one was first destroyed.

Contrary to the previous adjustment and liberalization reforms in the Global South or pro-market development-oriented 'transition' in China, transition in Eastern Europe has specifically targeted the social constitution of the affected nations. As well noted by Wedel (1998: 21), the neoliberal project in Eastern Europe has been not so much about exercising economic development but about exorcising the heresies of communism:

> The Second World had been 'misdeveloped', not 'underdeveloped' as the Third World, pundits said. Aid to India, as an example, tended to be couched mainly in terms of economic growth, not institutional and social change. But exorcising the legacies of communism in the Second World often required changing the very nature of recipient institutions, including those of banking, industry, international trade, social security, and health care.

Of course, cities of state socialism and post-socialism have been important players in these radical metamorphoses. Cities of socialism did not simply exist *within* socialism; they were *part* of socialist experiences. Likewise, cities of post-socialism do not simply exist *within* transition; they are *part* of transition. What is important is the ideological conflict that has emerged between the purpose and patterns of the socialist urban development and the new modalities since the fall of socialism. Let me exemplify these tensions by quoting from two books, both written by American political commentators, only divided by their ideological dispositions:

> Soviet cities face *problems*; ours face *crisis* . . . Our crisis-ridden great cities, from which increasing numbers are fleeing in terror, stands as the most powerful indictments of the inhumanism as well as obstructionism of our social system . . . [I]t is a deceased social system and not geography that is at the bottom of the urban crisis . . . Soviet cities are not decaying – they are flourishing. They are becoming increasingly liveable. Soviet cities are living proof that it is not population size . . . nor the complex problems of modern urban life that determines whether cities are in crisis or flourishing, manageable or unmanageable, liveable or unliveable. It is the *social system*. (*Cities without Crisis*: Davidow, 1976: 33–35, italic in original)

> From the perspective of today's market-economy imperative, looking back over Russia's history reveals that *misallocation* was the dominant characteristic of the Soviet period . . . . The system produced the wrong things. Its factories produced them in the wrong way. It educated its people with the wrong skills. Worst of all, communist planners put factories, machines, and people in the wrong places . . . Towns and cities grew to huge size in places they would never have developed under the influence of free-market forces (*The Siberian Curse*: Hill and Gaddy, 2003: 3, italic in original).

It is particularly entertaining to read these quotes from the vista of the present day, under the protracted crisis of global capitalism, when deficiencies of the free-market ideology culminate in the near-collapse of a number of national economies and when the sentiments about the need to change the dominant economic models are still sharp. In the wake of the financial crunch of 2007/2008, as Western governments were struggling to mitigate the consequences of neoliberal imperatives that produced so many 'wrong things', hopes did rise that the end of neoliberalism might be in sight. Neil Smith (2009) was eloquent in pronouncing that neoliberalism 'is badly wounded today, dominant but dead' (p. 54). However, with a foresight of the end of capitalism still largely absent even on the left, as Smith admitted himself, even moderate hopes for *post*-neoliberalism and the installation of a system a-la Keynesianism turned out to be premature (Aalbers, 2013; Brenner et al., 2010). Instead, they are overtaken by the reality of further austerity measures, privatization, and retrenchment of the welfare state. Stiglitz (2011) links this to the 'ideological crisis of western capitalism', a lack of vision of how capitalism can reform itself – which echoes Smith's argument about the intellectual crisis of imagining a different future.

'One of the greatest violences of the neoliberal era' – Smith (2009: 51) argued – 'was the closure of the political imagination', attributing it directly to the collapse of state socialism. In this light, 'the strange non-death of neo-liberalism' (Crouch, 2011) is not that strange at all: there is simply no longer an alternative vision in sight, from which to imagine an alternative future (Žižek, 1994).

The closure of the alternative economic and ideological imagination by post-socialist transition uncovers the full extent of its totalitarian nature and its truly planetary reach. It turns out to be much more than merely area-based neoliberalisation reforms. Transition effectively serves as the closure of global pluralism by neutralizing 'actually existing socialism' as an alternative point of reference, thus extolling capitalism as the only viable universal system – as expressed by Fukuyama's (1992) 'end of history'. The neoliberal ideology has relegated everything associated with the socialist regimes as 'erroneous' through its near-religious repetitive mantra of the heretical history of socialism. The social opposition to it was then thoroughly exorcised by the shock therapy terror – as brilliantly outlined in Naomi Klein's *The Shock Doctrine* (2007). There is no longer an intellectual point of reference from where to (out)source an alternative imagination – transition has discredited state socialism into a negative 'post-political' consensus. The geo-ideology of transition is thus bigger than the 'Second World', transforming the internal political economy of the West itself, as much as that of the Rest.

It is probably only now, with the collapse of state socialism, that Lukács's political imaginary becomes a diagnostic (1971: 91–92):

> the 'natural laws' of capitalist production have been extended to cover every manifestation of life in society; that – for the first time in history – the whole of society is subjected, or tends to be subjected, to a unified economic process, and that the fate of every member of society is determined by unified laws. . .

Producing the urban

Davidow, quoted above, supports the argument of many Marxist theorists that urban space is in dialectical relationships with the social system, acquiring, accumulating, and conveying a *particular* meaning only in a *particular* social and ideological context (e.g. Harvey, 1989; Lefebvre, 1991 [1974]). Thus, the social and physical conditions of cities, and their fates, may well seem to depend on their location and size, but the root causes of their crisis or otherwise are in the existing socio-political system – which produces space in its own image. This is why when under state socialism the geographical differences served the egalitarian project of equalizing development, under capitalism, as Harvey (2010: 290) contends, even minor inequalities 'get magnified and compounded over time into huge inequalities of influence, wealth and power'. By the same token, even small differences in relative space-economy as under socialism now get magnified into huge spatial inequalities (Golubchikov et al., 2014).

Under state socialism, cities were considered an essential part of the production of the socialist spatialities. The Soviet state, for example, was characterized by a hierarchically ordered space based on national economic planning and rigidly controlled and redistributive accumulation (Golubchikov, 2004, 2010). Industrialization was a key element of economic development, while urbanization was a necessary vehicle for industrialization. Urban planning was subservient to the complex hierarchy of economic planning (e.g. Bater, 1980; French, 1995). This approach suited well the existing accumulation and regulatory regime aiming at achieving generally high and egalitarian social standards for the masses, with cities being at the forefront of building a classless society. Pallot and Shaw (1981: 13) identified that the theory of the Soviet planning system was 'committed to helping to foster a society of unparalleled production and wealth, of social and spatial equality, including equality in welfare, liberty and opportunity, and which regulates its relations, including those with nature, in the most rational possible manner'. Certainly, the ideals were frequently far from the situation actually achieved – but these ideals did direct the vectors of social and spatial change.

Those vectors have completely changed since spaces in Eastern Europe embraced the new ideology. A now growing and already impressive body of literature explores various elements of the post-socialist city (for a few examples of the English-language edited compendia of international cases, see Andrusz et al., 1996; Diener and Hagen, 2015; Stanilov, 2007; Stanilov and Sýkora, 2014; Stenning et al., 2010; Tsenkova and Nedovic-Budic, 2006). While studies of post-socialist cities have already made a significant contribution, there is still much room to reveal how post-socialist urban space has been an intensive and oft-cruel battleground – over ideas, powers, social, economic, and political practices, identities, symbolism, understandings and meanings; to reveal the appropriation of urban space through various mechanisms – privatization and commodification, investment and disinvestment, violence and conformity, resistance and resilience, negation, interrogation and negotiation, location, relocation and displacement, exclusion and segregation, new representations of space and new spaces of representation; to reveal different agencies in these rapid and complex processes – state, markets, and people – in their different embodiment, organization, and personification.

What is particularly still missing in extant urban debates on post-socialism is that they tend to focus on forms and appearances of urban processes rather than on the meanings and indeed ontologies of the urban and the relationships between spatial processes and underpinning ideologies. City, however, should be understood not simply as a (physical) reflection or projection of new institutional and social order, this seen as a separate plain from that of the urban, but as a key mediating social space that 'mixes' the ideological and the everyday together and thus renders the new totalizing ideology its concrete practical contours and control over the production and reproduction of new social relationships (Lefebvre, 2003 [1970]).

Based on the understanding of 'neoliberalization' as a contextually embedded process, Stenning et al. (2010) rightly discuss how neoliberalism has been 'domesticated' in the everyday conditions of post-socialism – that is, how neoliberalism is understood, negotiated, renegotiated and remade by these conditions. However, what is also critically important is to approach the direction of the relationships between everyday life and neoliberalism from the other end: it is the process of neoliberalization that renegotiates the conditions of everyday in the first place, makes them internalize neoliberal practices and, most importantly, by changing their meaning, character, and behavior, uses them to its own ends. Domesticating neoliberalism is simultaneously the neoliberalization of the everyday, the appropriation of the everyday by capitalism and using it as the raw material, conduit, or agency of its expansion – that is, establishing itself not as an abstract market 'out there', but as a process going on and scaling up 'from within' post-socialist spatiality. The urban is this 'from within' spatiality through which neoliberalizing the everyday is negotiated.

It is important to properly account for such spatializing effects of the transition ideology – which is not simply 'domesticated', but *subsumes* pre-existing practices in the first place, alienates them from their own ideological history, and recasts them under the exigencies of capital(ism). As we argue elsewhere (Golubchikov et al., 2014), this ideological process of the subsumption of urban space produces 'hybrid spatialities of transition', where the appearances and forms may be understood as 'socialist legacies' (such as, for example, socialist-era housing estates), but such appearances actually only secrete their radically different social and economic meanings, functions, operations, and consequences under the new modalities of capitalism. Table 20.1 provides some schematic categories of the changing meaning-making in relation to urban space.

This totalizing reach of neoliberal 'transition' does not mean that everything can be reduced solely to the level of totality, but we do need to see the hierarchically structured inter-relationships between ideology and practice. This can be understood through the Lefebvrian conceptualization of totality as *synchronically co-present*

Table 20.1 Changing tendencies in the meaning of urban space

Socialist city	Post-socialist city
Part of production	Part of consumption
Planning	Markets
City as social contract	City as growth machine
Use-values	Exchange-values
Commons	Enclosures
Individual merits	Private wealth
Complementarity	Competition
Urban hierarchy	Centre and periphery
Spatial equalization	Uneven development
Social equity	Social divisions

levels of social practice in which 'one level mediates the other' and can dominate the other (Goonewardena, 2008: 127). Lefebvre (2003 [1970]) discusses three such levels: the macro-level, the mixed/urban level, and the micro/private level of social reality. To Lefebvre, these are not so much scalar levels, but rather tools with different granularity to jointly understand forces construing modern society, so each of these 'levels' can be traced, for example, at the scale of the city. *The macro-level* of social practice involves 'the most general, and therefore the most abstract, although essential, relations, such as capital market and the politics of space' (Lefebvre, 2003 [1970]). It is the level of 'society, the state, global power and knowledge, institutions, and ideologies' (p. 89); it is the level of political power that 'makes use of instruments (ideological and scientific)' to modify 'the distribution of resources, income, and the "value" created by productive labour (surplus value)' (Lefebvre, 2003 [1970]: 78). *The micro-level* involves the practice of everyday life, such as housing and habiting, typically seen as 'somewhat more modest, even unimportant' (p. 80) but in fact representing the very orientation of ideology. *The mixed or urban level* is then defined as a critical level of social practice that mediates between the distant/ideological and immediate/everyday order of social reality.

The production of urban space (or rather the production of the new social meanings of urban space) thus contributes to the production of new hegemony by fusing the immediate realm of lived space with ideological/capitalist modalities. Here, the production of space is not limited to the projection of regimes and ideologies onto the urban, but it is about conditioning social relationships, too. Lefebvre (2003 [1970]) argues that the latest stages of capitalism are characterized by a transition from industrialization to urbanization as the totalizing social 'episteme'. As Prigge (2008: 49) explains, 'It is no longer the *industrial* and its disciplines focusing on capital and labor, classes and reproduction that constitute the episteme (the possibility of knowing the social formation), but the *urban* and its forms focused on everydayness and consumption, planning and spectacle, that expose the tendencies of social development. . .' (see also Harvey, 1985, 1989).

Post-socialist transition, too, is aligned with the epistemic transition from indus-trialization to urbanization. While the logic of social development under socialism was much bound to industrialization (social and spatial regulations were contin-gent on the industrial), post-socialism makes a transition to consumption and urbanization (social and spatial regulations are contingent on the urban). Although the focus of the socialist development was on the real sector of production, city of socialism played a very important role as a social(ist) contract – providing quality of life to working people in exchange for their labor in the production process. This philosophy has been antagonistic to the capitalist logic of private profit maximiz-ing (as opposed to collective value maximizing). To all the previous discussions on whether cities of communism were structurally different from cities of capitalism or not so much so (Andrusz et al., 1996; Hirt, 2013), we can add that they were shaped by a very different political philosophy.

Making the urban dance to the tune of capitalism and alienating the inherited social and urban forms from the socialist ideology (that had either generated them or previously appropriated them from the pre-socialist regimes) creates serious ruptures with the previous philosophy of the city. The subsumption of urban spa-tialities to the capitalist logic has been achieved through profit-seeking invest-ments, expropriation of socialist commons, separation of people from the means of subsistence, especially through privatization, and the production of new meanings and discourses. Through the commodification, financialization, and revalorization of housing, real estate and other urban assets – strategies sought by both markets and regulations – urban space is surrendered to the operation of capital. Social inequalities, injustices, and uneven development are then naturalized by their mys-tification as the 'natural conditions' of the circulation of money and commodity and people's divergent skills and luck in acquiring personal wealth to accommodate themselves at different levels of consumption. Denouncing and de-legitimizing the previous practices of state socialism as an 'unnatural' experiment, national and urban regimes of post-socialist transition can legitimize their push of neoliberaliza-tion and austerity politics even further than the collective memory of the welfare state allows in Western Europe.

Even in academic research, there is frequently naturalization of the new construc-tion of socio-spatial relationships, such as spatial segregation and gentrification; these conditions are taken for granted and seen as law-like processes – worthy of analysis, but void of ethical questioning, normative reasoning, and workable alter-native strategy. In the next section, I will demonstrate how a surface-level gaze onto the urban form may miss the important role that the urban plays in making social relationships.

Mediating the social

An important social function of the post-socialist city is that the city's new con-sumption-based semiotic lubricates class transformation. While socialist societies were relatively egalitarian, the new society demands new etiquettes and ethics, new semiotics for distinguishing social class and status.

The period since the collapse of state socialism has seen a sharp rise of income inequalities. As the redistributive welfare mechanism was reduced by neoliberal reforms, income disproportions soared. These disproportions have constituted a major ground from which social inequalities are derived. However, high levels of income inequality per se are not a sufficient factor of social inequality; more significant is how income translates into life chances, consumption possibilities, and social privilege or disprivilege. The conversation between incomes and inequalities is mediated by varied social interactions; it is particularly the consumption of urban space and segregation (including in spaces of gentrification and suburbanization) that complete this 'translation' into class transformation.

In a settled class society, both in the Global North and the Global South, spatial segregation and its various derivatives reflect class division and participate in social reproduction. In the socialist city, especially in the countries of the 'more mature' socialism such as Soviet Russia, society was relatively egalitarian and spatially mixed. Although society ceased to be egalitarian with the start of transition, the legacy of socio-spatial mix has remained a more conservative element (partly due to the material legacies of high-density multifamily estates), while the notion of class itself is still blurred. Here, and in contrast to a more settled class society, the consumption of urban space plays a very significant structuration role for the *original* production of class and status, not only for social reproduction.

For example, the social topography of urban space changes in response to the new housing markets. Urban space becomes more strongly polarized along the lines of property markets and circuits of consumption. While housing privatization has formed the supply end of the residential market, socio-economic stratification has created differential demand for dwellings and differential ability to maintain the conditions of homes. Informed by the new symbolic meanings of what locations and types of housing are 'prestigious' or not, housing markets differentiate income groups, who are now in search of defining and securing their own lifestyles and status. Spatial segregation consequently works as a medium to transform income inequalities into class division. This is a mechanism of the establishment and reproduction of dominance in the urban society of consumers (more aligned with Weber) rather than a product of more explicit class struggle under industrial capitalism (as in Marx).

The everyday life in post-socialist cities is continuously evaded by the images of success and modernity, in which the ethos of consumption is given a privileged position. One of the benchmarks of modernity has become distance from the socialist era. It is not only that the function and morphology of the 'new capitalist city' have been considerably altered in response to commercialization, but also that the achievements of the socialist era (such as low levels of social-spatial segregation) are discredited as 'unnatural'. For example, the imaginaries of super-elite lifestyles have become an integral part of people's everyday experience. As property owner-ship has become a massive status symbol, the 'elite' real estate market has become a symbol of the transformation of the post-socialist metropolis.

What is also interesting is that the production of the post-socialist status and class, mediated by such spatial practices, is not necessarily limited nationally. The super-rich from Russia, for example, may produce their social status by owning properties or businesses in cities in other countries within the post-socialist world or beyond it. It is in this sense that we could talk of a further hybridization of post-socialist urban identities and their complex relationships with the global urbanity, where the production of class and status is not only happening *in situ* but is also outsourced to the symbolism of faraway places, thus making the whole world the playground of the post-socialist urban experience.

The mediascape is constitutive of all these processes. The language, which is circu-lated through the mass media, television, and other cultural products, has become a mechanism of constructing the audiences as consumers and forming their wishes by delivering them the ready-made meanings of what is desirable. Therefore, by manipulating people's needs and desires, satisfaction and dissatisfaction, the mass media serve as the key building block in what Lefebvre (1971) calls programmed everyday life in which the reality is charged with specific emotional or imaginative meanings suitable for hegemonic interests.

Pertaining to the new meanings are also new urban strategies of government. Their role is threefold: mechanical, symbolic, and political. First, as social integration and social equality have ceased to be principal tenets of state ideology, urban renewal programs often involve physical displacement of poorer dwellers and the construc-tion of new housing explicitly targeted on high-income groups or, alternatively, the construction of poorer-quality zones either for those who can hardly afford hous-ing or as public housing. This mediates segregation that mediates status. Second, urban development projects play a symbolic role for class definition. This is because they emphasize luxurious housing, which, mediated by the mass media, constitutes a status symbol. Such spaces serve to mobilize the identities of the rich by relating their consumption practices to the exclusionary forms of spatial practice (Badyina and Golubchikov, 2005). Third, being implemented within the local political con-texts, urban programs often preclude alternative political solutions and paths, and ignore and silence other voices and needs.

Urban space, thus constructed, essentially ceases to exist independently of consumption – it rather collapses into its endless circuits. The economic strati-fication and segmentation of consumption practice, which stem from underly-ing income inequalities, become a formative element of spatial practice itself. The splintered segments of urban space are then invested with signs and meanings and become valued according to these engineered meanings.

Conclusions

In this chapter, I invite a conceptualization of post-socialist urban change as inherently ideological. One direction further along that line is to decipher the urbanization of transition as the process of the appropriation of cities by the new political ideology, leading to particular forms of post-socialist urban transformation, at the cost of their alternatives. Research needs to analyze a broader institutional context of post-socialist urbanization and the resultant forms, focusing especially on the geometries of social and power relations which underpin the practices of urban development and change, such as the ideology, strategy, policy, and regulations.

In a similar way that state socialism produced a distinctive type of urbanization (Andrusz et al., 1996; Bater, 1980), post-socialist transition can be viewed as an inescapable compulsion which, while having originated at the regulatory level, has transformed life and circumstances in all cities – irrespective of the prior situations or aspirations in these cities. The introduction of the market economy resulted in a flood of new urban processes which have been rapidly changing the function and morphology of cities, and is particularly apparent in a rapid pace of commodification of urban space.

But even more fundamentally, the appropriation of ex-socialist society by capitalism has changed the very *raison d'être* of the city. Rather than being a vehicle for spatial equalization and re-distribution, for a purposeful evolution towards 'a fair and egalitarian society', the post-socialist city has become a dividing and divided experience – with increasing social and economic disparity and polarization at both inter-urban and intra-urban scales. It is not only that the principle of the egalitarian re-distribution of wealth has been replaced with the neoliberal principle of self-reliance, but that the new regime has also created preconditions for the extraction of wealth from the large majority of people and places and its re-concentration in the hands of the select few (people and places).

The urbanization of transition is a fulcrum of new social and spatial regulation. While cities are often portrayed as merely a projection on a local scale of larger societal changes, they are actually an important social and material framework for the production and reproduction of the new relationships of capitalism, including class (trans)formation and uneven development. In other words, urbanization is a major institutional *dimension* of transition, not simply its playground.

References

Aalbers, M. B. (2013) 'Neoliberalism is dead . . . long live neoliberalism!', *International Journal of Urban and Regional Research 37* (3): 1083–1090.

Andrusz, G., Harloe, M. and Szelenyi, I. (eds) (1996) *Cities After Socialism: Urban and Regional Change and Conflict in Post-Socialist Societies.* Oxford: Blackwell.

Badyina, A. and Golubchikov, O. (2005) 'Gentrification in Central Moscow – a market process or a deliberate policy? Money, power and people in housing regeneration in Ostozhenka', *Geografiska Annaler B 87* (2): 113–129.

Bater, J. H. (1980) *The Soviet City: Ideal and Reality*. London: Edward Arnold.

Brenner, N., Peck, J. and Theodore, N. (2010) 'Variegated neoliberalization: geographies, modalities, pathways', *Global Networks 10* (2): 182–222.

Burawoy, M. and Verdery, K. (1999) 'Introduction'. In M. Burawoy and K. Verdery (eds.), *Uncertain Transition: Ethnographies of Change in the Postsocial World*. Oxford: Rowman & Littlefield Publishers.

Collier, S. J. (2011) *Post-Soviet Social: Neoliberalism, Social Modernity, Biopolitics*. Princeton, NJ: Princeton Univeristy Press.

Crouch, C. (2011) *The Strange Non-Death of Neo-Liberalism*. Cambridge, UK: Polity.

Davidow, M. (1976) *Cities without Crisis*. New York: International Publishers.

Diener, A. C. and Hagen, J. (eds.) (2015) *From Socialist to Post-Socialist Cities: Cultural Politics of Architecture, Urban Planning, and Identity in Eurasia*. Abingdon, UK: Routledge.

French, R. A. (1995) *Plans, Pragmatism and People: The Legacy of Soviet Planning for Today's City*. London: UCL Press.

Fukuyama, F. (1992) *The End of History and the Last Man*. New York: Free Press.

Golubchikov, O. (2004) 'Urban planning in Russia: towards the market', *European Planning Studies 12* (2): 229–247.

Golubchikov, O. (2010) 'World-city entrepreneurialism: globalist imaginaries, neoliberal geographies, and the production of new St Petersburg', *Environment and Planning A 42* (3): 626–643.

Golubchikov, O., Badyina, A. and Makhrova, A. (2014) 'The hybrid spatialities of transition: capitalism, legacy and uneven urban economic restructuring', *Urban Studies 51* (4): 617–633.

Goonewardena, K. (2008) 'Marxism and everyday life: on Henri Lefebvre, Guy Debord, and some others'. In K. Goonewardena, S. Kipfer, R. Milgrom and C. Schmid (eds.), *Space, Difference, Everyday Life: Reading Henri Lefebvre* (pp. 117–133). Abingdon, UK: Routledge.

Gowan, P. (1995) 'Neo-liberal theory and practice for eastern Europe', *New Left Review 213*: 3–60.

Harvey, D. (1985) *Consciousness and the Urban Experience: Studies in the History and Theory of Capitalist Urbanization*. Baltimore, MD: Johns Hopkins University Press.

Harvey, D. (1989) *The Urban Experience*. Baltimore, MD: Johns Hopkins University Press.

Harvey, D. (2010) *A Companion to Marx's Capital*. London: Verso.

Hill, F. and Gaddy, C. G. (2003) *The Siberian Curse: How Communist Planners Left Russia Out in the Cold*. Washington, DC: Brookings Institution Press.

Hirt, S. (2013) 'Whatever happened to the (post)socialist city?', *Cities 32* (S1): S29–S38.

Klein, N. (2007) *The Shock Doctrine: The Rise of Disaster Capitalism*. London: Allen Lane.

Lefebvre, H. (1971) *Everyday Life in the Modern World*. London: Allen Lane, Penguin Press.

Lefebvre, H. (1991 [1974]) *The Production of Space*. Oxford: Blackwell.

Lefebvre, H. (2003 [1970]) *The Urban Revolution*. Minneapolis, MN: University of Minnesota Press.

Lukács, G. (1971) *History and Class Consciousness: Studies in Marxist Dialectics*. Cambridge, MA: MIT Press.

Pallot, J. and Shaw, D. J. B. (1981) *Planning in the Soviet Union*. London: Croom Helm.

Parker, S. (2015) *Urban Theory and the Urban Experience: Encountering the City* (2nd ed.). London: Routledge.

Prigge, W. (2008) 'Reading the urban revolution: space and representation'. In K. Goonewardena, S. Kipfer, R. Milgrom and C. Schmid (eds.), *Space, Difference, Everyday Life: Reading Henri Lefebvre* (pp. 46–61). Abingdon: Routledge.

Roy, A. (2009) 'The 21st-century metropolis: new geographies of theory', *Regional Studies 43* (6): 819–830.

Sjöberg, Ö. (2014) 'Cases onto themselves? Theory and research on ex-socialist urban environments', *Geografie 119* (4): 299–319.

Smith, D. M. (1994) *Geography and Social Justice*. Oxford: Blackwell.

Smith, D. M. (2000) 'Social justice revisited', *Environment and Planning A* 32 (7): 1149–1162.

Smith, N. (2009) 'The revolutionary imperative', *Antipode 41* (S1): 50–65.

Stanilov, K. (ed.) (2007) *The Post-Socialist City: Urban Form and Space Transformation in Central and Eastern Europe after Socialism*. Dordrecht, the Netherlands: Springer.

Stanilov, K. and Sýkora, L. (eds.) (2014) *Confronting Suburbanization: Urban Decentralization in Postsocialist Central and Eastern Europe*. Oxford: Wiley-Blackwell.

Stenning, A. and Hörschelmann, K. (2008) 'History, geography and difference in the post-socialist world: or, do we still need post-socialism?', *Antipode 40* (2): 312–335.

Stenning, A., Smith, A., Rochovska, A. and Swiatek, D. (2010) *Domesticating Neo-liberalism: Spaces of Economic Practice and Social Reproduction in Post-Socialist Cities*. Oxford: Wiley-Blackwell.

Stiglitz, J. E. (2011) 'The ideological crisis of Western capitalism', Project Syndicate, available: http://www.project-syndicate.org/commentary/stiglitz140/English, accessed November 2011.

Stuckler, D., King, L. and McKee, M. (2012) 'Response to Michael Gentile "Mass Privatisation, Unemployment and Mortality"', *Europe-Asia Studies 64* (5): 949–953.

Tsenkova, S. and Nedovic-Budic, Z. (eds.) (2006) *The Urban Mosaic of Post-Socialist Europe: Space Institutions and Policy*. Heidelberg: Physica-Verlag (Springer).

Tuvikene, T. (2016) 'Strategies for comparative urbanism: post-socialism as a re-territorialized concept', *International Journal of Urban and Regional Research 40* (1): 132–146.

Wedel, J. R. (1998) *Collision and Collusion: The Strange Case of Western Aid to Eastern Europe 1989–1998*. New York: St. Martin's Press.

Žižek, S. (ed.) (1994) *Mapping Ideology*. London: Verso.

Index

281